Taking a broad geographic scope from Virginia to South Carolina between 1820 and 1860, Jeff Forret scrutinizes relations among rural poor whites and slaves, a subject virtually unexplored and certainly under-reported until now. Forret's findings challenge historians' long-held assumption that mutual violence and animosity characterized the two groups' interactions. Evidence he draws from numerous sources reveals that while poor whites and slaves sometimes experienced bouts of hostility, often they worked or played in harmony and camaraderie.

Race Relations at the Margins is remarkable for its focus on lower-class whites and their dealings with slaves outside the purview of the slavemaster. Forret's research uncovers an interracial subculture of drinking, gambling, clandestine trade, and consensual sex. Daily commingling of poor white men and women with enslaved men and women both reinforced and challenged southern racial boundaries as the groups violated social convention to forge bonds of reciprocal interest, understanding, and affection. Race and class, Forret demonstrates, intersected in unique ways for those at the margins of southern society, challenging the belief

Race Relations at the Margins

Race Relations at the Margins

Slaves and Poor Whites in the Antebellum Southern Countryside

JEFF FORRET

Louisiana State University Press   Baton Rouge

Published by Louisiana State University Press
Copyright © 2006 by Louisiana State University Press
All rights reserved
Manufactured in the United States of America
First printing

Designer: Laura Roubique Gleason
Typeface: Adobe Caslon text, Clarendon Bold display
Typesetter: G&S Typesetters, Inc.
Printer and binder: Edwards Brothers, Inc.

Library of Congress Cataloging-in-Publication Data
Forret, Jeff, 1972–
    Race relations at the margins : slaves and poor whites in the
antebellum Southern countryside / Jeff Forret.
        p. cm.
    Includes bibliographical references and index.
    ISBN-13: 978-0-8071-3145-9 (cloth : alk. paper)
    ISBN-10: 0-8071-3145-8 (cloth : alk. paper)
1. Southern States—Race relations.   2. Slaves—Southern States
— Social conditions.   3. Poor whites—Southern States—Social
conditions.   4. Social interaction—Southern States—History.
5. Marginality, Social—Southern States—History.   6. Southern
States—Rural conditions.   7. Southern States—History—1775–
1865.   I. Title.
F220.A1F67 2006
305.800975—dc22

                                                        2005027531

Portions of this book were previously published as "Slaves, Poor
Whites, and the Underground Economy of the Rural Carolinas,"
Journal of Southern History 70 (November 2004): 783–824; and
"Slave–Poor White Violence in the Antebellum Carolinas," *North
Carolina Historical Review* 81 (April 2004): 139–167.

CONTENTS

ACKNOWLEDGMENTS

The idea for a study of the relationships between slaves and poor whites in the antebellum South struck me in 1997, while conducting research for my master's thesis. In subsequent years, I incurred a number of professional and personal debts that I am pleased to acknowledge here. My editor at LSU Press, Rand Dotson, guided my initial manuscript down the path of publication. I greatly appreciate the enthusiasm he showed for the project and his patience in dealing with someone as ignorant of the process as I. Copy editor Michael Baker's careful reading of the manuscript expunged it of embarrassing errors. I am grateful as well to Lee Sioles, Margaret Hart, and everyone at LSU Press who had a hand in making the book possible.

Dissertation advisor Peter Kolchin deserves the utmost thanks for taking me under his wing. He devoted a tremendous amount of time to this project, carefully reading several drafts and providing extensive and valuable feedback. His keen historical mind, exceptional patience, and knowledge of the profession all combine to make him a model mentor. Committee members Christine Leigh Heyrman, Howard Johnson, and Steven Hahn contributed penetrating criticisms and insightful comments that further helped develop and polish the finished work. Although they may not entirely agree with the contours of the final product, I am honored to have studied under the guidance and direction of such a distinguished panel of historians.

I must also express my gratitude to other scholars who had a direct influence on this work. Anne Boylan and Dan Dupre provided valuable comments on chapter 2 as I presented early versions of it at the University of Delaware history department and at the 68th Annual Meeting of the Southern Historical Association, Baltimore, Maryland, November 2002. Carole Haber, Tim Lockley, and others who attended these presentations deserve thanks for their comments and the different perspectives they brought to the subject of underground trade. Tim was generous enough to mail me a copy of a crucial primary source that was unavailable during my visit to the archives. The anonymous readers at the *Jour-*

nal of Southern History, Victoria Bynum, and Kevin Hardwick further helped sharpen the argument and argumentation of chapter 2, and I am extremely grateful. Two anonymous readers at the *Journal of Social History* offered the feedback that profoundly influenced the interpretation contained in chapter 3, while those at the *North Carolina Historical Review* made suggestions to refine chapter 4. Cindy Kierner's comments on a paper I delivered at UNC Charlotte's 15th Annual Graduate History Forum guided the construction of chapter 5, for which Thomas E. Buckley, S.J., graciously shared some of his own research on divorce in Virginia. J. William Harris, Leah Arroyo, and Larry Duggan offered support, encouragement, and advice at the early stages of research. I also appreciate the spirit of cooperation demonstrated by Cruce Stark and Shirley Samuels of the University of Delaware English department.

For their help in uncovering primary source material, I wish to thank the staffs at the North Carolina Department of Archives and History, especially Earl Ijames; the South Carolina Department of Archives and History; the South Caroliniana Library and the Coleman Karesh Law Library at the University of South Carolina; the Southern Historical Collection, in the University of North Carolina at Chapel Hill's Wilson Library; the Library of Virginia and the Virginia State Archives; the special collections room in the University of Delaware's Morris Library; and the reference room of North Carolina State University's D. H. Hill Library. A University Competitive Fellowship and a Bosley-Warnock Fellowship from the University of Delaware provided the funds to allow me to research and write expeditiously. The interlibrary loan department at James Madison University's Carrier Library located and obtained essential books and articles for use in revisions, and Madeleine Perez and Marilyn Schuster at UNC Charlotte's Atkins Library also came through in the clutch, supplying secondary sources and advice at the last minute.

While attending the University of Delaware, fellow graduate students John Davies, Christine Sears, Lyn Causey, Terry Johnston, Rick Demirjian, Alan Meyer, Tracey Birdwell, Karen Ryder, and Tom Rylko showed great interest in my work. At the North Carolina state archives, a fortuitous crossing of paths with Scott Giltner, from the University of Pittsburgh, provided not only intelligent conversation but also a frequent companion on research trips and at professional conferences. My indebtedness extends as well to friends and computer gurus Ryan Shovar, Travis Shovar, and Matt Parker for their technical expertise and advice. They bailed me out of more computer-related jams than I care to recall. Greg Lekavich, my teaching assistant for two years at James Madison

University, also merits recognition not only for his technical assistance but also for taking on more than his fair share of the grading in the U.S. history survey.

Finally, I appreciate the support of my family throughout this endeavor. This includes not only my mom, brother, sisters, and other relatives in the Midwest, but also my southern in-laws. James Hord, Joyce Mozingo Hord, and Michael, welcomed me into their family and in many ways made this project possible. Financially, they provided free accommodations, complimentary meals, and gas money during my research trips. More than that, James and Joyce blessed my marriage to their daughter Sharon, whose love and support sustained me throughout the writing of this book. For all of my wife's sacrifices over the years, I dedicate this book to her.

ABBREVIATIONS

NCDAH   North Carolina Department of Archives and History, Raleigh

SCDAH   South Carolina Department of Archives and History, Columbia

SCL   South Caroliniana Library, University of South Carolina, Columbia

SHC   Southern Historical Collection, Wilson Library, University of North Carolina at Chapel Hill

LVA   Library of Virginia, Richmond

Race Relations at the Margins

INTRODUCTION

Stereotypes marred the early historical scholarship on both slaves and poor whites in the Old South. In 1918, U. B. Phillips, the pioneering student of southern slavery, described the "predominant plantation type," identifying a series of traits common to bondspeople: "an eagerness for society, music and merriment, a fondness for display whether of person, dress, vocabulary or emotion, a not flagrant sensuality, a receptiveness toward any religion whose exercises were exhilarating, a proneness to superstition, a courteous acceptance of subordination, an avidity for praise, a readiness for loyalty of a feudal sort, and . . . a healthy human repugnance toward overwork." Furthermore, Phillips emphasized the malleability of the slave by the master, remarking that "a negro was what a white man made him." Stanley M. Elkins's seminal 1959 study, *Slavery: A Problem in American Institutional and Intellectual Life*, countered Phillips's racist assumptions but nevertheless perpetuated the objectification of the slaves themselves. Elkins drew an analogy between slaves in the American South and the victims of Nazi concentration camps. Subdued by the absolute authority Elkins claimed masters wielded over them, slaves, like Nazi prisoners, identified with their oppressors and were transformed into emasculated, docile, and childlike "Sambos." Elkins's controversial work sparked an onslaught of historical scholarship challenging the Sambo thesis. John W. Blassingame, for one, argued that Sambo-like behavior did not signify the infantilization of the slave but instead served as a defense mechanism, a clever ruse that helped bondspeople cope with their enslavement. Through studies of family, religion, community, and resistance, scholars including Blassingame and Eugene D. Genovese by the early 1970s began treating slaves not simply as objects of white treatment but also as subjects capable of shaping their own lives.[1]

1. Ulrich Bonnell Phillips, *American Negro Slavery: A Survey of the Supply, Employment and Control of Negro Labor as Determined by the Plantation Régime* (1918; reprint, New York: Peter Smith, 1952), 291; Stanley M. Elkins, *Slavery: A Problem in American Institutional and Intellectual Life*, 3rd ed. (Chicago: University of Chicago Press, 1976), ch. 3; John W. Blassingame, *The Slave Community: Plantation Life in the Antebellum South*, rev. ed. (New York: Oxford University Press, 1979), ch. 6; Eugene D.

The overwhelming number of secondary works on slavery dwarfs the paucity of historical literature examining the Old South's poor whites. Lacking in academic rigor, the first scholarship on poor whites, appearing in the 1930s as the Great Depression piqued interest in the poor, accepted uncritically the prevailing stereotypes found in the descriptions of northern travelers and foreign tourists to the antebellum South.[2] Travelers' accounts frequently disparaged the region's poor whites. Traversing North Carolina in the 1820s, geologist Denison Olmstead commented upon his bleak surroundings, recording that "the inhabitants are mostly poor and ignorant. . . . Here and there a log hut or cabin, surrounded by a few acres of corn and cotton, marks the little improvement which has been made by man." In the state's turpentine forests, Frederick Law Olmsted encountered a group of "entirely uneducated, poverty-stricken vagabonds . . . , people without habitual, definite occupation or reliable means of livelihood," who eked out a meager existence by hunting and herding, fishing and foraging. German-born Frederika Bremer met some "clay-eaters" during her southern travels. She described them as "a kind of wretched white people, found in considerable numbers both in Carolina and Georgia, who live in the woods, without churches, without schools, without hearths, and sometimes also without homes." Most mortifying to her was their habit, "induced by a diseased appetite[,] to eat a sort of unctuous earth, which is found here, until this taste becomes a passion with them, equally strong with the love of intoxicating liquors." English geologist George W. Featherstonhaugh considered the whole lot of poor whites a "vapouring, disgusting, and unprofitable set of beings, devoid of education, religion, or manners." These and many other travelers helped construct the stereotype of southern poor whites as idle, lazy, and indolent; ignorant, uneducated, and suspicious; impoverished and malnourished; dirty and disease-ridden; as well as drunken and immoral.[3] Whether labeled by their contemporaries as clay-

---

Genovese, *Roll, Jordan, Roll: The World the Slaves Made* (1974; New York: Vintage Books, 1976). For an overview of the enormous literature on slavery, see Peter Kolchin, *American Slavery, 1619–1877* (New York: Hill and Wang, 1993).

2. Paul H. Buck, "The Poor Whites of the Ante-Bellum South," *American Historical Review* 31 (October 1925): 41–54; Avery O. Craven, "Poor Whites and Negroes in the Ante-Bellum South," *Journal of Negro History* 15 (January 1930): 14–25; A. N. J. Den Hollander, "The Tradition of 'Poor Whites,'" in *Culture in the South*, ed. W. T. Couch (Chapel Hill: University of North Carolina Press, 1935), 403–431; Mildred Rutherford Mell, "Poor Whites of the South," *Social Forces* 17 (December 1938): 153–167; Shields McIlwaine, *The Southern Poor-White from Lubberland to Tobacco Road* (Norman: University of Oklahoma Press, 1939); W. O. Brown, "Role of the Poor Whites in Race Contacts of the South," *Social Forces* 19 (December 1940): 258–268.

3. Denison Olmstead, "On the Gold Mines of North Carolina," *American Journal of Science* 9

eaters, crackers, dirt-eaters, doughfaces, hillbillies, honkies, peckerwoods, rag tag and bob-tail, raw-gum chewers, rednecks, sandhillers, tackies, trash, po' white trash, or woolhats or wooly-hats, poor whites represented the dregs of southern society.[4]

Rather than attempting to explore poor whites' actual experiences in their daily lives, scholars throughout most of the twentieth century instead dealt with them as an undifferentiated mass. They labored to dispel the entrenched myth that the Old South consisted exclusively of planters, slaves, and a substantial and degraded poor white class. In an effort to correct this long-standing misconception, historian Frank L. Owsley and his students began exploring in the 1940s the "plain folk," the middling small slaveholding farmers, nonslaveholding landowners, and herdsmen, neither rich nor poor, who comprised the majority of all southern whites.[5] Although many of his specific findings were subsequently rebutted, Owsley nevertheless successfully resurrected the lives of plain folk from the historical dustbin and reestablished their important place in antebellum southern society. Whether describing their subjects as "plain folk," "yeomen," "common whites," or "non-elites," subsequent generations of scholars, including Steven Hahn, J. William Harris, Bill Cecil-Fronsman, Stephanie McCurry, and Tim Lockley, have deepened our knowledge of the southern white majority.[6] In

---

(1825): 6; Frederick Law Olmsted, *A Journey in the Seaboard Slave States, with Remarks on Their Economy* (New York: Dix & Edwards, 1856), 348–349; Frederika Bremer, *The Homes of the New World; Impressions of America*, vol. 1, trans. Mary Howitt (London: Arthur Hall, Virtue, & Co., 1853), 373; G. W. Featherstonhaugh, *A Canoe Voyage Up the Minnay Sotor*, vol. 2 (London: Richard Bentley, 1847), 195. On the poor white penchant for eating clay, see Robert W. Twyman, "The Clay Eater: A New Look at an Old Southern Enigma," *Journal of Southern History* 37 (August 1971): 439–448; and Rudolph M. Lapp, "The Ante Bellum Poor Whites of the South Atlantic States" (Ph.D. diss., University of California–Berkeley, 1956), 129–132.

4. The derogatory names applied to poor whites varied by locality. According to Alabama planter D. R. Hundley, "in the extreme South and South-west, they are usually called Squatters; in the Carolinas and Georgia Crackers or Sandhillers; in the Old Dominion, Rag Tag and Bob-tail; in Tennessee and some other States, People in the Barrens—but everywhere, Poor White Trash." See D. R. Hundley, *Social Relations in Our Southern States* (New York: Henry B. Price, 1860; reprint, New York: Arno Press, 1973), 257.

5. Frank L. Owsley, *Plain Folk of the Old South* (1949; reprint, Baton Rouge: Louisiana State University Press, 1982), xix–xxi, 1, 8.

6. Steven Hahn, *The Roots of Southern Populism: Yeoman Farmers and the Transformation of the Georgia Upcountry, 1850–1890* (New York: Oxford University Press, 1983); J. William Harris, *Plain Folk and Gentry in a Slave Society: White Liberty and Black Slavery in Augusta's Hinterlands* (Middletown, Conn.: Wesleyan University Press, 1985; reprint, Baton Rouge: Louisiana State University Press, 1998), 56–61; Lacy K. Ford, Jr., *Origins of Southern Radicalism: The South Carolina Upcountry, 1800–1860* (New York: Oxford University Press, 1988); Grady McWhiney, *Cracker Culture: Celtic*

the process, however, poor whites have fallen by the wayside, the continued victims of prejudice and misunderstanding. Only within the last decade or so have historians such as Charles C. Bolton revived the study of antebellum southern poor whites, this time on their own terms, as the subjects of legitimate scholarship.[7]

If stereotypes plagued the initial study of slaves and poor whites respectively, they have also shaped common misconceptions about relationships *between* slaves and poor whites. Scholars writing before the accomplishments of the American civil rights movement seemed to read the separation of the races backward into the antebellum years, attributing a timeless quality to Jim Crow segregation. When historians acknowledged contact between slaves and poor whites at all, they offered only a perfunctory comment that mutual hatred and animosity characterized their relationships.[8] This stock portrayal of slave–poor white relations has stubbornly resisted modification. Despite the prolific scholarship on slavery, and despite a few tantalizing hints of slave–poor white interaction in the literature on non-elite southern whites, no one has yet undertaken a comprehensive, book-length study exclusively of the relationship between slaves and poor whites in the Old South. Historians have tended instead to examine each group separately, in reference to southern planters. On one hand, they have analyzed the nature of the master-slave relationship, evaluating the degree to which concerns of capitalism or paternalism shaped slaveholders' treatment of their

Ways in the Old South (Tuscaloosa: University of Alabama Press, 1988); Bill Cecil-Fronsman, *Common Whites: Class and Culture in Antebellum North Carolina* (Lexington: University Press of Kentucky, 1992); Stephanie McCurry, *Masters of Small Worlds: Yeoman Households, Gender Relations, and the Political Culture of the Antebellum South Carolina Low Country* (New York: Oxford University Press, 1995); Edward E. Baptist, "Accidental Ethnography in an Antebellum Southern Newspaper: Snell's Homecoming Festival," *Journal of American History* 84 (March 1998): 1355–1383; Timothy James Lockley, *Lines in the Sand: Race and Class in Lowcountry Georgia, 1750–1860* (Athens: University of Georgia Press, 2001).

7. Charles C. Bolton, *Poor Whites of the Antebellum South: Tenants and Laborers in Central North Carolina and Northeast Mississippi* (Durham: Duke University Press, 1994); Charles C. Bolton and Scott P. Culclasure, eds., *The Confessions of Edward Isham: A Poor White Life of the Old South* (Athens: University of Georgia Press, 1998). One significant study of poor whites between the 1930s and the 1990s was Lapp, "Ante Bellum Poor Whites of the South Atlantic States."

8. Buck, "Poor Whites of the Ante-Bellum South," 52; Craven, "Poor Whites and Negroes in the Ante-Bellum South," 19; Den Hollander, "The Tradition of 'Poor Whites,'" 417; Brown, "Role of the Poor Whites," 262; Rosser H. Taylor, *Ante Bellum South Carolina: A Social and Cultural History* (Chapel Hill: University of North Carolina Press, 1942), 85; Lapp, "Ante Bellum Poor Whites of the South Atlantic States," 4.

bondspeople.[9] On the other hand, historians have questioned how southern slaveholders maintained hegemony over the numerically superior nonslaveholding southern white population and why many nonslaveholding whites ultimately sacrificed their lives for a Confederate cause that failed to serve their own best interests.[10] One by-product of the intense concern over slaves' and poor whites' relationships to their social superiors has been the neglect of slaves' and poor whites' relationship to each other. Eugene D. Genovese offered the initial, pioneering look at this topic in 1977, and a few historians have since addressed the subject in a brief article, a chapter, or a few pages of a book. Other scholars interested in interracial relationships have diluted the focus on poor whites by incorporating them into a much broader category of "non-slaveholders" or "non-elite whites." Thus, as J. William Harris recently observed, "The relationship between poor whites and slaves is certainly one that deserves more attention from future historians."[11]

This book investigates the social contacts between slaves and poor whites in antebellum North Carolina, South Carolina, and Virginia. The relative dearth of sources regarding slave–poor white contact encourages the investigation of a broad region rather than one state or a single portion thereof, and the older slave-holding states of North Carolina, South Carolina, and Virginia offer richer col-

9. Genovese, *Roll, Jordan, Roll;* James Oakes, *The Ruling Race: A History of American Slave-holders* (New York: W. W. Norton & Company, 1982).

10. W. J. Cash, *The Mind of the South* (New York: Alfred A. Knopf, 1941); George M. Fredrick-son, *The Black Image in the White Mind: The Debate on Afro-American Character and Destiny, 1817–1914* (New York: Harper & Row, 1971), ch. 2; Eugene D. Genovese, "Yeoman Farmers in a Slave-holders' Democracy," *Agricultural History* 49 (April 1975): 331–342; Bertram Wyatt-Brown, *Southern Honor: Ethics and Behavior in the Old South* (New York: Oxford University Press, 1982); Cecil-Fronsman, *Common Whites*, 84–85; and McCurry, *Masters of Small Worlds*, 47, 93.

11. Bolton and Culclasure, *Confessions of Edward Isham*, xxi. Those who have dealt with the topic of antebellum slave–poor white relations in a brief article, single chapter, or a few but significant pages include Genovese, *Roll, Jordan, Roll*, 22–25; Genovese, "'Rather Be a Nigger Than a Poor White Man': Slave Perceptions of Southern Yeomen and Poor Whites," in *Toward a New View of America: Essays in Honor of Arthur C. Cole*, ed. Hans L. Trefousse (New York: Burt Franklin & Company, Inc., 1977), 79–96; Philip D. Morgan and George D. Terry, "Slavery in Microcosm: A Conspiracy Scare in Colonial South Carolina," *Southern Studies* 21 (Summer 1982): 121–145; Harris, *Plain Folk and Gentry*, 56–61; Cecil-Fronsman, *Common Whites*, ch. 3; Bolton, *Poor Whites*, esp. 42–51, 105–110; Elizabeth Fortson Arroyo, "Poor Whites, Slaves, and Free Blacks in Tennessee, 1796–1861," *Tennessee Historical Quarterly* 55 (Spring 1996): 56–65; Bolton and Culclasure, *Confessions of Edward Isham;* and Lockley, *Lines in the Sand.* On the thorny issue of the categorization of poor whites, see note 19 below.

lections of primary sources than the newer slave states of the Old Southwest. Examining these three South Atlantic states affords at least a limited comparative vantage point through which one may consider slave–poor white interactions under different conditions. The area encompassed a range of agricultural economies, from tobacco in Virginia and portions of North Carolina to rice in the Carolina low country to cotton in much of South Carolina. It also witnessed numerous attempts to undertake nonagricultural enterprises, including iron production, coal and gold mining, and cotton textiles, affording a glimpse into slave–poor white relations in an industrial setting.

Diversity marked not only the region's economy but its demography as well. The black majority that developed in colonial South Carolina persisted throughout the antebellum period. Although blacks' percentage of the total population in the coastal districts declined somewhat between 1820 and 1860, their percentage actually increased in the middle districts during the same time, resulting in a population in which blacks outnumbered whites by a ratio of two, three, or more to one throughout most of the state. By 1850, South Carolina whites retained a clear majority only in the upper Piedmont districts that bordered North Carolina and Georgia. By contrast, whites were a majority of the population throughout most of the state of North Carolina, although their numerical superiority dwindled as one moved from west to east. In the western mountains, with some exceptions, slaves represented less than 15 percent of the total population. Slaves composed a greater percentage of the population in the North Carolina Piedmont, and in the eastern half of the state, slaves made up 35 percent or more of the population in most counties. In more than a dozen counties, most of which were located in the northeastern part of the state, slaves outnumbered whites. Virginia's slave population had begun to gravitate inland from the Tidewater region even during the colonial period, and by 1860, the bulk of that state's bondspeople resided in counties of the southern and central Piedmont. In 1860, slaves composed a majority of the population in no fewer than thirty counties in or near the Virginia Piedmont.[12]

The region under study, like most of the South, was rural. It embraces the cities of Charleston and Richmond, but because the combined slave populations of those two urban areas accounted for a mere 2.1 percent of the total number of

12. McCurry, *Masters of Small Worlds*, 34, 45, 46; Ford, *Origins of Southern Radicalism*, 45–46; John C. Inscoe, *Mountain Masters: Slavery and the Sectional Crisis in Western North Carolina* (Knoxville: University of Tennessee Press, 1989), 63, 64; Cecil-Fronsman, *Common Whites*, 72. For an excellent and easily accessible source of historical census data, visit on the web http://fisher.lib.virginia.edu/collections/stats/histcensus.

bondspeople in the Carolinas and Virginia in 1860, the emphasis here remains overwhelmingly rural, concentrating on slave–poor white relations in the southern countryside and small towns. This not only complements recent scholarship on nonslaveholders' relationships with slaves in significant urban areas such as Savannah, but also reflects settings more typical of the South as a whole.[13]

Evidence confirming the interaction between slaves and poor whites in the rural South proves elusive. Many valuable sources have been lost to the ravages of time. Poor whites, often illiterate, almost never left behind written records of their lives, either through diaries, correspondence, or memoirs. Almost all of the extant primary sources documenting slave–poor white contact are filtered through the eyes of slaveholders, slaves, or elite travelers to the South. Records of antebellum court cases at both the county and state levels, petitions to southern governors and legislatures, and census records provided the most helpful information. Surviving manuscript collections of southern planters show their frustration with neighborhood poor whites for mingling socially with their slaves and for forging passes for them. In slave runaway advertisements in local newspapers, masters also sometimes mentioned particular "low," "mean," or "degraded" whites who they suspected helped their chattel abscond. Slaves themselves occasionally discussed "po' white trash" or "po' buckra" in their autobiographies and narratives. African-American folklore, folk songs, and folk rhymes offer additional clues to slaves' perceptions of southern poor whites. Published travelers' accounts provide outsiders' perspectives on slave–poor white contact. Even though

13. Joseph C. G. Kennedy, *Population of the United States in 1860; Compiled from the Original Returns of the Eighth Census, Under the Direction of the Secretary of the Interior* (Washington: Government Printing Office, 1864), 513, 518–519, 357, 359, 451, 452. The slave population of Charleston (13,909) and Richmond (11,699) totaled 25,608 in 1860, 2.1 percent of the total slave population of 1,224,330 for all of the Carolinas and Virginia. In the three states under study, there were only fourteen urban areas in which more than 1,000 slaves lived in 1860. A total of 52,923 slaves lived in these fourteen cities and towns, or about 4.3 percent of the total slave population of North Carolina, South Carolina, and Virginia. After Charleston and Richmond, the next greatest concentrations of urban slaves could be found in Petersburg, Virginia (5,680); Wilmington, North Carolina (3,777); Norfolk, Virginia (3,284); Lynchburg, Virginia (2,694); and Newbern, North Carolina (2,383). The other seven urban areas —Alexandria and Fredericksburg, Virginia; and Fayetteville, Henderson, Hendersonville, Raleigh, and Salisbury, North Carolina—all had between 1,000 and 2,000 slaves in 1860. Because Charleston and Richmond were the two most distinctly urbanized areas in terms of both slave population and total population, I have elected to direct my attention elsewhere, focusing on the rural South and on smaller towns that would have retained much less of an urban sensibility than Charleston and Richmond. Nevertheless, I occasionally mention those two cities in the text as a point of comparison. Lockley's *Lines in the Sand* thoroughly examines interracial relationships in the urban context of Savannah.

poor white voices remain almost entirely silent, the use of wide-ranging sources begins to uncover slave–poor white relationships during the last four full decades of slavery.[14]

Although poor whites interacted with blacks both slave and free, enslaved blacks did so with greater frequency. In 1860, there were only 262,000 free blacks in the slave states, compared to four million bondspeople. Free blacks could be found in the greatest concentrations in the Upper South states of Delaware and Maryland, where they comprised 91.7 percent and 49.1 percent of the total African-American population, respectively. Free blacks' proportion of the black population decreased as one ventured farther south. In Virginia and the Carolinas, slaves greatly outnumbered free blacks, by a ratio of roughly nine to one in Virginia, eleven to one in North Carolina, and a staggering forty to one in South Carolina. Collectively, the more than 1.2 million slaves in the Carolinas and Virginia dwarfed the free black population of 98,000. Moreover, the South's free blacks were often concentrated in urban pockets. More than 36 percent of South Carolina's 9,900 free blacks, for instance, lived in Charleston District.[15] These figures suggest that poor whites had greater opportunities to come into contact with members of the numerically superior and more widely diffused slave population than with free blacks. Surviving court records suggest as much. Poor whites interacted with free blacks in many of the ways they did with slaves, but extant sources document far more of their contacts with the latter. Free blacks sometimes gathered promiscuously with slaves and poor whites, but slaves—primarily American-born field hands—remain the African Americans of interest here.

The poor whites under study prove far more difficult to define. Any examination of the Old South's poor whites is fraught with peril. First, the appellation "poor white" retains pejorative qualities today, conjuring negative images of trailer parks, intrafamily marriage, and cars on blocks, among many others. His-

14. Based on extant court records, the nine South Carolina districts I researched most closely are Fairfield, Greenville, Lancaster, Laurens, Spartanburg, Union, and York in the upcountry, as well as Marlboro and Williamsburg. In North Carolina, I examined thirty counties: Bertie, Carteret, Chowan, Craven, Edgecombe, Gates, Nash, New Hanover, Northampton, Pasquotank, Perquimans, Pitt, Richmond, Robeson, Wayne, and Wilson in the east; Caldwell, Chatham, Cleveland, Davidson, Granville, Guilford, Iredell, Orange, Randolph, Rockingham, Stanly, and Stokes in the Piedmont; and Haywood and McDowell in the mountains.

15. George Brown Tindall with David E. Shi, *America: A Narrative History*, vol. 1, 3rd ed. (New York: W. W. Norton & Company, 1992), 570; Kolchin, *American Slavery*, 82; Kennedy, *Population of the United States in 1860*, 515, 356, 451, 448–449.

torians must cast aside modern-day preconceived notions of poor whites to de-tach themselves from the present and deal with antebellum poor whites fairly. Second, most antebellum southerners made the sophisticated distinction be-tween whites who were poor and "poor whites." Whites who were poor suffered merely from depressed economic circumstances; "poor whites," usually but not necessarily quantitatively poor, possessed deficiencies in moral character, such as drunkenness or laziness. The mountain whites of North Carolina, for instance, were generally poor economically, but because as a rule they were hard working and industrious, contemporaries excluded most of them from the culturally de-fined category of "poor white." Petitions to southern governors frequently re-quested executive clemency for "poor but respectable" individuals convicted of crimes; almost no one rallied to defend degenerate, undeserving "poor whites."[16]

Complicating matters still further, antebellum southerners themselves—black and white—never reached a clear consensus on the criteria for inclusion in the poor white class. One former slave from Virginia explained to an inter-viewer that he "contemptuously" called those "persons who in old times owned no slaves" "po' white folks."[17] But definitions varied from person to person, and inconsistencies plagued individual judgments. In his *Recollections of Slavery Times,* Allen Parker, an ex-slave born in Chowan County, North Carolina, wrote that "my mother was let out to a poor white, that is a farmer who did not own any slaves." Slave ownership, however, could not have been the only marker of poor white-ness, for Parker himself was hired to John Littlefield, "a poor white who had two women slaves and a slave of his own." He also once lived with Eli-sha Buck, "a mean poor white who had a large farm, and owned some slaves."[18] In the first instance, Parker defines poor whites in strictly economic terms, as

16. Edward Ingle, *Southern Sidelights: A Picture of Social and Economic Life in the South a Generation Before the War* (Boston: Thomas Y. Crowell & Company, 1896), 22; J. Wayne Flynt, *Dixie's Forgotten People: The South's Poor Whites* (Bloomington: Indiana University Press, 1979), 8–9; F. N. Boney, *Southerners All* (Macon: Mercer University Press, 1984), 39; Barbara L. Bellows, "'My Children, Gentlemen, Are My Own': Poor Women, the Urban Elite, and the Bonds of Obligation in Antebellum Charleston," in *The Web of Southern Social Relations: Women, Family, & Education,* ed. Walter J. Fraser, Jr., R. Frank Saunders, Jr., and Jon L. Wakelyn (Athens: University of Georgia Press, 1985), 54; I. A. Newby, *Plain Folk in the New South: Social Change and Cultural Persistence, 1880–1915* (Baton Rouge: Louisiana State University Press, 1989), 9–13. See the *Raleigh Register,* March 25, 1830, for an account of "an industrious, respectable poor woman" deserving of public sympathy.

17. John W. Blassingame, *Slave Testimony: Two Centuries of Letters, Speeches, Interviews, and Autobiographies* (Baton Rouge: Louisiana State University Press, 1977), 488.

18. Allen Parker, *Recollections of Slavery Times* (Worcester, Mass.: Chas. W. Burbank & Co., 1895), 10, 84, 75.

whites without slaves. This, of course, conflates poor whites and nonslavehold-ing yeoman farmers, something historians have also been known to do.[19] In the second and third cases, the whites to whom Parker refers owned slaves, but still qualified in his mind as poor whites. Similarly, another North Carolina bonds-man recorded that his former master sold him for $50 to a Mrs. Wheeler, "a poor white woman of the neighborhood."[20] These instances suggest that character, and not wealth alone, somehow came into play in determining who counted among the South's poor whites.

The inability of antebellum southerners to arrive at a single, uniform defini-tion of poor whites makes the task that much more daunting for historians. Un-bothered by troublesome issues of definition, the early historians of poor whites did little to alleviate the confusion.[21] Recently, in by far the best work to date on the antebellum southern lower class, Charles C. Bolton defined poor whites in purely economic terms, as those southerners who owned neither land nor slaves. Bolton and Scott P. Culclasure have uncovered the details of the life of one ex-ceptional poor white man named Edward Isham, who was executed for murder in North Carolina in 1860. While an account of Isham's life fulfills virtually all of the unflattering stereotypes about his class's drinking, fighting, gambling, and carousing, it successfully depicts the South's disadvantaged poor whites' struggle to endure in a slaveholders' society.[22]

The definition of poor whites used in this book expands somewhat upon that of Bolton. Most of the poor whites under investigation here owned neither land nor slaves, and survived, as Bolton explains, as farm tenants and laborers. But, in contrast with Bolton, they may also have possessed a few paltry acres or an-other form of wealth, such as a grog shop. Furthermore, as Allen Parker's remi-niscences of slavery demonstrate, southern whites who owned one, two, or even more slaves could nevertheless be considered "poor whites" by their enslaved

19. See, for example, Michael Fellman, "Getting Right With the Poor White," *Canadian Re-view of American Studies* 18 (Winter 1987): 527–539. Bill Cecil-Fronsman's "common whites" and Timothy James Lockley's "non-slaveholders" lump poor whites together with a much larger seg-ment of the white population. See Cecil-Fronsman, *Common Whites*, 1; and Lockley, *Lines in the Sand*, xvi.

20. William Henry Singleton, *Recollections of My Slavery Days* (Peekskill, N.Y.: Highland Democrat, 1922), 5.

21. See note 2, above.

22. Bolton, *Poor Whites*, ix, 5, 11, 8; Bolton and Culclasure, *Confessions of Edward Isham*. On postbellum poor whites, see Flynt, *Dixie's Forgotten People*; J. Wayne Flynt, *Poor but Proud: Alabama's Poor Whites* (Tuscaloosa: University of Alabama Press, 1989); Newby, *Plain Folk in the New South*.

or slaveholding neighbors. The impossibility of determining individual character from the available sources, however, precludes an examination exclusively of
those whom antebellum southerners would have defined culturally as degraded
"poor whites." The definition of poor whites used here, therefore, straddles the
divide between Bolton's and the more authentic, antebellum southern usage by
embracing both quantitative and qualitative components. The poor whites appearing in these pages usually conform to Bolton's economically objective criteria, regardless of individual character, but in recognition of antebellum southerners' own empirical use of the term "poor white," or, the still more derogatory
"po' white trash," so do a handful of purportedly disreputable small slaveholders, crossroads merchants, and others who would otherwise violate Bolton's strict
economic parameters.

Eight million whites inhabited the South in 1860. In the first years of the Civil
War, Irish professor J. E. Cairnes estimated that the "mean whites" or "white
trash" comprised "no less than five millions of human beings," or "about seven-
tenths of the whole white population." According to Cairnes, the South accommodated an impoverished and degraded majority that "exist[ed] . . . in a condition little removed from savage life, eking out a wretched subsistence by hunting,
by fishing, by hiring themselves out for occasional jobs, [and] by plunder."[23] Like
Cairnes, many travelers to the South, whether from the North or from abroad,
failed to discriminate between poor whites and the southern yeomanry, and subsequently inflated the region's number of poor whites. Landless poor white farm
tenants and laborers actually made up between 30 and 50 percent of the southern white population, depending on locality.[24] If northern writer and one-time
cotton merchant James R. Gilmore (one of the few outsiders to appreciate the
subtle distinctions among nonelite southerners) may be believed, the so-called
trash numbered perhaps half a million, no more than 20 percent of the landless
white population and approximately 6 percent of southern white population as a

23. J. E. Cairnes, *The Slave Power: Its Character, Career, and Probable Designs*, 2nd ed. (New York:
Carleton, 1862), 54–55.

24. Bolton, *Poor Whites*, 5, 192; Lapp, "Ante Bellum Poor Whites of the South Atlantic States,"
10–11, 13–14, 15, 16, 18, 20. William L. Barney offers a somewhat more conservative estimate of 20 to
30 percent. See William Barney, *The Road to Secession: A New Perspective on the Old South* (Washington: Praeger Publishers, 1972), 42; William L. Barney, *The Secessionist Impulse: Alabama and Mississippi in 1860* (Princeton: Princeton University Press, 1974), 39. Work from Georgia and Tennessee
suggests higher rates. See Frederick A. Bode and Donald E. Ginter, *Farm Tenancy and the Census in
Antebellum Georgia* (Athens: University of Georgia Press, 1986); Fred Arthur Bailey, *Class and Tennessee's Confederate Generation* (Chapel Hill: University of North Carolina Press, 1987), 25, 171–172.

whole.[25] Certainly the "trash" left visitors with an impression disproportional to their overall numbers.

Membership in the social category of poor whites was fluid rather than static or fixed. Most poor whites in their thirties, forties, or older never improved their circumstances and remained permanently impoverished. But others identified as poor whites in this book, especially those in their late teens and twenties, were not condemned to a lifetime of poverty. Because of their youth, they had yet to acquire property of their own or to receive their inheritance. Take, for instance, the "nigger-breaker" Edward Covey, assigned the task of instilling discipline in the enslaved Frederick Douglass. Douglass described Covey as "a poor man, a farm-renter," "just commencing in life." Indeed, at the time of Douglass's stay, Covey was renting a 150-acre farm in Talbot County, Maryland, but in a few short years, he purchased a farm of 196 acres, and by the time of his death in 1875, he owned an estate worth a substantial sum of over $15,000.[26] It is rarely possible, however, to trace geographically mobile poor whites over a number of years. Historians must instead rely on the brief biographical snapshots census records provide, the quick glimpse of an individual at a particular moment in time. Relatively few poor whites appear in consecutive censuses in the same county, or even in the same state. Thus, some southerners identified here as poor whites undoubtedly were actually yeoman sons who rented land or worked as farm laborers prior to obtaining their own acreage. Through hard work and perhaps a little luck, some poor whites rose above their condition to become yeomen themselves, or even large slaveholders. But social mobility worked in both directions. A greater number of individuals fell into the poor white category over the course of the antebellum years. The vicissitudes of weather could easily destroy a struggling yeoman's crops, agricultural income declined during periods of depression, soil depletion in the older slave states reduced crop yields, and rising slave prices kept slaveholding out of reach of an increasing number of southern whites. All of these developments contributed to a downwardly mobile trend and to the swelling population of poor whites by the outbreak of the Civil War.[27]

25. James R. Gilmore, "Poor Whites of the South," *Harper's Magazine* 29 (June 1864): 115; James R. Gilmore [Edmund Kirke, pseud.], *Down in Tennessee, and Back By Way of Richmond* (New York: Carleton, 1864), 183, 190.

26. David W. Blight, ed., *Narrative of the Life of Frederick Douglass, An American Slave, Written by Himself* (New York: Bedford Books of St. Martin's Press, 1993), 71, 70, 73, 113.

27. Harris, *Plain Folk and Gentry*, 88–90; Lawrence T. McDonnell, "Work, Culture, and Society in the Slave South, 1790–1861," in *Black and White Cultural Interaction in the Antebellum South*, ed. Ted Ownby (Jackson: University Press of Mississippi, 1993), 126, 130–137; Ralph Mann, "Mountains,

The degree of contact between poor whites and slaves varied widely by location, based on the distribution of the two groups throughout the region. Many slaves and poor whites seldom came into contact with one another.[28] Scholars John Inscoe and Wilma A. Dunaway have crafted significant studies on slavery in the Appalachian setting, yet compared to the coastal plain and Piedmont regions of the South, relatively few slaves resided in the mountains of western North Carolina and Virginia, and many whites living in isolated valleys surely encountered slaves on only rare occasion, if ever.[29] Conversely, few poor whites lived on the most fertile lands of the black belt, where some of the densest populations of slaves cultivated tobacco and cotton for their masters. Slaveholders routinely purchased desirable poor white holdings to consolidate their own estates. Shunted to more marginal, unproductive, or depleted lands, poor whites had the greatest opportunities for regular contact with slaves at the ragged fringes of the plantation economy, in the Piedmont and the upper coastal plain.[30] Even then, masters sometimes forbade interracial interaction, or slaves and poor whites

---

Land, and Kin Networks: Burkes Garden, Virginia, in the 1840s and 1850s," *Journal of Southern History* 58 (August 1992): 411–434; Randolph B. Campbell, "Planters and Plain Folk: Harrison County, Texas, as a Test Case, 1850–1860," *Journal of Southern History* 40 (August 1974): 369–398; Gavin Wright, "'Economic Democracy' and the Concentration of Agricultural Wealth in the Cotton South, 1850–1860," *Agricultural History* 44 (January 1970): 63–93; James C. Bonner, "Profile of a Late Ante-Bellum Community," *American Historical Review* 49 (July 1944), 667, 679.

28. Hundley, *Social Relations*, 273; William W. Freehling, *The South vs. the South: How Anti-Confederate Southerners Shaped the Course of the Civil War* (New York: Oxford University Press, 2001), 22.

29. Slaveholding, while not widespread in the mountainous areas of the South, is nonetheless worthy of attention. See John C. Inscoe, "Mountain Masters: Slaveholding in Western North Carolina," *North Carolina Historical Review* 61 (April 1984): 143–173; Inscoe, *Mountain Masters;* and Wilma A. Dunaway, *Slavery in the American Mountain South* (New York: Cambridge University Press, 2003).

30. Stephanie McCurry deserves credit for demonstrating that the South Carolina low country did not consist exclusively of planters and slaves. Her analysis of the minority white population of the region reveals a host of "self-working farmers" who possessed varying quantities of land and slaves. See McCurry, *Masters of Small Worlds*, 43–55 (quotation 48). Her discovery of a yeoman majority among the white population in the low country, combined with the great planters who owned estates there, confirms that poor whites, while certainly not entirely absent from the low country, constituted a distinct minority of its total white population. On the geographic distribution of poor whites and their relatively small numbers in the low country, see Jacqueline Jones, "Encounters, Likely and Unlikely, between Black and Poor White Women in the Rural South, 1865–1940," *Georgia Historical Quarterly* 76 (Summer 1992), 337; Lapp, "Ante Bellum Poor Whites of the South Atlantic States," 22; and Robert Olwell, *Masters, Slaves, & Subjects: The Culture of Power in the South Carolina Low Country, 1740–1790* (Ithaca: Cornell University Press, 1998), 31.

made voluntary efforts to avoid one another. As a former Wake County, North Carolina, slave explained, "People didn't sociate together, pore whites, free niggers, slaves, and de slave owners. No dey didn' sociate much befo' de war."[31] Such may well have been the experience of that particular slave, but throughout the South, slaves and poor whites came into contact far more frequently than slaveholders wanted.

How, precisely, did slaves and poor whites interact in the Old South? Because racial slavery anchored the southern social order, historians have often assumed that animosity between blacks and whites divided the two groups. This contention contains some merit but fails to capture the complex range of relations between slaves and poor whites in the antebellum South. Slaves and poor whites interacted in different contexts with a number of potential outcomes. Chapter 1 surveys the many possible points of social contact between them. Slaves and poor whites sometimes worked together, whether harmoniously or otherwise, and relaxed with one another in their leisure time, occasionally in church but more often in a more profane and overwhelmingly male subculture of drinking and gambling. More than any other activity, trade in an array of goods brought slaves and poor whites together. The second chapter explores their frequent illicit economic exchanges that so alarmed southern slaveholders. Despite masters' anxiety over the underground trade, poor whites played crucial roles in the maintenance of the southern social hierarchy. As overseers, patrollers, and slave catchers, poor whites performed essential tasks for slaveholders. But as chapter 3 explains, poor whites occupied an ambiguous position with respect to the slave regime. When they aided fugitive slaves or, on rare occasion, helped them conspire to rebel, they fueled slaveholders' doubts about their commitment to the social order. Concerned planters were gratified to see violence erupt between slaves and poor whites, accepting it as evidence of their mutual animosity. Chapter 4, however, suggests that some of the violence that occurred resulted instead from erstwhile amicable socializing in a masculine interracial subculture hidden from masters' view. The fifth chapter explores both voluntary and involuntary sex between slaves and poor whites. The gendered experiences of poor white women and men confirmed the double standard that pervaded southern society. An examination of all of these points of contact sharpens historians' understanding of slave–poor white relations. In contrast to the stereotype of invariable hatred dividing them,

31. George P. Rawick, ed., *The American Slave: A Composite Autobiography*, vol. 15, pt. 2 (Westport, Conn.: Greenwood Publishing Company, 1972), 272.

it reveals a complex relationship between slaves and poor whites, a curious mix of love and hate, equality and inequality. At times, shared economic deprivation and impoverishment tempered racial hostilities and drew slaves and poor whites together into civil, cordial, and even intimate and loving relationships. On a daily basis, slave and poor white interaction both reinforced and challenged southern racial boundaries.[32]

The profoundly altered racial dynamics of the last third of the nineteenth century bequeathed us a legacy of racial animosity and segregation that has obscured our memory of the shared and complex interracial past between slaves and poor whites, at least in the antebellum decades. Several historians of early America have commented upon the relative openness and striking flexibility of race relations in the colonial era. Slaves, black indentured servants, and free blacks regularly fraternized with white indentured servants and other lower-class whites in their day-to-day lives, at work, at play, and in bed. After 1660, however, black slavery gradually supplanted indentured servitude in the South, a process that accelerated in Virginia after Bacon's Rebellion of 1676 and in the Carolina low country with the expansion of export staples in the 1690s. By the end of the seventeenth century, racial boundaries had solidified. Colonial legislatures passed new sets of laws designed to restrict black freedoms, and dark skin became an undeniable badge of inferiority. Lower-class whites continued to socialize and cooperate with slaves throughout the eighteenth century, but as Philip D. Morgan contends, "the trend was in the opposite direction," toward "reciprocal contempt."[33]

---

32. A few passing remarks in the early historical writings on poor whites suggested that relationships between slaves and poor whites were not always antagonistic. See, for example, Brown, "Role of the Poor Whites," 262. But the clearest expression to date of the cooperation-contention thesis may be found in Genovese, *Roll, Jordan, Roll,* and "Rather Be a Nigger Than a Poor White Man." Lockley's findings for his "non-slaveholders" also reflect this theme.

33. Winthrop D. Jordan, *White Over Black: American Attitudes toward the Negro, 1550–1812* (Chapel Hill: University of North Carolina Press, 1968); Edmund S. Morgan, *American Slavery, American Freedom: The Ordeal of Colonial Virginia* (New York: W. W. Norton & Company, 1975); Peter Wood, *Black Majority: Negroes in Colonial South Carolina from 1670 through the Stono Rebellion* (New York: W. W. Norton & Company, Inc., 1975); Ira Berlin, "Time, Space, and the Evolution of Afro-American Society on British Mainland North America," *American Historical Review* 85 (February 1980): 44–78; T. H. Breen and Stephen Innes, *"Myne Owne Ground": Race and Freedom on Virginia's Eastern Shore, 1640–1676* (New York: Oxford University Press, 1980); T. H. Breen, "A Changing Labor Force and Race Relations in Virginia, 1660–1710," *Journal of Social History* 7 (Fall 1993): 3–25; Philip D. Morgan, *Slave Counterpoint: Black Culture in the Eighteenth-Century Chesapeake & Lowcountry* (Chapel Hill: University of North Carolina Press, 1998), 310.

Yet despite the institutionalization of racial slavery and the maturation of the slave system, the colonial-era amity between slaves and lower-class whites never entirely disappeared. Even during the antebellum decades, race relations were not predetermined but rather negotiated continually by individuals acting in specific contexts. Slaves and poor whites in the Old South persisted in crossing racial lines in violation of social convention. As historians have contended for decades, mutual hostility shaped many of these interactions. Slaves and poor whites competed for work and committed violence and sexual assaults upon one another. Poor whites loyal to slaveholders contributed to the preservation of the slave regime by serving on slave patrol, tracking down runaways, and acting as extra sets of eyes and ears for the master. But at other times, slaves and poor whites overcame racial barriers to mingle in any number of ways that should not have occurred in a society rigidly divided by race. They worked side by side in a state of mutual dependence. They fraternized and socialized with one another, drinking, gambling, and attending church, and they conducted an informal underground network of trade to the detriment of the master. Potentially more subversive to the racially based slave society, slaves and poor whites sometimes consented to interracial sex. Poor whites also appeared to undermine the southern social structure when they aided fugitive slaves. Alienated from mainstream southern society and with few opportunities for upward mobility, poor whites had little to lose by consorting with slaves.[34]

The study of relations between slaves and poor whites promises to deepen our understanding of both groups. Poor whites have received precious little attention from historians, and their world remains relatively wide open for examination. By studying their range of contacts with slaves, both while at work and at play, this book provides insight into their daily lives and their ongoing struggle to survive in a slaveholding society that marginalized them socially and economically. While historians have largely neglected poor whites, they have constructed almost all of the scholarship on slavery around the reference point of the master. They have done excellent work exploring the dynamics of the master-slave relationship and slaves' efforts to build and sustain their own community and shape their own lives, socially, culturally, and economically. Yet masters and slaves did not coexist in a vacuum. Their neighbors often included poor whites, whom many planters loathed, and with whom slaves worked, socialized, traded, plotted, fought, and had sex. Like studies of the "slave community," this book shows

34. Cecil-Fronsman, *Common Whites*, 90.

slaves and poor whites described here demonstrate that interracial contacts were not governed exclusively according to a single, unifying racial principle. That poor whites did not always view their world in strictly racial terms permitted their often cordial interactions with slaves. Racial appeals for white unity carried less resonance among poor whites than among whites of any other class. As the group of southern whites with the least stake in slavery, poor whites lacked realistic aspirations of upward mobility within the system.[39] They were acutely aware that their material condition differed little from that of slaves, and among many, that realization engendered a sense of camaraderie rather than resentment.

A look at slave–poor white relationships thus helps refine our understanding of race relations in the antebellum South. The power of an omnipotent racism or blanket feelings of white supremacy to unite disparate classes of whites varied, in fact, by class. Slaves and poor whites lived parts of their lives independently from their social superiors. Their contact with one another occurred on a profoundly different level, in ways that did not mirror their relations with the slaveholding planter class. Slave–poor white relationships sometimes suggested racial animosity, but at many other times, slaves and poor whites overlooked their racial differences to interact in ways that bordered on equality and even inverted the normal social order. Even during slavery, compassion and cooperation sometimes prevailed. Slave–poor white contact often blurred racial distinctions and at times at least appeared to threaten the system of slavery itself. To the slaveholders who reigned over the Old South, these alarmingly frequent violations of southern racial etiquette were a genuine concern, but their best efforts could not prevent them.

39. Cecil-Fronsman, *Common Whites*, 90; Bolton, *Poor Whites*, 120, 84. Charles C. Bolton has suggested that slaveholders' racial appeals to unite whites of all socioeconomic classes probably exerted less influence on poor whites than on yeoman farmers, for impoverished, landless whites, though nonslaveholders, did not share the same interests as independent, landholding yeomen. J. Wayne Flynt, by contrast, argues that yeomen and poor whites shared common interests. See Flynt, *Dixie's Forgotten People*, 12.

CHAPTER I

THE SOCIAL WORLD OF SLAVES AND POOR WHITES

Work, Leisure, and Perception

Historians long ago commented on the mutual hostility that characterized relations between slaves and poor whites in the antebellum South. Despite more recent work to the contrary, misconceptions persist.[1] The long-standing myth of unwavering slave–poor white animosity has obscured a much broader range of relationships. To be sure, in some cases, slaves and poor whites did resent one another. But that enmity has concealed a far more complex set of relationships between slaves and poor whites that encompassed a wide spectrum of emotions and behavior. An examination of the work and leisure-time activities of slaves and poor whites reveals not only hatred but also friendship and camaraderie. Some bondspeople stepped outside the slave quarters and beyond the boundaries of the plantation, and some poor whites excused themselves from "respectable" white society to inhabit a shared, interracial social world in which antagonism succumbed to the realization of their collective degradation. Racial inequalities never disappeared, but slave–poor white fraternization nevertheless challenged the southern hierarchy of race.

The degree of contact between slaves and poor whites varied by location. Planter D. R. Hundley contended that "[t]he Poor Whites of the South seldom

1. Paul H. Buck, "The Poor Whites of the Ante-Bellum South," *American Historical Review* 31 (October 1925): 52; Avery O. Craven, "Poor Whites and Negroes in the Ante-Bellum South," *Journal of Negro History* 15 (January 1930): 19; A. N. J. Den Hollander, "The Tradition of 'Poor Whites,'" in *Culture in the South*, ed. W. T. Couch (Chapel Hill: University of North Carolina Press, 1935), 417; W. O. Brown, "Role of the Poor Whites in Race Contacts of the South," *Social Forces* 19 (December 1940): 262; Rosser H. Taylor, *Ante Bellum South Carolina: A Social and Cultural History* (Chapel Hill: University of North Carolina Press, 1942), 85; Rudolph M. Lapp, "The Ante Bellum Poor Whites of the South Atlantic States" (Ph.D. diss., University of California–Berkeley, 1956), 4. Eugene D. Genovese, "'Rather Be a Nigger Than a Poor White Man': Slave Perceptions of Southern Yeomen and Poor Whites," in *Toward a New View of America: Essays in Honor of Arthur C. Cole*, ed. Hans L. Trefousse (New York: Burt Franklin & Company, Inc., 1977), 79–96, offers a far more nuanced view of slave–poor white relations that serves as the foundation for my own work.

come in contact with the slaves at all, and thousands of them never saw a negro." Hundley's generalization exaggerated the social separation of slaves and poor whites in the Old South. Many slaves surely mingled little with poor whites, and a few probably never encountered them. In areas far removed from plantation districts, such as western Virginia and North Carolina, the relative paucity of slaves combined with the isolation of poor white cabins to limit their occasions for interaction. Similarly, in the heart of the black belt, slaveholders often bought out their poor white neighbors to obtain their valuable lands for the cultivation of cash crops. Thus, they essentially banished poor whites from those areas with the greatest concentrations of slaves. But at the margins of plantation society, where fertile soils gave way to less productive lands, poor whites owned or squatted on small, sterile lots amid the modest holdings of yeomen and the impressive tracts of large slaveholders. There, rich, middling, and poor lived side by side. The demographics and the spatial distribution of the population in these areas afforded the greatest opportunities for slave and poor white contact, cities such as Richmond and Charleston notwithstanding.[2]

Many poor whites did loathe slaves, but it was travelers to the South and slaveholders alike who fed the myth of all poor whites' unequivocal hatred of them. Touring the South, Frederick Law Olmsted reported that poor whites "seem . . . more than any other portion of the community, to hate and despise the negroes." Fellow traveler James Stirling concurred. "The 'white trash' of the South, though not themselves holding slaves," he recorded, "have all the passions and prejudices of slave-holders in the most exaggerated form." Slaveholders and poor whites both considered themselves racially superior to slaves, but only poor whites "have a personal dislike of the negroes," he noted. By contrast, "all planters of any heart or principle feel a certain interest in the welfare of their 'people,' and, in many cases, even affection for them." According to this widely held view, slaveholders' paternalist impulses and concerns with their own economic well-being prevented them from despising slaves as poor whites allegedly did. Masters also actively promoted poor whites' hatred of slaves to prevent interracial contact and possible class-based alliances. An ex-slave from North Carolina reported that "the poor

2. D. R. Hundley, *Social Relations in Our Southern States* (New York: Henry B. Price, 1860; reprint, New York: Arno Press, 1973), 273; Genovese, "Rather Be a Nigger Than a Poor White Man," 80–81; Craven, "Poor Whites and Negroes," 19; Orville Vernon Burton, *In My Father's House Are Many Mansions: Family and Community in Edgefield, South Carolina* (Chapel Hill: University of North Carolina Press, 1985), 48.

white man . . . was down on us. He was driven to it, by the rich slave owner."
One slaveholder insisted that poor whites harbored nothing but "downright envy
and hatred of the black man."[3]

Those poor whites who did feel "envy and hatred" toward slaves may have
resented the fact that their standard of living often differed little from that of
slaves. Despite the enslavement of one and freedom of the other, slave and poor
white levels of material existence were similar in many respects. Neither their
single-room homes, monotonous diets, nor homespun clothing clearly distinguished one from the other.[4] Some reports even gave a slight advantage to the
bondspeople. Traversing the North Carolina backcountry in 1833, New Englander Henry Barnard observed that "[t]he poor *whites* . . . are not as well off
in their physical condition as the slaves, and hardly as respectable." "Dere was a
heap of poor white folks in slavery time," agreed one South Carolina ex-slave,
"and some of them lived mighty hard, worse than the slaves sometimes." A former North Carolina slave likewise opined that "poor whites' living was not as
good as that of the average negro."[5]

Poor white men and women often labored at tasks similar to those performed
by their slave counterparts, sometimes alongside them and sometimes in competition. Members of both groups lived lives of hardship and toil. One landless
and impoverished white Civil War veteran acknowledged that "the poor class of
People was al most slaves them selves. [They] had to work hard and live hard."
Many slaves concurred. Robert Toatley, remembering a pair of poor white men
in his South Carolina neighborhood, commented, "Poor white people 'round in
slavery . . . had a hard time." "I don't know but two sets of white folks slaves up
my way; one was name Chatman, an' de tother one Nellovies," recalled a former
slave in Lunenburg County, Virginia. "Dese two families worked on [Colonel
Robert] Allen's farm as we did. Off from us on a plot called Morgan's lot, there

3. Frederick Law Olmsted, *A Journey in the Seaboard Slave States, with Remarks on Their Econ-*
omy (New York: Dix & Edwards, 1856), 85; James Stirling, *Letters from the Slave States* (London:
John W. Parker and Son, 1857), 86; George P. Rawick, ed., *The American Slave: A Composite Auto-*
biography, vol. 15, pt. 2 (Westport, Conn.: Greenwood Publishing Company, 1972), 319; Hundley,
Social Relations, 273.

4. Genovese, "Rather Be a Nigger Than a Poor White Man," 90; Craven, "Poor Whites and
Negroes," 16–17.

5. Henry Barnard, ed. Bernard C. Steiner, "The South Atlantic States in 1833, as Seen By a
New Englander," *Maryland Historical Magazine* 13 (December 1918), 338; Rawick, vol. 3, pt. 3, 51;
W. H. Robinson, *From Log Cabin to the Pulpit, or, Fifteen Years in Slavery*, 3rd ed. (Eau Claire, Wis.:
James H. Tifft, 1913), 22.

dey lived as slaves jes like us Colored fo'ks. Yes de poor white man had some dark an' tough days, like us poor niggers."[6]

But whereas prudent masters provided slaves food, clothing, and shelter, poor whites had to worry about obtaining these basic necessities on their own. As a result, a white man of Rockbridge County, Virginia, confidently declared in 1854 that slaves, "as a mass are better fed, housed and clothed than many of the poor white families in our community." By itself, this pronouncement merits skepticism as an exaggerated assertion of white paternalism, but many bondspeople concurred with the assessment. Some South Carolina poor whites "come to see the niggers an' et with us," an ex-slave noted, because "we had more to eat than them. They was sorry folks." A Wilmington, North Carolina, slave asserted that poor whites "lived in no better homes, and many of them not as good as the negro quarters." Antislavery forces in the North would have been hesitant to acknowledge any benefits of slavery, yet even abolitionist Maria L. Davis of Massachusetts conceded that many blacks were better off in bondage than in freedom, for as slaves, "they do as they please to enjoy more luxuries than the poor class of whites." Observers, both white and black, implicitly agreed with slave autobiographer H. C. Bruce's assertion that the "'poor white' class was held in slavery, just as real as the blacks." Bishop Henry Benjamin Whipple likely expressed the opinion of many when he asserted in the early 1840s that "I had rather be a *well treated* slave than one of the low & poor whites."[7]

What poor whites lacked in material comforts they gained in freedoms denied slaves. During his travels, Frederick Law Olmsted heard it said "that the

6. Quoted in Fred Arthur Bailey, *Class and Tennessee's Confederate Generation* (Chapel Hill: University of North Carolina Press, 1987), 24; Rawick, vol. 3, pt. 4, 165; Rawick, vol. 16, Virginia, 9–10. See also Charles L. Perdue, Jr., Thomas E. Barden, and Robert K. Phillips, eds., *Weevils in the Wheat: Interviews with Virginia Ex-Slaves* (Charlottesville: University Press of Virginia, 1976), 79.

7. James Mellon, ed., *Bullwhip Days: The Slaves Remember* (New York: Weidenfeld & Nicolson, 1988), 449; Henry B. Jones, "Farming in Virginia," *DeBow's Review* 18 (January 1855), 60; Rawick, vol. 13, pt. 3, 290; Robinson, *From Log Cabin to the Pulpit*, 21; Maria L. Davis to the Goddards, February 5, 1843, Folder 1, James S. M. Davis Papers, SCL; H. C. Bruce, *The New Man: Twenty-Nine Years a Slave, Twenty-Nine Years a Free Man* (York, Penn.: P. Anstadt & Sons, 1895; reprint, New York: Negro Universities Press, 1969), iv; Whipple quoted in Delma E. Presley, "The Crackers of Georgia," *Georgia Historical Quarterly* 60 (Summer 1976): 107 [italics mine]. Successful fugitive slave Charles Ball recorded in his autobiography that many poor white people occupied "wretched cabins, not half so good as the houses which judicious planters provide for their slaves. Some of these cabins of the white men are made of mere sticks, or small poles notched, or rather thatched together, and filled in with mud, mixed with the leaves . . . of the pine tree." See Charles Ball, *Fifty Years in Chains* (1837; reprint, New York: Dover Publications, Inc., 1970), 290.

poor white people, . . . although they may own a cabin and a little furniture, and cultivate land enough to supply themselves with (maize) bread, are worse off in almost all respects than the slaves." Olmsted disagreed with this assessment, however. He conceded that poor whites may have been "ignorant and immoral, as well as indolent and unambitious," but, he observed, they at least reserved the possibility of advancing socially. From the ranks of poor whites, Olmsted asserted, "men *sometimes* elevate themselves to positions and habits of usefulness, and respectability." Slavery denied bondspeople this same opportunity, and slaves knew it. That was precisely what made poor whites' "degradation . . . all the more condemnable," wrote former slave H. C. Bruce, "because being white, all the world was open to them, yet they *from choice,* remained in the South, in this position of *quasi* slavery." Poor whites did not need a pass to move about the countryside; no one had to give them permission to escape their degraded condition. Although poor, they enjoyed basic freedoms that slaves did not. Thus, Bruce found it baffling that poor whites "would have remained in the South, generations after generations, filling menial positions, with no perceptible degree of advancement." The ex-slave recounted some of the ways in which poor whites were subservient to slaveholders: poor whites faced an uphill battle in any dispute with a slaveholder; they were rarely permitted to mingle socially or intermarry with slaveholding families; and at election time they voted "just as the master class directed." Though "nominally free," Bruce concluded, poor whites "obeyed their masters as did the slaves."[8]

Many slaves reciprocated the feelings of hatred that some poor whites held for them. Escaped slave Charles Ball noted that, in low-country South Carolina and Georgia and in other rural areas, animosity divided slaves and poor whites. The son of a large slaveholder in Abbeville District, South Carolina, reminisced that his family's aristocratic slave Griffin, a renowned muleteer and talented fiddler, looked with unabashed "contempt" upon the "po' white trash." Griffin's exceptional skills, openly acknowledged by many local whites, likely explained his pride and sense of superiority, but many bondspeople without such extraordinary aptitudes shared Griffin's scorn for poor whites. Slave narratives and autobiographies suggest that the origins of slaves' antipathy lay in the fact that poor whites so often served as overseers, patrollers, and spies for slaveowners. Poor whites

8. Olmsted, *Seaboard Slave States,* 84; Bruce, *New Man,* iv, 38, 30. One ex-slave from Virginia reported that local poor whites did need a pass from the slaveholder to move about. See Rawick, vol. 16, Virginia, 9–10.

often served as cogs in the machinery of slavery, performing much of the dirty work for the slaveholders and therefore earning slaves' abhorrence. Their roles in enforcing the slave regime, H. C. Bruce stated frankly, marked "the cause of the intense hatred of slaves against the poor whites of the South." For that same reason, he added, slaves developed their pejorative nickname for poor whites: "poor white trash."[9]

Not every slave automatically looked with contempt upon all economically disadvantaged white people, however. A good number of slaves instead assessed white folks with an unappreciated degree of sophistication, taking several criteria into consideration. Lazy, disreputable whites qualified as "trash," but honest, hard-working poor white people did not. As a Civil War veteran from the North Carolina mountains reported, "The Negroes rather looked down on poor white trash who wouldn[']t work and were not respectable." Many bondspeople also privileged slave ownership in assessing rank. According to another white veteran, slaves "respected white men according to the number of slaves owned by them." They might observe that a particular master "has only 2 niggers" and not look upon him as highly as one with ten, twenty, or one hundred. They "had little respect for white men who owned no slaves [and] inclined to call them 'poor white trash.'" A former South Carolina slave confirmed this impression: "[T]hey was white folks in de neighborhood dat wasn't able to own slaves. All dis class of people was called by us niggers, poor white folks." Frederick Douglass recorded that he was familiar with a particularly "ignorant and poverty-stricken" nonslaveholding white man who had become "the laughing stock even of slaves themselves," and who had thus acquired the "poor white trash" label. No consistent criteria, however, governed slaves' evaluations of white people. Many bondspeople took into consideration a white person's character, degree of respectability, and wealth, with individual slaves assigning varying weights to each factor.[10]

Slaves commonly ranked themselves as well. They not only evaluated themselves on the basis of their own talents, skills, physiques, or occupations, but also

9. Hundley, *Social Relations*, 274; Ball, *Fifty Years in Chains*, 291; J. G. Clinkscales, *On the Old Plantation: Reminiscences of His Childhood* (Spartanburg, S.C.: Band & White, 1916), 12; Bruce, *New Man*, 30; Genovese, "Rather Be a Nigger Than a Poor White Man," 80–81.

10. Colleen Morse Elliott and Louise Armstrong Moxley, *The Tennessee Civil War Veterans Questionnaires*, comp. Gustavus W. Dyer and John Trotwood Moore, vol. 1 (Easley, S.C.: Southern Historical Press, Inc., 1985), 402; Elliott and Moxley, *Tennessee Civil War Veterans Questionnaires*, vol. 2, 482; Rawick, vol. 2, pt. 1, 67–68; Frederick Douglass, *My Bondage and My Freedom* (New York: Miller, Orten & Mulligan, 1855), 344.

constructed identities in reference to their white owners. They sometimes established their relative position in the slave hierarchy according to their assessments of their masters. Many slaves identified with their owners and took great
pride in belonging to a wealthy, respected, and socially prominent master—"de
quality," as slaves termed it. To slaves, all slaveholders were not created equal;
like poor whites, they could just as easily classify as trash.[11] "To be a slave, was
thought to be bad enough," Frederick Douglass explained, "but to be a poor
man's slave, was deemed a disgrace, indeed."[12]

Belonging to a prosperous master bestowed status upon a slave. According to
Virginia-born bondsman Louis Hughes, "A servant owned by a man in moder-
ate circumstances was hooted at by rich men's slaves. It was common for them to
say: 'Oh! don't mind that darkey, he belongs to po'r white trash.'" A female slave
sold in Richmond feared that her new master "wuz goin' ter be er poor white
trash owner, kaze he wuz dressed en coarse jeans pants en er ole common shirt,
with er big wide belt, en wore high top boots. Mos' all rich folks comin' ter sales
done wore pleated bosom shirts and broadcloth suits." To the slave's relief, her
master's outward appearance belied his apparent wealth, for "when Marse Hurts
open his belt he got jes' plenty money."[13]

No slaves wanted "trashy" masters to reflect poorly on them. A slave autobiographer from Prince William County, Virginia, "heard slaves object to being
sent in very small companies to labor in the field, lest that some passer-by should
think that they belonged to a poor man, who was unable to keep a large gang."
Prior to visiting their enslaved parents, spouses, or children residing on distant
plantations, some slaves solicited their masters for tokens or gifts to distribute.
Virginia's Parke Johnston requested "some little thing to take along with me
when I goes to see dem niggers of mine." Otherwise, he feared, "Dey be show to
think I b'longs to po' white folks." A North Carolina runaway reported that slave
men "let out to a poor white" had difficulty impressing their female sweethearts
and convincing them to marry, while one South Carolina slave mother scolded
her misbehaving son by telling him, "[Y]ou act jest like a nigger from some pore
white trashes poor land." Slave autobiographer Austin Steward lamented the fact

11. Genovese, "Rather Be a Nigger Than a Poor White Man," 81.

12. Quoted in Kenneth M. Stampp, *The Peculiar Institution: Slavery in the Ante-Bellum South*
(New York: Vintage Books, 1956), 338.

13. Louis Hughes, *Thirty Years a Slave: From Bondage to Freedom* (Milwaukee: South Side Printing Company, 1897), 63; George P. Rawick, ed., *The American Slave: A Composite Autobiography, Supplement, Series 1*, vol. 5, Ohio (Westport, Conn.: Greenwood Press, 1977), 285.

that many bondspeople gave so much weight to their white oppressors in esti-mating their own worth. He condemned the "foolish pride" of those "poor, de-graded and ignorant slaves" who "love[d] to boast of their master's wealth and influence" and to evaluate themselves on that basis, yet it remained a common means of appraisal among slaves.[14]

Other slaves preferred belonging to a prosperous master not for reasons of status but to help assure that they would receive the basic necessities for survival. Ex-slave Calline Brown loathed her impoverished owners. "My master and Miss was the meanest folks what ever lived," she complained bitterly. "They warn't nothing but poor white trash what had never had nothing in their lives. . . . There wasn't nothing on that place. Not a cow, not a hog, nothing—not even so much as a feather from a chicken." Her master's poverty forced her to endure substan-tial material deprivation. "They ain't got no money to buy us no clothes, or shoes, so we goes in rags, and barefooted, even in the winter," she grumbled.[15] Whether for reasons of status or material comfort, bondspeople hoped to be able to recite truthfully the widely known verse:

> My folks war'n' none o' yo' po'-white-trash;
> Nor, sah, dey was ob high degree—
> Dis heah nigger am quality![16]

As Eugene Genovese has argued, identifying with a "quality" master heightened slaves' self-esteem,[17] but a "quality" owner was also more likely to keep slaves well stocked in the essentials.

At the same time, masters cultivated in their bondspeople a sense of antipa-thy toward poor whites. Many slaveholders specifically forbade contact between slaves and poor whites, either to preclude poor white "corruption" of their slaves, to restrict illicit trade, or to prevent rebellious activity. Regardless of the exact

14. Austin Steward, *Twenty-Two Years a Slave, and Forty Years a Freeman* (Rochester, N.Y.: William Alling, 1857), 101; John W. Blassingame, *Slave Testimony: Two Centuries of Letters, Speeches, Interviews, and Autobiographies* (Baton Rouge: Louisiana State University Press, 1977), 491; Allen Parker, *Recollections of Slavery Times* (Worcester, Mass.: Chas. W. Burbank & Co., 1895), 23; Raw-ick, vol. 2, pt. 2, 70; Steward, *Twenty-Two Years a Slave*, 101.

15. Rawick, SS1, vol. 6, pt. 1, 235.

16. Thomas Nelson Page, "Uncle Gabe's White Folks," in *Library of Southern Literature*, vol. 9, ed. Edwin Anderson Alderman and Joel Chandler Harris (Atlanta: Martin & Hoyt Company, 1909), 3883. See also Shields McIlwaine, *The Southern Poor-White from Lubberland to Tobacco Road* (Nor-man: University of Oklahoma Press, 1939), xiii.

17. Genovese, "Rather Be a Nigger Than a Poor White Man," 82.

reason, slaves often commented that the "rich slave owner wouldn' let his Negroes sociate with poor white folks." As a slave born near Charlotte, North Carolina, remembered, "There was poor whites, all around us, but Master didn't
allow them on his place." Recalling the "pore white folks" in his master's neighborhood, another slave remarked that "de rich slave owners didn' 'low 'em to
come on dere plantations." But poor whites occasionally ignored masters' man-
dates and "slipped in dere at night when de marster didn' know it."[18]

Slaves witnessed the ways in which masters interacted socially with their poor
white neighbors and frequently adopted their owners' oftentimes haughty attitude toward them. Poor whites often felt ill at ease during visits to the "big
house." Perhaps a poor white man needed money, a temporary job, medical aid,
or any number of other favors. He arrived at the big house humbly, hat in hand,
to make his request. Usually slaveowners graciously extended aid to all of their
less fortunate neighbors,[19] but some used the occasion to overawe and humiliate
the poor white. Masters used slaves as their liaisons during these exchanges.
North Carolina ex-slave Willie Blackwell remembered the ritual:

> Poor white fo'ks don't have much go in dem days. W'en dey wants to
> speak to de Marster, dey comes up to de gate in de small yahd an' hollers.
> De Marster looks outer de winder an' says, "Looky yonder! Now I won-
> dah what he wants?" Den he calls fo' de slave, an' w'en Ise dere, he sends
> me. He tells weuns to go see what de man wants. Ise goes down an' asks
> what he wants. He say, "Ise wants to see youse Marster." Ise says, "M'ybe
> youse bettah tell me what youse wants, an' Ise go tell him.["] M'ybe he's
> bit stiff necked, an' he says, "Go tell youse Marster Ise wants to see him."
> Ise says, "Yes suh! Yes suh!["], den goes an' tells de Marster he wants to
> speak to him. M'ybe Marster looks outer de winder 'gain an' looks him
> ovah 'gain, or m'ybe not, but he always says, "Youse go tell him dat if'n he
> can't tell youse what he wants, he can go plum to hell!" An' he meant it.

If they wished to be heard, poor whites had to suffer the pretensions of house servants, and, in effect, bargain with a slave to gain access to the master.[20]

18. Ibid., 81; Rawick, vol. 15, pt. 2, 319; Rawick, SS1, vol. 9, pt. 4, 1712; Rawick, vol. 15, pt. 2,
273–274.

19. Eugene D. Genovese, "Yeomen Farmers in a Slaveholders' Democracy," *Agricultural History*
49 (April 1975), 337–338; Genovese, "Rather Be a Nigger Than a Poor White Man," 83.

20. George P. Rawick, ed., *The American Slave: A Composite Autobiography, Supplement, Series 2*,
vol. 2, pt. 1 (Westport, Conn.: Greenwood Press, 1979), 308–309.

To exacerbate the degradation, some masters demarcated plantation spaces as off limits to poor whites. Some did not extend to poor whites the privilege of entering the great house. One successful fugitive recalled a local poor white man whom planters "would not receive . . . into their houses as a visitor any sooner than they would one of their own slaves." Or, masters might deny poor whites entry by the front door. Like slaves, poor whites were sometimes relegated to a separate and less conspicuous entrance in the rear. In South Carolina, master Nick Peay had "no patience wid poor white folks. They couldn't come in de front yard; they knowed to pass on by to de lot, hitch up deir hoss, and come knock on de kitchen door and make deir wants and wishes knowed to de butler." In Virginia, too, when poor whites "would come 'roun to de big house, dey had to come to de back do', an' de white folks would ask dem, 'What in de hell do you want?'" Hardly a cordial welcome, but as one slave remarked, "Po' whites was just like stray goats."[21]

Parasitic poor white men and women tried slaveholders' patience as they repeatedly asked for handouts and favors. The wealthy Mary Boykin Chesnut of South Carolina recorded her experiences with local poor white women who called at the plantation. According to Chesnut, "gangs of these Sandhill women traipsed in with baskets to be filled by charity, ready to carry away anything they could get." But, she clarified, "They were treated as friends and neighbors, not as beggars. They were asked to take seats by the fire, and there they sat for hours, stony-eyed, silent, wearing out human endurance and politeness. . . . When patience was at its last ebb, they would open their mouths and loudly demand whatever they had come to seek." Chesnut remembered "a one-eyed virago" from her childhood named Judy Bradly, "who played the fiddle at all the Sandhill dances and fandangoes." "Her list of requests was always rather long," Chesnut reported. On one occasion, when Bradly's list of favors seemed particularly excessive, Chesnut's grandmother "hesitated," provoking the Sandhill woman to exclaim, "Woman, do you mean to let me starve?" "My grandmother then attempted a meek lecture as to the duty of earning one's bread," Chesnut recalled. "Judy squared her arms akimbo and answered, 'And pray, who made you a judge of the world? Lord, Lord, if I had 'er knowed I had ter stand all this jaw, I wouldn't a took your ole things,' but she did take them and came afterward again and again."[22]

21. Wm. Wells Brown, *My Southern Home: or, The South and Its People* (Boston: A. G. Brown & Co., 1880), 84; Rawick, vol. 3, pt. 4, 147–148; Perdue et al, *Weevils in the Wheat*, 326.

22. Isabella D. Martin and Myrta Lockett Avary, eds., *A Diary from Dixie, as Written By Mary Boykin Chesnut* (New York: D. Appleton and Company, 1914), 401.

Raised in an atmosphere of slaveholders' contempt and thinly disguised tolerance for local poor whites, many slaves embraced their masters' sense of superiority. So pervasive was this feeling that, even during bondage, it found expression in different folk songs and verses:

> Rare back, Sam! stand back, Davis!
> As soon kiss a monkey as a poor white man.[23]

Rhymes sometimes employed slaves' most stinging epithet for poor whites:

> I had a little dog,
> His name was Dash.
> I'd rather be a nigger
> Than po'h white trash.[24]

Most slave verses mocking lower-class whites, however, incorporated the ubiquitous saying, "rather be a nigger than a poor white man." "Even in slavery they used to sing that," remembered one former South Carolina slave.[25] One such popular slave song consisted of a series of cleverly rhymed couplets:

> My name's Ran, I wuks in de san';
> But I'd druther be a Nigger dan a po' white man.
>
> Gwineter hitch my oxes side by side,
> An' take my gal fer a big fine ride.
>
> Gwineter take my gal to de country sto';
> Gwineter dress her up in red calico.
>
> You take Kate, an' I'll take Joe.
> Den off we'll go to de pahty-o.
>
> Gwineter take my gal to de Hullabaloo,
> Whar dere hain't no Crackers in a mile or two.
>
> Interlocution:
> (Fiddler) "Oh, Sal! Whar's de milk strainer cloth?"
> (Banjo Picker) "Bill's got it wropped 'round his ole sore leg."

23. E. C. Perrow, "Songs and Rhymes from the South," *Journal of American Folk-Lore* 28 (April–June 1915): 189.

24. Robert Russa Moton, *What the Negro Thinks* (Garden City, N.Y.: Doubleday, Doran and Company, Inc., 1932), 21.

25. Rawick, vol. 10, pt. 5, 20.

(Fiddler) "Well, take it down to de gum spring an' give it a cold
 water rench;
I 'spizes nastness anyway. I'se got to have a clean cloth fer de milk."

He don't lak whisky but he jest drinks a can.
Honey! I'd druther be a Nigger dan a po' white man.

I'd druther be a Nigger, an' plow ole Beck
Dan a white Hill Billy wid his long red neck.[26]

Both during slavery and after emancipation, black humor poked fun at poor whites.[27] This version of the song succeeds exceptionally well in that respect, with its panoply of derisive references to poor whites, crackers, hillbillies, and rednecks. Through these folk rhymes, the slave masses demonstrated a resilient mental outlook despite their oppression. While slaves earnestly desired their freedom, the song suggests that they would not accept freedom at just any price. Specifically, they did not yearn to be white. Whiteness may have meant liberty, but it was not synonymous with wealth, prestige, or respect. "Racial slavery," Eugene Genovese reminds us, "by its very nature, taught the slaves to despise their color and to worship whiteness." But by identifying themselves with the master class—"de quality"—slaves successfully combated the self-loathing associated with blackness. Even in the twentieth century, former slaves of partial white descent distinguished their respectable Caucasian ancestors from lower-class whites. Reuben Rosborough of South Carolina stated that his grandfather was a white man, but specifically instructed his interviewer, "[Y]ou can put down dere dat deres no poor white trash blood in dese old veins." South Carolina slave Delia Thompson likewise claimed her grandfather "was a white man, and no poor white trash neither."[28]

 Slaves often articulated a three-tiered conception of humanity, placing themselves squarely in the middle on the scale of respectability. "You know boss, dese

26. Thomas W. Talley, *Negro Folk Rhymes Wise and Otherwise with a Study* (1922; reprint, Port Washington, N.Y.: Kennikat Press, 1968), 42–43. Talley notes that this is the "milder version" of the rhyme. See ibid., 248. Another verse went, "My name is Sam and I don't give a damn, / I'd rather be a nigger than a poor white man." See Newman I. White, *American Negro Folk-Songs* (Hatboro, Penn.: Folklore Associates, Inc., 1965), 197.

27. Lawrence W. Levine, *Black Culture and Black Consciousness: Afro-American Folk Thought from Slavery to Freedom* (New York: Oxford University Press, 1977), 300–320, esp. 307.

28. Talley, *Negro Folk Rhymes*, 248–249; Genovese, "Rather Be a Nigger Than a Poor White Man," 83; Rawick, vol. 3, pt. 4, 45; Rawick, vol. 3, pt. 4, 161.

days dere is three kind of people," said a South Carolina slave woman. "Lowest down is a layer of white folks, then in de middle is a layer of colored folks and on top is de cream, a layer of good white folks. 'Spect it'll be dat way 'till Jedgement day." Similarly, escaped slave Charles Ball referred to the "white man, who has no property, no possession[s], and no education" as "a third order of men . . . who . . . hold a separate station, occupying a place of their own." The poor white "is, in Carolina, in a condition no better than that to which the slave has been re-duced; except only that he is master of his own person, and of his own time, and may, if he chooses, emigrate and transfer himself to a country where he can bet-ter his circumstances." Many slaves acknowledged their subservience to "good white folks," whoever they were—kind masters or other nonslaveholding whites of good character. But, disregarding racial differences, they often rated them-selves higher than poor whites. As Ball wrote, "there is no order of men in any part of the United States, . . . who are in a more debased and humiliated state of moral servitude, than are those white people." Consequently, many slaves con-cluded "that however miserable they may be, in their servile station, it is never-theless preferable to the degraded existence of these poor white people." A num-ber of slaves, then, divided the white race into two distinct camps. Ball spoke for many bondspeople when he asserted that poor whites composed "a separate and distinct race of men from the planters, and appear to have nothing in common with them. If it were possible for any people to occupy a grade in human society below that of the slaves," he continued, ". . . certainly the station would be filled by these white families, who cannot be said to possess any thing in the shape of property."[29]

When slaves' actions publicly manifested this understanding of humanity, few slaveholders took notice. According to Charles Ball, masters supported slaves' notions of superiority over poor whites. Most of them wanted to foster the opinion among their bondspeople that slaves "are better off in the world than are many white persons," who, though free, had to fend for themselves. If masters could convince slaves of that, they extinguished slaves' aspirations for freedom and helped suppress discontent.[30] Many masters therefore found it amusing when slaves ridiculed or expressed contempt for poor whites.[31] A few slavehold-

29. Genovese, "Rather Be a Nigger Than a Poor White Man," 79; Rawick, vol. 3, pt. 3, 82; Ball, *Fifty Years in Chains,* 289, 290, 291.

30. Ball, *Fifty Years in Chains,* 291. See also *The Rev. J. W. Loguen, as a Slave and as a Freeman: A Narrative of Real Life* (1859; reprint, New York: Negro Universities Press, 1968), 144–145.

31. Stampp, *Peculiar Institution,* 380.

ers did grow upset when bondspeople's behavior was not commensurate with their status in society. Virginian Edward A. Pollard referred to the insolent *"slave gentry* of the South" as an utter "nuisance." More so in southern urban areas than in the countryside, Pollard complained, slaves "display a refinement and an ease which do not suit their condition, and which contrast most repulsively with the hard necessities of many of the whites." The poor white became the object of "scorn and sport of 'gentlemen of color,' who parade their superiority, rub their well-stuffed black skins, and thank God that they are not as he." Pollard could not tolerate witnessing free whites, however poor, "laughed at, scorned and degraded in the estimate of the slave." "Of all things," Pollard fumed, "I cannot bear to see negro slaves affect superiority over the poor, needy, and unsophisticated whites. . . . My blood boils when I recall how often I have seen some poor 'cracker,' dressed in striped cotton, and going through the streets of some of our Southern towns, . . . made sport of by the sleek, dandified negroes who lounge on the streets." "When I see a slave above his condition, or hear him talk insultingly of even the lowest white man in the land," Pollard admitted frankly, "I am strongly tempted to knock him down." Pollard's ultimate solution to the problem was to reopen the slave trade to make slave ownership accessible to poor whites. By entering the slaveholding ranks, poor whites would develop a stake in the slave system and elevate themselves above reproach. Pollard was among the very few slaveholders, however, who showed any hints of sympathy for poor whites as a class. Most masters pitied neighborhood poor whites and doled out charity, but nevertheless considered them a nuisance overall.[32]

Imbued with feelings of superiority over poor whites, some slaves took offense when masters violated class boundaries by fraternizing with their white social inferiors. "Our owner had one serious weakness which was very objectionable to us, and one in which he was the exception and not the rule of the master class," explained H. C. Bruce. "It was this: He would associate with 'poor white trash,' [and] would often invite them to dine with him."[33] Slaveholders occasionally hosted outdoor barbecues for all of their surrounding neighbors, regardless of wealth. They grudgingly invited poor whites to attend these public gatherings, but they virtually never received a poor white to sit at a table in the "big

32. Edward A. Pollard, *Black Diamonds Gathered in the Darkey Homes of the South* (New York: Pudney & Russell, 1859), 55, 56, 54–55, 57, 56, 52–54; William Barney, *The Road to Secession: A New Perspective on the Old South* (Washington: Praeger Publishers, 1972), 42.

33. Bruce, *New Man*, 28.

house" for a meal.[34] Some slaves found this every bit as objectionable as did their owners. How could masters tolerate the company of degraded poor whites—a group slaves judged no better than themselves—and suffer to eat with them? Most probably did not fully grasp slaveholders' need to cultivate good relations with neighborhood poor whites. As many slaves saw it, poor whites made inferior company. Their illiteracy, Bruce wrote contemptuously, limited even "their conversation" to "what they had seen and heard." Masters, however, depended upon poor white men to serve as patrollers, jurors, and voters in support of the slave regime. Mary Boykin Chesnut confessed her impatience with poor white women visiting her at the plantation. "But their husbands and sons . . . were citizens and voters!" she declared, and that alone demanded an increased tolerance of social inferiors. Slaveholders carefully balanced their own aversion for poor whites with enough flattery to maintain lower-class loyalty. Bruce reported that poor whites delighted in receiving an invitation to hobnob at the slaveholder's table. Practically speaking, they got a "good meal" and a rare opportunity to enjoy expensive coffee and other delicacies foreign to their palates. More than that, they received "the honor of dining with the 'BIG BUGS,'" slaves' term for distinguished gentlemen. If anyone deserved such special treatment, many slaves believed it should have been them.[35]

The evidence, then, supports the assertion of slaves' and poor whites' mutual resentment and contempt, but loathing coexisted with friendship and camaraderie. This side of the story merits equal consideration. From infancy, and in some cases from the very moment of birth, many slaves and poor whites lived in close contact with one another. One black woman in antebellum Cockeysville, Maryland, worked for a doctor, "gaining practical experience and knowledge of different herbs and roots" used in making medicine. "She was styled and called the doctor woman both by the slaves and the free people," her son explained. "She also delivered many babies and acted as a midwife for the poor whites and the slaves and free Negroes of which there were a number in Baltimore County." Traveling by rail from Washington, D.C., to Richmond, Virginia, Frederick Law Olmsted commented upon the "slovenly and dirty" homes of the "more common sort of inhabitants of the white people." "Swine, fox-hounds, and black and white children, are commonly lying very promiscuously together, on the ground about the doors," he remarked. "I am struck with the close co-habitation and

34. Genovese, "Yeomen Farmers in a Slaveholders' Democracy," 337; Genovese, "Rather Be a Nigger Than a Poor White Man," 82, 84–85.

35. Martin and Avary, *Diary from Dixie*, 401; Bruce, *New Man*, 29.

association of black and white—negro women are carrying black and white babies together in their arms; black and white children are playing together . . . black and white faces are constantly thrust together out of the doors, to see the train go by." [36]

It was not unusual in the antebellum South for white and black children to play together. Studying plantation life, historians have noted the striking degree of social interaction between slave and slaveholder children. Masters' children routinely played together with slave children and jointly engaged in mischief. In some cases, young bondspeople did not realize their enslaved condition. Walking the streets of Petersburg, Virginia, Olmsted "saw squads of negro and white boys together, pitching pennies and firing crackers in complete fraternization. The white boys manifested no superiority, or assumption of it, over the dark ones." Like the masters' children, many poor white boys and girls played with slave youngsters. "We thought well of the poor white neighbors," remembered an ex-slave from Chatham County, North Carolina. "We colored children took them as regular playmates." Janie Gallman of Union County remembered that, as a girl, she played with the children of the "poor white trash" overseer, "most of the time" jumping rope. As a child, Frederick Douglass bargained with some local poor white boys to achieve literacy. In terms of food, Douglass explained, "I was much better off . . . than many of the poor white children in our neighborhood." The clever young slave therefore traded them bread in exchange for furtive reading lessons. By token of their race, poor white youngsters could assist their slave friends in a number of ways. Sam T. Stewart of Wake County recalled one episode near the end of the Civil War when he "was caught by the patterollers in Raleigh." About twelve years old at the time, Stewart said, "I would have been whipped to pieces if it hadn't been for a white boy about my age by the name of Thomas Wilson. He told them I was his nigger, and they let me go." [37]

36. Rawick, vol. 16, Maryland, 14; Olmsted, *Seaboard Slave States,* 17. See also Frederick Law Olmsted, *The Cotton Kingdom: A Traveller's Observations on Cotton and Slavery in the American Slave States,* ed. Arthur M. Schlesinger (New York: Alfred A. Knopf, 1953), 31.

37. John W. Blassingame, *The Slave Community: Plantation Life in the Antebellum South,* rev. ed. (New York: Oxford University Press, 1979), 183–185; Eugene D. Genovese, *Roll, Jordan, Roll: The World the Slaves Made* (New York: Vintage Books, 1976), 515–519; David K. Wiggins, "The Play of Slave Children in the Plantation Communities of the Old South, 1820–1860," *Journal of Sport History* 7 (Summer 1980), 30–31; Olmsted, *Seaboard Slave States,* 113; Rawick, vol. 15, pt. 2, 345; Rawick, vol. 2, pt. 2, 98; David W. Blight, ed., *Narrative of the Life of Frederick Douglass, An American Slave, Written by Himself* (New York: Bedford Books of St. Martin's Press, 1993), 60; Rawick, vol. 15, pt. 2, 321–322.

Not all slave and poor white children lived in blissful harmony, however. Some masters projected their own notions of class onto their bondspeople and specifically instructed slave youngsters from keeping "the company of any of the poor white people." According to a former slave from Wilmington, North Carolina, "We child'en was told to play in our own yard and not have nothin' to do with . . . the common chil'en 'cross the street, white or colored, because they was'nt fitten to 'sociate with us. You see our owners was rich folks." As a young slave girl in Knox County, Tennessee, Rachel Cruze "used to get pretty lonesome sometimes because there wasn't a child of my age to play with." A nearby poor white woman named "Fanny Oldsby had a little girl . . . , but do you think Mis' Nancy would let me play with her? No, ma'am," Cruze replied. When Cruze ventured too close, her mistress promptly scolded her. According to the former slave, "Mis' Nancy would say, 'Don't you sit near her. Why, she'll bite you and she'll get your head full of lice.' The pore child would look at me and I'd look at her, but I didn't want her to bite me, so I didn't get close to her." Even when permitted to play with poor whites, some slave children "chose to tolerate them" only on occasion, perhaps imitating their parents' aversion for the "trash."[38]

When slave and poor white children did play together, fun could take a dark and menacing turn. One former bondsman from Goldsboro, North Carolina, remembered that during his boyhood he and his slave friends "used to have fights with the 'white trash' sometimes." Occasionally white children delighted in mimicking masters and overseers by tormenting or beating their black playmates. "Po' white kids useto ketch us an' whup us ontil dey make us call dem marser an' have us drapin' curtseys to dem," one ex-slave woman from Goldsboro recalled with displeasure. "Den dey beats us 'gain an' make us say, 'Oh pray marser! Please marser!'" This role-playing may not have signified any true feelings of superiority on the part of poor white children, but at the very least it does illustrate the process of socialization at work. In childhood, whites of even the lowest classes began learning the social privileges associated with whiteness.[39]

Simultaneously, slave children learned their subordinate place in society. Maryland-born freedman William Parker resented the fact that "many poor white lads of about my own age, . . . were [as] poor in personal effects as we were;

38. William Webb, *The History of William Webb, Composed By Himself* (Detroit: Egbert Hoekstra, 1873), 9; Rawick, vol. 15, pt. 2, 3; Mellon, *Bullwhip Days*, 209; William Parker, "The Freedman's Story. In Two Parts. Part I," *Atlantic Monthly* 17 (February 1866): 158.

39. Genovese, *Roll, Jordan, Roll*, 517; Wiggins, "Play of Slave Children," 31; Perdue et al., *Weevils in the Wheat*, 54–55; Rawick, vol. 16, Ohio, 40.

and yet, though our companions, . . . did not have to be controlled by a master."
According to Parker, "I felt I was the equal of those poor whites." But white society established social conventions to divest independent-minded slave children
of such notions. One slave autobiographer shared a rule governing interracial
childhood play: "If a white boy jumped on a colored boy and whipped him it did
not make any difference how poor he was[,] you were not allowed to touch him."
Nevertheless, a few slave children did retaliate. After one poor white boy hid the
clothes of "a colored boy of Mr. Dewitt's" who had gone for a swim, the irate
young slave stabbed the poor white trickster. Clearly this slave youngster had not
fully absorbed the lessons of properly subservient behavior.[40]

Some slaves and poor whites forged genuine friendships, with bonds that
held throughout their lives. The case of William Vandeford, a poor white man
of Anson County, North Carolina, illustrates that, while some poor whites displayed overt hostility toward slaves, others treated slaves as friends and equals.
Thus, the Vandeford incident perhaps captures best the complexity of the slave–
poor white relationship. In his fifties, Vandeford was variously described as
"an ignorant, obscure, moneyless man, without any kindred, or relations of any
standing," a "coward," a "pore . . . inoffensive drunkard," and a "goo[d] natured
honest fool . . . very little removed from an idiot."[41] In the spring of 1834, Vandeford and his poor white friends Warren Jones and Miles Williams returned to
Vandeford's home one evening after a day of vigorous drinking. The next morning, the three awakened early, retrieved their "Jug of brandy," and commenced
drinking again before breakfast. A slave belonging to Jeremiah Ingram, "with
whom Vandeford had lived for many years as a labourer," resided with Vandeford. The long-standing friendship between Vandeford and this slave became
the flash point for violence. Thoroughly marinated in alcohol, Warren Jones became enraged when the slave called Vandeford by his first name—Bill. Judging
this familiarity a certain sign of disrespect, Jones "threatened to whip the negro."
Vandeford objected, explaining "that he . . . and the boy had been raised together
and the boy alway[s] called him by that name." Unsatisfied with Vandeford's rea-
soning, Jones "took out his knife and made at the negro." The slave fled from the

40. Parker, "The Freedman's Story," 158; Peter Bruner, *A Slave's Adventures Toward Freedom: Not
Fiction, but the True Story of a Struggle* (Oxford, Ohio: n.p., 1918), 14.

41. A. Little to D. L. Swain, May 6, 1834, in Governor's Papers, Gov. David L. Swain, vol. 69,
561, NCDAH; William A. Morris to D. L. Swain, June 9, 1834, in Governor's Papers, Gov. David L.
Swain, vol. 69, 644, NCDAH; Jeremiah Benton to D. L. Swain, June 7, 1834, in Governor's Papers,
Gov. David L. Swain, vol. 69, 634, NCDAH.

house, Jones chasing him a short distance before he turned back, leaving the slave uninjured. At least in part out of loyalty to his slave friend, Vandeford ordered Jones from his premises. Jones, in reply, called Vandeford "a God damn Rascal," swore "God damn you I'll kill you," and pledged to "*mash his . . . damned heart out.*" Vandeford's wife Patsey cooled the two men's tempers, and they resumed drinking.[42]

When the feud renewed later that morning, Warren Jones ended up dead. Vandeford claimed that he planned to "shoot some pigeons," and that he shot Jones accidentally while cleaning his gun in preparation. According to witnesses, Vandeford blamed his wife for the incident, for he alleged that she and Jones "were too intimate" and that Jones planned to take her to Georgia, where she had children living. Vandeford reported "that the damned set had always been . . . trying to get all they could out of him," but at the same time declared that he "did not care" that Jones and his wife carried on "an illicit connexion," for, as Vandeford explained, "there was still enough left for him." He had reportedly even offered Jones "Fifty Dollars to take her with him" to Georgia. Disentangling the motive for the shooting, then, proves difficult. No one believed Vandeford's story that an accidental discharge killed Jones. But Vandeford's cavalier attitude toward his marriage suggests that the alleged affair may have had little or no bearing on the murder. Vandeford's anger likely originated, at least in good part, in that morning's mistreatment of his slave friend from childhood.[43]

42. Affidavit of Patsey Vandeford, March 26, 1834, in Governor's Papers, Gov. David L. Swain, vol. 68, 497, NCDAH; Affidavit of Willis McLendon, April 26, 1834, in Governor's Papers, Gov. David L. Swain, vol. 68, 538, NCDAH.

43. Petition, in Governor's Papers, Gov. David L. Swain, vol. 68, 498, NCDAH; Coroner's inquisition, March 29, 1834, in Governor's Papers, Gov. David L. Swain, vol. 68, 502, NCDAH. At Anson County Superior Court, March 1834, a jury convicted Vandeford of Jones's murder and sentenced him to die on Friday, April 18, 1834. Several members of the community petitioned the governor in favor of Vandeford's pardon. According to James Beverly, "Vandeford's death would be as small a loss to society as any other, but it is evident if his life is of little consequence his death could have but little influence." (James Beverly to D. L. Swain, April 15, 1834, in Governor's Papers, Gov. David L. Swain, vol. 68, 531, NCDAH.) Other petitioners disapproved of Jones and his history of violence. Coroner Jeremiah Benton wrote, "One of the Jury of inquest recognised a wound he had made on Jones some eight or ten years ago." (Jeremiah Benton to D. L. Swain, June 7, 1834, in Governor's Papers, Gov. David L. Swain, vol. 69, 634, NCDAH.) Another described Jones as "a turbulent troublesome man, always engaged in a *brawl* of some kind." (P. W. Kittrell to D. L. Swain, June 12, 1834, in Governor's Papers, Gov. David L. Swain, vol. 69, 649, NCDAH.) As one man concluded of Jones, "In his death neither society nor his family has sustained any loss." (A. Little to D. L. Swain, June 12, 1834, in Governor's Papers, Gov. David L. Swain, vol. 69, 651, NCDAH.) In consequence of these petitions, the governor issued respites and ultimately pardoned Vandeford on June 10, 1834. (Governor's Pa-

Whites' youthful attachments to slave playmates often disintegrated during adolescence, when the formalities of race asserted themselves. This tendency seemed particularly pronounced among wealthy slaveholders' sons. Masters groomed teenage sons to become responsible slaveholders in their own right. A wealthy young white man might make an erstwhile favorite black playmate a privileged body servant; other friendships with slaves dissolved entirely as former childhood friends went to the fields. Young women from slaveholding families faced less social disruption as they matured. As mistresses, they often worked around the home with some of the same female slaves they had played with as children. To maintain similar friendships, young white men in their late teens and early twenties had to make a more concerted effort. Except when the family owned but a few slaves, they did not go to work with their bondspeople. Furthermore, strictly social visits to the slave quarters undermined their newfound authority. This situation drove a wedge between boyhood friends. Poor whites, however, faced no such dilemma. Circumstances did not pressure them as much to distance themselves from their slave friends, and vibrant interactions between slaves and poor whites sometimes persisted into adulthood. That poor whites often worked and lived in close contact with slaves provided further opportunities to cultivate their interracial friendships.[44]

Despite widespread misconceptions of poor white laziness, and ubiquitous charges that they were too proud to perform "nigger work,"[45] poor white men and women sometimes labored together with slaves. Primarily as agricultural laborers, poor white men came into contact with slaves during the workday. Nearly 38,000 North Carolinians, or 22 percent of all white working-age men between the ages of fifteen and seventy, appear in the 1860 census as "farm laborers" or "laborers." More than 12,000 South Carolinians, or 15 percent of white working-

pers, Gov. David L. Swain, vol. 69, 648, NCDAH; and Governor's Letter Book, vol. 30, 218–219, NCDAH.)

44. Mechal Sobel, "Whatever You Do, Treat People Right: Personal Ethics in a Slave Society," in *Black and White Cultural Interaction in the Antebellum South,* ed. Ted Ownby (Jackson: University Press of Mississippi, 1993), 59; Ira Berlin, *Slaves without Masters: The Free Negro in the Antebellum South* (New York: Pantheon Books, 1974), 260; Wiggins, "Play of Slave Children," 31.

45. Olmsted, *Cotton Kingdom,* 19; Frederika Bremer, *The Homes of the New World; Impressions of America,* vol. 1, trans. Mary Howitt (London: Arthur Hall, Virtue, & Co., 1853), 374; Stirling, *Letters from the Slave States,* 230, 222; Basil Hall, *Travels in North America, the Years 1827 and 1828,* vol. 2 (Philadelphia: Carey, Lea & Carey, 1829), 179; J. S. Buckingham, *The Slave States of America,* vol. 1 (London: Fisher, Son, & Co., 1842), 554.

age men, are listed as holding those same occupations. These figures include many yeomen and the sons of slaveholders, and therefore should not be taken as accurate estimates of the male poor white population in those states. And certainly not every poor white laboring man worked with slaves. Those living in the Piedmont and at the periphery of plantation society probably had the greatest odds of doing so. Poor white women also had ample opportunities to work with slaves. In the 1860 census, more than 21,000 white North Carolinians, virtually all women, appear as "servants." As domestics, some poor white women probably encountered slaves in their employer's household. Some impoverished white women also engaged in field work with slaves. A fraction of the poor white men and women who worked as factory operatives in textile mills and various other industrial pursuits (poor whites probably comprised a majority of the 899 North Carolinians and 623 South Carolinians listed in the 1860 census as "factory hands") also came into contact with slaves. Many poor whites probably never worked with slaves, and those who did probably worked with them for only an abbreviated period, such as at harvest, when small slaveholders on modest holdings needed to augment their enslaved labor force. But for thousands of poor white men and women, the drive to make a living forced them to overcome any stigma attached to working for wages alongside slaves, either in the field or the factory.[46]

In the overwhelmingly rural South, poor whites were most likely to work with slaves at agricultural tasks on a plantation. Masters often hired not only poor white men but also poor white women to join the slaves in their labors. A North Carolina ex-slave remembered that "marster" gave the poor white neighbors "all the work he could. He hired both men an[d] women of the poor white class to work on the plantation. We all worked together." Most of the poor white men and women hired engaged in field work. In Georgia, traveler Emily Burke witnessed "white women and black women" laboring together in the fields "without distinction."[47]

46. Joseph C. G. Kennedy, *Population of the United States in 1860; Compiled from the Original Returns of the Eighth Census, Under the Direction of the Secretary of the Interior* (Washington: Government Printing Office, 1864), 350–351, 362–363, 448–449, 454–455. On the working life of the most famous poor white man, see Charles C. Bolton, "Edward Isham and Poor White Labor in the Old South," in *The Confessions of Edward Isham: A Poor White Life of the Old South*, ed. Charles C. Bolton and Scott P. Culclasure (Athens: University of Georgia Press, 1998), 19–31.

47. Rawick, vol. 15, pt. 2, 345; quoted in Timothy James Lockley, *Lines in the Sand: Race and Class in Lowcountry Georgia, 1750–1860* (Athens: University of Georgia Press, 2001), 36. Like poor white women, yeoman women also labored routinely in the fields. See Stephanie McCurry, "Producing Dependence: Women, Work, and Yeoman Households in Low-Country South Carolina," in *Nei-*

Poor white women also performed other essential tasks about the plantation. One former South Carolina slave recalled, for instance, that "old Miss Sallie Carlisle weaved and teached de slaves how it was done. . . . She show me how to spin and make ball thread, little as I was." The thirty-five-year-old Carlisle lived in Fairfield District, with no job, no land of her own, only $100 worth of property, and two young girls. She may have disliked teaching slaves to weave, but it offered her some form of employment.[48]

Paternalistic slaveholders who took on poor white laborers typically paid them a small wage in cash or in goods. A Rockingham County, North Carolina, master "done hire sev'ral poor white 'omans what done weavin' fer twenty five cents er day." Another North Carolina slaveholder "had plenty o' poor white trash help, what wuked fer flour, meal, syrup, en fer anything else he'd give em as pay fer dey wuk." Poor white Sallie Carlisle was fortunate to receive much more substantial compensation. For remuneration, "Marster give her a house to live in, and a garden spot on de place."[49]

Many slaveholders considered poor whites a convenient, supplemental labor force, a temporary expedient to draw upon in times of especial need. Travelers most often observed slaves and whites together in the fields at harvest time. Slave narratives provide hints that many poor whites fulfilled a secondary role in the South's agrarian economy. An ex-slave from Georgia remembered, "Shuh, dey was plenty of poor whites. . . . [W]en things git busy sometime Marzer he puts 'em to work in de fiel', only dey get money an' we don'." A former Alabama slave similarly recalled, "Dere was a bunch of po' white folks dat lived clos't to us and dey would help work sometimes when us was real busy." Many poor white men and women, then, did labor with slaves in the fields, not consistently but sporadically, as the slaveholder deemed necessary. Where slave labor was abundant, masters often avoided the added expense of hiring poor whites. Those slaveholders, remarked Frederick Law Olmsted, "need no assistance from the poor white man: his presence near them is disagreeable and unprofitable."[50]

---

ther Lady Nor Slave: Working Women of the Old South, ed. Susanna Delfino and Michele Gillespie (Chapel Hill: University of North Carolina Press, 2002), 55–71.

48. Rawick, vol. 3, pt. 4, 254; Eighth Census of the United States, 1860: Fairfield District, South Carolina, 277.

49. Rawick, SS1, vol. 5, Ohio, 386, 285–286; Rawick, vol. 3, pt. 4, 254. See also Charles Thompson, *Biography of a Slave; Being the Experiences of Rev. Charles Thompson, a Preacher of the United Brethren Church, While a Slave in the South* (Dayton, Ohio: United Brethren Publishing House, 1875), 62.

50. Rawick, SS1, vol. 5, Ohio, 362; Rawick, SS1, vol. 1, 279; Olmsted, *Seaboard Slave States,* 515.

Slaves and poor whites did not depend entirely upon planters to bring them together in the workplace, however. Their working lives also intersected off the master's plantation. Poor white women were often responsible for buying necessary goods for their households and for marketing whatever produce their families had to sell. One correspondent to the *New York Daily Times* mocked "the poor country people" traveling to an urban market in low-country South Carolina. According to his report, the roads virtually overflowed with the crude, hand-hewn "carts of the 'crackers'—the poor and uneducated peasantry." Poor white "[w]omen and children—often whole households—" piloted wagons laden "with corn, sweet potatoes, poultry, game, hides and peltry" to sell or trade. Rural poor white women who attempted to peddle their merchandise in the Old South's urban centers competed directly with the female slave vendors who dominated the marketplace. And when poor white women shopped for their families at the public market, they likely purchased needed commodities from slave women.[51]

A small number of poor whites worked with slaves whom they themselves had hired. Most poor whites lacked the resources to own slaves or to rent them for an entire calendar year as was the custom, but some must have had the wherewithal to hire a neighbor's slave for an hour or two, or for a day's worth of work— just long enough to complete a desired task. Several slaves testified that they had been hired to poor whites. Successful Chowan County, North Carolina, runaway Allen Parker worked with "a common poor white who owned or hired no [other] slaves. I being the only colored person on the place." He also spent time "on the farm of John Cofell, another poor white." That Parker spent two years with each, however, suggests that he perhaps mistakenly identified these nonslaveholding white men as poor whites when they may have been yeomen farmers struggling to improve their lot. The line dividing poor whites from yeomen proved blurry and permeable, however; surely a few poor whites did hire slaves. Though a prosperous man at the time of his death, Edward Covey was a poor farm renter in his late twenties when he hired Frederick Douglass from his owner Thomas Auld.

51. *New York Daily Times,* June 14, 1853; Betty Wood, *Women's Work, Men's Work: The Informal Slave Economies of Lowcountry Georgia* (Athens: University of Georgia Press, 1995), 81; Robert Olwell, "'Loose, Idle and Disorderly': Slave Women in the Eighteenth-Century Charleston Marketplace," in *More Than Chattel: Black Women and Slavery in the Americas,* ed. David Barry Gaspar and Darlene Clark Hine (Bloomington: Indiana University Press, 1996), 98, 99, 101, 103; Timothy J. Lockley, "Spheres of Influence: Working White and Black Women in Antebellum Savannah," in *Neither Lady Nor Slave: Working Women of the Old South,* ed. Susanna Delfino and Michele Gillespie (Chapel Hill: University of North Carolina Press, 2002), 109, 110.

Other poor whites hired slaves illicitly, without the master's knowledge. A black informant near Norfolk, Virginia, told Frederick Law Olmsted that the "poorer white men, owning small tracts" in the Dismal Swamp, sometimes employed runaway slaves. Elsewhere Olmsted observed that slaves occasionally worked for poor whites "at night and on Sundays," taking payment in liquor.[52] In extremely rare instances, slaves might invert the conventional social order by hiring poor whites. In one extraordinary case, Olmsted witnessed "a native, country fellow" taking orders from a slave. "[W]ithout consulting his master," the bondsman had hired the poor white man to erect a fence.[53]

Very small numbers of slaves and poor whites labored together not in agriculture but in an assortment of southern industries. Only about 5 percent of slaves, and probably a similarly minuscule proportion of poor white men and women, worked in industry.[54] Only a fraction of those would have been in positions that facilitated interracial contact. Employers desperate for laborers sometimes showed blatant disregard for the racial characteristics of their labor force. One North Carolina canal enterprise in 1823 wanted to "employ 15 or 20 good laboring Hands, black or white," along the Neuse River. With the rise in cotton prices in the 1850s, competition for laborers, black and white, reached unprecedented levels. A leading figure in North Carolina's antebellum gold-mining industry, English agent Captain John E. Penman, advertised three months in 1853 for "A LARGE number of HANDS, white or colored," to work his mines near Charlotte. Suffering from an apparently chronic labor shortage, a month later he placed another ad for "100 COLORED or WHITE MINERS" that ran almost weekly for a full year.[55] At the Gold Hill mines, one-third of the unskilled laborers were slaves, the majority of the remainder native-born whites.[56] Coal mines, too, employed

52. Parker, *Recollections of Slavery Times,* 41, 42; Blight, *Narrative of the Life of Frederick Douglass,* 113; Olmsted, *Seaboard Slave States,* 160; Olmsted, *Cotton Kingdom,* 121, 66. For other instances of slaves claiming that they were hired to poor whites, see Rawick, vol. 2, pt. 2, 77; Rawick, vol. 10, pt. 5, 149; Bruce, *New Man,* 66; Mellon, *Bullwhip Days,* 22.

53. Olmsted, *Seaboard Slave States,* 555.

54. Robert S. Starobin, *Industrial Slavery in the Old South* (New York: Oxford University Press, 1970), vii.

55. *Raleigh Register* (weekly), May 9, 1823; *North Carolina Whig* (Charlotte), June 8, 1853; October 4, 1853.

56. Brent D. Glass, "'Poor Men with Rude Machinery': The Formative Years of the Gold Hill Mining District, 1842–1853," *North Carolina Historical Review* 61 (January 1984), 25; Glass, "The Miner's World: Life and Labor at Gold Hill," *North Carolina Historical Review* 62 (October 1985), 430, 437–438.

a biracial work force. According to an 1845 advertisement, the Midlothian Coal Mining Company of Chesterfield County, Virginia, used slaves, "several free colored men," and "many white laborers."[57] Olmsted confirmed on a visit to a Virginia coal pit that "the majority of the mining laborers are slaves, and uncommonly athletic and fine-looking negroes; but a considerable number of white hands are also employed."[58] The Bath paper factory along Horse Creek, near Graniteville, South Carolina, employed fifty people, "one-half of that number being women and children." As one newspaper correspondent added, "About a dozen slaves are also employed."[59]

Although by the end of the antebellum era, laboring white men, women, and children dominated the Old South's most well-known industry—textiles— this had not always been the case. In the 1830s and early 1840s, slaves or a mix of slave and free white laborers worked in southern cotton mills. Textile entrepreneur William Gregg's Vaucluse cotton factory, which opened in 1831, employed twenty slaves and thirty white operatives in 1836, and continued with a mixed force in 1837.[60] The Saluda Manufacturing Company in South Carolina used a predominantly slave labor force when it opened in 1834 but some whites as well.[61] Camden's DeKalb Factory, erected in 1838, and North Carolina's Salem Manufacturing Company likewise made use of both slave and white laborers.[62] As British traveler James Silk Buckingham summarized, the South's textile mills in the late 1830s and early 1840s were "directed partly by free and partly by slave labor."[63]

That a given company employed both slaves and laboring whites did not necessarily mean that they worked together in an integrated setting, however. One newspaper reported that the closing of a cotton mill near Petersburg, Virginia, forced "a number of young white girls employed there" to seek work in predominantly slave-operated tobacco factories nearby. Although scholars have shown

---

57. *Richmond Enquirer,* December 19, 1845.

58. Olmsted, *Seaboard Slave States,* 47–48.

59. *Charleston Daily Courier,* February 11, 1860.

60. E. M. Lander, Jr., "Slave Labor in South Carolina Cotton Mills," *Journal of Negro History* 38 (April 1953): 165; Tom E. Terrill, "Eager Hands: Labor for Southern Textiles, 1850–1860," *Journal of Economic History* 36 (March 1976), 90; Norris W. Preyer, "The Historian, the Slave, and the Antebellum Textile Industry," *Journal of Negro History* 46 (April 1961): 77; Burton, *In My Father's House Are Many Mansions,* 53.

61. Terrill, "Eager Hands," 86.

62. Lander, "Slave Labor," 165–166; Terrill, "Eager Hands," 86.

63. Buckingham, *Slave States of America,* vol. 1, 43.

that poor white women labored extensively in the textile mills of the Old South, the "white girls" at this establishment and others worked "in separate rooms from the colored hands."[64] Chief engineer Ellwood Morris, in charge of the repair and improvement of North Carolina's Cape Fear & Deep River navigation works, related to that state's governor in 1859 that his "present working force" consisted of "about 160 hands, of all hues & classes."[65] Morris did his best, however, to keep his slave and white laborers separated. He explained to the governor in July that he planned to "raise a force of *white Men*" to work at locks two through four, using a "floating force of *negroes*" to finish locks five, six, and seven.[66] By mid-August, Morris had "20 pretty good *white* men" working at Jones' Lock, and "at Haw Ridge about the same chiefly *Blacks*." When a Mr. Cassiday offered Morris "20 men" to his operation, Morris, in an effort to maintain racial segregation, "wrote him to send them to Jones Lock if *white* & Haw Ridge if *black*." So when six black laborers—four slave and two free—arrived at Jones Lock, Morris directed them to Haw Ridge to supplement the black force there.[67]

Difficulties in attracting and retaining his workers, both black and white, forced a reluctant Morris to integrate a portion of his operation. As Morris reported in September, "[W]e are now compelled to work a mixed force, *White &* *Black*, which presents many inconveniences, in its management, & accom[m]odation." As Frederick Law Olmsted observed, "the employment of free and slave

64. *Petersburg Express*, quoted in *Richmond Enquirer*, August 3, 1855. It is impossible to generalize how frequently poor white female textile mill workers labored together with slave women. Bess Beatty notes that textile mills sometimes utilized mixed labor forces of black and white women, but most of the time, the workforce in that industry was exclusively white. Barbara J. Howe found no evidence of interracial contact in the textile mills she studied, while E. Susan Barber concedes only the possibility of an interracial female workforce. See Bess Beatty, "I Can't Get My Bored on Them Old Lomes: Female Textile Workers in the Antebellum South," in *Neither Lady Nor Slave: Working Women of the Old South*, ed. Susanna Delfino and Michele Gillespie (Chapel Hill: University of North Carolina Press, 2002), 251; Barbara J. Howe, "Patient Laborers: Women at Work in the Formal Economy of West(ern) Virginia," in *Neither Lady Nor Slave*, 121, 123–124; and E. Susan Barber, "Depraved and Abandoned Women: Prostitution in Richmond, Virginia, across the Civil War," in *Neither Lady Nor Slave*, 156.

65. Ellwood Morris to John W. Ellis, November 5, 1859, in Governor's Papers, Gov. John W. Ellis, box 1, folder November 1859, NCDAH. On Morris, see William S. Powell, ed., *Dictionary of North Carolina Biography*, vol. 4 (Chapel Hill: University of North Carolina Press, 1991), 327.

66. Ellwood Morris to John W. Ellis, July 3, 1859, in Governor's Papers, Gov. John W. Ellis, box 1, folder July 1859, NCDAH.

67. Ellwood Morris to John W. Ellis, August 18, 1859, and August 29, 1859, in Governor's Papers, Gov. John W. Ellis, box 1, folder August 1859, NCDAH.

labour together, is almost as difficult as working, under the same yoke, an un-broken horse and a docile ox." "Still," Morris wrote, "with patience, I hope to work thro' all our difficulties, tho' they are numerous."[68] In October, Morris em-ployed a mixed force of sixteen whites and twenty blacks at Green Rock's lock number six, but maintained segregated work forces at his other sites.[69]

In various other nonagricultural pursuits, slaves and poor whites sometimes labored promiscuously, side by side. Slave and free operatives worked alongside one another in several textile mills in South Carolina and other states.[70] At "a large brick cotton factory" not far from Charlottesville, Virginia, James Silk Buckingham reported that "both spinning and weaving are carried on; and whites and blacks work indiscriminately together."[71] Slaves and poor whites also worked together building railroads. During the construction of the Western North Carolina Railroad from Morganton to Asheville, they worked side by side, "digging track beds and laying track."[72] At the opposite end of the state, slaves and poor whites labored together in eastern North Carolina's turpentine forests.[73] Many more instances of slaves and poor whites laboring together in integrated work environments have been lost. Few company records from the antebellum South survive, and extant sources do not often list workers' names along with their race or status. Moreover, company records offer little indication of how the labor force was organized or distributed. Whites on the payroll may have occupied exclusively supervisory positions as superintendents or overseers. Or they may have performed the same tasks as slaves, but in segregated areas. Available sources make discerning the nature or degree of contact between slave and white laborers a formidable challenge.

The paucity of detailed company records means that historians must look elsewhere for indications of slaves and poor whites laboring together. Newspaper

68. Ellwood Morris to John W. Ellis, September 1, 1859, in Governor's Papers, Gov. John W. Ellis, box 1, folder September 1859, NCDAH; Olmsted, *Cotton Kingdom*, 19.

69. Ellwood Morris to John W. Ellis, October 4, 1859, in Governor's Papers, Gov. John W. Ellis, box 1, folder October 1859, NCDAH.

70. Lander, "Slave Labor," 172, 163–165, 161. See also his later work, Ernest McPherson Lan-der, Jr., *The Textile Industry in Antebellum South Carolina* (Baton Rouge: Louisiana State University Press, 1969).

71. Buckingham, *Slave States of America*, vol. 2, 411.

72. John C. Inscoe, "Mountain Masters: Slaveholding in Western North Carolina," *North Caro-lina Historical Review* 61 (April 1984): 167.

73. Robert B. Outland III, "Slavery, Work, and the Geography of the North Carolina Naval Stores Industry, 1835–1860," *Journal of Southern History* 62 (February 1996): 27.

accounts of industrial accidents offer a useful place to start. That single explosions in Virginia's coal pits killed both slave and white laborers suggests the workers' close proximity to one another in the mines. A catastrophic explosion at the Midlothian coal pits in 1855 resulted in a "shocking loss of life," newspapers estimating that only five of the fifty in the pit at the time of the explosion would survive. "Five white men, two white boys, and thirty colored men were killed," read the newspaper report. "All were shockingly burned."[74] In 1857, an accident at the Black Heath Pits in Chesterfield County killed three slaves, one free black, and one white. The "four negro men and a white lad" were descending the mine shaft, when "the cage which contained the men . . . detached from the rope" and plummeted three hundred feet down the shaft. According to reports, "The white person who lost his life was a lad, about thirteen years of age, son of Mr. James Pemberton, who resides near the pits." A James Pemberton appears in the 1850 census as a sixty-five-year-old carpenter with no land, but living alone, casting some doubt that he was the father of the deceased boy. Nevertheless, a thirteen-year-old forced to mine coal indicates dire economic need.[75] At Chesterfield's Bright Hope Coal Pits in 1859, a "terrible explosion" killed the "nine men in the shaft at the time, four whites and five negroes."[76] Subsequent reports stated that "the bodies of the unfortunate miners" were recovered, "found nearly stripped of their clothing, but . . . only slightly scorched and but little mutilated." The newspaper identified the masters of the deceased slaves, but did not list the slaves by name, only noting callously, "All the negroes were insured." But it did provide the names of the four whites killed: George Smith, Isaac Palmer (or Farmer), Richard Blankenship, and Albert Crump. "George Smith was thirty-five years of age, and leaves a wife and four children," wrote the *Petersburg Express* in an unusually factual piece of reporting. "Isaac Palmer was forty-five years of age, and leaves a wife and no children. Richard Blankenship, twenty years of age, single. Albert Crump, widower, about thirty-five years of age, and leaves two children." Of these four men, only Crump appears in the 1850 Chesterfield County census, listed as a miner. The others may have been skilled miners who arrived in Chesterfield after 1850, or poor whites seeking temporary labor in the mines.[77]

74. *Richmond Enquirer,* March 23, 1855.

75. *Richmond Enquirer,* January 23, 1857; Seventh Census of the United States, 1850: Chesterfield County, Virginia, 105.

76. *Petersburg Express,* April 14, 1859, reprinted in *Richmond Enquirer,* April 15, 1859.

77. *Petersburg Express,* April 18, 1859, reprinted in *Richmond Enquirer,* April 19, 1859; Seventh Census of the United States, 1850: Chesterfield County, Virginia, 63, lists Crump as a landless miner,

*   *   *

Were slaves and poor whites able to labor together civilly in integrated work environments? Very little credible evidence survives to answer the question. Much must have depended upon the circumstances that thrust them together. Competition for a limited number of jobs sometimes fueled hostilities between members of the two groups. Some poor whites confronted slaves head-on in the labor market, vying for jobs as farm hands, mill operatives, and other positions. Frequently venturing outside the home for employment, poor white women often earned wages as domestic servants or cooks, jobs traditionally held by female slaves. Poor whites of both sexes competed with slaves for positions as agricultural laborers. White Civil War veterans sometimes complained that the poor could not successfully challenge their slave rivals. "The slave holders could get the slave for almost nothing," said one, ". . . and the poor young men like myself could not get a job." A native-born white of eastern Virginia, identified in newspapers as "civis," expressed his concerns in the early 1830s that slavery "absorb[s] the whole labor of the community. . . . It first occupies all the agricultural labor of the country, and precludes the laboring white man from employment there." Once a master "finds himself possessed of more labor than he can advantageously use on his farm, his slaves are instructed in various trades, until at last, the laboring man," landless and unemployed, "is compelled to seek some more fortunate land, where the means of acquiring his daily bread are not denied him." The poor man's labor, "civis" warned, represented "his fortune, his only means of improving his condition, or supplying his wants. Deprive him of this, by depriving him of the means of using it, and you condemn him to a state of irretrievable and hopeless misery." Poor whites holding such emotionally charged convictions against the personal danger slave labor posed to them and their families likely resented ever having to work alongside the very people who they believed threatened their livelihood.[78]

Another possible source of hostility was the degradation that some poor whites must have felt working alongside slaves. In a society that valued the freedom and liberty derived from landholding, to work for wages entailed a loss of independence. When poor whites performed farm labor or factory work with slaves, they placed themselves on an uncomfortable level of dependency with

---

thirty-one years old. A Richard Blankenship appears on 118, but it cannot be the same individual described in the article.

78. Lockley, "Spheres of Influence," 102, 105, 112; quoted in Bailey, *Class and Tennessee's Confederate Generation*, 73; *Richmond Enquirer*, May 4, 1832.

them.[79] Travelers and other contemporary observers repeatedly mentioned "the insuperable repugnance of whites to labor side by side and on an equality with black slaves."[80] Slave autobiographer Charles Ball asserted that "[t]he white man . . . is too proud to go to work in the same field with the negro slaves by his side."[81] Circumstances forced many poor whites to overcome grudgingly any objections they may have had to working with slaves, but it is easy to imagine that they occasionally unleashed their simmering resentment physically upon some unfortunate slave.

If hostility characterized the relationship between some slave and poor white laborers, others worked together peaceably, and even amicably, whether in agricultural or industrial settings. In Christ Church Parish, South Carolina, entrepreneurs erected a factory "for the manufacture of Tubs, Pails and Brooms," employing in their establishment slaves "and also white operatives . . . whose residence is in such close proximity to the quarters of the negroes, that they must be instantly cognizant of any undue noise or disturbance." But, the small industrialists continued, "the premises have been thus occupied for several months, and there has not and probably will never occur, occasion for more than the ordinary control exercised throughout the State over the same number of Slaves." In the early 1840s, traveler James Silk Buckingham visited "three cotton factories" near Athens, Georgia, each employing "from 80 to 100 persons," with an equal proportion of whites and slaves. "There is no difficulty among them on account of colour," Buckingham asserted, "the white girls working in the same room and at the same loom with the black girls; and boys of each colour, as well as men and women, working together without apparent repugnance or objection." Slave and white workers in North Carolina's gold mines reportedly displayed a similarly striking degree of teamwork, digging together, in many instances side by side, with little evidence of racial hostility.[82] These positive assessments of integrated work forces must be regarded with caution. Southern industrialists preferred not to publicize incidents of racial unrest at their factories

79. Bolton, "Edward Isham," 25–26; J. William Harris, *Plain Folk and Gentry in a Slave Society: White Liberty and Black Slavery in Augusta's Hinterlands* (Middletown, Conn.: Wesleyan University Press, 1985; reprint, Baton Rouge: Louisiana State University Press, 1998), 78.

80. George M. Weston, "The Poor Whites of the South: The Injury Done Them By Slavery" (Washington, D.C.: Republican Executive Congressional Committee, 1860), 5.

81. Ball, *Fifty Years in Chains,* 290.

82. Petitions, Legislative Papers, 1851, item 78, SCDAH; Buckingham, *Slave States of America,* vol. 2, 112–113; Fletcher Melvin Green, "Gold Mining: A Forgotten Industry of Ante-Bellum North Carolina," *North Carolina Historical Review* 14 (January 1937): 15.

or mines, and they would surely have made conscious efforts to conceal evidence of racial hostility from the prying eyes of foreign travelers and other outsiders. Simultaneously, however, no records of poor white walkouts or strikes in opposition to slave laborers survive. The renowned Tredegar ironworkers' strike of 1847 involved not poor whites but skilled white laborers who objected to management's decision ordering them to teach their trade to slaves.[83] Skilled white tradesmen often petitioned state legislatures to take action to decrease competition from slave mechanics, but no evidence of specifically poor white discontent appears in the historical record.[84]

The narratives and autobiographies of ex-slaves provide a mixed assessment of slave–poor white working relationships. Some reports were favorable. A former bondsman from North Carolina's central Piedmont reminisced that slaves and poor whites on his master's plantation "all worked together. We had a good time. We worked and sang together and everybody seemed happy. In harvest time a lot of help was hired and such laughing, working and singing. Just a good time in general. We sang the songs 'Crossin' over Jordan' and [']'Bound for the Promised Land.'" Such glowing pronouncements merit skepticism, however. Slaves interviewed during the Great Depression as part of the Federal Writers' Project often viewed the antebellum era through rose-tinted glasses. They experienced a mild form of slavery, as children, that compared favorably to the suffering and deprivation of the 1930s. Other slaves nevertheless remembered their time working with or for poor whites less fondly. South Carolina ex-slave Aaron Ford recalled that his master once hired him to one of the "poor white neighbors." "Poor man give bout 1½ hours for noon whe' I get two hours back home," Ford complained, "en I never go back de next day." Former slave woman Charity Morris shared a similarly unpleasant experience. According to Morris, "When ah wuz very small dey rented me out tuh some very po' white fokes. Dey wuzn

83. Patricia A. Schechter, "Free and Slave Labor in the Old South: The Tredegar Ironworkers' Strike of 1847," *Labor History* 35 (Spring 1994): 171.

84. Some historians have taken cotton mill operatives' organizational inactivity as a sign of worker docility. Others have argued, however, that white antebellum mill hands viewed the employer-employee relationship from a traditional framework of reciprocity. Rather than thinking of themselves consciously as a working class, they regarded their relationship with management as a personal one, between individuals. On the first position, see, for example, Richard W. Griffin, "Poor White Laborers in Southern Cotton Factories, 1789–1865," *South Carolina Historical Magazine* 61 (January 1960): 38. On the more recent position, see Bess Beatty, "Textile Labor in the North Carolina Piedmont: Mill Owner Images and Mill Worker Response, 1830–1900," *Labor History* 25 (Fall 1984): 485–487; and Michael Shirley, "Yeoman Culture and Millworker Protest in Antebellum Salem, North Carolina," *Journal of Southern History* 57 (August 1991): 430, 452.

use tuh slaves so mah master made him promise not tuh beat me or knock me bout. Dey promise dey wouldn." But Morris found her situation insufferable. "Dey cahried me home," she related, "an ah clare dey wuz so mean tuh me till ah run off an tried tuh fin' de way back tuh mah marster. . . . De nex' mawnin dese white fokes sent word tuh Marster dat ah had lef' so Marster foun' me an took me home and let me stay dar too." In both of these instances, slaves made allegations of ill treatment at the hands of their poor white hirers. Neither poor white met the slaves' own expectations of what constituted proper management. Bridging these extremes, most slaves who worked with poor whites probably shared the experience of North Carolina slave autobiographer Allen Parker. Parker recorded that "I got along pretty well" with the "common poor white" Jacob Parker, but the "poor white" John Cofell, by contrast, "was a hard man to work for and I was glad when I got through with him." Clearly the mix of slaves' and poor whites' individual personalities had tremendous bearing on their working relationship. Sometimes, slaves and poor whites got along; other times, they did not.[85]

No doubt a few slaves and poor whites developed working relationships rooted in trust and friendship. In eastern North Carolina's Beaufort County, John Carmatt's slave Nat was indicted for hiring his own time. Nat "was engaged in running a boat on the river, and carrying turpentine" on Blount's Creek, "about twelve miles from the town of Washington." According to court records, "There was a white man, by the name of Pritchet in the boat with Nat, the first half of the year 1850." As Nat explained it, "he and Pritchet were partners in running the boat . . . they gave the owner of the boat one-half of what they made, and divided the balance between them." Although theirs was an exceptional case, Nat and Pritchet demonstrated that slaves and poor whites could view themselves as equals, at least in the world of business and commerce. While some slaves and poor whites labored in competition, others worked cooperatively in pursuit of their employers' goals, and perhaps even their own.[86]

At the conclusion of the workday or on weekends, some slaves and poor whites engaged in shared leisure-time activities. Most slaves had little time for relaxation. Those laboring under the gang system faced constant supervision from dawn until dusk. Bondspeople working by the task system had less regimented

---

85. Rawick, vol. 15, pt. 2, 345; Rawick, vol. 2, pt. 2, 77; Rawick, vol. 10, pt. 5, 149; Parker, *Recollections of Slavery Times*, 41, 42.

86. *State v. Nat*, 35 N.C. 154 (1851), 155.

schedules, but many of them spent whatever "free time" they had at work, often tending their own gardens or crops, producing food to sell or to supplement their own diet. This hardly qualifies as "leisure," strictly speaking, except in that it counted as time not at work *for someone else,* and for slaves, that made all the difference. To be sure, slaves did assert their right to free time, around Christmas, for example. Slaves welcomed the holiday break, but it benefited masters as well. The Christmas season provided paternalist slaveholders an opportunity to bestow gifts upon their bondspeople in carefully choreographed displays of charity and goodwill. In addition, as Frederick Douglass wrote, "holidays serve[d] as conductors, or safety-valves, to carry off the rebellious spirit of enslaved humanity." They gave slaves a brief respite and refreshed them in preparation for the next round of work. For these reasons, holiday seasons marked important times in the lives of both slaves and masters.[87]

Poor whites did not typically partake in holiday festivities with slaves, but they did associate socially with slaves the remainder of the year. During normal weekly routines, masters, patrollers, and exhaustion all circumscribed slaves' options for entertainment. Despite these impediments, slaves pursued leisurely diversions that sometimes reached beyond the slave quarters to include poor whites. Most slave–poor white social interactions have gone unrecorded, but the two most popular recreational activities, according to court records, were drinking and gambling. These were both overwhelmingly masculine pastimes. Compared to poor white men, poor white women probably spent less of their leisure time with slaves. Or, perhaps poor white women simply did not engage as often in leisurely pursuits with slaves that violated the law, or were more discreet about it. For whatever reason, the historical record provides far more evidence of the social interactions between slave and poor white men.

By modern standards, people in the antebellum United States consumed extraordinary amounts of alcohol. According to W. J. Rorabaugh, "Americans between 1790 and 1830 drank more alcoholic beverages per capita than ever before or since." They quaffed distilled liquors or spirits, especially whiskey, in the greatest quantities. Drinking pervaded all of American society, but differences in consumption patterns did exist. Generally speaking, men outdrank women, lower classes outconsumed upper classes, and unskilled laborers imbibed more than skilled employees. By these criteria, poor white men must have consumed

---

87. James Walvin, "Slaves, Free Time and the Question of Leisure," *Slavery & Abolition* 16 (April 1995): 5, 7, 11; Blight, *Narrative of the Life of Frederick Douglass,* 80. On slaves, poor whites, and the Christmas holiday, see the discussion of the John Canoe ritual in chapter 4.

more alcohol than any other group of whites. Whites as a group also drank more than blacks, in large part because masters, and various laws, forbade slaves from drinking. Masters did distribute alcohol to slaves for medicinal reasons, as an extra incentive at harvest time, or during holiday seasons, but under normal circumstances, they preferred keeping their charges from the damaging effects of the bottle. Slave runaway advertisements often noted a fugitive's "fondness" for alcohol, however, and to satisfy their thirst for liquor, slaves frequently sneaked to the nearest tavern or grog shop, trading goods they either produced or stole in exchange for a dram.[88]

Much of the convivial drinking between slaves and poor whites took place in the predominantly masculine realm of southern grog shops. Throughout the South, taverns were strategically positioned, in both urban and rural areas, for the convenience of passersby. High-traffic locations, along roads connecting important towns, or at the intersection of two well-traveled routes, earned the most business.[89] Grog shops, wrote one southerner, may be found "every where all over the land, in cities and towns, in the most retired hamlets, and at every crossroads." They typically consisted of "a small wooden building, with two rooms; one intended for a sleeping room but used mostly for playing cards in, and the other devoted to the retailing of ardent spirits."[90] While some establishments maintained reputations for respectability, most did not. The grand jury of Union District, South Carolina, expressed concern that "the country is overspread with grogg shops," dens "of all kinds of vice and immorality." One observer referred to the "reeking groggery" as the site of both "villainy and soul-murder." Poor men in particular "resort[ed] to the filthy, demoralizing rum-holes, . . . those terrible sinks of iniquity commonly called *dram-shops*." In Virginia, according to one traveler, "the lower classes" reveled in "the pandemonium of a whiskey-shop; where houseless, pennyless, famished idlers endeavour to 'keep their spirits up, by pouring spirits down.'" Slaves, too, frequented the grog shops. Most had access to either a small-town tavern or crossroads watering hole. Having encountered slave lumbermen in the Dismal Swamp, Frederick Law Olmsted wrote, "No liquor is sold or served to the negroes in the swamp, and, as their first want

88. W. J. Rorabaugh, *The Alcoholic Republic: An American Tradition* (New York: Oxford University Press, 1979), ix, 7, 20, 248, 12, 13. Ian R. Tyrrell, *Sobering Up: From Temperance to Prohibition in Antebellum America, 1800–1860* (Westport, Conn.: Greenwood Press, 1979), 321, largely ignores the South, noting that the temperance movement hardly penetrated the region.

89. Samples of advertisements offering taverns for sale may be found in *Richmond Enquirer,* July 5, 1836; September 27, 1836; and October 14, 1836.

90. Hundley, *Social Relations,* 225, 227.

when they come out of it is an excitement, most of their money goes to the grog-shops." Respectable citizens often petitioned state legislatures, conveying fears that the infestation of "Country Grog or retail shops" disturbed "the good order of society," corrupted "the morals of the community," and reduced entire families "to poverty & want."[91]

Like most slaveholders, planter D. R. Hundley looked with particular disfavor upon the individuals who ran southern grog shops facilitating interracial drinking. "A groggery-keeper in the South is usually a man of uncultivated mind, devoid of principle, habitually a blasphemer and Sabbath-breaker, a reviler of religion, and is sometimes also an abolitionist—owing to his secret traffic with the slaves," Hundley generalized. "He is usually stout of person, being bloated from constant imbibing, and possesses a coarse beard, a blotched and otherwise spotted face, a red nose, hard, cold, watery and inflamed eyes, a dirty and badly fitting dress from crown to sole; and in speech is low, vulgar and obscene, a retailer of stale jests and disgusting stories of scandal and intrigue, and with every sentence belches forth from his accursed throat oaths and blasphemy." Slaveholders such as Hundley considered grog-shop keepers not only personally reprehensible but also shady in their practices. According to Hundley, owners acquired whiskey and rum wholesale from a nearby town and used that as the base for their alcoholic beverages. Sometimes they merely watered it down prior to sale; at other times they brewed their own potent concoctions, adding "[l]ogwood, juniper berries, dog-leg tobacco, and even strychnine" for flavor. The physical effects of these intoxicating potions earned them "the expressive names of ['knock-'em-stiff,'] 'bust-head,' 'rifle-whiskey,' 'tangle-foot,' 'red-eye,' and 'blue-ruin.'" To prevent these reportedly immoral and unsavory men from dispensing liquor, slaveholders and other concerned citizens often called for laws requiring special licenses to sell ardent spirits or the word of respectable locals testifying to a vender's "good moral character."[92]

Those who owned the establishments where slaves and poor whites assembled together for drinking and entertainment faced criminal charges if detected. In

91. Grand Jury Presentments, Legislative Papers, 1831, item 25, SCDAH; Hundley, *Social Relations*, 226, 225; Arthur Singleton [Henry Cogswell Knight], *Letters from the South and West* (Boston: Richardson and Lord, 1824), 65–66; Olmsted, *Seaboard Slave States*, 155; General Assembly, Session Records, 1830–1831, folder Petitions (Miscellaneous), NCDAH.

92. Hundley, *Social Relations*, 226–227; General Assembly, Session Records, 1830–1831, folder Petitions (Miscellaneous), NCDAH. "Knock-'em-stiff" from James R. Gilmore [Edmund Kirke, pseud.], *Down in Tennessee, and Back By Way of Richmond* (New York: Carleton, 1864), 185.

Henrico County, Virginia, authorities arrested a poor white man named Christopher Kraft three different times for having "an unlawful assemblage of negroes in his house." Alvin G. Thornton was indicted in Wayne County, North Carolina, on a nuisance charge. Thornton, a young grocer, hosted "frequent" assemblies "of persons, white and black, in the day time and the night, on work-days and Sundays, at public and private times, in the town of Smithfield," in Johnston County. "[D]rinking and making loud noises by loud talking, cursing, swearing, and quarreling" accompanied these gatherings. According to court records, "The disturbances occasionally took place in the shop of the defendant, but more frequently in front of and around it." Thornton sold his black and white clientele liquor, possibly supplied by Alexander Findleson, a young distiller who lived with him.[93]

In the preindustrial South, a fine line divided work from leisure; work and leisure were not discrete activities. Barn raisings, quilting bees, and corn shuckings, for instance, brought both together. During these times, slave–poor white drinking took place outside the confines of the grog shop. In Johnston County, "several white persons & slaves" assembled in 1857 for a corn shucking. "Liquor was distributed very plentifully among the slaves & whites; & they all drank very freely" during their labors. "About midnight they ceased to work" and left for their homes. Curiously, although the slaves' and whites' homes "lay . . . in one common direction," the slaves took "a path which led around an enclosed field & the whites one which led through the field." The slaves and whites found shucking and drinking together perfectly acceptable, yet when the get-together ended, they took segregated routes home, the slaves taking the more roundabout path. Unwritten social rules governed the appropriateness of these interracial gatherings.[94]

93. *Richmond Enquirer*, August 26, 1853. The Seventh Census of the United States, 1850: Henrico County, Virginia, 345, lists Christopher Craft as a thirty-year-old laborer with no real estate, living in someone else's household. The Eighth Census of the United States, 1860: Henrico County, Virginia, 234, lists a C. Kraft as a forty-five-year-old shopkeeper with no real estate and $100 personal estate. *State v. Alvin G. Thornton*, 44 N.C. 252 (1853), 240–241. The Seventh Census of the United States, 1850: Johnston County, North Carolina, lists three in Thornton's household: A. G., a twenty-four-year-old grocer with $1,150 in real estate; William Thornton, a twenty-one-year-old clerk; and Alexander Findleson, a twenty-one-year-old distiller.

94. Governors' Papers, Thomas Bragg, G.P. 143, folder October 1857, NCDAH. This episode took place at the house of a Peden of Johnston County. The entire clan of Johnston County Pedens, near Boon Hill, owned only two slaves in 1860. Most were illiterate, straddling the boundary between poor whites and the lower yeomanry. See Eighth Census of the United States, 1860: Johnston County, North Carolina, 854, 855, 867, 871, 874, 875, 887.

Why did slaves and poor whites in the antebellum South drink together at all? Many possible answers present themselves. As the previous example suggests, slaves and poor whites sometimes worked together, and drinking and conviviality was an integral part of some work activities. For others, drinking together may have been a matter of convenience. Slaves and poor whites often obtained liquor at the same grog shops. Rather than retreating to the exclusive company of fellow slaves or poor whites to consume it, they drank at the point of purchase, in the social atmosphere of the dram shop and in the presence of each other. Most slaves must have preferred to drink their liquor as quickly and discreetly as possible or risk detection from carrying an unfinished bottle of whiskey with them. W. J. Rorabaugh has also discussed the symbolic meanings and psychological benefits of drinking—and drinking to excess—in the antebellum United States. "After 1800," Rorabaugh states, "drinking in groups to the point where everyone became inebriated had ideological overtones. For one thing, such drinking became a symbol of egalitarianism. All men were equal before the bottle." If drinking to intoxication effected a sense of social leveling among participants, he continues, "it also gave them a feeling of independence and liberty." People made the conscious choice to drink excessively and thereby alter their mental state or escape their troubles. Drinking, therefore, "increased a man's sense of autonomy. To be drunk was to be free."[95] This explanation goes a long way in explaining why lower-class white men drank with their social superiors: drinking released them from their problems as it generated feelings of equality and independence. But the question of why slaves and poor whites drank together remains. Poor whites did not consider slaves their social betters, and slaves likewise often regarded poor whites as their inferiors. Drinking, therefore, could not have generated feelings of equality with poor whites, since slaves often looked contemptuously upon them. Similarly, poor whites as a group derived no special psychological benefits from drinking with slaves. According to respectable white society, to associate socially with slaves signaled degradation. These explanations discounted, it seems clear that many slaves and poor whites drank together out of friendship and genuine feelings of camaraderie.

Gambling went hand in hand with drinking. Historians have written little about the seedy subculture of gambling in the nineteenth century, but many slave and poor white men found no more relaxing way to spend their leisure time on Sat-

95. Rorabaugh, *Alcoholic Republic*, 151.

urday or Sunday than at an interracial game of seven up, rattle-and-snap, pitch-and-toss, or chuck-a-luck.[96] As in the case with drinking, this may have reflected sincere friendships. On the other hand, it may suggest that slaves and poor whites each considered the other's money easy pickings. In runaway advertisements, masters often noted that their slaves were "fond of gaming." Milton A. Browder of Rockingham County, North Carolina, for instance, offered a $500 reward for his "artful" young "scoundrel" Manza, who "is said to play well for a negro—professes to be a good judge of paper money, and sometimes gets hold of one or two hundred dollars at a time, by gambling or otherwise." Poor white men of all ages likewise enjoyed gambling, and evinced no qualms about playing with slaves. "The poor and loafering class of whites, are about on a par in point of morals with the slaves in the South," wrote slave autobiographer Henry Bibb. "They are generally ignorant, intemperate, licentious, and profane. They associate much with the slaves; [and] are often found gambling together on the Sabbath." William Burton, for example, a twenty-year-old landless and unemployed poor white, "unlawfully did play at a game of dice with a slave" in Granville County, North Carolina, in 1857. Free blacks sometimes participated in these contests as well. In Fairfield District, South Carolina, poor whites William Wood and Jacob Barnadore gambled with a slave named Dennis and "free negro" John Oglesby. In Laurens District, a white man named Edward Neil played cards with

96. On the games of chance slaves and poor whites played, see Hundley, *Social Relations,* 223–224; and *State v. Nates,* 3 Hill 200 (S.C. 1836). Rattle-and-snap, sometimes called raffle-and-snap, and chuck-a-luck involved both cards and dice. Ann Fabian, *Card Sharps, Dream Books, and Bucket Shops: Gambling in 19th-Century America* (Ithaca: Cornell University Press, 1990), explores gambling's relationship to the emerging capitalist economy rather than to the gamblers themselves. On gambling among the gentry in the colonial era, see T. H. Breen, "Horses and Gentlemen: The Cultural Significance of Gambling among the Gentry of Virginia," *William & Mary Quarterly* 3d ser., 34 (April 1977): 239–257; and Randy J. Sparks, "Gentlemen's Sport: Horse Racing in Antebellum Charleston," *South Carolina Historical Magazine* 93 (January 1992): 15–30. Although Sparks neglects the issue of class, Breen contends that through high-stakes play, the gentry excluded lower-class whites from many contests, thereby helping establish their social superiority. In addition to poor whites, wealthy white youth coming of age composed another group likely to gamble with slaves. See York District, Clerk of Court of General Sessions, General Sessions Papers, case 803(704), reel 2660, SCDAH; and York District, Clerk of Court of General Sessions, General Sessions Papers, case 797(697), reel C2660, SCDAH. For firsthand accounts of professional gamblers, see John Morris [John O'Connor], *Wanderings of a Vagabond: An Autobiography* (New York: published by the author, 1873); and Martin Duralde Letter Book, 1846, LVA. On gambling as a pastime among slaves, see D. Wiggins, "Good Times On the Old Plantation: Popular Recreations of the Black Slave in Ante Bellum South, 1810–1860," *Journal of Sport History* 4 (Fall 1977): 274.

"four negroes," including Tom Wilson, a free black. Neil explained to authorities "that this Boy Tom owes him a dollar and that was how he came with those negroes." Lower-class men of all colors and statuses could potentially become equals in the presence of cards and dice.[97]

Impromptu games of chance broke out in any number of locations. The most popular venue for interracial play was the grog shop. A peek behind the front door of almost any urban watering hole or crossroads store shows slaves and poor whites placing their bets and mingling together familiarly. A Richmond County, North Carolina, jury indicted the nearly eighty-year-old poor white farmer Elisha Crowson "for permitting gambling with cards in his grog shop," as well as "for betting at cards," "for selling on the sabbath," for dispensing liquor to slaves Shepherd and Rich, and "for keeping a disorderly house and a nuisance." The most infamous poor white, Edward Isham, confessed that he "gambled with a negro" at "Franklins' grocery" and "won some money." Interracial games sometimes boldly took place directly under the master's nose, on or near his or her own plantation. In June 1857, four white men—including one overseer—gambled with John D. Williams's slave Allen "in Col. J. D. Williams' Mill House." A Granville County, North Carolina, man testified that he saw Alexander Humphreys, an illiterate poor white man in his twenties, on an April Sunday in 1840 "with several negroes in Peyton Purryears Plantation Setting or Squatting down & that they all broke & ran on discovering him." Another witness "went to the place where they ran from & saw Gambling Instruments & money & other things." Humphreys was charged with "play[ing] at a game of Cards for money liquor and property" with no fewer than ten "negro Slaves" belonging to at least seven different masters. Other games occurred "in the woods" or in an "old field," wherever the chances of detection seemed small.[98]

97. *Richmond Enquirer*, June 24, 1836; *Narrative of the Life and Adventures of Henry Bibb, an American Slave, Written by Himself with an Introduction by Lucius C. Matlack* (New York: published by the author, 1849), 24; Granville County, Criminal Actions Concerning Slaves and Free Persons of Color, 1857–1863, folder 1857, NCDAH; Seventh Census of the United States, 1850: Granville County, North Carolina, 172; Fairfield District, Court of General Sessions, Indictments, item 317, SCDAH; Laurens District, Court of Magistrates and Freeholders, Trial Papers, folder 45, SCDAH.

98. Richmond County, Slave Records, 1778–1866, Criminal Action Papers Concerning Slaves, 1850–1866; Seventh Census of the United States, 1850: Richmond County, North Carolina, 285, lists Crowson as seventy-six years old, a farmer, with $50 real estate; Bolton and Culclasure, *Confessions of Edward Isham*, 14; Laurens District, Court of General Sessions, Indictments, item 1086, SCDAH; Granville County, Criminal Actions Concerning Slaves and Free Persons of Color, 1838–1847, folder 1840, NCDAH; Sixth Census of the United States, 1840: Granville County, 126, lists an Alexander Humphrass as an illiterate nonslaveholder in his twenties, heading a household of five; Laurens Dis-

The close living and working quarters of some slaves and poor whites made illegal gaming a convenient pastime. Laboring poor white men in their twenties often gambled with slaves. Court records show, for example, that "about midnight" one November evening in 1856, "Ptolemy Funk did game with Cards with two negro men slaves said to belong to Lewis Froneberger, in a house in Yorkville," South Carolina. Funk, a poor mattress maker in his late twenties, occupied the dwelling with his wife Narcissa. He utilized it "as a work shop in the day time," but it was used "at night by the said two slaves . . . as a sleeping room." Likely other slave and poor white gamblers played cards and dice together after working side by side during the week. In Granville County, North Carolina, jurors presented James Tillotson, "laborer (being a white man[)]," for "play[ing] at divers games of chance with a certain slave named Herrod, the property of Lucy Bullock," in November of 1837. In May 1856, James Lain, an illiterate, laboring "white man" of Caldwell County, allegedly did "play at a game of cards with a slave named Lawson the property of John Jones." Likewise, Irish laborer Charles Gorman of Marlboro District, South Carolina, was accused of "playing at a game with cards and dice" with slaves Alfred and John in January 1860. Some slaves and poor whites who worked together certainly spent a portion of their free time together as well.[99]

Like poor white laborers, tenant farmers, often in their thirties and forties but with no land to call their own, found slaves suitable gaming partners. In Richmond County, North Carolina, jurors presented "Nathan Baldwin a white person" for playing at "an unlawful game of chance called raffling with a certain negro called Harry the property of one Thomas Robinson." In February 1857, Caldwell County's Jacob Wilson, "a white man" in his early thirties, purportedly "play[ed] at a game of hazard with Dick a slave, the property of one Powell." Ed-

trict, Court of Magistrates and Freeholders, Trial Papers, folder 45, SCDAH; Laurens District, Court of General Sessions, Indictments, item 903, SCDAH.

99. York District, Clerk of Court of General Sessions, General Sessions Papers, case 906(815), reel C2661, SCDAH; Eighth Census of the United States, 1860: York District, South Carolina, 372, lists Ptolemy Funk as a native of Virginia, thirty-one years old with $100 in real estate; Granville County, Criminal Actions Concerning Slaves and Free Persons of Color, 1838–1847, folder 1838–1839, NCDAH; Sixth Census of the United States, 1840: Granville County, North Carolina, 130, lists Tillotson as a nonslaveholder; Caldwell County, Slave Records, n.d., 1842–1866, folder 1856, NCDAH; Seventh Census of the United States, 1850: Caldwell County, North Carolina, 38, lists Lain as an illiterate laborer of twenty-nine with no real estate; Marlboro District, Court of General Sessions, Indictments, item 721, SCDAH; Eighth Census of the United States, 1860: Darlington District, South Carolina, 406, lists Charles Gorman as a native Irishman, twenty-three years old, a laborer, with no real or personal estate.

ward Blanton, "a white person" of Cleveland County in his midforties, "unlaw-fully did play at a game of cards for money with a slave named Andy" in Febru-ary 1859. A South Carolina court found James C. Brown of Greenville District, South Carolina, guilty of playing "a certain prohibited game with cards called seven up," one Sunday in May 1851, with Archibald Owings's slave Clark. In each of these cases, poor, struggling farmers turned to slaves for entertainment.[100]

Slaves and poor whites both faced harsh penalties if caught gambling with one another. A North Carolina law that went into effect in May 1831 entirely forbade slaves from gambling. Any violator "receive[d] a whipping on his or her bare back, not exceeding thirty nine lashes." The same act warned whites and free blacks not "to play at any game of cards, dice, nine pins or any game of chance or hazard, whether for money, liquor, or any kind of property, or not, with any slave or slaves." The law awarded free blacks convicted of gambling with bondspeople the same thirty-nine lashes granted slaves, while whites who dis-regarded the prohibition faced a fine and a maximum of six months in jail.[101] South Carolina went one step further. That state inflicted as many as thirty-nine stripes on whites—men only—caught gambling with slaves or free blacks, in addition to fines and imprisonment that both men and women faced. Laurens District court doled out "Twenty Lashes" to poor white James C. Brown for playing seven up with a slave in 1851. For betting at cards with a slave named Allen, George Grant earned "20 lashes, then imprisonment one month & . . . 19 lashes more, afterwards to be imprisoned one month longer." The Fairfield

100. Richmond County, Slave Records, 1778–1866, Criminal Action Papers Concerning Slaves 1848, folder 1831–1838, NCDAH; Sixth Census of the United States, 1840: Orange County, North Carolina, 200, lists Baldwin as a nonslaveholder in his twenties; Caldwell County, Slave Records, n.d., 1842–1866, folder 1858, NCDAH; Eighth Census of the United States, 1860: Caldwell County, North Carolina, 308, lists Jacob Wilson as a thirty-five-year-old illiterate farmer with no real estate and $200 personal estate; Cleveland County, Records of Slaves and Free Persons of Color, 1841–1869, folder 1850–1859, NCDAH; Seventh Census of the United States, 1850: Cleveland County, North Carolina, 124, lists Blanton as thirty-five years old, an illiterate farmer with no real estate; Eighth Census of the United States, 1860: Cleveland County, North Carolina, 803, lists him as forty-four, illiterate, and a farmer with neither real nor personal estate; Laurens District, Court of General Ses-sions, Indictments, item 903, SCDAH; Seventh Census of the United States, 1850: Greenville Dis-trict, South Carolina, 337, shows James C. Brown as a forty-one-year-old farmer with no real estate.

101. *Acts Passed By the General Assembly of the State of North Carolina, at the Session of 1830–31* (Raleigh: Lawrence & Lemay, 1831), 14–15. See also laws ratified in January 1839, in *Laws of the State of North Carolina, Passed By the General Assembly, at the Session of 1838–'39* (Raleigh: J. Gales and Son, 1839), 32; and in January 1851, in *Laws of the State of North-Carolina, Passed By the General Assembly, at the Session of 1850–'51* (Raleigh: T. J. Lemay, 1851), 498.

District court in the spring of 1853 found Jacob Barnadore guilty of gaming with a slave and ordered him "[t]o pay a fine of two hundred dollars: to be imprisoned 'till the first Monday in November next, and on that day to receive publickly thirty nine lashes on the bare back." Fines and jail sentences of less than the maximums the law allowed were the rule for whites convicted of gambling with slaves, and there is no way to tell whether those South Carolina offenders who were ordered whipped did suffer the lash. That such severe punishments existed at all reveals the seriousness with which lawmakers viewed interracial gambling.[102]

Some slaves and poor whites engaged in still other rowdy and boisterous pastimes. Immersed in the Old South's culture of competition, they sometimes wagered at horse races or at blood sports such as cockfights. Less the preserve of the gentry than horse racing, cockfighting in particular attracted men from all ranks of society, slave as well as free.[103] In the piney woods of eastern North Carolina in 1857, one observer happened upon a cockfight taking place near a tavern. He witnessed "a crowd of shabby-looking white men and negroes collected in an open space behind the stable," placing wagers of ten to twenty-five cents on the outcome of the spectacle.[104] Slaves and poor whites might also gather together to partake in the excitement of gander-pulling contests. At one gander pull, a traveler observed "thousands of spectators—ladies as well as gentlemen, the *elite* as well as the vulgar—assembled to engage in or witness the favorite sport." Gan-

102. David J. McCord, *The Statutes at Large of South Carolina; Edited, Under Authority of the Legislature*, vol. 7 (Columbia: A. S. Johnston, 1840), 469–470; Laurens District, Court of General Sessions, Indictments, item 903, SCDAH; Laurens District, Court of General Sessions, Indictments, item 1086, SCDAH; Eighth Census of the United States, 1860: Laurens District, South Carolina, 228, lists George W. Grant as a twenty-two-year-old overseer for Adolph Fuller; Fairfield District, Court of General Sessions, Indictments, item 317, SCDAH; Seventh Census of the United States, 1850: Fairfield District, South Carolina, 238, lists Barnadore as a fifty-one-year-old man with neither an occupation nor real estate; Eighth Census of the United States, 1860: Fairfield District, South Carolina, 260, shows Barnadore as a sixty-four-year-old illiterate laborer with no real estate but $300 personal estate.

103. Richard E. Powell, Jr., "Sport, Social Relations and Animal Husbandry: Early Cockfighting in North America," *International Journal of the History of Sport* 10 (December 1993): 362, 370–371, 372, 375, 376; Rhys Isaac, *The Transformation of Virginia, 1740–1790* (New York: W. W. Norton & Company, 1982), 102, 103; B. W. C. Roberts, "Cockfighting: An Early Entertainment in North Carolina," *North Carolina Historical Review* 42 (July 1965): 308; Guion Griffis Johnson, "Recreational and Cultural Activities in the Ante-Bellum Town of North Carolina," *North Carolina Historical Review* 6 (January 1929): 31.

104. Porte Crayon [David Hunter Strother], "North Carolina Illustrated. II. —The Piny Woods," *Harper's New Monthly Magazine* 14 (May 1857): 751–752. Quotation on p. 751.

der pulling involved taking a goose, greasing its head and neck, binding its legs together with a cord, and suspending the unfortunate creature upside-down from a tree branch. Participants paid a small entry fee to the owner of the goose. Riding on horseback at full gallop, they charged at the helpless, dangling bird and attempted to tear off its head as they rode underneath it. The slick, well-oiled neck and head, combined with the unwilling gander's flailing, made this an exceedingly difficult challenge. Moreover, an observer wrote, "A 'nigger,' with a long whip in hand, was stationed . . . about two rods from the gander, with orders to strike the horse of the puller as he passed by." The startled horse might rear up, veer in an unexpected direction, or unleash an abrupt burst of speed as it passed the gander. Many riders missed the head altogether; others broke the bird's neck without snapping off the head. He who successfully detached the goose's head from its body won the privilege of eating the bird. At the contest one traveler witnessed, "An old Cracker—with a sandpaper glove on—pulled off his head at last, amid the shouts of a wondering host of intoxicated competitors."[105]

Public punishments and court days provided additional occasions for the social elbow rubbing of slaves and poor whites. To inculcate a message of obedience among slaves, masters often dispatched their bondspeople to see whippings meted out to other transgressing chattel. "The negroes from the neighboring plantations were summoned to witness the scene," remembered successful Maryland fugitive Josiah Henson, but the area's "illiterate, besotted poor whites" also came to observe and delight in the spectacle. During court days, poor whites sat for hours watching legal proceedings, idle slaves sometimes viewing from a back bench or gallery. Noting the "dilapidated condition" of the ceiling in Richmond's Mayor's Court, the editor of the *Richmond Enquirer* expressed with jeering contempt his desire "that some of the plaster might fall unexpectedly on the heads of the loafers who, to gratify a depraved curiosity, poke their unwashed faces over the rail each day to hear the disgusting matter which comes before His Honor, instead of being at work or at home doing something useful."[106]

105. C. G. Parsons, *Inside View of Slavery: or A Tour Among the Planters* (Boston: John P. Jewett and Company; Cleveland: Jewett, Proctor and Worthington, 1855), 136, 137, 138. For another firsthand account of a gander-pulling contest, see G. W. Featherstonhaugh, *A Canoe Voyage Up the Minnay Sotor*, vol. 2 (London: Richard Bentley, 1847), 196–197.

106. *An Autobiography of the Reverend Josiah Henson* (Reading, Mass.: Addison-Wesley Publishing Company, 1969), 14; *Richmond Enquirer*, May 4, 1860.

Poor whites also sometimes enjoyed the music and dance of the slaves. A Virginia ex-slave fondly recalled the Saturday night dances in his master's barn. "A banjo player would be dere an' he would sing," he remembered. "De niggers would be pattin' dey feet an' dancin' for life. Master an' dem would be settin' on de front porch listenin' to de music, 'cause you could hear it for a half mile. . . . We had a time of our life." Their festivities attracted neighborhood poor whites in search of entertainment. "Po' whites would come over to see de dance," he continued. "De master wouldn't 'low de po' whites on his place an' dey would have to steal in to see de dance." Investigating echoes of music and laughter, a patrol in the South Carolina upcountry found "a collection of free blacks, slaves and some white folks, fiddling and frolicing generally" in 1857. Music continued during the workday as well, slaves working to the cadence of their tunes. Their songs possessed the power not only to ease slaves' psychological burdens but to bring even the most seemingly antagonistic blacks and whites together. A former South Carolina slave recollected a time when "one of the overseers, a white man, Andy Odom, got so happy that he fell offen a rail fence . . . where he was watching the hands as they chopped cotton. They got to singing an finally broke out on 'Am I a Soldier of the Cross.' Mr. Odom got so happy he went to shouting and fell off the fence."[107]

As this last bondsman's remarks suggest, some slaves and poor whites shared a spiritual link. In the antebellum South, slaves often attended the same evangelical churches, camp meetings, and revivals as whites of all economic backgrounds.[108] Slaves participated in their own religious rituals, but respondents in

107. Perdue et al., *Weevils in the Wheat*, 326; quoted in Berlin, *Slaves without Masters*, 260; Rawick, SS2, vol. 3, pt. 2, 860. On music and dancing, see Bill C. Malone, "Blacks and Whites and the Music of the Old South," in *Black and White Cultural Interaction in the Antebellum South*, ed. Ted Ownby (Jackson: University Press of Mississippi, 1993), 149–170; and Wiggins, "Good Times," 274–276. For indulgent small slaveholders who permitted interracial gatherings with music and dancing, see the case of Bray Parker in Gates County, Slave Records, n.d., 1783–1867, Criminal Actions Concerning Slaves, n.d., 1803–1861, folder 1835, NCDAH; and the case of Jacob Boyce in Perquimans County, Slave Records, 1759–1864, folder 1840–1849, NCDAH. The latter case went before the state supreme court. See *State v. Boyce*, 32 N.C. 536 (1849).

108. Donald G. Mathews, *Religion in the Old South* (Chicago: University of Chicago Press, 1977), 193; Dickson D. Bruce, Jr., *And They All Sang Hallelujah: Plain-Folk Camp-Meeting Religion, 1800–1845* (Knoxville: University of Tennessee Press, 1974), 3; John B. Boles, "Introduction," in *Masters & Slaves in the House of the Lord: Race and Religion in the American South, 1740–1870*, ed. John B. Boles (Lexington: University Press of Kentucky, 1988), 1–2, 9; Randy J. Sparks, "Religion in Amite County, Mississippi, 1800–1861," in *Masters & Slaves in the House of the Lord*, 67; Robert L. Hall, "Black and White Christians in Florida, 1822–1861," in *Masters & Slaves in the House of the Lord*, 84;

the Federal Writers' Project interviews of the 1930s routinely observed that slaves also attended the "white folks' church." Masters sometimes forced their bonds-people to go and hear white preachers' message of obedience to authority; other slaves went willingly.[109] Enslaved church members comprised only a small fraction of some congregations, but a substantial majority of others. When Antioch Baptist Church opened in Society Hill, South Carolina, in 1830, its members included thirty-three whites and eight blacks, at least five of whom were slaves. The First Baptist Church in Edgefield boasted both greater numbers and a much larger percentage of black members. By August 1858, its congregation included 175 blacks—almost all slaves—and 104 whites.[110]

When slaves joined white churches, they subjected themselves to new sets of stringent rules and regulations under church oversight. Their everyday transgressions were opened to the censure of the congregation. For minor infractions, slave members helped govern the behavior of black congregants. Serious offenses, however, invited white intervention. At an 1829 meeting of Ebenezer Baptist Church in Darlington District, South Carolina, slave member Philip was brought before the church to answer to a charge of absconding from his master. Philip explained that "[t]wo white men . . . overtook him one Evening on the Publick Road between his Master's & a Neighbours" and warned him of an impending "agitation" that would result in the death of "all the people in this Neighbourhood." According to Philip, the whites "gave him a pass" and advised that he flee to the safety of Charleston. The alarmed slave ran off with his wife only to return home a short time later. The church, "not . . . altogether pleased with the plausibility of the account given by Philip," believed the slave had intended to escape aboard a vessel in Charleston's harbor, then reconsidered. They expelled him for running away and telling falsehoods.[111]

Charles A. Johnson, *The Frontier Camp Meeting: Religion's Harvest Time* (1955; reprint, Dallas: Southern Methodist University Press, 1985), 113.

109. Boles, "Introduction," 16; Genovese, *Roll, Jordan, Roll,* 202–209.

110. Minutes of Antioch Baptist Church [1830–1895], 1830, SCDAH; Minutes of First Baptist Church [1823–1900], August 1858, 64, SCDAH.

111. Minutes of Ebenezer Baptist Church [1823–1908], March 1829, SCDAH. Just as whites had the power to censure African-American congregants, black churchgoers also retained the power to bring disciplinary action against their white coreligionists. Only within the confines of the church did blacks in the Old South have the ability to testify against whites. See Betty Wood, "'For Their Satisfaction or Redress': African Americans and Church Discipline in the Early South," in *The Devil's Lane: Sex and Race in the Early South,* ed. Catherine Clinton and Michele Gillespie (New York: Oxford University Press, 1997), 110, 114.

Like a number of slaves, some poor whites also joined evangelical churches. In their formative decades in the eighteenth century, the evangelical Baptists and Methodists had challenged the Anglican hierarchies of rank and race, and appealed to poor and nonslaveholding whites and to slaves for membership. The economic chasm that separated poor whites from the gentry permitted some to view slaves as possible brothers in Christ and to countenance biracial worship.[112] By the early nineteenth century, in fact, many in society's upper ranks mocked Methodism as a "religion for 'Niggers and poor whites.'" Not every poor white welcomed slave membership, however. When asked why he missed church, one poor white Virginian told his neighbor, "I thank you I dont go to church whare negros set above the white folks." Poor white Edward Isham temporarily "joined the Methodist Church" in Georgia, but as he reported, "I got into a difficulty with a negro about a fishing pole and tried to cut him but was prevented, and for this they turned me out of the church."[113] Many antebellum poor whites displayed indifference, if not overt hostility, toward "institutional religion" generally.[114] Evangelicals' unwavering strictures against the sinfulness of drinking and gambling, horse racing and cockfighting, fiddling and dancing—all among many poor whites' favorite pastimes—deterred them from embracing evangelical religion en masse.[115] And poor whites as a group never proved particularly dogmatic. Those who attended services often preferred churches based on ties of kinship rather than religious affiliation. Charles C. Bolton has found that poor whites in North Carolina's central Piedmont who joined a particular church entered congregations composed of familiar family and kinship groups, consisting of both rich and poor, black and white. Poor whites cared less about church doc-

112. Christine Leigh Heyrman, *Southern Cross: The Beginnings of the Bible Belt* (Chapel Hill: University of North Carolina Press, 1997), 11, 13, 15; Bruce, *And They All Sang Hallelujah,* 5; Boles, "Introduction," 8–9; Sylvia R. Frey and Betty Wood, *Come Shouting to Zion: African American Protestantism in the American South and British Caribbean to 1830* (Chapel Hill: University of North Carolina Press, 1998), 101.

113. Guion Griffis Johnson, *Ante-Bellum North Carolina: A Social History* (Chapel Hill: University of North Carolina Press, 1937), 430; Elliott and Moxley, *Tennessee Civil War Veterans Questionnaires,* vol. 5, 1823; Bolton and Culclasure, *Confessions of Edward Isham,* 2. See also Charles C. Bolton, *Poor Whites of the Antebellum South: Tenants and Laborers in Central North Carolina and Northeast Mississippi* (Durham: Duke University Press, 1994), 2.

114. Bertram Wyatt-Brown, "Religion and the Formation of Folk Culture: Poor Whites of the Old South," in *The Americanization of the Gulf Coast, 1803–1850,* ed. Lucius F. Ellsworth (Pensacola: State of Florida; Department of State; Historic Pensacola Preservation Board, 1972), 28.

115. Heyrman, *Southern Cross,* 8–9, 15, 17, 18, 25.

trine, a professionalized ministry, and missionary work, than worshiping with those with whom they felt comfortable, regardless of class or race.[116]

When poor whites did attend church, only four thin walls separated the sacred from the profane. Outside, during services in one "less than usually rude meeting-house," Frederick Law Olmsted discovered "circles of negroes and white boys, roasting potatoes in the ashes" of two campfires. This scene was relatively tame. Often, slaves, poor whites, and free blacks sold alcoholic refreshments near church grounds and at the fringes of camp meetings. At one camp meeting, a slave autobiographer encountered a "crowd of eaters, drinkers, gamblers, prostitutes and other rowdies of every class, who swarm around these places." In Caldwell County, North Carolina, landless white laborer Washington Anderson allegedly committed the unholy offense of "Playing Cards with a negro slave belonging to William B. Dula near a meeting house on the sabath day during publick worship for money." While the saints prayed, the sinners played.[117]

Inside, preachers stirred up their flocks. Planter D. R. Hundley mocked poor whites' and yeomen's parsons as "ignorant men of the Whang Doodle description, illiterate and dogmatic, and blessed with a nasal twang. . . . They very seldom know any thing about their Bibles."[118] What they lacked in theological training they compensated for with charisma, guiding their interracial audience toward religious ferment. Black exhorters had their chance to preach at the conclusion of the main service, after the whites had departed. They also ministered to black audiences at camp meetings, but rarely stood before whites in any religious setting. Rebel slave Nat Turner, however, claimed to commune frequently with a spirit and to experience apocalyptic visions that he shared with "both white and black, in the neighborhood." Turner told of his visions "to a white man (Etheldred T. Brantley) on whom it had a wonderful effect—and he ceased from his wickedness."[119]

116. Wyatt-Brown, "Religion and the Formation of Folk Culture," 29; Bolton, *Poor Whites*, 57.

117. Olmsted, *Seaboard Slave States*, 454; *The Rev. J. W. Loguen*, 144–145; Caldwell County, Slave Records, n.d., 1842–1866, folder "no date," NCDAH; Seventh Census of the United States, 1850: Caldwell County, North Carolina, 36, lists Anderson as a twenty-four-year-old laborer with no real estate.

118. Hundley, *Social Relations*, 218; see also 266.

119. Bruce, *And They All Sang Hallelujah*, 75; *The Confessions of Nat Turner, the Leader of the Late Insurrection in Southampton, Va., As Fully and Voluntarily Made to Thomas R. Gray* (Baltimore: Thomas R. Gray, 1831), reprinted in William L. Andrews and Henry Louis Gates, Jr., eds., *The Civitas Anthology of African American Slave Narratives* (Washington, D.C.: Civitas/Counterpoint, 1999),

Slaves and poor whites differed little in their ecstatic responses to evangelical preaching. The kinetic behavior and audible vocalizations of the evangelicals had both European and African roots, but in biracial gatherings, their traditions reinforced one another—to a point. D. R. Hundley wrote that yeomen, and presumably poor whites as well, "are prone to shout at camp-meetings, and to see visions and dream dreams." He reported with disdain that "they are led not infrequently, to mistake animal excitement for holy ecstasy, and seem to think . . . that God is not to be entreated save with loud prayers, and much beating of the breasts, and clapping of the hands, accompanied with audible groans and sighs." W. E. B. DuBois would later assert that lower-class whites copied the "emotional fervor" of blacks. Blacks often despised it when whites sent up cries, shouts, and choruses of "amens," believing the exclamations weak imitations of their own worship style. Frederick Law Olmsted reported blacks' indifference to the preaching during biracial church services: "[T]here may have been a sympathetic groan or exclamation uttered by one or two" of the black congregants, he wrote, "but generally they expressed only the interest of curiosity in the proceedings." They were saving themselves, Olmsted discerned, and patiently biding their time until the whites departed and they began their separate service. The next day, the blacks "were so hoarse that they could scarcely speak," for "the religious exercises they most enjoy are rather hard upon the lungs." Amid the religious frenzy of camp meetings, slaves made a concerted effort to outshout the whites and to remain long after the whites had gone, singing and praying in voices growing ever louder. Slaves and poor whites, then, sometimes attended the same services, and shared similar outward forms of religious expression, but they did not compose a unified spiritual community.[120]

The biracial membership of evangelical churches belied the persistent inequalities between black and white behind church doors. Whites accepted blacks into fellowship, worshiped with them, enforced church discipline upon them, and permitted black baptism, but in many ways blacks remained incomplete members of the religious community. The spatial arrangement of bodies within the church, for one, implied inequality. During the colonial period, Anglican

92. See also Herbert Aptheker, *American Negro Slave Revolts* (New York: Columbia University Press, 1943), 296.

120. Sylvia R. Frey, "Shaking the Dry Bones: The Dialectic of Conversion," in *Black and White Cultural Interaction in the Antebellum South*, ed. Ted Ownby (Jackson: University Press of Mississippi, 1993), 33, 37; Frey and Wood, *Come Shouting to Zion*, 121; Hundley, *Social Relations*, 217, 218; Olmsted, *Seaboard Slave States*, 460, 454, 461; Genovese, *Roll, Jordan, Roll*, 239–240.

churches had introduced the tradition of separate seating for black and white members to appease poor white churchgoers anxious to demonstrate their rank and privilege above their black coreligionists. In the nineteenth century, evangelical churches continued to seat blacks in segregated areas within the church, either in the back, in a separate balcony or gallery, or in an apse. Olmsted witnessed fifty "crackers" at one meeting house, where a "dense body of negroes" sat in and under a gallery in the rear.[121] At camp meetings, too, blacks and whites lived in separate camps, their tents sometimes divided by a plank fence.[122] The use of the terms "Brother" and "Sister" for black congregants in no way symbolized their equality with whites or full inclusion into the church. Black members were prohibited from voting for church officers, and clerks listed them on separate pages in church records. In short, blacks and whites attended biracial—but not "integrated"—religious services.[123] One folk song expressed the widespread belief among slaves that, despite their earthly subjugation, they would achieve social equality in the afterlife, if not with masters then at least with poor whites:

> You may be a white man, white as de drippin's [*sic*] of snow,
> But if you ain' got Jesus on yo' min', to hell you'll sho'ly go.
> Little nigger baby, black face an' shinin' eye,
> Jes' as good as de po' white trash in de sweet bye an' bye.[124]

Evangelical religion competed with superstition for slaves' and poor whites' spiritual loyalties. Throughout the antebellum era, many slaves and poor whites persisted in their belief in the supernatural and in witchcraft as part of their folk cultures. Fortunes, spells, potions, and signs all held real meaning for them. A former Maryland bondsman turned minister asserted that poor whites shared "all the superstitions of the negroes." As ex-slave H. C. Bruce observed, "Superstition in some form has always existed, especially among illiterate people, re-

121. Boles, "Introduction," 12; Larry M. James, "Biracial Fellowship in Antebellum Baptist Churches," in *Masters & Slaves in the House of the Lord: Race and Religion in the American South, 1740–1870*, ed. John B. Boles (Lexington: University Press of Kentucky, 1988), 52; Hall, "Black and White Christians in Florida," 85, 97; Heyrman, *Southern Cross*, 67–69, 217–218, 255; Frey and Wood, *Come Shouting to Zion*, 141, 77–80; Olmsted, *Seaboard Slave States*, 454. Men and women of both races sat apart as well. See Olmsted, *Seaboard Slave States*, 454; Boles, "Introduction," 12; Bruce, *And They All Sang Hallelujah*, 73.

122. Johnson, *Frontier Camp Meeting*, 46, 114; Bruce, *And They All Sang Hallelujah*, 73.

123. Sparks, "Religion in Amite County," 71, 77–78; Hall, "Black and White Christians in Florida," 85.

124. John A. Lomax, "Self-Pity in Negro Folk-Songs," *The Nation* 105 (August 9, 1917): 144.

gardless of color."[125] Slaveholder D. R. Hundley described southern poor whites as "very superstitious, being firm believers in witches and hobgoblins" and in "fortune-telling after the ancient modes—such as palm-reading, card-cutting, or the revelations of coffee-grounds left in the bottom of the cup." Poor white parents admonished their children to behave for fear of witches or the "Big Nig." Civil War chronicler Mary Boykin Chesnut recorded the death of the alleged witch Milly Trimlin, "a perfect specimen of the Sandhill 'tackey' race, sometimes called 'country crackers,'" with her "yellow and leathery" skin, jaundiced eyes, and lean, sharp features: "Three times she was buried in consecrated ground in different churchyards, and three times she was dug up by a superstitious horde, who put her out of their holy ground." Chesnut considered the "poor Sandhill" a "good, kind creature," despite her purported mystical ties to the occult. "Where her poor, old, ill-used bones are lying now I do not know," she wrote. "I hope her soul is faring better than her body." A colporteur informed a Charleston newspaper that the poor whites of the North Carolina pine barrens "seemed to be totally given up to a species of mental hallucination, which carried them captive at its will. They nearly all believed implicitly in witchcraft, and attributed everything that happened, good or bad, to the agency of persons whom they supposed possessed of evil spirits." The agents of northern missionary associations who traveled among South Carolina's illiterate poor routinely noted the strong "state of ignorance and superstition in the population." Many of the poor whites they encountered attended no organized church.[126]

A few select slaves acted as the depositories of magical knowledge and ethereal traditions transported from Africa. Slave conjurors commanded tremendous respect among plantation slaves, who believed that ties to the supernatural granted them powers even over the master. Conjurors mesmerized slaves, but their clientele also included poor white believers. An ex-slave from North Carolina recalled that blacks and whites alike placed their faith in spells and charms. "One colored man used to make charms, little bags filled with queer things," she

125. Wyatt-Brown, "Religion and the Formation of Folk Culture," 29, 20; Rev. John Dixon Long, *Pictures of Slavery in Church and State,* 2nd ed. (Philadelphia: published by the author, 1857), 354; Bruce, *New Man,* 57. On supernaturalism in the early national period, see Alan Taylor, *Liberty Men and Great Proprietors: The Revolutionary Settlement on the Maine Frontier, 1760–1820* (Chapel Hill: University of North Carolina Press, 1990), 79–82, 178–180; and Heyrman, *Southern Cross,* ch. 1.

126. Hundley, *Social Relations,* 266; Bertram Wyatt-Brown, *Southern Honor: Ethics and Behavior in the Old South* (New York: Oxford University Press, 1982), 160; Martin and Avary, *Diary from Dixie,* 401, 400; Olmsted, *Seaboard Slave States,* 350, 509–510.

reported. "He called 'em 'jacks' an' sold 'em to the colored folks an' some white folks too."[127] A former Virginia slave asserted that whites adhered to superstitions even more than slaves. In a possibly apocryphal story, he claimed that "slaves used superstition to fool the white man":

> There was one nigger on our plantation that even the overseer feared. He had a red flannel jacket which he could make talk. He would hang the jacket on a nail, say something, squeeze it and the jacket would groan, moan and carry on. If anyone else touched it, the jacket didn't move. The solution was this: the nigger had a huge bullfrog sewed in his jacket so that the frog could breathe. When others touched it, the frog sat still; when the nigger touched it, he stuck a pin in the frog and the frog yelled and jumped. The ignorant overseer couldn't see through that and gave the slave very few orders.

Another slave on the same plantation reportedly "caught snakes, and kept them as pets," extracting their fangs but feeding them alcohol to make them "vicious." "They were huge snakes and everybody feared them," the ex-slave said, "especially the poor white overseer," who apparently did not realize the fangs had been removed: "The overseer never beat him because he feared the nigger would call out his snakes on him." By the same token, poor whites manipulated slaves' superstitious beliefs to their own financial advantage. Editorial writer "Powhatan" warned of wandering "gipsies" in his neighborhood who "are likely to prowl about, browsing on the credulity and superstition of ignorant whites and blacks." The gypsies, he complained, made their living "by trafficking with, and duping negroes, who levy upon their masters, to have their fortunes told." To the contributor's dismay, these fortunes almost inevitably "intoxicated" slaves with the "delusive hope" "of a glorious dawn of freedom."[128]

Through all of these social contacts—work and play, drinking and gambling, music and dance, religion and superstition—slaves and poor whites often developed an understanding of the other, one that permitted them to shed their racial fears and hatreds and to forge interracial relationships. While mutual contempt and resentment indeed characterized the relationships of some slaves and poor whites, many others transcended such animosity. Despite differences of color and status, they recognized that they both resided in a slaveholder's society that

127. Blassingame, *Slave Community*, 109–110, 113; Genovese, *Roll, Jordan, Roll*, 217–218; Rawick, SS1, vol. 11, North Carolina, 19–20.

128. Perdue et al., *Weevils in the Wheat*, 155–156; *Richmond Enquirer*, March 17, 1859.

shunted them to the margins in different ways. Slaves and poor whites sometimes expressed their feelings of superiority over the other, but on other occasions, their words or actions declared their equality. "We looked upon the poor
white folks as our equals," said one North Carolina ex-slave. "They mixed with
us and helped us to envy our masters. They looked upon our masters as we
did."[129] Take as well the notions of equality espoused in the slave verse "Black
Molasses":

> Cawn bread en black molasses
> Is better dan honey en hash
> Fer de fahm-han' coon
> En de light quadroon,
> Along wid de po' white trash.[130]

The fraternity that developed between slaves and poor whites owed much to
the similarity of their material conditions and their subordinate positions in relation to the master. Slaveholding society denied slaves freedom and relegated
them to grudging lives of unpaid labor. Though nominally free, poor whites suffered similar degradation, barely able to eke out their own existence. Both depended in large degree on the noblesse oblige of wealthy whites for their survival.[131] Masters supplied slaves basic necessities in the same way they dispensed
charity upon local poor whites. "I 'member all the po' white trash that lived near
us," reported a former South Carolina slave. "Marster all time send 'em meat an'
bread an' help 'em with they crop. Some of 'em come from Goldsboro, North Ca'-
lina to git a crop whar we lived. They was so sorry they couldn't git no crop whar
they come frum, so they moved near us." Using the Gullah term for "white man,"
another South Carolina ex-slave recalled a "poor buckra" named "Mr. Reed dat
lived down on Wateree, passin' our house sometime. He was a God-forsaken
lookin' man dat marster or mistress always give somethin'." "Many was de poor
white folks dat 'most lived on Master John," reported a third. In situations like
these, slaves could see for themselves that whiteness did not imply superiority.
Masters oversaw a dependent population of slaves as well as poor whites. Simultaneously, slaves beheld the disrespect some masters showed poor whites, receiving them at a back door of the "big house" and treating them as less than equal.

129. Rawick, vol. 14, pt. 1, 267.

130. John Charles McNeill, *Lyrics from Cotton Land* (Charlotte: Stone Publishing Co., 1907), 98.
See also McIlwaine, *Southern Poor-White*, xx.

131. Genovese, "Rather Be a Nigger Than a Poor White Man," 83.

"Ol' Marster was more hard on dem poor white folks den he was on us niggers," claimed one sympathetic Virginia slave. Slaves, too, knew what it meant to be regarded as inferior.[132]

In striking displays of compassion, slaves themselves sometimes helped sustain suffering poor whites. According to one ex-slave from Tennessee, "Many pore white folks would have starved if it had not been for slaves who stole food from their masters to feed the white folks." Former Maryland bondsman G. W. Offley reminisced that his mother had given "good victuals" to "the poor whites" on more than one occasion. Some slaves' generosity seemingly knew no bounds. In Richland District, South Carolina, bondspeople reportedly provided for the family of a local slave catcher, who eked out a meager living tracking and capturing runaways. "Mr. Black, the slave hunter, was very poor, and had a large family; he had a wife, with eight or ten helpless children," wrote successful fugitive Jacob Stroyer. "But as cruel as Mr. Black was to runaway slaves, his family was almost wholly supported by negroes; I have known in some cases that they stole from their master to help this family. The negroes were so kind to Mr. Black's family that his wife turned against him for his cruelty to runaway slaves." Slaves who pilfered from their owners' stores sometimes provoked their masters' wrath. To aid "[a] very poor white woman" who "lived within about a mile of the plantation house," recalled slave autobiographer Lewis Clarke, "[a] female slave named Flora, knowing she was in a very suffering condition, shelled out a peck of corn and carried it to her in the night." Her altruistic efforts to feed the destitute poor white woman earned her 150 lashes. But as former Granville County, North Carolina, slave Willie Blackwell proudly proclaimed, "W'en de niggers sees a poor white man's wife an' daughtah aint got no clothes, no food, dey steals old Mistez's dress right off de line, an' goes into de smokehouse fo' rations, den totes 'em to de poor fo'ks. Yes suh! Dat's de nigger slave all ovah. Can't stand to see no suffer'n." Some poor whites may have felt ashamed to receive slaves' assistance, but their desperate need of supplies compelled them to swallow their pride.[133]

132. Rawick, vol. 13, pt. 3, 290; John Solomon Otto and Augustus Marion Burns III, "Black Folks and Poor Buckras: Archeological Evidence of Slave and Overseer Living Conditions on an Antebellum Plantation," *Journal of Black Studies* 14 (December 1983): 185; Rawick, vol. 3, pt. 3, 2; Rawick, vol. 3, pt. 3, 119; Rawick, vol. 16, Virginia, 9–10.

133. Mellon, *Bullwhip Days*, 208–209; *A Narrative of the Life and Labors of the Rev. G. W. Offley* (Hartford, Conn., 1859), 6; William Loren Katz, comp., *Flight from the Devil: Six Slave Narratives* (Trenton: Africa World Press, Inc., 1996), 200; *Narrative of the Sufferings of Lewis Clarke, During a Captivity of More Than Twenty-Five Years, Among the Algerines of Kentucky, One of the So Called Chris-*

Slaves and poor whites established patterns of social interaction that lasted, potentially, from the cradle to the grave. The interracial ties of infancy and childhood sometimes fell by the wayside as parents socialized their youngsters to the mores of southern society, but that same spirit of camaraderie sometimes continued into adulthood in the shared work and leisure-time activities of slaves and poor whites. Their interactions provided occasional, fleeting glimpses of a genuinely integrated world; at other times, such as at church, slaves and poor whites merely coexisted peacefully in a biracial but segregated setting. All of the interracial contacts outlined here, however, help dismantle the stubborn myth of an invariable, mutual hatred between blacks and whites that has been read backward in time from the postbellum years and imposed on the antebellum era. To the alarm of slaveholders, no impermeable line divided slaves and poor whites in the years before the Civil War.

---

tian States of North America (Boston: David H. Ela, 1845), 28; Rawick, SS2, vol. 2, pt. 1, 309. On Flora, see also Genovese, "Rather Be a Nigger Than a Poor White Man," 86.

CHAPTER 2

THE UNDERGROUND ECONOMY

Historians have paid a great deal of attention over the past two decades to the so-called "slave," "internal," or "informal" economy, studying slaves' independent activities as producers and consumers. In the rice-growing low country of South Carolina and Georgia, where the task system predominated, slaves had the opportunity to use their free time toward the end of the day as they saw fit, within certain constraints that their masters imposed. Many slaves diligently worked their own garden plots, raised and sold their own crops, and tended horses and livestock. As Southern Claims Commission records make clear, through their own hard work, some slaves amassed impressive amounts of property. Outside the low country, various forces circumscribed slaves' ability to produce for themselves, market their goods, and accumulate wealth. Limited available land in the Piedmont and in the upcountry precluded masters from supplying slaves their own provision grounds. Moreover, slaveholders in those regions tended to organize their slave labor forces according to the gang system. Under the gang system, slaves labored under close supervision from sunup to sundown, providing them time only at night and on Sundays to work for themselves. Across the South, however, internal economies proliferated. Slaves sometimes earned payments in money, perhaps for performing additional chores on the plantation or "extra work" in industry. Armed with the money and commodities they earned from or through the largesse of their masters, slaves were no strangers to the antebellum marketplace.[1]

1. In the low country, see Philip D. Morgan, "Work and Culture: The Task System and the World of Low Country Blacks, 1700–1880," *William & Mary Quarterly* 3d ser., 39 (October 1982): 563–599; Philip D. Morgan, "The Ownership of Property by Slaves in the Mid-Nineteenth-Century Low Country," *Journal of Southern History* 49 (August 1983): 399–420; Betty Wood, "'White Society' and the 'Informal' Slave Economies of Lowcountry Georgia, c. 1763–1830," *Slavery & Abolition* 11 (December 1990): 313–331; Betty Wood, *Women's Work, Men's Work: The Informal Slave Economies of Lowcountry Georgia* (Athens: University of Georgia Press, 1995); and Robert Olwell, *Masters, Slaves, & Subjects: The Culture of Power in the South Carolina Low Country, 1740–1790* (Ithaca: Cornell University Press, 1998), ch. 4. For works dealing with areas outside the low country, see John Campbell, "As 'A Kind of Freeman'?: Slaves' Market-Related Activities in the South Carolina Up Country, 1800–1860," *Slavery & Abolition* 12 (May 1991): 131–169; and John T. Schlotterbeck, "The Internal

Running parallel to slaves' economic activities sanctioned by the master were those that lacked such authorization. Several historians have recognized that an illicit, underground slave economy flourished throughout the antebellum South, rooted largely in theft and consequently anathema to slaveholders. Slaves' surreptitious dealings often brought them into contact not only with other bondspeople and with free blacks, but also with "unscrupulous" whites who ignored racial distinctions and eagerly traded with slaves without the masters' consent.[2] But

---

Economy of Slavery in Rural Piedmont Virginia," *Slavery & Abolition* 12 (May 1991): 170–181. Other important works on the slave economy include Alex Lichtenstein, "'That Disposition To Theft, With Which They Have Been Branded': Moral Economy, Slave Management, and the Law," *Journal of Social History* 21 (Spring 1988): 413–440; Lawrence T. McDonnell, "Money Knows No Master: Market Relations and the American Slave Community," in *Developing Dixie: Modernization in a Traditional Society,* ed. Winfred B. Moore, Jr., Joseph F. Tripp, and Lyon G. Tyler (Westport, Conn.: Greenwood Press, 1988), 31–44; Loren Schweninger, "The Underside of Slavery: The Internal Economy, Self-Hire, and Quasi-Freedom in Virginia," *Slavery & Abolition* 12 (September 1991): 1–22; Loren Schweninger, "Slave Independence and Enterprise in South Carolina, 1780–1865," *South Carolina Historical Magazine* 93 (April 1992): 101–125; Joseph P. Reidy, "Obligation and Right: Patterns of Labor, Subsistence, and Exchange in the Cotton Belt of Georgia, 1790–1860," in *Cultivation and Culture: Labor and the Shaping of Slave Life in the Americas,* ed. Ira Berlin and Philip D. Morgan (Charlottesville: University Press of Virginia, 1993), 138–154; Larry E. Hudson, Jr., "'All That Cash': Work and Status in the Slave Quarters," in *Working Toward Freedom: Slave Society and Domestic Economy in the American South,* ed. Hudson (Rochester: University of Rochester Press, 1994), 77–94; Larry E. Hudson, Jr., *To Have and to Hold: Slave Work and Family Life in Antebellum South Carolina* (Athens: University of Georgia Press, 1997), ch. 1; and Dylan C. Penningroth, *The Claims of Kinfolk: African American Property and Community in the Nineteenth-Century South* (Chapel Hill: University of North Carolina Press, 2003), ch. 2. For a previous generation of scholarship that touches on a similar theme, see John Hope Franklin, "Slaves Virtually Free in Ante-Bellum North Carolina," *Journal of Negro History* 28 (July 1943): 284–310; Clement Eaton, "Slave-Hiring in the Upper South: A Step toward Freedom," *Mississippi Valley Historical Review* 46 (March 1960): 663–678; and John Hebron Moore, "Simon Gray, Riverman: A Slave Who Was Almost Free," *Mississippi Valley Historical Review* 49 (December 1962): 472–484.

2. The best work on slave theft remains Lichtenstein, "Disposition To Theft." For historians who acknowledge the presence of an underground slave economy, see many of the works listed in note 1 above as well as Eugene D. Genovese, *Roll, Jordan, Roll: The World the Slaves Made* (New York: Vintage Books, 1976), 22; Eugene D. Genovese, "'Rather Be a Nigger Than a Poor White Man': Slave Perceptions of Southern Yeomen and Poor Whites," in *Toward a New View of America: Essays in Honor of Arthur C. Cole,* ed. Hans L. Trefousse (New York: Burt Franklin & Company, Inc., 1977), 87–88; J. William Harris, *Plain Folk and Gentry in a Slave Society: White Liberty and Black Slavery in Augusta's Hinterlands* (Middletown, Conn.: Wesleyan University Press, 1985; reprint, Baton Rouge: Louisiana State University Press, 1998), 56–61; Bill Cecil-Fronsman, *Common Whites: Class and Culture in Antebellum North Carolina* (Lexington: University Press of Kentucky, 1992), 92–94; Charles C. Bolton, *Poor Whites of the Antebellum South: Tenants and Laborers in Central North Carolina and Northeast Mississippi* (Durham: Duke University Press, 1994), 46–47, 107–108; Stephanie McCurry, *Mas-*

while scholars acknowledge the existence of this interracial, underground trade, they have devoted surprisingly little energy to its study. Timothy J. Lockley has uncovered evidence of a thriving clandestine network of exchange between slaves and white shopkeepers in the city of Savannah,[3] but the preponderance of southerners lived not in urban but in rural areas. It must have been much more difficult for slaves to sustain systems of underground trade with whites in the countryside. In the rural South, the white population was more isolated and scattered across a wide geographical area. Small, close-knit communities in which everyone knew one another and kept a watchful eye on their neighbors supplanted the anonymity of the bustling city. Furthermore, the relatively few foreigners who settled in the South—among the whites most likely to collaborate and trade clandestinely with slaves—tended to congregate in the region's urban centers.[4]

This chapter calls attention to the underground economy of the rural South through an investigation of slaves' unlawful trade with poor whites in the antebellum Carolinas and Virginia. Lockley's work has examined the economic exchanges between slaves and a broad and diverse group of "non-slaveholders" or "non-elite" white shopkeepers, but merchants notwithstanding, there existed an inverse relationship between a white person's wealth and his or her likelihood of engaging in the unlawful trade with slaves. Slaves' most frequent white trading

---

ters of Small Worlds: Yeoman Households, Gender Relations, and the Political Culture of the Antebellum South Carolina Low Country (New York: Oxford University Press, 1995), 116–121; and Elizabeth Fortson Arroyo, "Poor Whites, Slaves, and Free Blacks in Tennessee, 1796–1861," *Tennessee Historical Quarterly* 55 (Spring 1996): 60–62.

3. Timothy J. Lockley, "Trading Encounters between Non-Elite Whites and African Americans in Savannah, 1790–1860," *Journal of Southern History* 66 (February 2000): 25–48; and Timothy James Lockley, *Lines in the Sand: Race and Class in Lowcountry Georgia, 1750–1860* (Athens: University of Georgia Press, 2001), ch. 3. See also Betty Wood, *Women's Work, Men's Work*, chs. 6–7; and Richard C. Wade, *Slavery in the Cities: The South, 1820–1860* (New York: Oxford University Press, 1964), 84–90, 149–160, 252–258.

4. The overwhelming majority of those identified in this book as poor whites are native-born Southerners. On foreigners in the South, see Ira Berlin and Herbert G. Gutman, "Natives and Immigrants, Free Men and Slaves: Urban Workingmen in the Antebellum Southern South," *American Historical Review* 88 (December 1983): 1175–1200; and Randall M. Miller, "The Enemy Within: Some Effects of Foreign Immigrants on Antebellum Southern Cities," *Southern Studies* 24 (Spring 1985): 30–53. Many immigrants brought antislavery traditions with them from their native countries—traditions that permitted them to think nothing of trading with slaves. German and Irish immigrants, especially, were either ignorant of or dismissive of southern racial etiquette. As Noel Ignatiev cautions, however, antislavery traditions from the mother country did not necessarily transfer to American soil. See Noel Ignatiev, *How the Irish Became White* (New York: Routledge, 1995), ch. 1.

partners appear to have been the poor white farmers, laborers, and other marginal members of white society who comprised between 30 and 50 percent of the southern white population, depending on the locality.[5] Exploring in depth the important place that these poor whites occupied within slaves' underground trading networks, this chapter argues that, while anxious slaveholders found such economic cooperation inimical to a society stratified on the basis of race, the calculated, rational nature of slave–poor white exchange blunted its potentially subversive character.

Slaves and poor whites conducted a thriving illicit trade throughout the antebellum era. Although they were generally illiterate and left few records in voices of their own, by analyzing court records, census returns, slave narratives, and other sources, it is possible to investigate these unsanctioned economic interactions in the rural antebellum Carolinas and Virginia, and answer a series of basic but fundamental questions. What commodities did slaves and poor whites trade? Who were the poor whites willing to flout the law and conduct business with slaves, and who were the slaves who partnered with them? How did they safely establish their economic relationships, and how long did they last? Did these transactions involve cash or merely an exchange of goods? What benefits did each derive from the clandestine trade? How did masters detect unlawful trading and attempt to curb it? And perhaps most important, did poor whites' willingness to trade with slaves signal a repudiation of the southern social order?

Poor whites made likely trading partners for slaves in the antebellum Carolinas and Virginia. As Charles C. Bolton has explained, the Old South's poor whites marked an economically dependent population that typically survived by working as farm tenants and laborers. Without the security and independence derived from land ownership, these poor whites sometimes hunted or herded animals to make a living, but most belonged to a highly mobile labor force, offering a variety of marketable skills and frequently relocating to where they could

5. Bolton, *Poor Whites*, 5, 192; Rudolph M. Lapp, "The Ante Bellum Poor Whites of the South Atlantic States" (Ph.D. diss., University of California–Berkeley, 1956), 10–11, 13–14, 15, 16, 18, 20. William L. Barney offers a somewhat more conservative estimate of 20 to 30 percent. See William Barney, *The Road to Secession: A New Perspective on the Old South* (Washington: Praeger Publishers, 1972), 42; and William L. Barney, *The Secessionist Impulse: Alabama and Mississippi in 1860* (Princeton: Princeton University Press, 1974), 39. Work on Georgia and Tennessee suggests higher rates. See Frederick A. Bode and Donald E. Ginter, *Farm Tenancy and the Census in Antebellum Georgia* (Athens: University of Georgia Press, 1986); and Fred Arthur Bailey, *Class and Tennessee's Confederate Generation* (Chapel Hill: University of North Carolina Press, 1987), 25, 171–172.

find work.[6] Poor whites' standard of living often did not differ markedly from that of slaves, whether in their housing, diets, or clothing. Indeed, antebellum travelers and slaves themselves sometimes gave a slight advantage in material existence to the bondspeople. Struggling, impoverished, and dwelling at the social and economic margins of southern white society, poor whites made attractive potential economic allies for enterprising slaves in the region.[7]

Several factors, including the organization of slave labor, the sheer numbers of slaves and poor whites in a given area, individual masters' own managerial styles, and the size of land holdings all helped determine the likelihood of illicit slave–poor white commerce. Take South Carolina, for example. In the low country, the prevalence of the task system encouraged independent production by slaves. Ambitious bondspeople could complete their assigned task in an abbreviated work day, then turn to their own pursuits on a plot of land granted by the master. Their efforts produced commodities that they could theoretically have traded with local poor whites, but many low-country masters purchased their slaves' goods themselves, and relatively few potential poor white trading partners inhabited the immediate coast. The pool of possible poor white business associates was much greater in the upcountry. There, however, the greater prevalence of the gang labor system combined with the generally smaller land holdings of the region to limit slaves' opportunities to produce for themselves.[8] These facts suggest that the slave–poor white economy of the upcountry would have been driven more by theft than that of the low country. On the other hand, the greater incidence of absentee landownership in the low country likely encouraged stealing. No master, in short, could claim complete immunity from victimization by the unlawful traffic between slaves and poor whites. Even those slaveholders

6. Bolton, *Poor Whites*, ix, 5, 11, 8. For a fascinating, detailed look at the life of one exceptional poor white man's struggle to survive in a slaveholder's society, see Charles C. Bolton and Scott P. Culclasure, eds., *The Confessions of Edward Isham: A Poor White Life of the Old South* (Athens: University of Georgia Press, 1998).

7. Genovese, "Rather Be a Nigger Than a Poor White Man," 90; Avery O. Craven, "Poor Whites and Negroes in the Ante-Bellum South," *Journal of Negro History* 15 (January 1930): 16–17. For declarations of slaves' superior living conditions, see Henry Barnard, ed. Bernard C. Steiner, "The South Atlantic States in 1833, as Seen By a New Englander," *Maryland Historical Magazine* 13 (December 1918): 338; George P. Rawick, ed., *The American Slave: A Composite Autobiography*, vol. 3, pt. 3 (Westport, Conn.: Greenwood Publishing Company, 1972), 51; and W. H. Robinson, *From Log Cabin to the Pulpit, or, Fifteen Years in Slavery*, 3rd ed. (Eau Claire, Wis.: James H. Tifft, 1913), 22.

8. Morgan, "Work and Culture"; Campbell, "As 'A Kind of Freeman'?" 132–133; Schlotterbeck, "Internal Economy," 170; Hudson, *To Have and to Hold*, chap. 1.

who provided a market for their slaves' produce withheld alcohol and other goods their bondspeople desired. For those items, slaves needed to rely on their own initiative. Thus, in most locations, but particularly outside the low country, the clandestine trade between slaves and poor whites likely outpaced their licit commerce.

Although the degree and nature of the clandestine traffic surely varied by locality, a geographically inequitable distribution of extant court records prohibits advancing definitive judgments. Sources permitted the close examination of only nine of the thirty districts in South Carolina on the eve of the Civil War: Fairfield, Greenville, Lancaster, Laurens, Marlboro, Spartanburg, Union, Williamsburg, and York. Of these, only Williamsburg was located in the low country. The thirty North Carolina counties that merited close consideration were more evenly scattered across the state, though concentrated, like slaves themselves, in the eastern coastal plain and, somewhat less, in the Piedmont.[9] As a result, this chapter is based primarily on those illicit slave–poor white transactions occurring in a broad swath stretching from upcountry South Carolina, northeast through the North Carolina Piedmont, and east to the Atlantic coast—a region that the historiography of the slave economy, with its emphasis on the rice-producing low country, has largely neglected.[10]

Slaves and poor whites conducted their illicit transactions in any number of locations: at the humble cabin of the poor white; at a concealed, prearranged site; and especially at the local dram shop. Onslow County, North Carolina, planter James Battle Avirett described "the constant temptation of the servants, coming

9. The presence of surviving Court of General Sessions indictments determined the South Carolina districts under close scrutiny here. Of the thirteen districts with extant indictments, I found no applicable records from either Anderson or Kershaw Districts. Charleston and Pendleton Districts' indictments were not indexed and therefore regrettably eliminated from this study. In North Carolina, I examined with greatest care the counties of Bertie, Carteret, Chowan, Craven, Edgecombe, Gates, Nash, New Hanover, Northampton, Pasquotank, Perquimans, Pitt, Richmond, Robeson, Wayne, and Wilson in the east; Caldwell, Chatham, Cleveland, Davidson, Granville, Guilford, Iredell, Orange, Randolph, Rockingham, Stanly, and Stokes in the Piedmont; and Haywood and McDowell in the mountains. These thirty counties represent all of the counties in North Carolina for which the North Carolina Department of Archives and History has extant slave records.

10. Campbell, "As 'A Kind of Freeman'?" on upcountry South Carolina, and Schlotterbeck, "Internal Economy," and Schweninger, "Underside of Slavery," both on Virginia, are among the few historians who have dealt at length with areas outside the South Carolina and Georgia low country. A number of other works discuss South Carolina without clearly differentiating regions within the state. By contrast, North Carolina has been almost entirely ignored.

from the hurtful influence of small stores, kept by the lower class of whites" as "the curse of the plantation." "These people were ready, by night," he reminisced bitterly, "to carry on a system of demoralizing barter, taking at their own price articles stolen by the servants, to wit, corn, poultry, pigs; in short, anything the negro might carry in his bag, in any sense marketable." In return, proprietors dispensed "mean whiskey or other articles at high prices to compensate for the great risk they took." [11]

As in urban areas, the commodity slaves in the countryside most commonly sought from their poor white trading partners was liquor. Masters provided slaves alcohol only on rare occasion, at Christmas holiday and perhaps as an incentive at harvest. Liquor temporarily bolstered slaves' spirits and offered them a momentary release from the severity of their condition, but it was also used medicinally, in cooking, and to share in fellowship with bondspeople back in the quarters. Moreover, barring a special agreement with the master, slaves lacked a secure depository for any money they might have earned through their own labor. They therefore usually geared their spending more toward immediate gratification, and the local grog shop served as a convenient repository for slaves' earnings. [12]

Slaves also traded with poor whites for clothing. In Gates County, North Carolina, Enoch Jones allegedly sold "one sun-shade," "one coat," and "one pair of pantaloons," respectively, to slaves Wilson, Jerry, and Jim. Nash County's John L. B. Woodard purportedly supplied "coats, vests & calico" to no fewer than six slaves in 1857. Other slaves traded for shoes, blankets, and rugs. All of these items served a vital role in protecting slaves from the elements, and in that sense the trade with poor whites may have compensated for a master's neglect, but they also allowed for a modicum of self-expression. Even if they already owned garments and footwear supplied by the master, many slave men and women still enjoyed exercising their own independent judgment in selecting their outfits, and acquiring perhaps fancier apparel than the cheap, drab raiment their masters provided. [13]

11. James Battle Avirett, *The Old Plantation: How We Lived in Great House and Cabin Before the War* (New York: F. Tennyson Neely Co., 1901), 118.

12. Peter H. Wood, *Black Majority: Negroes in Colonial South Carolina from 1670 through the Stono Rebellion* (New York: W. W. Norton & Company, Inc., 1974), 209; Schlotterbeck, "Internal Economy," 177. On the illicit liquor trade in Savannah, see Lockley, "Trading Encounters."

13. Gates County, Slave Records, n.d., 1783–1867, Criminal Actions Concerning Slaves, n.d., 1803–1861, folder 1847, NCDAH; Seventh Census of the United States, 1850: Chowan County, North Carolina, 105, lists Jones as a thirty-two-year-old merchant from Virginia with no real estate; Nash County, Slave Records, Civil Action Records and Criminal Action Records, 1796–1863, folder

In contrast, slaves rarely traded with poor whites for food. Not only did many poor whites probably not have surplus victuals to exchange, but slaves were also resourceful enough to procure most foods without them. In addition to the sometimes scanty provisions allotted them by the master, many slaves routinely supplemented inadequate diets with the produce from their own garden plots. They could also easily appropriate the master's or the neighbors' foodstuffs for their own use, secretly killing a hog, picking apples or peaches from the orchard, or gathering vegetables from the garden. They generally consulted poor whites only to acquire nonessential, luxury, or specialty foodstuffs, particularly sugar and sweets, cakes and candies. These items were not as readily obtained on the plantation through their own efforts, so slaves with a sweet tooth sought out other suppliers, such as Kannon Parham of Granville County, North Carolina. A tenant farmer with only $50 worth of personal property, Parham was indicted in 1858 for selling "one pound of candy" to a slave.[14]

Whereas slaves bought few comestibles from poor whites, foodstuffs marked the commodities poor whites most often purchased from slaves. Poor whites represented a convenient market for surplus produce from slaves' garden plots or for the edibles stolen from their masters and from surrounding plantations. Many poor whites subsisted on meager and monotonous diets, and eagerly accepted an increase in their caloric intake, from any source. Furthermore, in most cases, they could buy food from slaves more cheaply than elsewhere, making their decision to trade with slaves a rational choice. Slaves supplied poor whites with chickens, turkeys, beef, and fish, but none of these protein sources appear in court records as frequently as pork. Poor whites commonly purchased "one side of Bacon," "twenty pounds of pork," or "one dead hog" from their slave associates.[15] Poor

---

1857, NCDAH; Seventh Census of the United States, 1850: Nash County, North Carolina, 298, lists Woodard as a house carpenter with no real estate. Wood, *Women's Work, Men's Work*, 58–61; Shane White and Graham White, *Stylin': African American Expressive Culture from Its Beginnings to the Zoot Suit* (Ithaca: Cornell University Press, 1998), 5–7, 9–10, 13, 31; Stephanie H. M. Camp, "The Pleasures of Resistance: Enslaved Women and Body Politics in the Plantation South, 1830–1861," *Journal of Southern History* 68 (August 2002): 534, 544, 558–566.

14. Granville County, Criminal Actions Concerning Slaves and Free Persons of Color, 1857–1863, folder 1858, NCDAH; Eighth Census of the United States, 1860: Granville County, North Carolina, 524, provides information on a Kenan Parham. Slaves also purchased sweets from whites in Rockingham and Nash counties.

15. Caldwell County, Slave Records, n.d., 1842–1866, folder 1847, NCDAH; Seventh Census of the United States, 1850: Caldwell County, North Carolina, 50; Northampton County, Slave Records, 1830–1867, folder 1850–1859, NCDAH; Seventh Census of the United States, 1850: Northampton County, North Carolina, 19.

whites also purchased various cereal crops from slaves, such as rice, in the low country, or wheat, in the Piedmont. But regardless of location, corn was the grain most widely traded to poor whites.[16] Slaves also kept poor whites stocked in other staples, including potatoes, butter, flour, and molasses. "[T]he poor whites were truly glad to buy the molasses caught in the hands of our mothers," wrote an ex-slave of Wilmington, North Carolina: "they ate it and asked no questions."[17]

Less frequently, poor whites purchased from slaves inedible agricultural commodities, including cotton and tobacco, flax and wool. In 1852, the elderly John Ross, who two years earlier had been listed in the census as a pauper living in the Laurens District, South Carolina, poor house, was indicted for trading with slave Jack "for Two Bales of Cotton."[18] In Brunswick County, Virginia, "tobacco dealer" Benjamin W. Lynch purportedly received "three hundred pounds" of the leaf from Daniel Huff's slave Mack.[19] In these and many other cases, the poor white buyers presumably planned to carry the goods acquired from slaves to market to sell as their own. Other poor whites purchased feed for livestock from slaves. South Carolina's Nancy Blanton allegedly traded with a slave "for one Bushel of Oats," while Jackson Pittman of Wilson County, North Carolina, purportedly bought "two bundles of fodder" from Larry D. Farmer's slave Dick.[20] Poor whites sometimes purchased stolen iron or farm implements, such as hoes, probably for their own use. In the dense pine forests of North Carolina, they traded for turpentine, planks, and shingles. Poor whites, in short, bought a far greater variety of goods from their enslaved trading partners than slaves bought

16. See, for example, Union District, Court of General Sessions, Indictments, file 3034, SCDAH; Union District, Court of General Sessions, Indictments, file 2966, SCDAH; Seventh Census of the United States, 1850: Union District, South Carolina, 33.

17. Robinson, *From Log Cabin to the Pulpit*, 12; Granville County, Criminal Actions Concerning Slaves and Free Persons of Color, 1848–1856, folder 1853, NCDAH; Spartanburg District, Court of General Sessions, Indictments, file 10, SCDAH; Spartanburg District, Court of General Sessions, Indictments, file 14, SCDAH.

18. Laurens District, Court of General Sessions, Indictments, file 897A, SCDAH; Seventh Census of the United States, 1850: Laurens District, South Carolina, 299.

19. Governor's Papers, Gov. John W. Ellis, box 1, folder May 1859, NCDAH; Seventh Census of the United States, 1850: Mecklenburg County, Virginia, 105.

20. Spartanburg District, Court of General Sessions, Indictments, Fall 1857, file 23, SCDAH; Seventh Census of the United States, 1850: Spartanburg District, South Carolina, 238; Eighth Census of the United States, 1860: Spartanburg District, South Carolina, 299; Wilson County, Slave Records, 1855–1864, folder Buying of Slave 1857, NCDAH; Eighth Census of the United States, 1860: Edgecombe County, North Carolina, 391, lists Pittman as twenty-eight, with no occupation, no real estate, and no personal estate. The census taker also labeled him a "Lunatic."

of them, a fact that underscores not only the economic deprivation of southern poor whites but also the resourcefulness of the slaves themselves.

Rather than indiscriminately delivering to poor whites whatever goods they could get their hands on, however, some slaves evinced sophisticated market behavior, carefully calculating which items were best suited for trade. "Tobacco was our favorite crop," wrote successful Virginia runaway Ralph Roberts. "Its value, compared with its weight, was much greater than that of grain, and a man's shoulders could bear off, in one night, what would bring a sum sufficient for a week or two." [21] For the identical reasons of price and weight, cotton was also a popular item in the clandestine trade between slaves and poor whites in areas producing that staple. Slaves endowed with less business savvy could still participate successfully in the illegal trade with poor whites. Only a bondsperson's imagination, combined with the resources available in a given locality, seemed to limit what poor whites proved willing to buy. As ex-slave Sallie Paul of South Carolina declared, "de colored people sell dem things day white folks never [even] want. Oh, dey take anything you carry dem." [22]

Most economic relationships between slaves and poor whites focused on trade, but poor whites also sometimes conducted business on slaves' behalf. As Chowan County, North Carolina, runaway Allen Parker recorded, "There was always some poor white who would . . . sell [goods] for the benefit of the slaves, for a consideration." Less restricted than slaves in their access to public markets, some poor whites willingly functioned as intermediaries, or middlemen, for bondspeople, selling merchandise that slaves had either produced or stolen, in return for a share of the profits from the sale. Parker himself recalled one instance in which he pilfered a pig, dressed it, and "carried him on my shoulder about three miles, and turned him over to a 'poor white' who took him to a neighboring town the next day, and sold him for me." Surrendering the porker to a poor white man to take to market insulated Parker from the dangers of commerce, sparing him the barrage of questions that would almost inevitably have accompanied a slave's arrival at market with a dressed pig for sale, without a ticket from the master. Whoever purchased the pig from Parker's white accomplice must have had no idea that it had been stolen by a slave. This arrangement, however, required a tremendous amount of trust on the slave's part. A slave could not find redress in the law or in the master for a deal gone sour. With only an unenforce-

21. Ralph Roberts, "A Slave's Story," *Putnam's Monthly Magazine of American Literature, Science, and Art,* 9 (June 1857): 617.

22. Rawick, vol. 3, pt. 3, 234.

Wealth of Masters Whose Slaves Engaged in Illicit Trade with Poor Whites

SOUTH CAROLINA

Slaveholder	# of Slaves	Value of Real Estate (in $)	Date of Crime	Census	District
Samuel W. Evans	109	40,000	1860	1860	Marlboro
Joseph Leach	45	18,500	1857	1850/60	York
Margaret Young	39	20,000	1855	1860	Union
Nathan B. Thomas	31	7,750	1848	1850	Marlboro
Daniel M. Crosland	24	6,000	1852	1850	Marlboro
Christopher Brandon	21	9,016	1857	1850/60	Union
Jabish N. Townsend	15	5,720	1855	1850/60	Marlboro
Henry B. Covington	14	10,413	1854	1850/60	Marlboro
John W. Farrow	13	5,332	1854	1850/60	Spartanburg
Micah Jenkins	12	13,600	1859	1860	York
George Spencer	11	3,900	1855	1850/60	Union
Samuel W. Anderson	6	2,000	1857	1850	Laurens
Lewis Blanton	1	2,800	1857	1860	Spartanburg
Totals	341	145,031			
Averages	26	11,156			

Six South Carolina masters—Brandon, Covington, Farrow, Leach, Spencer, and Townsend—appear in both the 1850 and 1860 census records. In calculating their assets, I have assumed a steady accumulation of wealth in land and slaves over the course of the decade. Thus, rather than using 1850 or 1860 figures, or an average of the two, I arrived at a prorated figure based on the year in which his slave committed the trade with a poor white. For example, Joseph Leach owned $23,000 in real estate in 1860, but only $8,000 in 1850. When his slave traded with a poor white in 1857, I am assuming that he owned approximately $18,500 worth of land (23,000 − 8,000 = 15,000; 15,000/10 = 1,500; 1,500 × 7 = 10,500; 10,500 + 8,000 = 18,500). Similarly, his slave family increased from thirty-seven in 1850 to forty-nine in 1860, so I have calculated that he owned forty-five slaves in 1857 (49 − 37 = 12; 12/10 = 1.2; 1.2 × 7 = 8.4, which rounds down to 8; 8 + 37 = 45). These exceptions notwithstanding, the figures cited for both South Carolina and North Carolina do not account for fluctuations in wealth in land or slaves that occurred between the time of the alleged crime and the arrival of the census taker.

able verbal agreement binding the poor white to the bondsperson, the slave confronted a high likelihood of being swindled. Thus, like other slaves, Parker surely chose his poor white agent carefully. As a result, he reported, "In due time the 'poor white' gave me my share of the money he got for the pig."[23]

Who, exactly, were the slaves and poor whites who traded with one another? Little can be determined from extant records about the slaves, although available

23. Allen Parker, *Recollections of Slavery Times* (Worcester, Mass.: Chas. W. Burbank & Co., 1895), 58, 76, 77.

Wealth of Masters Whose Slaves Engaged in Illicit Trade with Poor Whites

NORTH CAROLINA

Slaveholder	# of Slaves	Value of Real Estate (in $)	Date of Crime	Census	County
George Costen	62	10,000	1853	1850	Gates
Thomas Riddick	50	5,000	1847	1850	Gates
William D. Cobb	47	8,000	1850	1850	Wayne
Larry D. Farmer	34	11,220	1857	1860	Wilson
Perry Tyler	34	9,000	1850	1850	Bertie
Thomas J. A. Cooper	25	4,000	1857	1860	Nash
James Turner	23	8,000	1852	1850	Granville
Noah Roundtree	20	5,000	1851	1850	Gates
Samuel Simpson	20	3,000	1851	1850	Chowan
Parker Quince	18	3,500	1854	1850	New Hanover
Robert V. Eaton	17	2,800	1852	1850	Granville
William W. Barnes	13	6,000	1859	1860	Wayne
Elizabeth Gilliam	9	3,000	1847	1850	Gates
Edward Wood	7	3,500	1847	1850	Chowan
Margaret McLauchlin	4	2,200 (son)	1848	1850	Robeson
Totals	383	84,220			
Averages	26	5,615			

evidence suggests that most of those who transacted business with poor whites lived on the medium-sized estates of ten to forty-nine slaves that comprised roughly half of all southern holdings.[24] More than one hundred cases of illegal trading between slaves and poor whites appear in North Carolina and South Carolina court records between 1845 and 1860 alone. Indictments for unlawful trading often listed the names of accused slaves' masters. By cross-referencing the names of these masters with their census record entries, it is possible to gain a general sense of the size of the estates on which the accused slaves lived. While slaveholder mobility prevents many masters from being positively located in census records, twenty-eight of them, or roughly one-quarter of the total, can be traced back successfully to the free and slave population schedules of 1850 and/or 1860 — a sample sufficiently large to hint that most slaves who traded with poor whites belonged to relatively prosperous masters. The sample of thirteen slave-holders in five South Carolina districts, and fifteen scattered across nine counties in North Carolina shows that the average North Carolina master of a slave

24. Peter Kolchin, *American Slavery, 1619–1877* (New York: Hill and Wang, 1993), 101, 243.

indicted for trading illicitly with poor whites owned approximately $5,600 in real estate—barely more than half the figure for South Carolina masters—but an identical twenty-six total slaves. Twenty-three of the twenty-eight masters in the sample owned more than ten slaves, and fifteen, or more than half, counted among the "planter" class, owning at least twenty slaves.

Because a sizeable majority of all bondspeople lived on holdings of ten or more slaves, these figures for both North and South Carolina come as little surprise. It is a statistical probability that the preponderance of those slaves who traded stolen goods with poor whites would have resided on larger holdings. But what factors prompted or invited these slaves to steal from their owners in the first place? Masters with few slaves tended to oversee their hands personally, perhaps providing their bondspeople fewer opportunities to purloin their goods. On larger holdings, where the owner was less likely to labor side by side with his bondspeople, slaves perhaps felt less personal attachment to the master, and therefore had fewer scruples about robbing him and trading pilfered goods to local poor whites. Slaves on larger holdings also likely had access to a greater variety of commodities to carry away and exchange. The house servants of wealthy masters met with countless opportunities to smuggle foodstuffs out of the kitchen or storeroom. It may have been precisely because the slaves who traded with poor whites resided on larger holdings that bondspeople tended to acquire nonessentials such as liquor in exchange for their plunder. Slaves belonging to more prosperous masters were more likely to have an adequate food allowance and perhaps even a plot of land for raising their own crops.

Slave men conducted virtually all of the documented unlawful trade with poor whites. Male slaves were more likely than slave women to be hired out or sent on errands off the plantation, so they were the ones more likely to develop contacts with neighborhood poor whites. That they most often went in search of liquor suggests that they may have desired a channel through which to counter the harsh realities of slave life. Yet many other economic exchanges, for clothing, carpets, and the like, may well have represented efforts on the part of slave men, not to ameliorate their own personal suffering, but to provide for their families independently from the master. Stepping beyond the boundaries of the plantation to secure consumer goods for their families marked an autonomous bid of slave men to serve as genuine husbands and fathers.[25]

25. On slavery's tendency to emasculate slave men by stripping them of power and authority, and slave men's own efforts to protect and provide for their families, see Genovese, *Roll, Jordan, Roll,* 482–494; John W. Blassingame, *The Slave Community: Plantation Life in the Antebellum South,* rev. ed.

Occasionally, slave women ventured into the masculine world of unlawful interracial commerce. As historians such as Betty Wood and Robert Olwell have shown, female slaves played a dominant role in the informal slave economy as vendors in the South's urban markets.[26] Possibly because their economic energies were focused on these legitimate marketing activities, slave women do not often appear in court records as active participants in the countryside's slave–poor white underground economy. But there were exceptions. In Robeson County, North Carolina, one poor white man purchased "ten pounds of bacon" from William Thompson's slave woman Flora, in 1850. A rare trade involving exclusively women took place in Union District, South Carolina, in December 1853. Two young, illiterate white women named Sarah and Jemima Woodward, presumably sisters, bought "a quantity of meat and flour of the value of one dollar" from a female slave named Bet.[27]

Court records, however, almost certainly camouflage slave women's important place in the clandestine trade between slaves and poor whites. While sources suggest that female slaves only rarely participated in the direct, physical transaction of business with poor whites, slave women likely played a significant but elusive role in procuring the goods for slave men to trade. Compared to slave men, slave women who stopped by the kitchen or borrowed the keys to the storeroom raised less suspicion. Their work in food production and meal preparation provided them ample opportunity to steal goods from the master that they could then deliver to husbands and brothers, fathers and sons, who, in turn, could sell them to local poor whites. Slave women's relative invisibility in court records also suggests that their underground exchanges with poor whites may have taken different form. Whereas slave men swapped goods with local poor whites, slave women were probably more likely to trade their services, performing washing or

(New York: Oxford University Press, 1979), 172–173, 178–179; and Herbert G. Gutman, *The Black Family in Slavery and Freedom, 1750–1925* (New York: Pantheon Books, 1976), esp. 306–307.

26. Wood, "White Society," 321; Wood, *Women's Work, Men's Work*, 81; Robert Olwell, "'Loose, Idle and Disorderly': Slave Women in the Eighteenth-Century Charleston Marketplace," in *More Than Chattel: Black Women and Slavery in the Americas*, ed. David Barry Gaspar and Darlene Clark Hine (Bloomington: Indiana University Press, 1996), 98, 99, 101, 103; Olwell, *Masters, Slaves, & Subjects*, 20.

27. Robeson County, Records Concerning Slaves and Free Persons of Color, 1848–1855, folder 1850, NCDAH; Union District, Court of General Sessions, Indictments, file 2645, SCDAH. For examples of interracial female economic exchange in the colonial era, see Kathleen M. Brown, *Good Wives, Nasty Wenches, and Anxious Patriarchs: Gender, Race, and Power in Colonial Virginia* (Chapel Hill: University of North Carolina Press, 1996), 305.

sewing for poor white neighbors. Their poor white female counterparts some-times completed these kinds of chores for slaves. North Carolina bondsman Allen Parker, for instance, used the money he acquired from his pilfered pig to buy "some cloth, which a white woman made into a coat and a pair of pants for me."[28] By their very nature, these types of exchanges would have been in-credibly difficult to detect or to prove in court. Perhaps masters did not find such traditionally "feminine" activities as washing or sewing sufficiently threatening to merit much attention anyway. As long as their stores of food remained safe, they may have tolerated some degree of unapproved interracial fraternization.

Such a wide variety of poor whites traded with slaves that they are not easily categorized. Age made little difference in determining the likelihood of a poor white to do business with a slave. Poor whites accused of unlawful trading in-cluded young laboring men in their twenties, not necessarily condemned to re-main poor whites their entire lives. Landless, laboring men in their thirties and forties, likely among a more entrenched or permanent class of poor whites, also routinely traded illicitly with slaves. Less often, the elderly conducted a furtive business with them. Poor whites struggling to support large families, as well as those trying to subsist alone, all found the illicit trade with slaves advantageous.

Court records show that poor white women participated directly in the slave–poor white economy more than female slaves apparently did. Poor white women heading their own households comprised perhaps as much as 20 or 25 percent of all poor whites connected with the illicit trade. Most of these women were single, either abandoned by their husbands, widowed, or in rare cases, divorced. In other instances, their partner may have simply been away in search of work when the census taker passed through the neighborhood. In any event, poor white moth-ers often traded with slaves, almost exclusively for food. In Wayne County, North Carolina, Sally Lee, a thirty-four-year-old, illiterate mother of four, allegedly obtained "a peck of corn" from William D. Cobb's slave Jim. Women, both slave and free, successfully penetrated the informal, illicit marketplace, but typically men of both races dominated the documented activities of the underground, slave–poor white economy.[29]

28. Parker, *Recollections of Slavery Times*, 77. See also the case below, of poor white sisters Mary and Elizabeth Cumbo and the slave Ralph.

29. Wayne County, Records of Slaves and Free Persons of Color, n.d., 1783–1869, folder State vs. Sally Lee, 1850, NCDAH; Seventh Census of the United States, 1850: Johnston County, North Carolina, 25; Greenville District, Court of General Sessions, Indictments, file 2264, SCDAH; Sev-enth Census of the United States, 1850: Greenville District, South Carolina, 355; Eighth Census of the United States, 1860: Greenville District, South Carolina, 453.

Slaves conducted most of their trade with poor whites personally, face to face, at night. North Carolina ex-slave Allen Parker described the usual process. "The slave would eat his supper and take a nap," he explained. Then, after any patrols had already passed by or had turned in for the evening, the slave awoke, retrieved his stolen loot from its hiding place, put it in a bag that he slung over his shoulder, and "start[ed] for the house of the poor white." Most of these meetings must have been prearranged, to save the slave the time and trouble of locating a buyer in the precious few hours before dawn.[30]

Occasionally, concerns over being detected militated against slaves and poor whites exchanging goods with one another directly. Some trading partners instead agreed upon a secluded location where they could deposit their goods for the other to retrieve. In this manner, North Carolina fugitive William Kinnegy traded a pig to "a poor white man with whom I accidentally became acquainted." Kinnegy left the hog "in a place designated," then returned later to pick up the gun that he had requested of the poor white. "I took the gun and he took the pig," Kinnegy noted, "of course without meeting each other." The slave later exchanged a cowhide for powder and shot in the same furtive manner. Of his poor white associate, Kinnegy explained, "I saw him but rarely, as my acquaintance was too dangerous a thing for him."[31]

Slaves and poor whites rarely acted in concert to pilfer from a wealthy slaveholder; rather, slaves usually committed the theft, then delivered the stolen goods to a poor white recipient. In one notable exception to this pattern, "laborer" Alford Hartly of Davidson County, North Carolina, collaborated with Madson Davis's slaves "to carry away two Chickens from the hen Ruste." Detected, Hartly was charged with "stealing Chickens and Conspiring with negro slaves." According to Davis, Hartly had propositioned Davis's slaves "to assist him . . . steal som[e] pottry [poultry]."[32] But because southern courts did not permit the tes-

30. Parker, *Recollections of Slavery Times*, 57.

31. Vincent Colyer, *Brief Report of the Services Rendered by the Freed People to the United States Army in North Carolina, in the Spring of 1862, after the Battle of Newbern* (New York: Vincent Colyer, 1864), 20.

32. Davidson County, Records of Slaves and Free Persons of Color, n.d., 1826–1896, folder 1840, 1843, 1844, NCDAH; Sixth Census of the United States, 1840: Davidson County, North Carolina, 242, lists an Alfred Hartly as an illiterate nonslaveholder in his twenties; Seventh Census of the United States, 1850: Davidson County, North Carolina, 302, lists Alfred Hartley as a thirty-eight-year-old laborer with no real estate. For an example from Georgia, see Timothy J. Lockley, "Partners in Crime: African Americans and Non-Slaveholding Whites in Antebellum Georgia," in *White Trash: Race and Class in America*, ed. Matt Wray and Annalee Newitz (New York: Routledge, 1997), 57–58, 61–63.

timony of slaves against whites of any class, Hartly faced practically no danger in approaching Davis's slaves.

The limitations of southern law meant that even loyal, well-intentioned slaves accomplished nothing by intimating illicit plans to the master. At best, slaves who informed their masters of underground trading might provoke an extralegal response against a local poor white. Informing the master of poor whites engaged in the underground trade entailed a separate set of dangers for bondspeople themselves, however. If slaves who participated in such clandestine activity revealed it to the master, they incriminated themselves and provided the slaveholder with a motive to whip them. As one former North Carolina bondsman explained, the white buyer "knew that the slave could not complain of him without getting into trouble himself." [33] Slaves who dared betray their poor white trading partners also risked depriving themselves of desired contraband goods. [34] Moreover, if, in an effort to curry favor with the master, a slave tattled on a fellow bondsperson engaged in the illicit trade, he or she invited social ostracism in the quarters.

Establishing a trading relationship between a slave and a poor white must have been a much riskier proposition for a slave to initiate. "A great audacious piece of presumption indeed," reflected North Carolina teacher and lawyer William Valentine, "if the negro had not cause or reason to believe the white man would buy of him." Slaves needed to exercise the utmost discretion when approaching poor whites with commodities for sale. Poor whites could easily report the transgressing slave to the master, or take matters into their own hands and administer a whipping. [35]

Despite the dangers, slaves developed an astute sense of which whites could be trusted as business associates. In the early morning hours of February 10, 1819, slaves Morris, Moses, and Simon robbed William Dabney's store on the wharf in the coastal town of New Bern, North Carolina. Morris and Moses then went to the shop and residence of John Campbell and Polly Brown, roused them from sleep, and delivered them the contraband goods. When authorities discovered

33. Parker, *Recollections of Slavery Times*, 15–16.

34. D. R. Hundley, *Social Relations in Our Southern States* (New York: Henry B. Price, 1860; reprint, New York: Arno Press, 1973), 230.

35. William D. Valentine Diary, January 1, 1851, folder 11, #2148, SHC. See also Genovese, *Roll, Jordan, Roll*, 601; Cecil-Fronsman, *Common Whites*, 74. Valentine recalled that, during his boyhood, "a few men and occassionaly [*sic*] scoundrally families did for a long time keep a familiarity and traffic with our black portion of the family." Quoted in Cecil-Fronsman, *Common Whites*, 93.

ſ

the stolen merchandise at Campbell's shop, Campbell deposed that the two slaves

> knocked at the door. They asked me . . . if I would buy a barrel of wine. I told them I will, and asked the prices. I then asked them where did you get this wine. They the negros answered it was none of my business where they got it. I might as well have a bargain as any other person. I then asked them the price particularly. Their answer was thirty dollars. I told them I will give twenty. They then brought in the wine, and I gave them the money. . . . They asked me also if I did not want to buy Coffee, that I should have a bargain. I told them I would give twenty cents. . . . They asked me do you want to buy cheese. I said I did not, but they answered you might as well have it as another. We will give you a bargain also in the cheese. They then brought [them] right into the shop, and left them. I again asked the negros where do [they] get these cheeses. They said it was none of my business, and then parted.

If Campbell's testimony may be believed, it proves quite instructive. The slaves deflected questions about the provenance of their goods, and instead highlighted the great values they offered. Their willingness to deal correlated with the urgent need to dispose of the stolen goods before daybreak. It must have been difficult to find more than one or two buyers over the course of a single night, so slaves sold what they stole below its actual value rather than hold out for its market price. Other evidence, however, casts some doubt on the white shopkeeper's account of that night. Although Campbell's remarks predictably shifted blame from himself to implicate the bondsmen as the instigators of the trade, the slave Moses claimed to have overheard Campbell conspiring with Morris before the night of the robbery, urging him to steal from Dabney's store. Indeed, it seems doubtful that the slaves picked Campbell's shop at random. Attempting to dispose of contraband wares by seeking out potential buyers haphazardly would have been an inefficient and risky method of conducting the underground trade.[36]

36. Craven County, Criminal Actions Concerning Slaves and Free Persons of Color, n.d., 1781–1839, folder 1820–1822, NCDAH. Campbell was found guilty of receiving stolen goods and sentenced "to stand in pillary two hours." Morris was also found guilty of larceny and sentenced to thirty-nine lashes. See Craven County, Superior Court, State Docket, 1815–1829, April term 1819, NCDAH. Campbell's punishment was subsequently reduced to one hour in the pillory. See Craven County, Superior Court, Minutes, 1801–1820, April term 1819, NCDAH.

Slaves preferred dealing repeatedly with the same, familiar poor whites to branching out to others with unknown loyalties. William Kinnegy recalled that, as a runaway in the forests and swamps of eastern North Carolina, "I dared not permit myself to be seen by a white man for months, and then only by one or two of the very poorest, who traded with me in small things." Kinnegy and other slaves felt more at ease trading recurrently with particular poor whites who had proven themselves trustworthy. Poor whites who gained reputations as reliable economic allies invited further clandestine dealings, which in turn gave those poor white accomplices continued access to the cheap goods or other monetary rewards obtained through their cooperation with slaves. As a matter of good policy, then, slave–poor white trading relationships sometimes spanned several years.[37]

Slave and poor white economic transactions usually consisted of an exchange of goods, with slaves most often taking liquor in return for whatever they sold their poor white trading partner. But a portion of the slave–poor white economy operated along a cash nexus. Former bondsman Charles Ball remarked that, in the early nineteenth century, white shopkeepers welcomed slave customers who, unlike most whites, purchased goods with cash rather than on credit. By the 1840s and 1850s, however, slaves did not often pay poor whites with money, a finding consistent with historian John Campbell's contention that cash became increasingly scarce among South Carolina upcountry slaves as the antebellum years wore on. In contrast, it was not at all unusual for poor whites in the 1840s and 1850s to pay a slave a small sum for the goods he or she received. In Marlboro District, South Carolina, one poor white man paid a dollar to a slave for "[e]ight pounds of bacon." Another spent one dollar in exchange for "one fiddle, one pair of pantaloons, one vest and one cotton handkerchief." Poor white woman Maria Davis used specie, reportedly giving a slave named Dave "twenty five cents in Silver" for "one peck of wheat." Slaves apparently welcomed the influx of cash and coin into their economy, but proved cautious in their expenditure of currency.[38]

37. Colyer, *Brief Report of the Services Rendered*, 19. See also Roberts, "A Slave's Story," 617.

38. Charles Ball, *Fifty Years in Chains* (1837; New York: Dover Publications, Inc., 1970), 191; Campbell, "As 'A Kind of Freeman'?" 132; Marlboro District, Court of General Sessions, Indictments, item 572, SCDAH; Eighth Census of the United States, 1860: Marlboro District, South Carolina, 157; Marlboro District, Court of General Sessions, Indictments, item 629, SCDAH; Seventh Census of the United States, 1850: Marlboro District, 128; Eighth Census of the United States, 1860: Marlboro District, South Carolina, 169; Marlboro District, Court of General Sessions, Indictments, item 571, SCDAH; Seventh Census of the United States, 1850: Marlboro District, 159, lists Davis as fifty years old, illiterate, with no occupation and no real estate. Hudson, "All That Cash," stresses the importance of cash to slaves.

With so little money and property to their name, poor whites needed to make calculated economic decisions for their households, and they discovered that trading with slaves offered them opportunities to strike remarkable bargains. One former bondsman wrote that poor whites made "enormous profits by their trade with slaves."[39] Another remembered that slaves sold nearby "poor white folks" "their master's corn, hogs, chickens and many other things" "for practically nothing."[40] When shopkeeper John Campbell bought coffee, wine, and cheese from Morris and Moses, Polly Brown deposed, "The money given in payment of this property appeared to me to be but a trifle."[41] Poor whites routinely paid the grossly discounted price of twenty-five or fifty cents for an entire hog worth between five and ten dollars, and they frequently exchanged goods of unequal value.[42] One poor white in South Carolina, for instance, traded a slave a ten-cent "quart of molasses" in return for "one half bushel of corn" worth "twenty five cents," earning himself a net profit of fifteen cents.[43] Certainly, had the underground trade not offered such bargains, poor whites would have had little incentive to engage in it. If forced to pay market price, they might as well have traded legitimately through more conventional economic channels.

Poor whites often did take advantage of their enslaved business associates, who needed to dispose of their contraband goods quickly and quietly. "There could always be found a market among the poor whites, for whatever a slave had to sell," explained ex-slave Allen Parker, "though the price was often very low, for the slave was in a measure at the mercy of the buyer."[44] On the other hand, trading with poor whites secured slaves access to products their masters denied them, such as alcohol. Contraband liquor, tobacco, and clothing all made slaves' lives materially more bearable. Moreover, if slaves had stolen the items they sold, they made a respectable profit no matter what price they received; all it cost them was the time and effort to pilfer and deliver their masters' goods to a poor white buyer.[45]

39. Roberts, "A Slave's Story," 617–618.

40. Rawick, vol. 7, 112.

41. Craven County, Criminal Actions Concerning Slaves and Free Persons of Color, n.d., 1781–1839, folder 1820–1822, NCDAH.

42. Northampton County, Slave Records, 1830–1867, folder 1850–1859, NCDAH; Marlboro District, Court of General Sessions, Indictments, item 694, SCDAH; Hundley, *Social Relations*, 229.

43. Marlboro District, Court of General Sessions, Indictments, item 494, SCDAH; Seventh Census of the United States, 1850: Marlboro District, 159.

44. Parker, *Recollections of Slavery Times*, 15. See also Wood, "White Society," 316.

45. Campbell, "As 'A Kind of Freeman'?" 138–139; Lockley, "Trading Encounters," 39.

If slaves and poor whites each derived material benefits from their trade with one another, they may have also earned psychological rewards as well. Poor whites largely set the terms of the negotiations, using their superior bargaining position over their enslaved business associates to acquire contraband goods for prices well below their actual value. Poor whites' underground trade with slaves perhaps also sometimes marked a form of "Snopesian" retaliation, allowing them to strike back in a subtle and indirect yet potent way against certain neighborhood slaveholders with whom they maintained some unresolved grievance.[46] For their part, slaves could enjoy a fleeting moment of empowerment as they transacted business with poor whites. The buying, selling, and bartering of consumer goods fostered among slaves feelings of independence and autonomy, and signaled their fundamental humanity. The choices they made in the underground marketplace affected their own lives and inherently marked a denial of their enslaved condition.[47]

The mutual benefits of the illicit trade between slaves and poor whites made such transactions pervasive in many localities across the rural Carolinas and Virginia. Wherever slaves and poor whites came into contact, especially in the South Carolina upcountry and in the coastal plain and Piedmont regions of North Carolina and Virginia, the possibility of interracial trade loomed. Although impossible to quantify, the magnitude of the slave–poor white economy dismayed and disturbed contemporary white observers, who frequently decried the epidemic proportions of the clandestine traffic. Petitioners in North Carolina described the unlawful trade with slaves in spiritous liquors alone as "alarming." In South Carolina, one Barnwell District memorial asserted that "the illicit traffic with slaves . . . pervades . . . the whole State." And slaveholders were likely aware of only a small fraction of their slaves' underground dealings with poor whites. Explained one former slave, "as the parties to it are interested in keeping the secret, it is not often the masters find out how much they are robbed."[48]

46. Bertram Wyatt-Brown, "Community, Class, and Snopesian Crime: Local Justice in the Old South," in *Class, Conflict, and Consensus: Antebellum Southern Community Studies*, ed. Orville Vernon Burton and Robert C. McMath, Jr. (Westport, Conn.: Greenwood Press, 1982), 173–206.

47. McDonnell, "Money Knows No Master," 35, 31–32, 34; Olwell, "Loose, Idle and Disorderly," 103. See also Victoria E. Bynum, *Unruly Women: The Politics of Social and Sexual Control in the Old South* (Chapel Hill: University of North Carolina Press, 1992), 4; Campbell, "As 'A Kind of Freeman'?" 136; Hudson, "All That Cash," 81.

48. General Assembly, Session Records, 1854–1855, folder Petitions (2), NCDAH; Petitions, Legislative Papers, 1850, item 27, SCDAH; L. A. Chamerovzow, ed., *Slave Life in Georgia: A Narra-*

Slaveholders typically blamed not their own slaves but neighborhood poor whites for instigating the underground trade. A few slaves concurred, assigning direct responsibility for the illicit trade to their poor white trading partners. According to one former bondsman, "when these poor whites cannot obtain a living honestly, which they very seldom do, they get the slaves in their neighborhood to steal corn, poultry, and such like, from their masters, and bring these things to them."[49] Poor whites were always "encouraging slaves to steal from their owners, and sell to them, corn, wheat, sheep, chickens, or any thing of the kind which they can well conceal."[50]

State legislatures therefore passed a series of laws designed to quell the illicit trade, imposing a combination of fines and imprisonment for those convicted of trading with slaves illegally. An 1819 North Carolina law punished anyone who "shall deal, trade or traffic with any negro slave . . . for any cotton, tobacco, flax, corn, wheat, rice, rye, oats, barley, bacon, pork, spiritous liquors or beef" without written permission of the master. If convicted, the offender faced a maximum fine of $50 and a jail sentence of up to three months. An 1826 law replacing the one of 1819 enumerated more than two dozen additional articles forbidden to trade. The law continued to allow trade, however, if the slave had the master's written permission, but "in the day time only, Sundays excepted."[51] Despite the intent of such legislation, the ticket system permitted a few literate slaves and poor whites to circumvent the law by forging trading permits. A Virginia law of 1831 contained penalties slightly harsher than those in North Carolina. Anyone convicted of illegally trading with slaves received a fine from $10 to $50 and a prison sentence from one to sixth months.[52]

South Carolina's punishments for whites who traded with slaves easily outranked the North Carolina and Virginia law codes in severity. In 1817, the state legislature passed an act prohibiting anyone from trading with slaves for "any . . .

tive of the Life, Sufferings, and Escape of John Brown, a Fugitive Slave, Now in England (London: n.p., 1855), 54.

49. Chamerovzow, ed., Slave Life in Georgia, 53.

50. Gilbert Osofsky, ed., Puttin' on Ole Massa: The Slave Narratives of Henry Bibb, William Wells Brown, and Solomon Northup (New York: Harper & Row, 1969), 69. See also William Parker, "The Freedman's Story. In Two Parts. Part I," Atlantic Monthly 17 (February 1866): 158.

51. Laws of the State of North-Carolina, Enacted in the Year 1819, Transmitted According to Law, to One of the Justices of the Peace for the County of . . . (Raleigh: Thomas Henderson, Jr., 1820), 23–24; Acts Passed By the General Assembly of the State of North Carolina, At Its Session, Commencing on the 25th of December, 1826 (Raleigh: Lawrence & Lemay, 1827), 7.

52. Acts Passed at a General Assembly of the Commonwealth of Virginia (Richmond: Thomas Ritchie, 1831), 130.

article whatsoever," without the master's knowledge. Offenders were subject to a fine "not exceeding one thousand dollars, and imprisonment not exceeding a term of twelve months, nor less than one month." In reality, most penalties were far more mild, probably adjusted to an individual's ability to pay. Setting the fine at a ridiculous $1,000 — a sum very few southerners could have afforded — served primarily as a symbolic act, suggesting the seriousness with which law-makers viewed the underground trade. An 1834 South Carolina law went a step further, banning all trade with slaves, whether they possessed a permit from the master or not. In effect, a slave could trade legally with a white person only while in the master's presence.[53] Many South Carolina slaveholders considered this an undue inconvenience, however, dismissed the law, and continued to send trusted slaves on shopping errands.[54] Their disregard for a law intended to protect their own interests revealed masters' ambivalence toward legislative remedies. Slave-holders wanted to ban not all trade with their slaves, but rather only that of which they disapproved.

Despite tightening laws, the number of indictments for unlawful trading with slaves increased each decade from the 1820s to the outbreak of the Civil War. In many North Carolina counties and South Carolina districts, indictments mush-roomed from one every several years during the 1820s and 1830s to two, three, four, or more per annum in the late 1840s and 1850s. The growth of the southern population, both white and black, over this time period accounts for some natu-ral rise in the number of such cases from decade to decade. The stiffening laws designed to curtail the surreptitious trade also helps explain the increasing num-bers of whites who landed in court, charged with trading with slaves; however, no sudden spike in the number of illicit trading cases followed the passage of new legislation. The most dramatic increase came instead in the 1840s and 1850s. Those decades saw far more white defendants in the courtroom than had the 1820s or 1830s.

Why, then, did the clandestine trade reach such unprecedented levels in the 1840s and especially in the 1850s? A number of factors contribute to the trend. First, growing tensions with northern abolitionists sensitized slaveholders to po-tentially disloyal behaviors of whites in their own midst. They therefore took the

53. David J. McCord, *The Statutes at Large of South Carolina; Edited, Under Authority of the Legis-lature*, vol. 7 (Columbia: A. S. Johnston, 1840), 454 (both quotations); David J. McCord, *The Statutes at Large of South Carolina; Edited, Under Authority of the Legislature*, vol. 6 (Columbia: A. S. Johnston, 1839), 516.

54. *Richmond Enquirer*, August 17, 1849.

crime of trading with slaves more seriously than in the past and prosecuted violators more aggressively. Second, wealth in the Old South became concentrated in fewer and fewer hands by the end of the antebellum era. The poor white population swelled in the 1850s, and poor whites' increasing poverty likely made them more desperate for the goods that slaves had either produced or stolen.[55] Finally, the increase in unlawful trading in the 1840s and 1850s coincided with new restrictions masters imposed on slaves' independent market-related activities. As John Campbell and Joseph P. Reidy have argued, masters in upcountry South Carolina and Georgia cracked down on the slaves' economy during this period. By establishing credit accounts at reputable local stores and by disposing of slaves' crops on their behalf, slaveholders took steps to extricate bondspeople from the roles of buyer and seller in the antebellum marketplace. This effort to limit slaves' control over their own lives and to increase their dependency upon the master had the unintended and paradoxical effect of fueling an escalation of the underground slave–poor white economy.[56]

The laws that southern legislatures enacted to end the clandestine trade with slaves did not lead to easy convictions. In South Carolina, conviction rates for all whites brought up on charges of trading with slaves varied by district, from 20 to 48 percent, distressingly low for masters who believed themselves "unmercifully robbed." At best, not even half of the whites alleged to have traded with slaves were found guilty. Likewise in North Carolina, a sample of twelve superior courts and twenty-seven county courts reveals that, for the year 1839, thirty-seven prosecutions for trading with slaves yielded only nine convictions.[57] Surely not

55. Harris, *Plain Folk and Gentry*, 88–90; Lawrence T. McDonnell, "Work, Culture, and Society in the Slave South, 1790–1861," in *Black and White Cultural Interaction in the Antebellum South*, ed. Ted Ownby (Jackson: University Press of Mississippi, 1993), 126, 130–137; Ralph Mann, "Mountains, Land, and Kin Networks: Burkes Garden, Virginia, in the 1840s and 1850s," *Journal of Southern History* 58 (August 1992): 411–434; Randolph B. Campbell, "Planters and Plain Folk: Harrison County, Texas, as a Test Case, 1850–1860," *Journal of Southern History* 40 (August 1974): 369–398; Gavin Wright, "'Economic Democracy' and the Concentration of Agricultural Wealth in the Cotton South, 1850–1860," *Agricultural History* 44 (January 1970): 63–93; James C. Bonner, "Profile of a Late Ante-Bellum Community," *American Historical Review* 49 (July 1944): 667, 679.

56. Campbell, "As 'A Kind of Freeman'?" 143–147; Reidy, "Obligation and Right," 154; Frederick Law Olmsted, *A Journey in the Seaboard Slave States, with Remarks on Their Economy* (New York: Dix & Edwards, 1856), 442–443.

57. H. M. Henry, *The Police Control of the Slave in South Carolina* (1914; reprint, New York: Negro Universities Press, 1968), 86–87; Guion Griffis Johnson, *Ante-Bellum North Carolina: A Social History* (Chapel Hill: University of North Carolina Press, 1937), 670. The "unmercifully robbed" quote is from Roberts, "A Slave's Story," 617. Conviction rates for trading with slaves conform to a

every white person accused of trading with slaves actually was guilty, but many who were probably were did escape punishment due to the hassle, expense, and, ultimately, the perceived futility of pursuing the matter in court. "Three-fourths of the persons who are guilty, you can get no fine from," reported one newspaper, "and, if they have some property, all they have to do is to confess a judgment to a friend, go to jail, and swear out. . . . The State, or the party injured, has the cost of all these prosecutions and suits to pay, besides the trouble of attending Court."[58] Traveler Frederick Law Olmsted further suggested that nonslaveholding jurors, themselves beneficiaries of the unlawful trade, refused to convict whites accused of underground dealing.[59]

A lack of evidence marks a more important reason for the paucity of convictions. As the Union District, South Carolina, grand jury explained, "The grate [sic] difficulty in suppressing this crime consists in obtaining proof of its having been committed."[60] Southern courts did not permit slaves to testify against whites, so the very individual who participated in the illegal transaction could offer no assistance in securing a conviction against a white trader. "The negro, not being competent to give testimony in court," rendered it "exceedingly difficult to convict his white accomplice in crime," acknowledged one southern editor. Olmsted, too, recognized the legal dilemma of southern prosecutors. "The law which prevents the reception of the evidence of a negro in courts," he wrote, "here strikes back, with a most annoying force, upon the dominant power itself." Paradoxically, the inadmissibility of slave testimony, designed to ensure white hegemony over blacks, prevented slaveholders from enforcing class supremacy over the poor of their own race.[61]

In lieu of slave testimony, slaveholders devised other means to substantiate claims of the illicit trade between slaves and poor whites. For accusations of trading with slaves to hold up in court, slaveholders needed white witnesses. They therefore formulated various schemes to ferret out suspicious whites. Poor white Josiah

broad pattern of low conviction rates for crimes in the South. See Michael Stephen Hindus, *Prison and Plantation: Crime, Justice, and Authority in Massachusetts and South Carolina, 1767–1878* (Chapel Hill: University of North Carolina Press, 1980), 89–97.

58. Henry, *Police Control,* 88; *Charleston Standard,* November 23, 1854, in Olmsted, *Seaboard Slave States,* 441.

59. Lockley, *Lines in the Sand,* 80.

60. Henry, *Police Control,* 88; Union District, Grand Jury Presentments, Legislative Papers, 1831, item 25, SCDAH.

61. *Raleigh Register* (weekly), November 30, 1859; Olmsted, *Seaboard Slave States,* 441.

Lassiter of Richmond County, North Carolina, fell victim to one of these plots in 1847. Eli Watkins, the overseer for slaveowner William Covington, Jr., suspected Lassiter of trading with Covington's slaves. One December night, the overseer caught "the negro Jerry in the road" with "some corn in a basket . . . going in the direction of Lassiters." He whipped the slave, then instructed him to try and sell the corn to Lassiter. Watkins followed, secretly watching as Lassiter ushered the slave inside a crib, where "the negro put the corn in a tub." Hidden just a few yards away, peering through a crack in the wall, the overseer overheard Lassiter tell the slave Jerry that "there was about half [a] bushel of corn," so "he ought not to give him more than a pint of Liquor," since the alcohol "cost him so much." Lassiter "filled one bottle" and one "tickler" full of liquor. He apparently recognized the latter container from previous dealings, remarking, "[A]heh! you got that again." The transaction completed, Jerry delivered the alcohol to his master as Watkins had directed, and Lassiter was subsequently ordered to appear before the Richmond County court in 1848, charged with trading "one pint of whiskey" for "one peck of indian corn."[62]

In their efforts to squelch the clandestine trade, slaveholders frequently marked goods that they anticipated would be stolen. Olmsted reported that one planter executed a "strategem" to uncover the slave who had been stealing cotton from him, and, more important, "to discover for whom the thief worked." The planter prepared some cotton "by mixing hair with it, and put it in a tempting place. A negro was seen to take it, and was followed by scouts, to a grog-shop, several miles distant, where he sold it—its real value being nearly ten dollars—for ten cents, taking his pay in liquor." The adulterated cotton allowed the planter to prove the grog shop owner had received stolen goods, while white "scouts" were able to verify what transpired. Authorities arrested the white trader.[63] A similar ruse in York District, South Carolina, led to the apprehension in early 1848 of David Scates, a landless and illiterate poor white laborer. According to court records, slaveholder Edward Bird sent his slave "Dick with a piece of marked pork to a certain barrel in which Scates was supposed to receive such wares as negroes might deposit." Dick placed his master's pork in the barrel next to Scates's smokehouse around 10:00 p.m. one January night, with his master's white accomplices hiding a short distance away behind a tree. The next

62. Richmond County, Slave Records, 1778–1866, Criminal Action Papers Concerning Slaves 1848, folder 1840–1848, NCDAH; Sixth Census of the United States, 1840: Randolph County, North Carolina, 72, lists Lassiter as a nonslaveholder in his thirties, with no occupation.

63. Olmsted, *Seaboard Slave States*, 440.

morning, Scates went outside, peered into the barrel, "looked about and took the meat into his smoke house." Scates thus fell into the trap. Armed with a warrant, a magistrate found "the very piece of meat" in Scates's possession. A York District jury convicted Scates of buying "a certain shoulder of Pork" valued at "Ten Cents," from the slave Dick, and sentenced him to three months in jail and a $25 fine.[64] By luring suspected traders into their snares, slaveholders successfully framed some poor whites guilty of transacting business with slaves.[65]

A coincidental crossing of paths sometimes substituted for these types of overt trickery, as vigilant whites kept their eyes open for unlawful traders. This was more often true in urban rather than rural areas, but the greater concentration of people in even the smallest of hamlets increased the likelihood that a white witness would spy a particularly bold or careless interracial trade in progress. In the town of Wilmington, North Carolina, Dianah Bohnstedt repeatedly observed storekeeper Charles Hamburg (probably a German immigrant but not listed in the New Hanover County census) openly trading with the slaves of Parker Quince. On a Saturday night in the early 1850s, Bohnstedt was buying groceries when she saw Quince's slave Peter trade "one bushel and a peck of whole rice" for "some silver money," with which he purchased a three-cent glass of liquor and a few other articles before parting. Probably that same evening, Bohnstedt watched as Parker Quince's Ned left Hamburg's shop with a pistol, powder, and shot, apparently without paying anything. On another Saturday, she saw Ned collect "Ten Dollars"—nine in paper and one in silver—for "five bushels of whole & three bushels of half Rice" that she had seen delivered by "an old Negro man with a cart" earlier in the week. Dianah Bohnstedt seem-

---

64. *State v. Scates*, 3 Strobhart 106 (1848), *South Carolina Law Reports*, vol. 34; York District, Clerk of Court of General Sessions, General Sessions Papers, case 688(585), reel C2658, SCDAH; Seventh Census of the United States, 1850: York District, South Carolina, 284, lists a David Skates as a forty-six-year-old laborer, illiterate, with no real estate; Eighth Census of the United States, 1860: York District, South Carolina, 483, lists Skates as sixty years old, a "hired laborer," with no real estate and $75 personal estate. For other instances of the entrapment of whites who traded with slaves in South Carolina, see *State v. Sonnerkalb*, 2 Nott & McCord 280 (1820), *South Carolina Law Reports*, vol. 11; *State v. Fife*, 1 Bailey 1 (1828), *South Carolina Law Reports*, vol. 17; *State v. Berhman and Peters*, Riley 92 (1836), *South Carolina Law Reports*, vol. 22; *State v. Lefronty*, Riley 155 (1836), *South Carolina Law Reports*, vol. 22; *State v. Hardy*, Dudley 236 (1838), *South Carolina Law Reports*, vol. 23; *State v. Turner*, 2 McMullan 399 (1842), *South Carolina Law Reports*, vol. 27; *State v. Anderson*, 1 Strobhart 455 (1847), *South Carolina Law Reports*, vol. 32. See also *State v. Schroder*, 3 Hill 61 (1836), *South Carolina Law Reports*, vol. 21.

65. For other instances of entrapment, see McCurry, *Masters of Small Worlds*, 118, 119n47; Lichtenstein, "Disposition To Theft," 432.

ingly spent an inordinate amount of time shopping at Hamburg's store, and Hamburg certainly exhibited gross indiscretion in dealing so openly with slaves. As a result, Bohnstedt's testimony formed the backbone of the case against the shopkeeper.[66]

Whether through spying, entrapment, or sheer carelessness, slaveholding society unearthed and brought to justice only a minority of those whites who traded with slaves. Slaves and poor whites, however, questioned the purity of slaveholders' motives for seeking them out. While slaveholders often emphasized the ubiquitous thefts from their plantations and the dangers to slaves' physical health associated with liquor, slaves and poor whites themselves felt certain that masters contrived allegations of slave–poor white trading relationships to evict pesky poor whites from the neighborhood. With no poor whites in the area, slaveholders reasoned, no one would "corrupt" their chattel, and they could appropriate the poor whites' abandoned acreage for their own personal use. According to one ex-slave from Wake County, North Carolina, "Some of the slave owners, when a poor white man's land joined theirs and they wanted his place would have their Negroes steal things and carry them to the poor white man, and sell them to him. Then the slave owner, knowing where the stuff was, . . . would go and find his things at the poor white man's house." The ostensibly benevolent planter then pledged not to prosecute if the poor white would "sell out to him, and leave." "That's the way some of the slave owners got such large tracks [*sic*] of lands," the former slave explained.[67]

In 1838, slaveholder Charles Townsend may have hoped that a conviction for trading with slaves would force poor white sisters Mary and Elizabeth Cumbo from his Robeson County, North Carolina, neighborhood. A feud had been simmering between Townsend and the Cumbo sisters for some years. Mary and Elizabeth, in their late forties or fifties, shared a dwelling near Townsend's estate. They had complained in 1836 that Townsend's slave Ralph pilfered "a large Fat Hog" from their enclosure. The following year, Townsend alleged that the Cumbos had purchased stolen corn from Ralph on numerous occasions. Elizabeth, however, called Townsend's claims "false and Groundless," and maintained that the slaveholder "had continued to intrap" them "by sending his Negroes to deposit Corn at their house privately & without their knowledge for the purpose

66. New Hanover County, Records of Slaves and Free Persons of Color, 1786–1888, NCDAH.

67. Rawick, vol. 15, pt. 2, 319. See also Frederick Law Olmsted, *A Journey in the Back Country* (1860; reprint, New York: Burt Franklin, 1970), 75; and James Mellon, ed., *Bullwhip Days: The Slaves Remember* (New York: Weidenfeld & Nicolson, 1988), 208.

of laying a foundation for his warrant & claim." Townsend denied that he had any "agency in furnishing the Negroes with the corn or sending them for trade" with the Cumbos, but he undoubtedly did want to put an end to the illicit trade he suspected was going on. In 1838, Charles's relative William Townsend went in company with two others to monitor the sisters' dwelling. The three men secreted themselves near the house, when they saw Ralph "approach the front door with a Bag." Ralph "gave a whistle" to signal Elizabeth, who then "came out of the house & entered into a conversation" with the slave. William Townsend overheard Ralph "inquire '*if the cloth was ready*' '*That he must go into the house with his bag to the light*' '*for he did not know but there was some rotten ears*' '*for he had got it in a hurry.*'" Elizabeth and Ralph then went around the house and entered the dwelling by the back door. Townsend soon heard a "sound . . . like ears of corn poured out upon a naked floor." To gain a closer look, he attempted to make his way nearer the house, when Mary Cumbo, who had been outdoors, spotted him. She called out to her sister to "*mind what you are about somebody is watching.*" With the warning, "Elizabeth ordered the slave Ralph out of the house & to clear himself or she would knock him down with the axe." Ralph quickly departed, at which point the three men in hiding "examined" him and "found him with a Bag, empty with the exception of some grains of corn." William, however, denied that Charles Townsend had ordered him to the Cumbos to spy on them. "I know of no plot to entrap or ensnare the defendants," William stated. Whether part of a slaveholder's conscious scheme to oust a pair of irritating poor whites from the neighborhood or not, Townsend did successfully detect the Cumbo sisters in the process of exchanging cloth they had woven for the slave Ralph's stolen corn.[68]

When slaveholders successfully secured convictions against poor whites for trading with slaves, local citizens did not necessarily unite in support of the ruling. In a handful of cases, if a guilty party was unusually young or old, in bad health, or (prior to the conviction) a respectable member of society with no previous run-ins with the law, magnanimous neighborhood whites might petition for a pardon or a reduced sentence.[69] Poor whites, however, rarely benefited from

68. Robeson County, Records Concerning Slaves and Free Persons of Color, 1814–1839, folder 1838, NCDAH; Sixth Census of the United States, 1840: Robeson County, North Carolina, 215, lists both women as illiterate and in their fifties.

69. For petitions on behalf of whites convicted of trading with slaves, see Governor's Papers, Gov. John M. Morehead, G.P. 104, folder May 1843, NCDAH; Governor's Papers, Gov. John M. Morehead, G.P. 108, folder undated, NCDAH; Governor's Papers, Gov. William A. Graham, G.P. 119, folder December 1847, NCDAH; Governor's Papers, Gov. Thomas Bragg, G.P. 144, folder April 1858, NCDAH.

neighborhood benevolence; instead, they became the subjects of controversy. In one instructive case, more than one hundred petitioners from Mecklenburg County, North Carolina, begged clemency on behalf of Samuel McCracken, a laboring Irish immigrant convicted on three counts of "unlawful trading with negroes." According to the memorial, McCracken "is a man extremely poor, in bad health, [and] has a wife and family to maintain." The signers, including many of the most prominent professional men of Charlotte, protested that there existed "no positive proof of any sale," suggesting the shakiness of the evidence upon which McCracken had been convicted.[70] Mecklenburg County solicitor S. Nye Hutchison, however, wrote the governor, describing McCracken as "wholly unworthy [of] executive clemency. His house is [a] most perfect nuisance. Without license he retails liquor. In addition his house is the general rende[z]vous for negroes." It took "a long period of fruitless effort" before authorities successfully "detected & convicted" the man, so the solicitor wanted to uphold the convictions. Moreover, he added, "His wife is more degraded than himself and therefore no family consideration should move you." Wealthy Charlotte merchant H. B. Williams mailed his own letter to the governor, explaining that McCracken "is a miserable drun[k]en fellow [who] has done nothing for the last 18 months but drink and sell whisky to slaves at night [and on] Sunday and at all times keeps the most disprate [*sic*] house in the county." As Williams saw it, "his family are better without his services and if he could be kept in prison . . . it would be a great relief to the community. . . . I hope he will remain in Gaol."[71]

Many white observers perceived that the laws against trading with slaves provided an insufficient deterrent to the crime. An editorial from "SEVERAL SUFFERERS" of Beaufort District, South Carolina, maintained that "the laws, as they now stand, are indeed *impotent* to suppress the traffic. Truly they may be said to encourage it, the punishment being so trifling in proportion to the magnitude of

70. Governor's Papers, Gov. Charles Manly, G.P. 123, folder May–August 1849, NCDAH; Seventh Census of the United States, 1850: Mecklenburg County, North Carolina, 96–97, lists Samuel McCracken as an Irish-born "labourer," fifty-three years old. His wife also hailed from Ireland, but their oldest daughter was born in New York, suggesting that they had lived there before moving to the South. Most of the signers appear on pages 93–101 of the census.

71. S. Nye Hutchison to Manly, August 23, 1849; H. B. Williams to Manly, August 18, 1849; both in Governor's Papers, Gov. Charles Manly, G.P. 123, folder May–August 1849, NCDAH. What happened to McCracken is not clear. In another unusual case, almost one hundred citizens of Lincoln and Mecklenburg counties signed a petition for the release from jail of Peter Cansler, a white man who chronically traded with slaves, because Cansler promised to leave the state if freed. See Governor's Papers, Gov. William A. Graham, G.P. 111, folder September 1845, NCDAH.

the offence, and the large profits which tempt to its commission." The Beaufort District correspondents claimed that, when whites who received the maximum punishment under the law for trading with slaves were released from jail, they defiantly resumed their illicit traffic, "more openly than before conviction."[72]

Such blatant defiance of the law led many slaveholders to demand stricter measures against trading with slaves. A South Carolina act of 1817 required that anyone who traded with slaves must keep the permit, for the burden of proof fell on the white person involved to show that a given transaction adhered to the law. The state's revised act of 1834 contained a presumptive proof clause that dispensed with the need for direct proof of illicit trading. The North Carolina legislature had passed a similar law eight years before, in 1826. By these statutes, to convict someone of trading unlawfully with a slave, one need only show that the slave entered the "shop, store, or house used for trading" with an article and left without it, or departed with an article they did not take in.[73] In either case, the law presumed the white inside to have traded with the slave. These acts, in effect, held a white person guilty until proven innocent. No one actually saw Darlington District, South Carolina, shopkeeper William D. Rollins trade with a slave, but according to court records, "The proof was, that the slave went into [the] defendant's shop with five pounds of bacon and an empty bottle, and came out without the bacon and with a bottle of whiskey."[74] Similarly, the South Carolina Court of Appeals upheld the conviction of York District's David Scates because "circumstantial evidence is legally competent, . . . especially in cases of illicit trading and retailing of spirits, in which ingenious devices are so common."[75]

Feeling besieged by illicit traders, some South Carolinians wanted the law to go a step further. In 1860, fifty-two petitioners from Orangeburg District complained that current state laws rendered it "almost impossible" to secure a conviction for "negro trading." They wanted to amend the 1834 law so that "if a negro is seen to go into a shop, remain long enough to trade & comes out with an article kept for sale in such shops it will be prima facie evidence of trading &

72. *Charleston Daily Courier*, November 4, 1857.

73. McCord, *Statutes at Large of South Carolina*, vol. 7, 454, 469; *Acts Passed By the General Assembly of the State of North Carolina, At Its Session, Commencing on the 25th of December, 1826*, 7–8.

74. *State v. Rollins*, 12 Richardson 297 (1859), *South Carolina Law Reports*, vol. 46; Seventh Census of the United States, 1850: Darlington District, South Carolina, 326, lists Rollins as thirty-one years old, with no occupation and no real estate.

75. *State v. Scates*, 3 Strobhart 106 (1848), *South Carolina Law Reports*, vol. 34, 107 (first quotation), 106 (second quotation).

the trader must prove his innocence or be held guilty of negro trading."[76] To crack down on the ever-increasing clandestine trade, many South Carolinians felt no reservations about sacrificing the civil liberties of the state's white population. One contributor to the *Charleston Mercury* suggested the even more radical step of allowing slaves to testify in court against their white trading partners, provided the master attested to the truth of the slave's remarks.[77]

A few South Carolina whites recommended that white men convicted of trading with slaves suffer complete disfranchisement. This idea reached a crescendo in the early 1850s. A Charleston District grand jury reasoned that "white men so degraded" as to sell liquor to slaves deserved nothing less than "a forfeiture forever, of the right of suffrage." The Darlington District grand jury concurred that men who traded with slaves sacrificed their privilege to vote. This proposed penalty did not affect white women, since they were already denied the ballot. Nevertheless, it marked a significant change in thinking, turning away from the usual retributive punishments of fines and imprisonment to strike at one of the very markers of white men's freedom: the franchise. The state legislature's Committee on Colored Population looked with favor upon the suggestion, although the proposal never garnered enough support to make it into law. In 1857, the "SEVERAL SUFFERERS" of Beaufort District were still recommending disfranchisement as a possible solution to the epidemic of trading with slaves.[78]

More vocal, probably more numerous, and ultimately more successful, were those who advocated that whites convicted of trading with slaves suffer the punishment of whipping. Like disfranchisement, whipping was fraught with symbolic significance. A punishment normally reserved exclusively for slaves, whipping humiliated the victim. For at least a brief moment, flogging degraded the white man, reducing him to the level of slaves and temporarily suspending his membership in white society. During the 1850s, as tensions over slavery heightened and the South rallied to defend its peculiar institution, many whites in both North and South Carolina concluded that trading with slaves warranted such a severe punishment. After some of his family's slaves received a flogging for attempting to sell a stolen hog to a neighborhood poor white man, North Carolina's William D. Valentine reflected in his diary that it was actually "some white

76. Petitions, Legislative Papers, 1860, item 24, SCDAH.

77. Henry, *Police Control*, 88.

78. Charleston District, Grand Jury Presentments, Legislative Papers, 1851, item 20, SCDAH; Darlington District, Grand Jury Presentments, Legislative Papers, 1852, item 9, SCDAH; Committee Reports, Legislative Papers, 1852, item 36, SCDAH; *Charleston Daily Courier*, November 4, 1857.

people" who "deserve all the whipping these poor slaves received last evening."[79] Acting on similar sentiments, James Graham petitioned the North Carolina state legislature. He asked that body to consider passing a law that would punish those convicted of trading with slaves with "one or more whippings on the bare back at the whipping post. . . . Those persons who live by corrupting and hiring negroes to steal for their benefit, deserve and ought to receive the most severe and exemplary punishment."[80]

The South Carolina legislature received many more such requests. As early as 1831, the grand jury of Spartanburg District recommended "that whipping should be superadded to the punishment of those convicted of trading with slaves."[81] In 1850, forty-one petitioners from Barnwell District requested the passage of a law "imposing corporal punishment for the second conviction for trafficking with slaves."[82] Even the governor chimed in that unlawful trading marked "perhaps one of the very few offenses deserving of corporal punishment."[83] The state legislature referred the matter to the Judiciary Committee, which ruled the proposal "inexpedient." The Committee on Colored Population explained "that the infliction of corporal punishment in a slave holding community and in the presence of slaves is calculated to create improper feelings & notions on that class of our population—to degrade the white man to a level with the negro would be bad policy in our state."[84] But petitions and grand jury presentments continued to pour in, reaching a peak in 1857. With whites from Chesterfield, Darlington, Kershaw, Spartanburg, Union, and Williamsburg districts all clamoring for action, the South Carolina legislature passed a law in December 1857, stating that anyone convicted of trading with slaves a second time "shall, for such second, or other subsequent offence, in addition to the penalties now prescribed by law, be whipped not exceeding thirty-nine lashes." This act excluded white women, and may never have been invoked in the punishment of white men. It instead served primarily as a deterrent, and demonstrated the gravity with which South Carolina whites viewed the unlawful traffic with slaves. Although also plagued with the problem of illicit trade, North Carolina was never as radically wedded to the

79. Valentine Diary, January 1, 1851, SHC. See also Genovese, *Roll, Jordan, Roll,* 601.

80. General Assembly Session Records, 1850–1851, folder Petitions (5), NCDAH.

81. Committee Reports, Legislative Papers, 1831, item 51, SCDAH. The Judiciary Committee found the idea "inexpedient," December 5, 1831. See also Spartanburg District, Grand Jury Presentments, Legislative Papers, 1831, item 35, SCDAH.

82. Petitions, Legislative Papers, 1850, item 27, SCDAH.

83. Quoted in Henry, *Police Control,* 90.

84. Committee Reports, Legislative Papers, 1850, item 39, 48, SCDAH.

institution of slavery as its southern neighbor, and eschewed the whipping of whites for the offense.[85]

In this case, the South Carolina legislature acquiesced to public opinion, but in general lawmakers dismissed pleas to enact new statutes strengthening the penalties against whites convicted of trading with slaves. They repeatedly insisted that current laws "afford[ed] ample & stringent remedies" and were "adequate to prevent the evil complained of."[86] The legislature was convinced that "further legislation would only accumulate threats of punishment, which the public by their indifference and inaction, would render as impotent as those which had been made before." Politicians thus blamed citizens' own inertia for allowing the clandestine trade to continue unchecked. Legislators held it the people's responsibility to report suspected violations to the authorities, and they believed South Carolina's citizens negligent in their duty. If people just "shut their eyes" to the unlawful trade, reported one committee, laws cannot substitute for "what is deficient in the public spirit of the citizen." Rather than passing additional legislation, lawmakers endorsed community vigilance and activism.[87]

In its mildest form, community activism meant the expulsion of white men and women from local churches. Congregations took suspicions of trading with slaves seriously. Members of New Providence Baptist Church "withdrew our fellowship from Bro. Richard Jordan for trading with negroes."[88] Likewise, Barnwell Baptist Church "excommunicated" Nancy Barden "for her unchristian conduct in retailing spiritous liquors and trading with negroes."[89] A committee in Anti-

---

85. Chesterfield District, Grand Jury Presentments, Legislative Papers, 1855, item 7, SCDAH; Kershaw District, Grand Jury Presentments, Legislative Papers, 1857, item 10, SCDAH; Henry, *Police Control*, 90; *Acts of the General Assembly of the State of South Carolina, Passed in December, 1850* (Columbia: I. C. Morgan, 1850), 615. An earlier act of 1829 stated that any person who bought or received stolen goods, "knowing the same to have been stolen," was guilty of a misdemeanor and "shall be punished by imprisonment and whipping." See McCord, *Statutes at Large of South Carolina*, vol. 6, 393.

86. Committee Reports, Legislative Papers, n.d., item 1218, SCDAH (first quotation); Committee Reports, Legislative Papers, 1860, item 31, SCDAH (second quotation).

87. Committee Reports, Legislative Papers, 1856, item 25, SCDAH.

88. Minutes of New Providence Baptist Church [1808–1922], May 25, 1833, SCDAH; Fifth Census of the United States, 1830: Darlington District, South Carolina, 218, lists a Richard Jordon, Sr., as a nonslaveholder.

89. Minutes of Barnwell Baptist Church [1812–1912], December 5, 1840, 129, SCDAH; Sixth Census of the United States, 1840: Edgefield District, South Carolina, 110, lists five Barden households consecutively. Of the twenty-two total individuals in these households, only one was a slave.

och Baptist Church charged a Brother Howle with immoral conduct because he "had procured a supply of spirit[s] and had disposed of it in too short a time to have used it temperately in his family and some circumstances occurred which gave suspicion that he had disposed of it clandestinely." Howle refused to confess to any sale, denied any wrongdoing, and was eventually "excluded by a majority of two votes."[90]

Community censure of poor whites and others must have acted as a potent deterrent against trading with slaves. Virtually no whites wished to be ostracized by their neighbors. So powerful was the desire to maintain one's reputation in the community that some whites accused of unlawful trading took their detractors to court. Poor white overseer John T. Moss of Virginia levied an allegation of slander against his employer, slaveholder Edward H. Moseley. Moss overheard Moseley accuse him of selling the master's bacon to local slaves, who then carried it to nearby coal pits to sell. "I consider him a damned scoundrel," Moseley said of his overseer. "I could not trust him, [and] I consider his wife the worst, the damndest of the two." Such words personally insulted Moss and his spouse, opened him to "public scandal and disgrace," and jeopardized "the good opinion and credit of all his neighbours." Moreover, the aspersions were magnified in their effect by the nature of Moss's profession. They not only had the potential to injure his reputation, but also to extinguish effectively his means of making a livelihood, for Moseley's defamatory language implied that Moss "was dishonest and untrustworthy in his calling and occupation as an overseer."[91] In the Old South's culture of honor, southern whites proved so sensitive to attacks on their character that even slaves found themselves on the defensive, suggesting that their word carried at least some influence locally. Although legally their testimony was inadmissible against a white defendant, slaves could still fuel a community's doubts and contribute to the erosion of a white person's standing. Thus, in Union District, South Carolina, an injudicious remark landed slave Henry in court, accused of "saying that William Lawson and Spencer Lawson assisted in stealing cotton and received stolen cotton."[92]

90. Minutes of Antioch Baptist Church, [1830–1895], 1842, SCDAH.

91. *Moseley v. Moss*, 6 Grattan 534 (1850), 47 Va. 534 (quotations 534, 536–537). The Powhatan circuit court found a verdict in favor of Moss, and awarded him $400.

92. Union District, Court of General Sessions, Indictments, item 1927, SCDAH; Sixth Census of the United States, 1840: Union District, South Carolina, 198, lists two William Lawsons, as well as a man named Scum Lawson. In December 1842, the case went before the Magistrates and Freeholders Court, which acquitted Henry of the charge of "slandering white men." See also *State v. Jim and Dick* (1849), Anderson District, Court of Magistrates and Freeholders, Trial Papers, microfilm reel 2918, case #215, SCDAH.

If the community at large pressured poor whites to curb their unlawful trade with slaves, so did the proactive steps of individual slaveholders. The "SEVERAL SUFFERERS" from Beaufort District asserted that "inefficient" laws necessitated that the master "depend on his own private means, and not on the law, to suppress the traffic."[93] As one planter explained to Frederick Law Olmsted, the law "is entirely inadequate to protect us against these rascals; it rather protects them than us. They easily evade detection in breaking it; and we can never get them punished, except we go beyond or against the law ourselves."[94] Runaway slave Charles Ball recalled one instance in the first decade of the nineteenth century when a South Carolina overseer administered his own extralegal remedy. When two bags of cotton turned up missing from the plantation, the overseer immediately suspected that slaves had stolen the cotton "and sold [it] to a poor white man, who resided at the distance of three miles back in the pine woods." Ball looked with pity upon the man and his wife: "The lowest poverty had, through life, been the companion of these poor people, of which their clayey complexions, haggard figures, and tattered garments, gave the strongest proof." Their very "state of destitution," Ball believed, "afforded very convincing evidence that they were not in possession of the proceeds of the stolen goods of any person." But the overseer knew "that black people often called at his house." As Ball himself confessed, "I had often been at the cabin of this man, in my trapping expeditions." To the overseer, these facts offered "conclusive evidence" that the poor white man conducted a "criminal intercourse" with slaves, and had been "a receiver of their stolen goods, for many years."[95] Determined to locate the pilfered bags of cotton, the overseer commanded Ball to search both inside and outside the humble cabin, as the alarmed poor white family fled their dwelling. Upon finding nothing, the enraged overseer set their home ablaze. Later, Ball's master bragged that "he had routed one receiver of stolen goods out of the country, and that all others of his character ought to be dealt with in the same manner."[96]

At times, frustrated planters joined forces to oust irksome poor whites from the community. Slaveholders and other "respectable" members of society often conferred with one another to devise wonderfully creative techniques to cleanse their neighborhoods of undesirable poor whites. In the mid-1820s, neighbors in Charleston District cooperated in an effort to evict the poor white shopkeeper

93. *Charleston Daily Courier,* November 4, 1857.

94. Frederick Law Olmsted, *The Cotton Kingdom: A Traveller's Observations on Cotton and Slavery in the American Slave States,* ed. Arthur M. Schlesinger (New York: Alfred A. Knopf, 1953), 258.

95. Ball, *Fifty Years in Chains,* 307–308.

96. Ibid., 312.

Andrew S. Rhodes from his "small house . . . near Monk's Corner." Rhodes had apparently rented the dwelling, an insubstantial shack "of no great value," for eighteen months, when his neighbors decided "to get rid of him, believing that he was dealing with their negroes and was a troublesome neighbor." Rhodes "was regarded as a nuisance in the parish, and a great vagabond, with whom no white man associated, and who cultivated no land, and owned no other property, than . . . which were only fit for negro trading." According to court records, Rhodes "had been an inmate of the Charleston gaol for seven or eight years, the greater part of the time for perjury." Authorities in Charleston had also imprisoned him briefly for uttering incendiary comments during the Denmark Vesey unrest of 1822. Fearing the poor white's corrupting influence on their slaves, neighbors, including the owner of the house, entered the shack during Rhodes's absence. They "seized upon such articles as were in the house, which were very few and of little value, being such as were suitable only for the lowest retail grog shop, worth about $5 or $10," meticulously removed Rhodes's meager belongings, and, at the invitation of the owner, systematically dismantled the humble dwelling. Upon his return, the stunned Rhodes sued his neighbors for trespassing. The defendants vindicated themselves, saying, "The object in pulling down the house was to prevent . . . Rhodes, [from] getting possession again, and to expel him thereby from the neighborhood; as he was trading illicitly with the negroes." Clearly siding with the vigilantes, the sympathetic judge awarded Rhodes one paltry cent in compensation.[97]

Slaveholders sometimes threatened those whites suspected of trading with slaves and physically punished them. Planters in Onslow County, North Carolina, "closely banded together" for protection, paying spies to ferret out their "midnight enemies." When they identified a suspicious grog shop keeper, they tried to persuade him to abandon his establishment and relocate elsewhere. Several planters would pay a visit to the proprietor, offer "cash for his acres and storeroom," and insinuate that if he did not accept the offer within forty-eight hours, he would face "a coat of tar with a full ruffling of feathers."[98] One white man in South Carolina did suffer such a punishment for allegedly receiving "stolen goods from negroes" in 1838. According to a tantalizing fragment of a letter, "a lot of fellows . . . strip[p]ed him to the pantaloons," coated him with the contents of a "barrel of Tar," and "daubed him" with cotton. The mob then "drove him through the most publick [streets?] applying the cowskin to the cotton every few

97. *Rhodes v. Bunch*, 3 McCord 66 (1825), *South Carolina Law Reports*, vol. 14; Genovese, *Roll, Jordan, Roll*, 796n25.
98. Avirett, *Old Plantation*, 118, 119.

minutes." A witness to the event considered the episode "the most disgraceful thing I ever saw don[e to a] white man; death to me before that." The mob undoubtedly hoped other whites shared this witness's sense of shame and would be dissuaded from participating in the unlawful traffic.[99]

Some frustrated slaveholders throughout South Carolina formed official vigilance associations with the express intent of curbing the illicit trade. Vigilance associations began as early as the mid-1840s, reaching their peak in 1859, probably by no coincidence the same year the fanatical northern abolitionist John Brown raided Harpers Ferry.[100] Observing "a visible change . . . in the last few years in the conduct of our Slaves," James Henry Hammond and other planters in Barnwell and Edgefield districts founded the Savannah River Anti–Slave Traffick Association in 1846, "for the purpose of preserving proper subordination among our slaves, and putting down unlawful traffick with them." By the 1850s, committees also sprang up in Abbeville, Darlington, Kershaw, Lancaster, Orangeburg, Sumter, and other rural South Carolina districts.[101] The Abbeville vigilance committee organized in 1859 "for the purpose of taking measures to prevent illicit traffic between mean white men and the slaves," the association hoping "to rid the neighborhood of these pests." Elsewhere, citizens in Cartersville confidently asserted that "these rascals can be conquered," and resolved to "boycott any attorney who would undertake to prosecute their society."[102] When one Darlington District shopkeeper ignored warnings in 1857 to cease trading with slaves, a mob of seventy-five burned down his store and exchanged gunfire with him, killing the man.[103]

Many slaveholders had long suspected a link between illicit trade and slave unrest. More than two hundred petitioners from Mecklenburg, Iredell, and Cabarrus counties in North Carolina attributed the "crime and insubordination" of their slaves "to the cupidity of evil-disposed persons located in our midst, who carry on an unlawful traffic with slaves." The Charleston District grand jury explained that selling liquor to slaves "is subversive of public safety by bringing the

99. William M. Leary to Daniel O. Leary, August 26, 1838, Henry Calvin Conner Papers, SCL. See also McDonnell, "Money Knows No Master," 43.

100. Henry, *Police Control*, 88.

101. *Preamble and Regulations of the Savannah River Anti–Slave Traffick Association*, n.p., SCL; Henry, *Police Control*, 159–160; McDonnell, "Money Knows No Master," 36; McCurry, *Masters of Small Worlds*, 117–118. See also Drew Gilpin Faust, *James Henry Hammond and the Old South: A Design for Mastery* (Baton Rouge: Louisiana State University Press, 1982), 98.

102. Quoted in Henry, *Police Control*, 89.

103. McDonnell, "Money Knows No Master," 36.

negro slave in such familiar contact with the white man, as to excite his contempt, or invite the assertion of equality, or draw from him exhibitions of presumption and insubordination." When slaves and poor whites colluded in criminal intercourse, they dissolved the racial barriers that ordered southern society. The bondspeople tied to the illicit trade thus became increasingly "refractory and ungovernable." If the clandestine traffic persisted unchecked, many southern whites feared, they would sacrifice all feelings of security, for it seemed only a short step from participation in the underground trade to participation in outright rebellion.[104]

Many southern whites complained that the illicit traffic not only bred slave discontent but also struck at the very institution of slavery. In North Carolina, one petitioner informed the state legislature of the "numerous class of the worst sort of Abolitionists dwelling in our midst . . . who clandestinely trade with slaves and receive stolen goods in payment for ardent spirits and other articles, thereby corrupting and destroying the value of servants. Many of these malefactors are insolvent persons."[105] As the "SEVERAL SUFFERERS" from Beaufort District saw it, "These are practical abolitionists, who are really destroying the value of our slave property."[106] Countless planters agreed with one South Carolina master who recorded that the "mean democratic white men" who kept slaves stocked in liquor "are no better than abolitionists,"[107] and the Savannah River Anti–Slave Traffick Association declared the dealer in stolen goods even "more potent than the abolitionist," encouraging "insurrection, burning and murder."[108] The "swarm" of whites who traded with slaves marked "an internal enemy" who sold liquor to "debase the slave, and in this manner our very slave system is being . . . weakened." The clandestine traffic "strikes at the vitals of our domestic Institutions" through "base and nefarious means,"[109] and "aim[s] an insidious but most effectual blow at the system itself."[110]

104. General Assembly, Session Records, November 1860 to February 1861, folder Petitions, NCDAH (first and second quotations); Charleston District, Grand Jury Presentments, Legislative Papers, 1851, item 20, SCDAH (third quotation); *Richmond Enquirer,* September 14, 1852 (fourth quotation).

105. General Assembly Session Records, 1850–1851, folder Petitions (5), NCDAH.

106. *Charleston Daily Courier,* November 4, 1857.

107. Quoted in Genovese, *Roll, Jordan, Roll,* 642.

108. *Preamble and Regulations of the Savannah River Anti–Slave Traffic Association,* 5, 6.

109. Petitions, Legislative Papers, 1850, item 27, SCDAH.

110. Charleston District, Grand Jury Presentments, Legislative Papers, 1851, item 20, SCDAH. Much the same could be said of clandestine activity in antebellum southern cities. "[B]y deteriorating our negros morally and physically," asserted Charleston mayor William Porcher Miles, "the base,

In the slave–poor white economy, slaveholders detected a grievous threat to southern society. As Alex Lichtenstein has argued, the interracial trade called into question masters' hegemony over race and class relations in the Old South.[111] When bondspeople systematically pilfered from gardens, smokehouses, and corn cribs, then ventured off the plantation to trade in underground markets, they defied plantation discipline and exhibited an independence inconsistent with their enslaved status. Likewise, poor whites who exchanged commodities with slaves contested their subordination as lower-class members of white society. Through their clandestine traffic, both slaves and poor whites challenged planter pretensions of domination. As active participants in the slave–poor white economy, they disregarded elite constrictions on their behavior in order to improve their material standards of living. Moreover, these economic interactions bred what slaveholders considered a disconcerting intimacy between black and white. The clandestine trade had the potential to awaken shared sympathies between slaves and poor whites and to forge among them a common identity as an impoverished, inferior, and biracial southern lower class. Such a reorientation along class lines could menace the existing social fabric.[112] In those scant few cases in which poor whites supplied guns to slaves—no insignificant purchase but one likely for slaves' own personal use in hunting—southern planters could not help but see the revolutionary implications of the interracial trade. Abolitionists' mounting attacks upon the institution of slavery in the late 1840s and 1850s only magnified planter fears. No wonder, then, that anxious slaveholders complained incessantly of the unlawful traffic, agitated for harsher penalties, and even took the law into their own hands to suppress it. Given the growing social and psychological tensions of the late antebellum period, slaveholders' reactions represented perfectly legitimate responses to a perceived threat upon their way of life.

Upon closer inspection, however, the slave–poor white economy does not appear as disruptive or subversive as southern planters feared. A detailed examination of the underground trade between slaves and poor whites shows that racial boundaries were maintained and even reinforced within the slave–poor white economy itself. Although slave–poor white economic exchanges probably did occasionally blossom into genuine friendship or produce feelings of cama-

---

demoralizing and illicit traffic with slaves . . . is doing more daily to undermine the institution . . . than all the insane rant of the Garrisons, Parkers, and other fanatical abolitionists of the North." See *Charleston Daily Courier*, December 27, 1856. See also the mayor's remarks in the *Charleston Daily Courier*, May 24, 1856.

111. Lichtenstein, "Disposition To Theft," 415–417, 426–427.

112. Hundley, *Social Relations*, 230.

raderie on both sides, the overwhelming majority of these contacts remained strictly business relationships—mutually beneficial exchanges of goods or cash. As one runaway recalled, "There were, in our vicinity, plenty of *poor white folks,* as we contemptuously called them, whom we cordially despised, but with whom we carried on a regular traffic at our master's expense." Another one-time fugitive added that "many persons will sell a slave any article that he can get the money to buy. Not that they sympathize with the slave, but merely because his testimony is not admitted in court against a free white person."[113] The unlawful trade between slaves and poor whites undoubtedly did erode racial barriers somewhat, but the mutual benefits to marginalized southerners, both black and white, muted its threat to the broader social structure. Through their exchanges in the underground economy, poor whites maintained a precarious superiority over slaves, frustrated and annoyed their own social betters, and found an avenue to secure cheap food and consumer goods. Though unequal partners in trade, slaves successfully used the underground economy to resist the terms and conditions of their enslavement and to improve the material standards of their day-to-day lives. Slaves and poor whites, in short, each engaged in the underground trade for their own rational motives. Poor whites' illicit commerce with slaves should not be construed as a sign either of solidarity with bondspeople or of animosity toward planters. On the contrary, the clandestine trade effectively channeled lower-class discontent within the established social framework, and never seriously threatened to undermine the southern social order. But amid the growing abolitionist challenges and the increasingly tension-filled political atmosphere of the late 1840s and 1850s, planters viewed the underground slave–poor white economy as one more part of a nefarious conspiracy against them.

113. Roberts, "A Slave's Story," 617; William L. Andrews and Henry Louis Gates, Jr., eds., *The Civitas Anthology of African American Slave Narratives* (Washington, D.C.: Civitas/Counterpoint, 1999), 421.

CHAPTER 3

POOR WHITE ROLES IN SLAVE
CONTROL AND SLAVE RESISTANCE

Proslavery intellectual George Fitzhugh wrote during the antebellum years that poor whites "constitute our militia and our police. They protect . . . and . . . secure men in possession of a kind of property which they could not hold a day but for the supervision and protection of the poor."[1] To preserve slavery as an institution, masters needed to maintain control of their slave property. As overseers and patrollers, spies and slave hunters, poor white men performed vital roles for slaveowners, and, by extension, the slave system. Through these functions, they kept slaves in their oppressed condition, as they reassured slaveholders of their own allegiance to the Old South's racial hierarchy. Simultaneously, however, poor whites also possessed the means to subvert the slave system. By assisting slave runaways and rebels, they, whether consciously or not, undermined the very social structure that slaveholders expected them to defend. Poor whites thus played a contradictory role in regulating the slaves of the Old South, both sustaining and challenging planter authority and the southern social order.

Scholars have debated for decades the nature of the relationship between slaveholders and nonslaveholders in the antebellum South. When poor whites cooperated with slaveowners by serving as overseers, patrollers, or slave catchers, they gave credence to the argument of such historians as Frank Owsley and Clement Eaton that southern whites exhibited little class consciousness. Several other scholars, however, have found that nonslaveholding whites were acutely aware of class differences and often resented slaveholders.[2] Poor whites who aided

1. Quoted in Rudolph M. Lapp, "The Ante Bellum Poor Whites of the South Atlantic States" (Ph.D. diss., University of California–Berkeley, 1956), 124.

2. Frank L. Owsley, *Plain Folk of the Old South* (1949; reprint, Baton Rouge: Louisiana State University Press, 1982), 133; Clement Eaton, "Class Differences in the Old South," *Virginia Quarterly Review* 33 (Summer 1957): 357–370; Fred Bailey, "Tennessee's Antebellum Society from the Bottom Up," *Southern Studies* 22 (Fall 1983): 262; Fred Arthur Bailey, *Class and Tennessee's Confederate Generation* (Chapel Hill: University of North Carolina Press, 1987), ch. 5; Wayne K. Durrill, *War of Another Kind: A Southern Community in the Great Rebellion* (New York: Oxford University Press, 1990); David Williams, *Rich Man's War: Class, Caste, and Confederate Defeat in the Lower Chattahoochee Valley* (Athens: University of Georgia Press, 1998); William W. Freehling, *The South vs. the South: How Anti-*

slave runaways and rebels implicitly affirmed the presence of class tension. Taken together, the multifarious and conflicting roles that poor whites played in slave control and slave resistance illustrate the ambiguous position of poor whites vis-à-vis the slave regime.[3]

Somewhere between one-fourth and one-third of the South's rural slaves toiled under the watchful eyes of white overseers. Overseeing was a booming profession in the 1850s. Census returns from 1850 reported nearly 1,000 overseers statewide in North Carolina, and more than 1,800 in South Carolina. Ten years later close to 1,800 and more than 2,700 were listed with that occupation in North and South Carolina, respectively—increases of 80 and 50 percent.[4] The larger the size of the landholding, the greater the likelihood of a resident overseer. Although most overseers came from a yeoman background, historians have identified three broad categories of overseer: planters' sons learning the art of plantation management; the largest group, a professional or semiprofessional class who planned to oversee either as a career or just until they could earn enough to become independent farmers; and a smaller floating class of amateur young men whose incompetence tarnished the reputation of the entire profession. Poor whites comprised many of those in the third category. One Civil War veteran from Stokes County, North Carolina, commented that "menny poor young men overseered for slave holders." Slaves, too, confirmed that poor whites often served as overseers, to do the master's "dirty work." Low-country rice planter Robert F. W. Allston, for one, typically relied on "overseers from the poorer class who had settled in the pinelands of Georgetown District." For white men unable to afford to buy a small plot of land of their own or to find other employment, overseeing provided an avenue of escape, giving them some means to earn a wage. Most of them lacked special skills as overseers, but they asked for less remuneration than the professionals and could therefore secure em-

Confederate Southerners Shaped the Course of the Civil War (New York: Oxford University Press, 2001); David Williams, Teresa Crisp Williams, and R. David Carlson, *Plain Folk in a Rich Man's War: Class and Dissent in Confederate Georgia* (Gainesville: University Press of Florida, 2002).

3. One article that briefly touches on this theme is Philip D. Morgan and George D. Terry, "Slavery in Microcosm: A Conspiracy Scare in Colonial South Carolina," *Southern Studies* 21 (Summer 1982): 121–145. See also Robert Olwell, *Masters, Slaves, & Subjects: The Culture of Power in the South Carolina Low Country, 1740–1790* (Ithaca: Cornell University Press, 1998), 45.

4. J. D. B. DeBow, *The Seventh Census of the United States: 1850* (Washington: Robert Armstrong, 1853), 318, 344; and Joseph C. G. Kennedy, *Population of the United States in 1860; Compiled from the Original Returns of the Eighth Census, Under the Direction of the Secretary of the Interior* (Washington: Government Printing Office, 1864), 363, 454.

ployment, at least temporarily. Regardless of their economic standing, overseers rarely stayed at any one plantation for more than two or three years at most.[5]

Overseers occupied an ambiguous position on the plantation. Slaveowners demanded much of them. They tried to recruit overseers with experience and competence in whatever crops they planned to grow in the upcoming season, and often required references or testimonials from applicants' previous employers. They constantly kept an eye out for overseers possessing the perfect combination of character traits, including honesty, sobriety, industry, integrity, humanity, and faithfulness. Some specifically requested men of a particular age or marital status. Whatever the precise mix of qualities masters sought in an overseer, they expected him to run a smooth plantation for little compensation or job security. But even if an overseer met all of a slaveholder's requirements, the master still usually treated him as the social inferior he was. With the slaveowner outranking him in social status, the overseer found getting slaves to obey him a frustrating task, as the slaves themselves recognized that he lacked ultimate power over them. Throughout the antebellum era, overseeing remained a thankless job involving, as one historian has noted, "maximum responsibility with minimum authority."[6]

Slaveowners across the South constantly disparaged overseers for their alleged shortcomings in character or management. British traveler Captain Basil Hall detected a tendency of masters "to abuse these overseers as a class." One master in Virginia called overseers "the curse of this country, . . . the worst men in the community." In low-country South Carolina, rice planters described the character of the overseers they left in charge of their absentee estates as "exceedingly bad," chosen from among the small pool of white men "born and reared in the miasmatic district of the coast" who could tolerate the locality's asphyxiating

5. William Kauffman Scarborough, *The Overseer: Plantation Management in the Old South* (Baton Rouge: Louisiana State University Press, 1966), 5, 12, 41; Eugene D. Genovese, *Roll, Jordan, Roll: The World the Slaves Made* (New York: Vintage Books, 1976), 13; Colleen Morse Elliott and Louise Armstrong Moxley, *The Tennessee Civil War Veterans Questionnaires*, comp. Gustavus W. Dyer and John Trotwood Moore, vol. 2 (Easley, S.C.: Southern Historical Press, Inc., 1985), 752; W. H. Robinson, *From Log Cabin to the Pulpit, or, Fifteen Years in Slavery*, 3rd ed. (Eau Claire, Wis.: James H. Tifft, 1913), 20; Allston quoted in Scarborough, *Overseer*, 41. For other testimony from slaves that poor whites served as overseers, see George P. Rawick, ed., *The American Slave: A Composite Autobiography*, vol. 16, Maryland (Westport, Conn.: Greenwood Publishing Company, 1972), 49; and Rawick, vol. 2, pt. 1, 68.

6. Orville Vernon Burton, *In My Father's House Are Many Mansions: Family and Community in Edgefield, South Carolina* (Chapel Hill: University of North Carolina Press, 1985), 52; quote from Scarborough, *Overseer*, 6.

heat, humidity, and disease. According to the planters, "They were almost universally drunken and dissolute, and constantly liable to neglect their duties." Masters routinely accused such overseers of managing their land and slaves poorly. In the low country, many rice planters turned instead to black drivers to manage their estates.[7]

All overseers confronted challenges and criticism in the administration of their duties, but this must have been doubly the case for poor whites. Overseeing provided poor white men at least a meager source of income to meet immediate needs. The job was certainly frustrating and unrewarding for most, but many of them probably saw it as the first step to acquiring land and to becoming independent farmers in their own right. To planters, however, poor white overseers were obvious social inferiors. Some masters treated them with a veneer of respect, but others could not hide their contempt, and hired them only as a last resort or merely because they came cheaper than the professionals.[8]

Slaves were no more generous in their feelings toward poor white overseers. As overseers, poor whites gained authority over slaves, and the right to boss them, at least in theory. Across the South, however, slave men and women looked down upon them every bit as much as their masters did. Poor white overseers must have presented a striking visual contrast to wealthier and more refined slaveholders. Moreover, as one study has shown, their level of material comforts and diet differed little from that of the slaves themselves.[9] Under such circumstances, poor white overseers commanded far less respect than the master or a professional overseer. At one plantation, the slave women objected to the various "poor white folks" their master repeatedly hired as overseer. As one slave explained, "The women didn't like none of that for their boss, so they would not do nothing he tell them."[10] That even slaves disregarded his orders must have been a maddening reminder to the poor white overseer of his lowly social station.

7. Basil Hall, *Travels in North America, in the Years 1827 and 1828,* vol. 2 (Philadelphia: Carey, Lea & Carey, 1829), 217; Frederick Law Olmsted, *A Journey in the Seaboard Slave States, with Remarks on Their Economy* (New York: Dix & Edwards, 1856), 45, 485, 486. See also Olwell, *Masters, Slaves, & Subjects,* 211.

8. Scarborough, *Overseer,* 44–47.

9. John Solomon Otto and Augustus Marion Burns III, "Black Folks and Poor Buckras: Archeological Evidence of Slave and Overseer Living Conditions on an Antebellum Plantation," *Journal of Black Studies* 14 (December 1983): 195–197.

10. George P. Rawick, ed., *The American Slave: A Composite Autobiography, Supplement, Series 1,* vol. 9, pt. 4, 1712.

Slaves maintained their own notions of which whites merited deference and obedience, and poor white overseers typically did not count among that number. To the contrary, asserted one former bondsman, "the slave feels a contempt for the overseer as 'poor white trash.'" Slaves often used the opprobrious "trash" label when referring to poor white overseers. "The overseers and patterollers in the time of slavery were called poor white trash by the slaves," former Cumberland County, North Carolina, slave John C. Bectom remembered. "Yes," corroborated Ella Kelly of the South Carolina low country, "de overseer was de poor buckra, he was what you calls dis poor white trash." Slaves such as South Carolina carriage driver Andy Marion often refused to show respect to the "poor white trash" overseers they deemed "not as good as de niggers." "All de overseer done was to wake us up, see to feeding stock and act biggity," he complained.[11]

Were the overseers whom slaves deemed "poor white trash" actually poor whites? The few overseers mentioned by name in slave narratives as "trash" can rarely be located in census records, a reflection of the transience of the profession. Some of them may have been not poor whites at all but yeoman or planter sons instead. Evidence suggests, however, that slaves did not indiscriminately bandy about the "poor white trash" label; rather, many slaves made shrewd distinctions between those overseers who did and did not deserve that designation. According to former slave George Fleming, the overseers on his master's Laurens District, South Carolina, plantation "wasn't poor whites. All Marse Sam's overseers was good men. Dey lived wid deir families, and Marse's folks 'sociated wid dem, too." Another former South Carolina slave remembered that his overseer was named Mike Melton, a landless and illiterate man who appears in the 1860 census as a well digger: "No sir, he poor man but come from good folks, not poor white trash." If every single overseer who forced slaves to rise early and directed their work in the fields was trash, then all overseers would have been trash. As these examples suggest, at least some slaves assessed their overseers in part on the basis of character. Even an economically poor overseer did not automatically become "trash" in all slaves' minds.[12]

---

11. J. W. C. Pennington, *A Narrative of Events of the Life of J. H. Banks, an Escaped Slave, from the Cotton State, Alabama, in America* (Liverpool: M. Rourke, 1861), 16; Rawick, vol. 14, pt. 1, 98; Rawick, vol. 3, pt. 3, 82; Rawick, vol. 3, pt. 3, 168–169. For similar sentiments, see also Rawick, vol. 3, pt. 3, 2; Rawick, vol. 2, pt. 2, 306; Rawick, vol. 7, Oklahoma, 211; and Rawick, vol. 14, pt. 1, 119.

12. Rawick, SS1, vol. 11 (Westport, Conn.: Greenwood Press, 1977), 132; Rawick, vol. 2, pt. 1, 206; Eighth Census of the United States, 1860: Chester District, South Carolina, 39.

Slaves did, however, tend to use the term freely when referring to overseers whom they adjudged unreasonably cruel. The actual level of brutality varied from overseer to overseer, plantation to plantation. Much depended on the temperaments of the particular slaveowner and overseer involved. Outside Augusta, Georgia, foreign traveler Frederika Bremer encountered a "clay-eater" who had given up overseeing because "the office was one of so much cruelty. . . . He could not endure having to flog the slaves himself. . . . But his master would not permit him to abstain from it." Most overseers Bremer encountered, however, "displease me by a certain severity, a certain savage expression in their countenance." Yet as Captain Basil Hall indicated while touring the South Carolina low country, planters and overseers had a shared interest "to use the slaves well." Masters wanted to preserve their slave property and put it to profitable use. An overseer who gained a reputation for undue severity jeopardized his prospects for future employment. Such considerations tempered the use of the lash among some, but by no means all, slaveholders and overseers.[13]

More than anything, the fact that overseers administered whippings shaped slave perceptions of them. "De overseer, whose name I'se plumb forgot, wuz pore white trash an' he wuz meaner dan de meanest nigger," remembered former Union County, North Carolina, slave Mandy Coverson. A fellow slave born in North Carolina agreed. "The overseer was nothing, just common white trash," she complained. "If the niggers didn't get to the field by daylight, he would beat them." The physical pain these slaves either endured firsthand or saw overseers inflict remained etched into their memories more than seven decades after emancipation.[14]

More than one former slave suggested that the strict control some overseers attempted to exercise over them compensated for the overseers' own humble origins. According to one South Carolina slave, on his master's plantation, "De overseer was poor white folks . . . and dat is one thing dat made him so hard on de slaves of de plantation." Others concurred. "Often de overseers acted meaner den de masters in slav'ry days, just to prove dey wuz on de job and watchin' things," a former South Carolina bondsman explained. The youth of this particular respondent spared him from any beatings, but "wuz dem overseers mean to de

13. Frederika Bremer, *The Homes of the New World; Impressions of America,* vol. 1, trans. Mary Howitt (London: Arthur Hall, Virtue, & Co., 1853), 375, 376; Hall, *Travels in North America,* 217.

14. Rawick, vol. 14, pt. 1, 180; Rawick, SS1, vol. 7, pt. 2, 365–366. See also Rawick, vol. 14, pt. 1, 418; Rawick, SS1, vol. 6, pt. 1, 130.

darkies!" he exclaimed. "[D]ey used to lick de field hands somethin' awful." An ex-slave born in Albemarle County, Virginia, remembered a brutal overseer on a neighboring plantation, who "tied three slaves, Daniel Myers, Edmond Clarke, and Joe Prosser, up to a tree and lashed them with a big bull whip 'til they could hardly stand up; then he cut the ropes loose and made them go back to work." During rainstorms, he continued, "the ole poor white overseer would want some of the slaves to go out into the wood to get the cattle or other stock and if the slaves refused they would get a whipping." Poor white overseers treaded a fine line, balancing the need to produce a good crop for the slaveowner without falling completely out of favor with the slaves.[15]

Slave women resented poor white overseers for inflicting sexual violence and abuse. A female slave near Camden, South Carolina, remembered "a mean overseer" on a nearby plantation who "tuk 'vantage of the womens in the fiel's. One time he slammed a niggah woman down that was heavy [pregnant], en cause her to hev her baby—dead. The niggah womens in the Quarters jumped on 'im and say they gwine take him to a brushpile and burn him up. But their mens hollered for 'em to turn him loose." The slaveowner defused the situation, telling the women to return to the slave quarters. When he threatened to whip the women the upcoming night, "all de womens hid in the woods dat evenin'." After that episode, the master "sent the over seer away en never did hev no more."[16]

On rare occasions, a few particularly frustrated or enraged slaves lashed out violently against their poor white overseers. One former Virginia slave reported that, when her father disobeyed an order and the overseer cursed at him, "dat ole po' white trash got jumped. My pappy reached down an' pull out his knife; was gonna cut dat debil's th'oat. All de niggers run an' shake de knife out'n my father's han'. I tell you dat overseer was on his way to de debil." In Henrico County, Virginia, authorities charged six slaves of William Boulware with assault with intent to kill poor white overseer John H. Dodd on July 27, 1857. All were found guilty. In a sensational story that defies credibility, an ex-slave from Virginia described the murder of "Ole Saunders," a brutal overseer who "was de meanes' po' white debbil dat ever drawed a breath." Ordered to burn a pile of tree limbs and brush, the slaves "crep up behin'" Saunders "an' all at once pushed him over

15. Rawick, vol. 2, pt. 1, 67–68; Rawick, SS1, vol. 5, 484–485; Charles L. Perdue, Jr., Thomas E. Barden, and Robert K. Phillips, eds., *Weevils in the Wheat: Interviews with Virginia Ex-Slaves* (Charlottesville: University Press of Virginia, 1976), 166.

16. Rawick, SS1, vol. 7, pt. 2, 441–442.

in de fire. Down he went on his face in de middle of de pile, an' all of us kep' pilin' brush on top of him." When Saunders's remains were found in the ashes, the slaveowner assumed he had gotten sick and fallen into the fire on his own.[17]

These few instances of unleashed rage against poor white overseers should not disguise a far more complex range of feelings toward them. At one extreme, an ex-slave from King William County, Virginia, recalled that "overseers was white and of the lowest grade. The slave always hated them." At the other extreme, former slave Annie Coley of South Carolina remembered that her "overseer was a po' white man, but he was good to us cullud folks." Such positive remarks must be regarded with caution, however, since they may reflect the former slaves' obsequiousness toward their white interviewers. One South Carolina ex-slave probably best captured the complex reality of overseeing. He noted that his poor white overseer, John Parker, "was mean to us sometimes. He was good to some and bad to others." The very nature of the occupation dictated that all overseers were "mean" sometimes, and "bad" to some slaves more than others.[18]

One former slave woman displayed a tremendous amount of understanding toward poor white overseers, despite the overseers' assigned task of slave management. Ninety-six-year-old Lucretia Hayward recollected that her overseer was named Edward Blunt. "He been poor white trash," she said, "but he wuk haa'd and save he money and buy slave. He buy my Ma and bring she to Beaufort to wuk in he house by da Baptist chu'ch. I been born den." Though her remarks fell shy of admiration per se, she did acknowledge Blunt's efforts to improve his condition. "Does I hate Mr. Blunt?" Hayward asked. "No, I ain't hate um. He poor white trash but he . . . hab he self to look out for, enty? He wuk, he sabe he money for buy slabe and land. He git some slabe, but he nebber git any land—de war cum." Hayward's comments demonstrate that at least some slaves realized that poor white overseers, much like slaves themselves, struggled to get by, and that they, too, often failed to achieve their dreams.[19]

To aid in the South's system of slave control, poor white men not only served as overseers but also performed patrol duty. By the end of the eighteenth cen-

17. Perdue et al., *Weevils in the Wheat,* 317; *Richmond Enquirer,* August 21, 1857; Seventh Census of the United States, 1850: Henrico County, Virginia, 485, lists John H. Dodd as a thirty-one-year-old farmer with no real estate; Perdue et al., *Weevils in the Wheat,* 346–347. For other examples of slave violence on overseers, see *Richmond Enquirer,* November 1, 1839; and March 8, 1859.

18. Perdue et al., *Weevils in the Wheat,* 85; Rawick, SS1, vol. 7, pt. 2, 441; Rawick, vol. 2, pt. 1, 67.

19. Rawick, vol. 2, pt. 2, 279, 281.

tury, South Carolina, Virginia, and North Carolina had all established a formalized system of slave patrol. During patrols, a small group of southern white men traveled on horseback by night, in all types of inclement weather, to detect slaves sneaking about without a pass from their master and to disperse unlawful assemblies of blacks. Based largely on interviews with former slaves, historians have long contended that this onerous duty fell overwhelmingly to poor whites.[20] "Most of them there patrollers was poor white folks, I believes," said former slave Samuel Boulware of South Carolina. According to a Virginia ex-slave, "Patrol duty was always performed by the poor whites, who took great pride in the whipping of a slave." While some poor white patrollers certainly did relish the opportunity to vent their frustrations on an unfortunate slave, even those disinclined to beating bondspeople wielded the whip on occasion to remain in good standing with local slaveholders. "De patrollers was nothin' but poor white trash, mammy say," said one slave descendant, "and if they didn't whip some slaves, every now and then, they would lose deir jobs." Few ex-slaves expressed such an understanding of the difficult position of a naturally peaceable poor white man. Seared into their memories instead were the nightmarish encounters with unnecessarily brutal patrollers. "Why de good white folks put up wid them poor white trash patarollers I never can see or understand," pondered former slave Manda Walker of South Carolina. "You never see classy white buckra men a patarollin'. It was always some low-down white men, dat never owned a nigger in deir life, doin' de patarollin' and a strippin' de clothes off men, . . . right befo' de wives and chillun and beatin' de blood out of him." "No, sir," she concluded, "good white men never dirty deir hands and souls in sich work of de devil as dat." As in the case of overseers, however, it remains unclear which patrollers in slaves' memories were actually poor whites, for hatred, anger, resentment, and stereotypes from the postbellum years all shaded their recollections.[21]

In her recent study of slave patrols in Virginia and the Carolinas, Sally E. Hadden contends that the majority of patrollers were not poor whites at all but a middling sort. From the eighteenth century and into the nineteenth, she finds, patrollers consisted of "a representative cross-section of citizens." Men from all social classes participated in slave patrols. One ex-slave born in Laurens Dis-

20. See, for example, Lapp, "Ante Bellum Poor Whites," 124–125.
21. Rawick, vol. 2, pt. 1, 68; H. C. Bruce, *The New Man: Twenty-Nine Years a Slave, Twenty-Nine Years a Free Man* (York, Penn.: P. Anstadt & Sons, 1895; reprint, New York: Negro Universities Press, 1969), 96; Rawick, vol. 2, pt. 1, 252; Rawick, vol. 3, pt. 4, 171; Sally E. Hadden, *Slave Patrols: Law and Violence in Virginia and the Carolinas* (Cambridge, Mass.: Harvard University Press, 2001), 90–91.

trict, South Carolina, said as much: "Patrollers was made up of jes' anybody dat wanted to jine 'em," he remarked, "poor white trash and all." In North Carolina, it was slaveholders who comprised the majority of patrollers until the 1850s. Elsewhere, however, nonslaveholders did most of the patrolling for their slaveholding neighbors, a point of friction between the two groups. Some masters happily paid the fine for not serving on patrol to enjoy the privilege of sitting at home at night, leaving the unpleasant task for their social inferiors. According to Hadden, the nonslaveholders on patrol were not disproportionately poor whites, except in the South Carolina low country, where absentee landownership increasingly shifted the burden of patrolling to the poor, who could not afford to flee the area to evade patrol duty. Poor whites might also perform more than their fair share of patrolling by consenting to serve as paid substitutes for wealthier neighbors. "Rich folks stay in their house at night, 'less they has some sort of big frolic amongst theirselves," explained a former South Carolina slave. "Poor white folks had to hustle 'round to make a living, so, they hired out theirselves to slave owners and rode de roads at night and whipped niggers if they ketched any off their plantation widout a pass." Chowan County, North Carolina, slave autobiographer Allen Parker similarly recorded that "generally poor whites . . . did the work" of patrolling, "partly for the money they could get out of the business, and partly on account of the excit[e]ment there was in it." In at least some cases, then, poor whites served on patrol voluntarily, compelled by economic necessity or a desire for a diversion, without having slaveholders force the burden upon them in any coercive, heavy-handed way.[22]

Although poor whites did not constitute a majority of all patrollers, they were the ones about whom elite whites complained incessantly. Planters especially disapproved of overly aggressive poor whites who treated patrol duty as an opportunity for drunken revelry and who assumed that it granted them license to torment and abuse slave property indiscriminately. A daughter of the wealthy Nash family of North Carolina felt that patrollers unfairly disrupted the peace and quietude of the plantation. "This is a poor country I think," she lamented, "where the lowest set of white men can come on your place, search your kitchen and whip your negroes." An anonymous slaveholder writing to the *Richmond Enquirer* bemoaned at great length "the *character* of those appointed as patrol." "[E]ver

22. J. Michael Crane, "Controlling the Night: Perceptions of the Slave Patrol System in Mississippi," *Journal of Mississippi History* 61 (Summer 1999): 120, 129; Hadden, *Slave Patrols*, 64, 99, 102, 65; Rawick, SS1, vol. 11, 133; Rawick, vol. 2, pt. 1, 68–69; Allen Parker, *Recollections of Slavery Times* (Worcester, Mass.: Chas. W. Burbank & Co., 1895), 28.

since I was a boy," he explained, ". . . it was a common practice to appoint the very rag, tag and bob tail of society, the idle, unfeeling, brutal 'poor white folks,' inferior to the negro in many qualities, and despising him." Poor white patrollers, he explained, "glory in this sort of temporary military authority . . . , and, making it the occasion of a *frolic*, their bad passions stirred up by drink, they maltreat the quiet, inoffensive, home staying negro" and "the faithful old family servant." "[I]n fact," he continued, "they often perform their whole task with a noisy, swaggering vulgarity very offensive to the feelings of a humane master." According to the slaveholding author, "I would rather run all the risk of insurrection . . . than to have my premises visited by such gangs." He considered it the masters' duty to protect their slaves from any abuse at the hands of poor white patrollers, urging "the magistrates everywhere to appoint men of the right stamp, . . . [and] to *instruct* them as to the propriety of making their companies demean themselves properly, and to require rigidly . . . that there be *no drinking*" during patrol.[23] A handful of vindictive poor whites surely did serve on patrol with depraved enthusiasm, taking advantage of the opportunity to project physically their resentment toward planters onto valuable slave property or to distinguish themselves from slaves in a way that economics did not. That poor whites could gain psychological rewards from patrol duty alarmed slaveholders. If a poor white's violent assault resulted in the death or permanent maiming of a slave, the aggrieved master had little hope of ever receiving compensation from the impoverished offender.[24]

Whereas "A Slaveholder" feared the drunken, unbridled excesses of poor white patrollers, other masters dreaded that men of such low caliber would use patrolling to develop economic networks with the very slaves the patrols were designed to control. They had reason to worry. One ex-slave from the coastal plain of North Carolina recalled that "de patrollers was low white trash! We all knowed dat if a patroller jest rode right by and didn't say nothing dat he was doing his honest job, but iffen he stopped his hoss and talked to a nigger he was after some kind of trade." Although a secondary duty, patrollers' responsibilities

23. Quoted in Bertram Wyatt-Brown, "Community, Class, and Snopesian Crime: Local Justice in the Old South," in *Class, Conflict, and Consensus: Antebellum Southern Community Studies*, ed. Orville Vernon Burton and Robert C. McMath, Jr. (Westport, Conn.: Greenwood Press, 1982), 183; *Richmond Enquirer,* December 23, 1856.

24. Hadden, *Slave Patrols,* 103; H. Hoetink, *Slavery and Race Relations in the Americas: Comparative Notes on Their Nature and Nexus* (New York: Harper & Row, 1973), 14–15; Lapp, "Ante Bellum Poor Whites," 125; Bill Cecil-Fronsman, *Common Whites: Class and Culture in Antebellum North Carolina* (Lexington: University Press of Kentucky, 1992), 78.

included checking on suspicious whites as well as slaves. In North Carolina, a law of 1830 gave patrollers the authority to investigate, ferret out, and apprehend "all persons guilty of trading with slaves," including white people. Yet poor whites themselves, while on patrol duty, sometimes traded liquor to slaves for stolen goods. To curb poor white patrollers' opportunities for illicit trade with slaves, South Carolina planter Robert F. W. Allston declared that elite whites should compose a portion of any patrol. Precisely because patrollers also kept watch over the "shadowy underworld" of slaves and poor whites, Sally Hadden observes, the slave patrol required men of "discretion, prestige, and good character."[25]

The very nature of patrol duty left slaves little room to sympathize with white patrollers. Patrols, though often lax (except during periods of rumored slave conspiracies and actual rebellions), restricted slaves' freedom in profound ways. Slaves devoted entire days to working for their master. Yet even when the work day ended, patrols impeded slaves' mobility and shaped the ways in which they spent their precious few hours of free time. Slaves knew full well that "de paddyrollers would give 'em a beatin' if dey caught dem off de plantashun without a pass." According to a former slave born in Nottoway County, Virginia, "If dem old po' white overseers an' paterrollers fin you ain' got no pass dey would nigh beat you to death." Slaves tempted to stray from the plantation needed to weigh the risk of capture and physical punishment against the possible benefits of leaving the quarters without permission. Upon reflection, the idea of attending an unsanctioned religious meeting or other social gathering might not seem so inviting. To be sure, patrols proved far from omnipresent, and the likelihood of capture by patrol "varied from community to community and from county to county." All of these factors came into play when a slave pondered an independent excursion off the plantation.[26]

Even if detected by the patrol, slaves had recourse. In the case of a group of North Carolina slaves, a timely bribe of liquor spared them a whipping. "Yes, we seed the patterollers, we called 'em pore white trash, we also called patterollers pore white pecks," remembered Hannah Crasson. "They came to our house one night when we were singin' and prayin'. . . . My daddy told us to show 'em de

25. Rawick, vol. 7, Oklahoma, 66; *Acts Passed By the General Assembly of the State of North Carolina, at the Session of 1830–1831* (Raleigh: Lawrence & Lemay, 1831), 17; Hadden, *Slave Patrols*, 90, 104.

26. Rawick, SS1, vol. 5, 484–485; Perdue et al., *Weevils in the Wheat*, 125; Freddie L. Parker, *Running for Freedom: Slave Runaways in North Carolina, 1775–1840* (New York: Garland Publishing, Inc., 1993), 42. Slaves virtually never said anything positive about patrollers. For one exception, see Rawick, vol. 15, pt. 2, 209.

brandy our marster gib us, den dey went on a way." Other slaves whipped by the patrol reported the incident to their master. If the slaveowner deemed the punishment inflicted too harsh, he or she could confront the offender personally or take the case before a local court. The planter had no desire to see his valuable bondspeople unnecessarily mistreated by poor white patrollers. Slaves singled out patrollers for retribution at their own hands, too. They could destroy a patroller's property or burn his buildings as easily as they could the master's.[27]

Slaves' trickery in dealing with poor white patrollers became the stuff of legend. Stories abound of how slaves successfully passed off scraps of paper or random scribbles as authentic passes. "I have heard of many jokes played on these patrols by slaves, tending to show how easy it was to fool them," wrote one slave autobiographer, "because they were as a rule illiterate, and of course could not read writing." Slaves "would take a portion of a letter . . . and palm it off on them as a pass when arrested," he explained. The patroller, not wishing to betray his illiteracy, would take the pass, pretend to examine it, and hand it back to the slave, permitting him to proceed unmolested. Other accounts tell of slaves taking revenge upon patrollers through the grapevine trick. "We set traps to catch the patterollers," explained a former Wake County, North Carolina, slave. "The patterollers were poor white men. We stretched grape vines across the roads, then we would run from them. They would follow, and get knocked off their horses." Thrown to the ground from the impact with the taut vine, the riders sometimes suffered serious injuries. The widespread recollection of these grapevine stories among ex-slaves leads some historians to doubt their authenticity. One scholar describes the grapevine stories as "probably apocryphal, their common elements suggesting folklore origins." These tales of inversion, in which slaves prevail over their white oppressors, surely had roots in a small handful of actual events; that they resonated with all slaves explains their diffusion. Such a shared story of triumph over white patrollers swelled slaves' "sense of empowerment and group accomplishment."[28]

In addition to serving patrol duty, poor whites also acted as spies for slaveholders, providing extra sets of eyes to monitor local slaves. Ex-slave H. C. Bruce remembered "two poor white men, better known at the South as 'poor white trash,'" who lived near his master's farm in Prince Edward County, Virginia, in

27. Rawick, vol. 14, pt. 1, 190; Rawick, vol. 14, pt. 1, 64; Herbert Aptheker, *American Negro Slave Revolts* (New York: Columbia University Press, 1943), 147.

28. Bruce, *New Man*, 96–97; Rawick, vol. 15, pt. 2, 321–322; Crane, "Controlling the Night," 132.

the 1840s. John Flippen and Sam Hawkins "were too lazy to do steady work and made their living by doing chores for the rich and killing hawks and crows at so much a piece, for the owner of the land on which they were destroyed. These men would watch us and report to our master everything they saw us do that was a violation of the rules." Catering to the slaveholder, the poor whites "told everything they had seen the slaves do, and oftener more." On one occasion, Sam Hawkins told a lie leading to Bruce's being punished. Bruce twice refuted Hawkins's story, and twice received a whipping. His master administered the floggings not for Bruce's alleged indiscretion but "for disputing a white man's word." The slave felt nothing but contempt for the poor white man whose falsehood led to the beating. Almost as much as slaves, Bruce concluded, poor whites considered slaveholders "their masters."[29]

A few poor whites made their living from slaveholders as professional slave hunters assigned to track down runaways. More commonly, poor white slave catchers were illiterate, marginal farmers who found apprehending runaways a lucrative side job.[30] Slaveowners hired these poor whites to capture runaways, paying them by the day or by the mile.[31] The most effective slave catchers used specially trained dogs. According to Frederick Law Olmsted, "No particular breed of dogs is needed for hunting negroes: blood-hounds, fox-hounds, bull-dogs, and curs were used." Bloodhounds, however, seemed the dog of choice for tracking runaway slaves. Successful fugitive William Wells Brown recalled "an inferior white man" named Tabor who kept bloodhounds to pursue runaways. Planters routinely hired him "to hunt down their negroes." According to a former North Carolina bondsman, "Dar wus a man in Raleigh what had two blood houn's an' he made his livin' by ketchin' runaway niggers. His name wus Beaver an' he ain't missed but onct." Another ex-slave from North Carolina remembered the names of Kenyan Jones and Billy Pump, both "po' white trash," who "owned blood houn's, an' chased de niggers an' whupped dem shamful." Slaves despised

29. Bruce, *New Man*, 28–29. The Seventh Census of the United States, 1850: Prince Edward County, Virginia, 51, lists John Flippen as a forty-seven-year-old farmer with $520 real estate, Sam Hawkins as a fifty-year-old farmer with $75 real estate. Hawkins more closely approximates poor white status, but this rare example illustrates how slaves extended the phrase "poor white trash" upward to include individuals historians would usually label "yeomen."

30. Kenneth M. Stampp, *The Peculiar Institution: Slavery in the Ante-Bellum South* (New York: Vintage Books, 1956), 153, notes that a poor white fortunate enough to capture a runaway found it a "financial windfall."

31. John Hope Franklin and Loren Schweninger, *Runaway Slaves: Rebels on the Plantation* (New York: Oxford University Press, 1999), 156. See also 149, 160, 163.

tracking dogs and would kill them and bury them in the fields whenever they had the chance. Some masters stipulated that slave catchers bring their slaves back "unbruised and untorn by their dogs," but others did not. Slaveholders compensated the poor white slave catcher upon the successful capture of his prey.[32]

Poor white slave hunters sometimes violently abused those fugitives they captured. Ex-slave Jacob Stroyer remembered a "heartless" and "cruel" professional slave catcher named Black, who appears in a petition to the South Carolina legislature and in census and court records as William Blackledge. Blackledge lived in Richland District, South Carolina. He was illiterate, "very poor, and had a large family," including "a wife, with eight or ten helpless children." Not listed as having any occupation in the 1850 census, Blackledge made his living by hunting runaways with his dogs and a gaunt, decrepit horse. Rumors swirled that he had murdered slaves he had captured in the woods, but no solid evidence had been assembled against him.[33]

In 1853, however, Blackledge and a white companion named Thomas Motley overstepped their authority. That year, the pair journeyed to a portion of Colleton District "comparatively uninhabited by white persons" and "committed many outrages, with their ferocious dogs, upon Slaves." At Parker's Ferry, they inflicted "the most outrageous and inhuman barbarities" upon one unlucky fugitive named Joe.[34] Joe, twenty-two years old and reportedly "humble . . . as a dog," had recently been taken up as a runaway by a man named Grant, who transferred possession of the slave to Blackledge until he could convey him to jail. Claiming that Joe refused to identify his owner, Blackledge and Motley stripped and beat their

32. Olmsted, *Seaboard Slave States,* 160–161. See also Olmsted, *A Journey in the Back Country* (1860; reprint, New York: Burt Franklin, 1970), 214–217; and Olmsted, *The Cotton Kingdom: A Traveller's Observations on Cotton and Slavery in the American Slave States, 1853–1861,* ed. Arthur M. Schlesinger (New York: Da Capo Press, 1996), 122, 387, 389–390; Wm. Wells Brown, *My Southern Home: or, The South and Its People* (Boston: A. G. Brown & Co., 1880), 82, 84; Rawick, vol. 14, pt. 1, 397; Rawick, vol. 14, pt. 1, 293; William Loren Katz, comp., *Flight from the Devil: Six Slave Narratives* (Trenton: Africa World Press, Inc., 1996), 199, 201. Solomon Northup recalled that in Louisiana, a "mean white" considered it his good fortune to encounter "an unknown negro without a pass." Sue Eakin and Joseph Logsdon, eds., *Twelve Years a Slave, by Solomon Northup* (Baton Rouge: Louisiana State University Press, 1968), 118–119.

33. Katz, *Flight from the Devil,* 198, 200, 201. In the Seventh Census of the United States, 1850: Richland District, South Carolina, 48, William Blackledge is listed as thirty-five years old, illiterate, and with no occupation. He headed a household of five, including a wife Eliza and three children, ages five, four, and two.

34. Petitions, Legislative Papers, 1854, item 47, SCDAH. Motley does not appear in the 1850 census for South Carolina.

captive mercilessly. Three individuals not only witnessed "the cruel and barbarous treatment" but also reported hearing the slave disclose his master's name as requested. Joe then either escaped "or was permitted to fly," with Blackledge, Motley, and their dogs pursuing him in macabre sport.[35] According to Jacob Stroyer, the slave resisted capture, killing several of Blackledge's canines, so Blackledge shot him, and with Motley's assistance, "cut him up and gave his remains to the living dogs," burying what was left.[36]

Blackledge and Motley might still have gotten away with the crime. The community suspected the slave hunter Blackledge of the murder, but in the absence of witnesses, nothing could be done. During a drunken spree sometime later, however, Blackledge confided to another white man of Richland District that he had committed the crime, commenting coldly that "that is the way I put a nigger in his place." Blackledge's anonymous acquaintance alerted authorities, who arrested the pair of slave catchers.[37] Hoping for immunity, Blackledge fingered Motley as the murderer. His confession "led to the discovery of the bones and hair of a negro concealed behind a log in a swamp, not far from the place where Joe was supposed to have been killed." The remains could not be positively identified as those of the unfortunate fugitive, but they did match Joe's five-foot-six frame. A jury composed exclusively of slaveholders convicted the two men and sentenced them to death for their exceptionally cruel murder of the runaway slave, and the state court of appeals denied their motion for a new trial.[38] At some point during these proceedings, Blackledge and Motley escaped from jail. Possibly for fear of their own lives, "no Constable or Deputy Sheriff could be induced to go in pursuit of them." It took a specially appointed constable to track the felons fifty miles, apprehend them, and return them to justice. Blackledge and Motley both hanged for their crime before a crowd of onlookers outside the Colleton District courthouse. Clearly an exceptional case, that of Blackledge and Motley reveals in starkest form the brutal excesses of poor whites' role in slave control.[39]

35. *State v. Thomas Motley; State v. William Blackledge,* 7 Richardson 327 (1854), *South Carolina Law Reports,* vol. 41, quotes 329, 328.

36. Katz, *Flight from the Devil,* 201.

37. Ibid., 202. Stroyer claims the incident happened in Barnwell District.

38. Historical Sketch of DeTreville House (Walterboro, S.C.), SCL, 5; *State v. Thomas Motley; State v. William Blackledge,* 7 Richardson 327 (1854), *South Carolina Law Reports,* vol. 41, quote 328. According to Jacob Stroyer, a runaway slave had stumbled upon the murdered slave's shallow grave and returned home to report the gruesome discovery to his master. See Katz, *Flight from the Devil,* 201.

39. Petitions, Legislative Papers, 1854, item 47, SCDAH. Rumors circulated that relatives of Motley would engineer the rescue of the two condemned men, prompting South Carolina's gover-

*   *   *

As overseers, patrollers, spies, and slave hunters, poor whites lent valuable support to the preservation of the southern slave regime. In all of these ways, they helped slaveholders maintain control over their bondspeople and reassured them of poor white allegiance to the South's racially based social structure. But at other times, poor whites' actions implicitly called their commitment to the slave regime into question. For all of the assistance most poor whites gave slaveholders, a few also challenged planter hegemony by aiding slave runaways and rebels. To be sure, the vast majority of poor whites made no effort to undermine slavery. Planter fears of poor white disloyalty always exceeded actual subversive behavior. Nevertheless, in hundreds of scattered, isolated incidents, poor whites aided slave fugitives and malcontents. Undoubtedly most of these occurrences have gone undocumented, but dozens of confirmed cases in the Carolinas and Virginia attest to the alliances, however fleeting, poor whites occasionally forged with slaves. These instances of cooperation troubled slaveholders, for they cast doubt on poor whites' attachment to the society the masters ruled. When poor whites falsified passes and free papers, harbored runaways, stole slaves off the plantation, and, in exceptionally rare cases, played some small part in slave rebellions or conspiracies, they called their commitment to the slave regime into question. Perhaps most vexing to slaveholders, the poor whites who engaged in such seditious activities could be the very same individuals who so loyally served as their overseers, patrollers, and slave catchers.

From the colonial period to the end of the Civil War, masters suspected "unscrupulous" whites of helping slaves run away. Poor whites proved no less willing to assist slave runaways than other classes of whites. Indeed, in the seventeenth and eighteenth centuries, white indentured servants often ran away *with* black slaves, a consequence of their shared economic status. Many slaveowners, unable to conceive that slaves would abscond by their own volition, felt certain that whites enticed or persuaded their slaves away. Slave runaway advertisements frequently warned whites not to carry off, harbor, or employ fugitive slaves, and promised to prosecute those who did "under penalty of law." Masters commonly offered a greater reward to someone who discovered a runaway secreted by a white person than by a black.[40] Most runaway advertisements conveyed only the

---

nor to muster the militias from Charleston, Edisto Island, and Colleton District. No attempt to liberate Motley and Blackledge from the gallows occurred. See Historical Sketch of DeTreville House, 6. See also Katz, *Flight from the Devil*, 203.

40. Freddie L. Parker, *Stealing a Little Freedom: Advertisements for Slave Runaways in North Carolina, 1791–1840* (New York: Garland Publishing, Inc., 1994), 136, 137, 154.

vaguest suspicions of white complicity, although a tiny fraction did mention specific white persons alleged to have helped runaways. Any slave who placed confidence in a white person, however, took a calculated risk. Loyalty to a local slaveholder or the potential reward for a missing slave meant that at any point a white person could betray a slave's trust.[41]

The simplest way a white person could help a runaway slave was to forge a pass or free papers that afforded the bondsperson mobility. Slaveholders often expressed their suspicions that "some villain," "rascal," or "*worthless* white man" supplied runaways tickets that allowed them to move freely about the countryside.[42] Denying that slaveholders themselves furnished slaves any reason to ab-

---

41. The best published collections of slave runaway advertisements are Daniel Meaders, ed., *Advertisements for Runaway Slaves in Virginia, 1801–1820* (New York: Garland Publishing, Inc., 1997); Parker, *Stealing a Little Freedom;* Billy G. Smith and Richard Wojtowicz, *Blacks Who Stole Themselves: Advertisements for Runaways in the* Pennsylvania Gazette, *1728–1790* (Philadelphia: University of Pennsylvania Press, 1989); and Lathan A. Windley, comp., *Runaway Slave Advertisements: A Documentary History from the 1730s to 1790,* 4 vols. (Westport, Conn.: Greenwood Press, 1983). The scholarship on slave runaways is extensive. On slave runaways in the colonial era, see Gerald W. Mullin, *Flight and Rebellion: Slave Resistance in Eighteenth-Century Virginia* (New York: Oxford University Press, 1972); Daniel E. Meaders, "South Carolina Fugitives as Viewed Through Local Newspapers with Emphasis on Runaway Notices, 1732–1801," *Journal of Negro History* 60 (April 1975): 288–319; Marvin L. Michael Kay and Lorin Lee Cary, "'They are Indeed the Constant Plague of Their Tyrants': Slave Defence of a Moral Economy in Colonial North Carolina, 1748–1772," *Slavery & Abolition* 6 (December 1985): 37–56; Philip D. Morgan, "Colonial South Carolina Runaways: Their Significance for Slave Culture," *Slavery & Abolition* 6 (December 1985): 57–78; Marvin L. Michael Kay and Lorin Lee Cary, "Slave Runaways in Colonial North Carolina, 1748–1775," *North Carolina Historical Review* 63 (January 1986): 1–39; Jonathan Prude, "To Look Upon the 'Lower Sort': Runaway Ads and the Appearance of Unfree Laborers in America, 1750–1800," *Journal of American History* 78 (July 1991): 124–159; Lathan Algerna Windley, *A Profile of Runaway Slaves in Virginia and South Carolina from 1730 through 1787* (New York: Garland Publishing, Inc., 1995); and David Waldstreicher, "Reading the Runaways: Self-Fashioning, Print Culture, and Confidence in Slavery in the Eighteenth-Century Mid-Atlantic," *William & Mary Quarterly* 3d ser., 56 (April 1999): 243–272. For the postcolonial era, see Elwood L. Bridner, Jr., "The Fugitive Slaves of Maryland," *Maryland Historical Magazine* 66 (Spring 1971): 33–50; Michael P. Johnson, "Runaway Slaves and the Slave Communities in South Carolina, 1799–1830," *William & Mary Quarterly* 3d ser., 38 (July 1981): 418–441; Freddie L. Parker, *Running for Freedom: Slave Runaways in North Carolina, 1775–1840* (New York: Garland Publishing, Inc., 1993); David S. Cecelski, "The Shores of Freedom: The Maritime Underground Railroad in North Carolina, 1800–1861," *North Carolina Historical Review* 71 (April 1994): 174–206; Franklin and Schweninger, *Runaway Slaves.* Only a few of these sources note that any whites, much less poor whites, helped slaves run away. See, for example, Mullin, *Flight and Rebellion,* 112–116; Windley, *Profile of Runaway Slaves,* 15–19; and Franklin and Schweninger, *Runaway Slaves,* 30–33.

42. *North Carolina Journal* (Halifax), September 21, 1801, and February 15, 1802, in Parker, *Stealing a Little Freedom,* 72, 75; *Raleigh Register* (weekly), September 8, 1847. Whites took a substantial risk in writing a pass for a slave. According to the *Acts Passed at a General Assembly of the Common-*

scond, such pronouncements deflected blame for a bondsperson's disappearance onto poor white scapegoats. Not every poor white possessed the ability to write, and therefore to falsify a pass, and the elementary writing skills of those who did betrayed their lack of formal schooling. In Chatham County, North Carolina, nonslaveholder Jordan Holliman allegedly forged free papers for Thomas Bell's slave Willis in 1829. The poorly scribbled document was signed by the fictitious James O'Kelly on behalf of Willis's free black alias, Isaac Evans:

> This Will Certify that the Barrer (Isaac Evans) a Man of Color is of Free Parrantage Was Born'd and Raised in the County afores[d] and a person of a Morral Carrector is about six feet high and served [h]is apprentiship under me as a farmer and was of age the 15 of December in the year of our Lord Eightteen Hundred and nine and the same Registered in s[d] County.

Had education been widespread among whites in the antebellum South, such a forgery could immediately have been recognized as a fake, drawn up by a semi-literate slave. But because even some respected southern white citizens never had the benefit of formal education, errors in spelling and grammar did not automatically signal deception.[43] Landless laborer Nelson J. Cook went too far, however, by allegedly furnishing slave Lewis "with forged free papers purporting to come from Winslow Robinson Clerk of Charlotte County Court." Cook appeared before a Lunenburg County, Virginia, court in 1851 to answer to the offense.[44] Charles G. Spann of Chester District, South Carolina, swore an affidavit in 1832 "that his negro man Jacob" ran off, aided by "a ticket signed by and in the hand writing of one Jacob Hoppes, otherwise called Jacob Hoppers," of

---

wealth of Virginia (Richmond: Thomas Ritchie, 1829), 25, the Virginia assembly passed a law in 1829 that sentenced anyone convicted of "procuring, furnishing or delivering" a permit or pass to a slave to a three- to twelve-month prison sentence. An 1834 law stated that "if any free person shall entice, advise or persuade any slave to abscond" by supplying a pass, "money, clothes or provisions," upon conviction that individual would be jailed for two to five years. (*Acts Passed at a General Assembly of the Commonwealth of Virginia* [Richmond: Thomas Ritchie, 1834], 80.) In South Carolina, a law passed in 1836 sentenced anyone found guilty of giving a slave a ticket or permit to a fine up to a thousand dollars (given to the informer) and a prison sentence of up to one year. (David J. McCord, *The Statutes at Large of South Carolina; Edited, Under Authority of the Legislature*, vol. 6 [Columbia: A. S. Johnston, 1839], 552.)

43. Chatham County, Records of Slaves and Free Persons of Color, 1782–1870, NCDAH. The Fifth Census of the United States, 1830: Wake County, North Carolina, 474, lists Jordan Holliman as a nonslaveholder in his forties, heading a household of nine.

44. Lunenburg County, Justice of the Peace Records, Box 1, Virginia State Archives, Richmond. The Seventh Census of the United States, 1850: Lunenburg County, Virginia, 53, lists Nelson J. Cook as a twenty-two-year-old laborer with no real estate or household of his own.

Burke County, North Carolina. The slave "exhibited the said ticket at different times & places by which he was enabled to pass publicly" on his way to Hoppes's house, until his apprehension near Lincolnton, North Carolina. Spann assumed Hoppes "did inveigle and entice the said negro to abscond away," and believed that the nonslaveholding white man planned to meet up with the runaway for some invidious purpose.[45]

To planters' satisfaction and delight, slaves sometimes exposed whites willing to forge them free papers. In November of 1857, Union County, North Carolina, native Joseph Underwood accosted a slave belonging to David Parks in Charlotte and asked him "if he did not desire to be set free." Underwood offered to write the slave a pass "and have him, with others, conveyed off next Saturday night." The slave assented to the proposal "and invited him to his master's Kitchen for the purpose of making arrangements." The faithful slave "immediately informed his master of the conversation," however, and participated in a plot to arrest Underwood. By the time Underwood arrived at Parks's kitchen, authorities had taken position near the door to eavesdrop. After eliciting all of the information from Underwood that he could, the slave overpowered the suspicious white man for the constable, who then "marched him off to Jail." Underwood "did not write the negro a pass," reported the newspaper, "for it appears that he is uneducated and cannot write." Why Underwood would offer to forge a pass if he himself could not write defies explanation. Perhaps the newspaper exaggerated its retelling of events to underscore Underwood's depravity and the loyalty of David Parks's slave. Or perhaps the bondsman falsely accused Underwood out of revenge or to curry favor with his master, earning himself a reward for his ostensible faithfulness.[46]

Watchful neighbors also alerted slaveholders if they spied a slave they recognized roaming where he or she did not belong. Apparently dissatisfied with work at the Burke County, North Carolina, gold mines, in 1832, slave Tom ran away from master William A. Burwell, to his former home with William's father Spotswood Burwell, in Mecklenburg County, Virginia. Tom managed to travel

45. Governor's Papers, Gov. Montfort Stokes, vol. 64, 161, NCDAH. The Fifth Census of the United States, 1830: Burke County, North Carolina, 128, lists Jacob Hoppes as a nonslaveholder in his twenties, with eight in his household.

46. *Western Democrat* (Charlotte), November 10, 1857. According to the Eighth Census of the United States, 1860: Union County, North Carolina, 878, the only Underwood listed in Union County is William Underwood, a well digger with no real estate and $100 personal estate. William may be considered a poor white, and through a likely kinship, I have placed Joseph Underwood in that category as well.

nearly 150 miles from Burke County before being recognized in Caswell County, North Carolina, adjacent to the Virginia border. By sheer coincidence, two acquaintances of the elder Burwell, who happened to be visiting an uncle in Caswell County, saw Tom passing on his way to Virginia. They stopped the slave, who carried with him a pass allegedly signed by William Burwell. The two men realized that the handwriting did not match the younger Burwell's, but since Tom had already journeyed so far, they allowed him to continue the remaining sixty miles or so to Spotswood's plantation. "Tom says a Mr. Griffin who keeps a grog shop or a confectioners house was the man that gave him the pass," Spotswood Burwell informed his son. Two brothers, James and Robert Griffin, lived with their mother in Burke County, a mile from William. The slave Tom explained that one of them gave him the ticket, instructing him not "to let the pass be seen" until he had proceeded beyond the Catawba River—or Griffin's handwriting would be recognized—and to "destroy the pass" once safely home.[47]

Spotswood Burwell seemed uncertain how precisely to handle the situation with Griffin. Like any slaveholder, he weighed several options. Initially, he suggested a personal, though coercive, approach rather than a legal one. He recommended that his son go with someone to Griffin's grog shop. "I would mention the facts to Griffin in a mild manner," Burwell advised, and "give him to under stand that if he would act in a[n] up right way I would not expose him nor prosecut[e] him for the offence." Judging his interests "injured at le[a]st $50 or $100," Burwell wrote that "if [Griffin] will pay you that sum I will not prosecute him." Not following Griffin's instructions, slave Tom had only partly destroyed the white man's pass. Burwell recovered the fragments and enclosed them with his letter to William, instructing his son to "give Griffin a scare."[48]

Burwell reconsidered the matter, however, and sent his son revised advice three days later. After sending his first missive, Burwell spoke with a Mr. Hamilton, who "wants me to bring suit against Griffin," Burwell explained, for "[t]his same man Griffin . . . was strongly suspected of giving Major Hunts man a pass at the time he left Burke."[49] Apparently at the encouragement of Hamilton, Burwell resolved to prosecute Griffin through formal legal channels. He therefore desired concrete evidence of the poor white man's crime. "I think if you

47. Spotswood Burwell to William A. Burwell, July 31, 1832, Folder 10, Burwell Family Papers #112, SHC.

48. Ibid.

49. Spotswood Burwell to William A. Burwell, August 9, 1832, Folder 11, Burwell Family Papers, SHC.

will manage the affair Judicious, you may trap Griffin," Burwell wrote. "I should think that his hand writing could be detected from the pieces of the pass that I sent you. If you have not disclosed the matter to Griffin befour you received this letter I would get some friend to get him to rite a few lines on a piece of paper in order that you may have his hand writing to compair with the pieces of the pass." Matching a sample of Griffin's handwriting with that on the pass would bolster any case against him in court. As for the runaway slave, Burwell wrote frankly, "Tom is a vile raskal I dont intend to keep Tom long." The fates of Tom and his poor white accomplice unfortunately go unrecorded.[50]

While some poor whites forged passes, others harbored, concealed, or "entertained" fugitive slaves. This reflected an even greater level of involvement in a slave's effort to abscond. When North Carolina slave Allen Parker ran away one night from his employer, he found shelter at "the house of a poor white woman who had been a friend to my mother."[51] Another successful fugitive wrote that he "stayed with the poor white people in the mountains."[52] Convinced that "low" or "mean" whites frequently harbored runaways, masters offered extra rewards in many slave runaway advertisements, should a fugitive be found under the care of a white person. Slaveowners looked with revulsion upon those whites willing to conceal a fugitive slave, perhaps masking fears of an interracial alliance against them. As one North Carolina attorney articulated, "[C]harging a man with harboring a runaway negro . . . imputes an act of moral turpitude which subjects a man to indictment and punishment, and degrades him in the eyes of the community."[53] Whites who did "entertain" fugitive bondspeople took a substantial risk. An 1822 North Carolina law penalized anyone convicted of harboring or maintaining a runaway up to $100 in fines and a prison sentence of up to six months. The year before that, South Carolina had passed similar but more severe legislation that allowed for a maximum $1,000 fine and one year's imprisonment.[54]

50. Spotswood Burwell to William A. Burwell, August 3, 1832, Folder 11, Burwell Family Papers, SHC.

51. Parker, *Recollections of Slavery Times*, 82.

52. Peter Bruner, *A Slave's Adventures Toward Freedom: Not Fiction, but the True Story of a Struggle* (Oxford, Ohio: n.p., 1918), 29. Bruner was a slave in Kentucky.

53. *Skinner v. White*, 18 N.C. 471 (1836), 462.

54. *The Laws of North-Carolina, Enacted in the Year 1821* (Raleigh: Thomas Henderson, 1822), 40; David J. McCord, *The Statutes at Large of South Carolina; Edited, Under Authority of the Legislature*, vol. 7 (Columbia: A. S. Johnston, 1840), 460.

The likelihood of poor whites harboring runaways correlated neither to gender, nor age, nor marital or family status. Poor whites accused of sheltering runaways included women such as Elizabeth Blackwell of Spartanburg District, South Carolina, and Elizabeth Copeland of Gates County, North Carolina.[55] Poor white men also seemed willing to assist slaves fleeing their masters. During his travels across the South, Frederick Law Olmsted learned that poor white men living in the Dismal Swamp frequently harbored fugitive slaves.[56] Bordering the Dismal, in Gates County, North Carolina, Thomas Blanchard appeared before the superior court in 1850 for allegedly "harbouring a slave." An illiterate and unemployed man of forty-five with a wife and small family and only $20 worth of land, Blanchard purportedly deprived slaveholder David Parker of the services of his slave Isaac for an entire month.[57] At the Granville County Court of Pleas and Quarter Sessions in 1854, jurors presented two landless white men, William E. and Thomas Norwood, charging them with enticing and persuading "a certain negro slave, named Mason, the property of Edward A. Lewis," to abscond. William E. Norwood was close to forty, did not head his own household, and, as of the 1850 census, held no job. In his midtwenties, Thomas Norwood, by contrast, was just starting out in life as a farmer with a young wife named Mary. The two poor whites allegedly "did maintain & harbor" the runaway slave once they drew him away from his master.[58] Fairfield District, South Carolina, jurors found Rightman and John A. Bagley not guilty in 1848 of harboring and maintaining James Hinkle's runaway slave Bob. Rightman, a propertyless man of eighty-three years, lived alone, although nearby to John, a forty-eight-year-old man with no real estate, a wife, and nine children.[59]

Under certain conditions, some southerners gave a select few poor whites convicted of harboring slaves the benefit of the doubt and rallied to their defense.

55. Spartanburg District, Court of General Sessions, Indictments, Spring 1857, file 2, SCDAH; Eighth Census of the United States, 1860: Spartanburg District, South Carolina, 290; Gates County, Slave Records, n.d., 1783–1867, Criminal Actions Concerning Slaves, n.d., 1803–1861, folder 1844, NCDAH; Sixth Census of the United States, 1840: Gates County, North Carolina, 173; Seventh Census of the United States, 1850: Gates County, North Carolina, 42.

56. Olmsted, *Seaboard Slave States*, 160.

57. Gates County, Slave Records, n.d., 1783–1867, Criminal Actions Concerning Slaves, n.d., 1803–1861, folder 1850, NCDAH; Seventh Census of the United States, 1850: Gates County, North Carolina, 41.

58. Granville County, Criminal Actions Concerning Slaves and Free Persons of Color, 1848–1856, folder 1854, NCDAH; Seventh Census of the United States, 1850: Granville County, 189.

59. Fairfield District, Court of General Sessions, Indictments, file 227, SCDAH; Seventh Census of the United States, 1850: Fairfield District, South Carolina, 287, 284.

Three cases from North Carolina in the early 1830s illustrate the point. In each instance, concerned citizens petitioned Governor Montfort Stokes on behalf of a poor white, asking him to grant a pardon. "[A] number of respectable petitioners" from Pasquotank County begged clemency for William Shaw, "an old & poor man . . . in a low state of health," who had been sentenced to six months in jail for harboring a slave of Exum Newby's.[60] Another memorial expressed concern for "a poor Man by the Name of Stephen Wells now confined in the Goal [*sic*] in Columbus County he was found guilty of harbouring a Negro Woman the property of Josiah Powel within two years past" and sentenced to six months' imprisonment. Thirty-one petitioners prayed the governor "to pitty the poor Man Who has a desent [*sic*] wife and a promising Son about five years old and they are Suffering for want of the labour of Mr. Wells." The signers observed that Wells was "the Son of a honest Man," and that he "was convicted only by the oath of one witness Whoes Name is Braziel Kook and a Suspicious character he swore he seene the Negro one time in Mr. Welses house on a cold Snowey day."[61] Similarly, petitioners for "a very poor man" named Abraham Connor explained that his case "was an extremely doubtful one." Connor was "convicted of the crime of harbouring a runaway negro" belonging to Francis Ingram of South Carolina and sentenced to a $50 fine and three months in jail. Connor, petitioners observed, lived in Rockingham County but went to trial in Stokes, where he was a stranger and his family's character unknown to the jury.[62]

Fifteen and thirteen signers, respectively, of the petitions for Stephen Wells and Abraham Connor may be positively identified in the 1830 census. Eleven of the fifteen petitioners on Wells's behalf were slaveholders. Two owned but one slave apiece; the largest possessed fifteen. The average slaveholder had six slaves to his name. Those who endorsed Connor's pardon were, on average, significantly more wealthy. Of the thirteen who signed his petition, only two were nonslaveholders. The remaining eleven individuals owned from between four and seventy-two slaves, for a total of 229 between them. The average signer, then, officially belonged to the "planter" category, owning more than twenty slaves. For any of a number of reasons—age, health, a family in need, erstwhile respectability, and questionable evidence—some slaveholding as well as nonslaveholding southern whites proved willing to suspend the punishment of a poor white guilty of harboring a runaway. In all three cases, North Carolina's governor pardoned the poor white offenders.

60. Governor's Papers, Gov. Montfort Stokes, vol. 64, 89, NCDAH.
61. Ibid., vol. 63, 439, NCDAH.
62. Ibid., vol. 64, 109, 122, NCDAH.

Not limited simply to harboring runaway slaves, some poor whites actively conveyed them away from their masters. Slaveholders often suspected as much, although most had no definite proof of white complicity. They could make only vague comments, like one Raleigh slaveholder, who expected his slave "has got in with some base white man to take him out of the State." A Johnston County, North Carolina, master warned readers to watch out for "his runaway slave Wilson," who "is now lurking in the neighborhood, with a debased white woman, or with an unprincipled white man, disguised in female apparel."[63]

It must have been both advantageous and reassuring for runaway slaves to have a white person accompany them. Whites could more readily obtain necessary provisions than slaves, provide transportation, pose as the slave's master, or merely offer companionship. During an attempt to escape an exceptionally brutal South Carolina master, runaway slave Moses Roper encountered "a poor man" near Salisbury, North Carolina, who "took me up in his cart." En route to Virginia, the poor white man conducted the fugitive northward to the bondsman's birthplace in Caswell County. Whites also sometimes masqueraded as slaveowners. James Camak, for instance, advertised for "a negro man FREDERICK, . . . an excellent fiddler, and very fond of the company of white people." Frederick was last seen in Greenville District, South Carolina, "riding a small poor horse, his fiddle tied behind him, and in company with a suspicious looking white man, who was on foot, and said that he had bought the negro of me." Camak offered a reward of $20 for the slave, $30 for the white man. The higher reward for the white suggests the seriousness with which masters viewed the carrying off of their slave property.[64]

Poor whites thus engaged in highly ambivalent relations with both slaveholders and slaves. The overwhelming majority of poor whites aided in the control of slaves and helped monitor their behavior, dutifully reporting to masters any transgressions they witnessed. Yet under certain conditions, poor white loyalty shifted away from slaveholders toward the slaves, and poor whites willingly forged passes, harbored fugitives, or conveyed them away. What motivated them to do so?

Some poor whites who aided slaves did so inadvertently as unwitting ac-

---

63. *Raleigh Star and North Carolina Gazette,* July 10, 1834; *North Carolina Standard* (Raleigh), August 19, 1840; both in Parker, *Stealing a Little Freedom,* 502, 863.

64. Moses Roper, *A Narrative of the Adventures and Escape of Moses Roper, from American Slavery; with a Preface, by the Rev. T. Price, D.D.* (London: Darton, Harvey and Darton, 1838; reprint, New York: Negro Universities Press, 1970), 30; *Raleigh Register* (weekly), October 7, 1825.

complices, the victims of slave deception. When a poor white man took fugitive Moses Roper up in his cart, he may not have realized that Roper was a runaway. Prudent fugitives did not freely divulge their circumstances, allowing them to trick poor whites into providing assistance. Poor whites whom slaves knew to be illiterate made especially likely targets. A bondsperson could claim any scrap of paper with scribbles jotted on it was a pass, and, lacking the ability to read and perhaps too proud to admit that weakness, the poor white had to accept the slave's word on it.[65] Occasionally, slaves also had the ability to manipulate whites into conducting them to freedom. A singular case from North Carolina demonstrates that slaves could mastermind their own "kidnapping." In the town of Washington, slave Albert worked as a tailor for Edward C. O. Tinker, alongside Daniel O'Rafferty, a naive young laboring man who "had not been long in this Country." Albert reportedly "enjoyed uncommon privileges and immunity as a Slave and possessed the entire confidence" of O'Rafferty. Some Craven County residents suggested that the literate and artful Albert had brainwashed his white co-worker. O'Rafferty, they claimed, "was greatly under the influence and controul" of Albert. The slave "had repeatedly advised & informed" O'Rafferty that "he was to be free" when their employer Tinker died. That day arrived in 1846. According to the slave, Tinker "declared on his deathbed" that Albert should be emancipated. Apparently unaware that Tinker's uncle John L. Durand of New Bern had purchased Albert shortly before Tinker's death, O'Rafferty did as instructed and conveyed the slave to Goldsboro. Detected and sent to trial, O'Rafferty "was convicted and sentenced to be hung" for carrying Albert away "with the intent and for the purpose of enabling said slave to Effect an Escape." The jury issued its verdict, however, "with their unanimous recommendation" that Governor William A. Graham pardon him. A petition containing 143 signatures from Craven County residents and a letter from Albert's owner both urged the same. Under these unusual circumstances, they agreed, O'Rafferty deserved clemency, and the governor complied with their request.[66]

In some cases, those poor whites who conspired with slaves had befriended them. When his slave Jeff absconded, Jeremiah Cureton of Lancaster District, South Carolina, implicated Jeff's "friend" John Underwood, a white man, for harboring the fugitive and assisting him in the covert, "underhanded" mining

65. Roper, *Narrative of the Adventures and Escape of Moses Roper*, 30; Bruce, *New Man*, 96–97.

66. Governor's Papers, Gov. William A. Graham, G.P. 116, folder December 1846, NCDAH; Governor's Papers, Gov. William A. Graham, G.P. 116, folder November 1846, NCDAH; Gov. William A. Graham, Letter Book, G.L.B. 37, 268, NCDAH. O'Rafferty does not appear in the 1850 North Carolina census. On O'Rafferty, see also Cecil-Fronsman, *Common Whites*, 88.

of gold in neighboring Mecklenburg County, North Carolina. A scandalous and mysterious figure, "John Underwood, at this time, is absent from his family," Cureton related. He "possesses a mean look and is a shoemaker by trade, is fond of spirits and lying in negro kitchens."[67] Poor white outcasts or those living alone, including the elderly and others without families, may have placed particular value on the companionship of slaves. Under circumstances such as these, white assistance represented an act of kindness or camaraderie. Individual poor whites may have at times identified with individual slaves, viewing them as darker-skinned reflections of themselves, brothers and sisters in a fraternity of shared economic deprivation.

Suggestive runaway advertisements imply that a few slave and poor white allies went beyond friendship and may have been lovers. One North Carolina master suspected "a white man, by the name of Tynes," of writing his slave woman a pass. "I have lately discovered," the slaveowner wrote, that Tynes "has had an intercourse and connexion with her for some time." In a potentially similar situation, slave Phil absconded from "Mrs. Warren's in Wake County," North Carolina, "with a base white woman by the name of SALLY POWEL." One North Carolina master believed it no coincidence that his slave Gilbert absconded about the same time that "an idle Girl of the name of Sally Henderson, left this neighborhood." According to the aggrieved slaveholder, "there are strong reasons to believe that she seduced the boy away with her."[68]

More frequently than bonds of affection, economic opportunism motivated poor whites to help bondspeople resist the terms and conditions of their enslavement. Poor whites probably only rarely offered their assistance unconditionally; for the majority, aiding a fugitive slave afforded them the chance to secure a desired product. Fugitive slave John Brown recorded that he "obtained a forged pass

67. *Miners' & Farmers' Journal* (Charlotte), September 14, 1833. See also Jeff Forret, "Slave Labor in North Carolina's Antebellum Gold Mines," *North Carolina Historical Review* 76 (April 1999): 153; and Jeffrey P. Forret, "African Americans and Gold Mining in North Carolina," in *Gold in History, Geology, and Culture: Collected Essays*, ed. Richard F. Knapp and Robert M. Topkins (Raleigh: Division of Archives and History, North Carolina Department of Cultural Resources, 2001), 212. The Fifth Census of the United States, 1830: Lancaster District, South Carolina, 61, identifies John Underwood as a household head between the ages of twenty and twenty-nine, with a wife, also in her twenties, and two children under five.

68. *North Carolina Journal* (Halifax), July 15, 1805; *The North Carolina Minerva and Raleigh Advertiser*, July 9, 1813; and *The North Carolina Minerva and Raleigh Advertiser*, August 31, 1819, all in Parker, *Stealing a Little Freedom*, 81, 116, 123. Sally Powel also appears as Sally Powell in *The Star* (Raleigh), July 9, 1813, in Parker, *Stealing a Little Freedom*, 412.

from a poor white man, for which I gave him an old hen." [69] Virginia master Spotswood Burwell strongly suspected that his former bondsman Tom, whom he had dispatched to the western North Carolina gold-mining region, paid the poor white shopkeeper Griffin for a permit with gold stolen from the slaveholder's son. [70] In cases of slave–poor white cooperation such as these, slaves bargained with poor whites in exchange for free passes, shelter, or other aid. If slaves offered their poor white abettors compensation, by supplying them with food or other useful articles stolen from the master, for example, or by helping them with household chores or farm labor, poor whites benefited from the arrangement every bit as much as the slaves. They recognized an economic opportunity and seized it.

One can readily imagine that poor whites, who could not afford to purchase bondspeople of their own, welcomed the labor of slaves they may have appropriated without the master's permission. This seems especially likely in the case of poor white women trying to raise families by themselves, without a male provider. Poor white women who harbored fugitive slaves typically headed households of their own, with any number of children but no resident adult male. A jury in Spartanburg District, South Carolina, convicted Elizabeth Blackwell in March 1857 because she "did unlawfully wilfully and knowingly harbor, conceal, and entertain" a runaway slave named Andy "for a long space of time," from mid-December 1856 to mid-February 1857. In her late thirties, the illiterate Blackwell owned neither real nor personal estate, and struggled to support four girls between the ages of four and sixteen. Nevertheless, the jury sentenced her to one month in jail. [71] In Gates County, North Carolina, Elizabeth Copeland stood accused in 1844 of harboring and maintaining a runaway slave belonging to George W. Granbery. Like Blackwell, Copeland also likely led a hard life. In 1840, at about the age of thirty, she headed a household of her own, raising four girls, the youngest under five, the oldest between fifteen and nineteen. The 1850 census listed her as forty years old and illiterate, with three teenage daughters but no occupation or real estate. Unusual in Copeland's case was that the fugitive she allegedly harbored was not a man, as were the overwhelming majority of slave

69. L. A. Chamerovzow, ed., *Slave Life in Georgia: A Narrative of the Life, Sufferings, and Escape of John Brown, a Fugitive Slave, Now in England* (London: n.p., 1855), 72.

70. Spotswood Burwell to William A. Burwell, July 31, 1832, Folder 10, Burwell Family Papers, SHC.

71. Spartanburg District, Court of General Sessions, Indictments, Spring 1857, file 2, SCDAH; Eighth Census of the United States, 1860: Spartanburg District, South Carolina, 290.

runaways, but a woman named Martha.[72] Any speculation about the motivations of these poor white women demands caution, as neither of them speak for themselves in surviving court records. Blackwell and Copeland may have sympathized with the slaves or counted them as friends. But it seems almost certain that they would have appreciated any infusion of extra hands around their busy households.

In addition to harboring and concealing, slave stealing marked yet another category of poor white behavior that planters considered subversive. Based on available court records, the minute fraction of poor whites who engaged in this crime almost always did it for economic gain. Most often, they kidnapped slaves to appropriate the unfree laborers for their own use, to collect reward money, or to profit by selling the fugitives to others. Whatever the reason, as the most egregious violation of property rights in a slaveholding society, slave stealing brought the harshest penalties. Legislators in North Carolina made slave stealing a felony punishable by death without the benefit of clergy in 1779.[73] In South Carolina, kidnapping a slave carried the death penalty after 1754.[74] A conviction for slave stealing in Virginia brought a relatively mild two to ten years in the penitentiary.[75] These punishments made the abduction of slaves a high-stakes activity. The financial rewards proved great, but so did the risk.

For some poor whites, slave stealing was a scam, the first step in an artful con game. After abducting a slave, the poor white waited patiently until the master advertised a reward, then produced the hostage and collected the money. No

72. Gates County, Slave Records, n.d., 1783–1867, Criminal Actions Concerning Slaves, n.d., 1803–1861, folder 1844, NCDAH; Sixth Census of the United States, 1840: Gates County, North Carolina, 173; Seventh Census of the United States, 1850: Gates County, North Carolina, 42.

73. Parker, *Running for Freedom*, 49. According to the *Laws of the State of North Carolina, Passed By the General Assembly, at the Session of 1852* (Raleigh: Wesley Whitaker, Jr., 1853), 160, anyone "who shall steal, or by violence, seduction or any other means, take or convey away any slave or slaves, the property of another, with an intention to sell or dispose of to another, or appropriate to his, her or their own use . . . shall be deemed guilty of felony, and, upon conviction thereof, shall suffer *death* without the benefit of clergy." An 1825 law strictly forbade ship masters, mariners, and sailors from stealing or concealing slaves aboard vessels, or suffer the death penalty. See *Acts Passed By the General Assembly of the State of North Carolina, At Its Session, Commencing on the 21st of Nov. 1825* (Raleigh: Bell & Lawrence, 1826), 13–14.

74. Jack Kenny Williams, *Vogues in Villainy: Crime and Retribution in Ante-Bellum South Carolina* (Columbia: University of South Carolina Press, 1959), 43.

75. *Acts of the General Assembly of Virginia* (Richmond: Samuel Shepherd, 1848), 101, 102. At Richmond Circuit Court, one man found guilty of slave stealing received a sentence of six years in the penitentiary. See *Richmond Enquirer*, April 14, 1857.

poor white could have implemented this scheme on such a scale as to make a living by it, but it could supply some welcome extra cash. Moses Dean's story provides the best example of this technique. Approximately thirty-seven years old in 1851, the landless Dean lived in Guilford County and appears in the sources as a "laborer" and an "insolvent" person. His failure to profit from the kidnapping of a slave guaranteed the preservation of his story in North Carolina court records. In October 1850, slave Lewis ran away from the Anson County plantation of Philip G. Smith. Two white men, James White and James Brown, apprehended Lewis in Guilford County the following January. They "were makeing arrangements to carry him to jail in Greensboro," when Moses Dean "passed by the house where they were, with his wagon." Since White and Brown "had no vehicle to carry the negro to jail in," they asked to borrow Dean's wagon. Dean consented to transport the two men and the slave to Greensboro "for the sum of one dollar and fifty cents." During the trip, it occurred to Dean that he was squandering an opportunity to make far more money. Dean proposed to his traveling companions that they "turn back with the slave and keep him until a reward should be offered." Furthermore, Dean reasoned, "the weather [was] very cold" and "his horse was worried." The two other white men dissented, and proceeded according to their original plan. Passing a roadside inn or tavern, Dean proposed that the party stop "to get liquor." White and Brown went inside to procure the spirits, while Dean drove with slave Lewis in the wagon "about seventy five yards beyond the house" and stopped. White and Brown soon returned to the wagon with the liquor, and "they all drank together," but it seems likely Dean hatched a plan with Lewis during their absence. Dean renewed his complaint that "his horse was too much fatigued to proceed" and offered "to take the negro and keep him for a few days in a vacant house of his in order to give time for a reward to be offered." Once Lewis's master advertised a reward, Dean pledged to take the slave to jail. White and Brown grudgingly assented to this plan, and subsequently spread a fabricated story of Lewis's escape.[76]

But dissent grew among the plotters. With the help of fellow "laborer" Abram M. Weaver, Moses Dean had hidden Lewis in an undisclosed location. When White later confronted Dean, Dean said he expected to go see Lewis but vowed to "shoot any one whom he should discover watching him." At their next encounter, Dean explained that Weaver "had taken the negro off where no one could get him." Brown then threatened to go public with the men's plot, to which

76. *State v. Moses Dean*, 35 N.C. 63 (1851), Supreme Court Original Case 6985; Seventh Census of the United States, 1850: Guilford County, North Carolina, 411.

Dean replied that White and Brown "alone had been seen with the slave." No one knew of Dean's involvement at all. Court records do not make plain the details, but eventually, authorities arrested all three men for slave stealing and lodged them in the same Greensboro jail for which Lewis had been destined. After suffering to listen to White and Brown criticize him in jail, Dean decided to take full responsibility for the abduction. Court proceedings revealed that Weaver had taken slave Lewis to Virginia with a horse matching the description of Dean's. Two witnesses also spotted Dean and Weaver at an election, "walk[ing] off together" in close conversation. A North Carolina official recovered Lewis in Tazewell County, Virginia, and there arrested Weaver, who confessed that he had conveyed the slave to Virginia as Dean's "agent." Lewis's master picked up his runaway slave from a Virginia jail in May 1851, but a Guilford County court found Dean guilty of slave stealing and sentenced him to hang in November of the same year. With no evidence to the contrary, Dean likely was executed as scheduled.[77]

Not content simply to collect oftentimes paltry monetary rewards, some poor whites charged with kidnapping slaves had attempted to sell apprehended runaways like Lewis as their own. This marked a more profitable way for the poor white to utilize the bondsperson. Along with four others, the landless and illiterate Benjamin Mechum captured slave George, who had run away from his Salisbury, North Carolina, master, in 1857. At Danville, Virginia, the five white men appointed Mechum to carry the slave to Richmond, sell him, and then return to divide the proceeds among the group.[78] On the railroad cars, Mechum "claimed the servant as his property" and "said he came in possession of him at the death of his father." He maintained "that he was on his way to Richmond to learn the trade of painter," but doubtless intended to head to the slave auction there, the South's second largest, to dispose of George.[79]

A few particularly bold poor whites kidnapped slaves directly off the planta-

77. *State v. Moses Dean*, 35 N.C. 63 (1851), Supreme Court Original Case 6985.

78. *Richmond Whig*, reprinted in *Richmond Enquirer*, May 1, 1857. The Seventh Census of the United States, 1850: Anson County, North Carolina, 222, lists a Benjamin Meacham as a twenty-four-year-old illiterate farmer with no real estate, recently married to a twenty-year-old woman named Prudence. They had an unnamed three-month-old girl. The Eighth Census of the United States, 1860: Anson County, North Carolina, 585, lists a Benjamin Meacham as a thirty-five-year-old illiterate overseer with no real or personal estate. He lived with Emeline, thirty-two, and three children, ages six, four, and two. These individuals may well not be the same person, but both qualify as poor whites.

79. *Richmond Dispatch*, reprinted in *Richmond Enquirer*, May 1, 1857.

tion with the intention of reselling them on the sly and turning a quick profit for themselves. These poor whites must be distinguished from slave traders, however. Slave trading was a full-time profession, one that required an ample supply of money to buy slaves at auction and to traverse the South in search of buyers or other markets. Many masters found slave traders' character as objectionable as that of poor whites,[80] but unlike slave traders, poor whites who stole slaves were simply opportunists. Their occasional clandestine trafficking in stolen slaves offered them not a livelihood but a chance to make a few extra dollars. The typical poor white slave stealer, a man in his twenties or thirties struggling to support an extensive family, needed to gain whatever supplemental income he could. In 1821, for instance, North Carolina nonslaveholder Willis Edge, a self-described "poor and friendless" man heading a household of seven, allegedly stole "with force and arms in Hertford County one Negro Man Slave, named Archer," worth $100, as well as a slave named Sampson and a slave woman. The bill of indictment against him charged that Edge "did . . . feloniously take by seduction carry and convey away with intention . . . to sell and dispose of" the bondspeople.[81]

The number of cases of poor whites stealing slaves increased in the 1850s as slave prices skyrocketed. A Richmond County, North Carolina, slaveholder accused landless laborer John McQueen of stealing "negro woman" Olive and her two children in 1855, with the intent of selling them.[82] In Stanly County, Eben Herne reported in November 1858 that he saw David Perry, a landless man about forty years of age, "passing through the streets of Albemarle, with two likely negro men, tolerably black." When questioned, Perry claimed the slaves as his own, saying that he purchased them in Robeson County and planned to resell one of them—"a good mechanic"—in Salisbury. Nine days later, Perry told Herne a conflicting story, claiming that "an old gentleman in the lower part of Robeson County" had requested Perry hire out the two slaves for him. Suspicions raised, Herne consulted the authorities, who arrested Perry, charging him with "kidnaping or secretly Runing slaves and holden them unlawfully."[83]

80. D. R. Hundley, *Social Relations in Our Southern States* (New York: Henry B. Price, 1860; reprint, New York: Arno Press, 1973), 139.

81. Chowan County, Slave Records, Criminal Actions Concerning Slaves, 1767–1829, folder 1823, NCDAH; Fifth Census of the United States, 1830: Bladen County, North Carolina, 87.

82. Richmond County, Slave Records, 1778–1866, Criminal Action Papers Concerning Slaves, 1850–1866, folder 1854–1857, NCDAH; Seventh Census of the United States, 1850: Richmond County, North Carolina, 292. McQueen's partner in crime, William Melton, does not appear in the census records.

83. Stanly County, Records of Slaves and Free Persons of Color, 183–1868, folder 1851–1854, 1856–1859, NCDAH; Seventh Census of the United States, 1850: Stanly County, North Carolina, 27.

*   *   *

Though probably the most significant reason that poor whites aided or stole slaves, profiteering did not motivate all such subversive behaviors. Some poor whites helped slaves despite anticipating no material benefit for themselves. They sometimes viewed assisting slaves as a channel through which to take vengeance upon a certain master. Many poor whites resented the way in which planters lorded over southern society and humiliated lower-class whites. They therefore sometimes assisted runaways or stole slaves to redress a perceived grievance against a particular slaveholder. By depriving masters of their slaves' services, poor whites enjoyed a potent form of revenge—a nonviolent "Snopesian crime" —against slaveholders they considered excessively haughty, condescending, or uncharitable toward their less fortunate neighbors. Some efforts to aid runaways surely evinced the animus that some poor whites felt toward slaveholders.[84]

Poor whites also possessed legitimate, practical reasons of their own to oppose slavery. Some held strong convictions against the institution because they resented competition with slave labor. Although court records painted the young immigrant O'Rafferty as the unwitting dupe of the exceptionally clever slave Albert, O'Rafferty, like poor whites across the South, may be easily imagined to have opposed slavery in his own right for the competition it produced for work. Poor immigrants to the United States generally gravitated more toward the North than the South. With its more rapidly expanding industrial sector, the North offered greater employment opportunities. Moreover, the presence of slavery in the South repelled foreigners from the region. Most of the relatively few immigrants who made the South their home did not agree with its organizing social principles. Immigrants valued the right to control one's own labor and viewed slavery as a threat to their own freedom. They believed competition with slave labor undermined their own ability to make a decent living and degraded white workers. Immigrant laborers loathed comparisons to black slaves or accusations that they performed "nigger work." In short, the antislavery sentiments and traditions that foreign newcomers brought with them from Europe did not mesh well with the southern social structure. Native-born poor whites often shared these identical sentiments.[85]

---

84. Wyatt-Brown, "Snopesian Crime."

85. Bailey, *Class and Tennessee's Confederate Generation*, 73; *Richmond Enquirer*, May 4, 1832; Ira Berlin and Herbert G. Gutman, "Natives and Immigrants, Free Men and Slaves: Urban Workingmen in the Antebellum South," *American Historical Review* 88 (December 1983): 1176–1177, 1189, 1194–1198; Randall M. Miller, "The Enemy Within: Some Effects of Foreign Immigrants on Antebellum Southern Cities," *Southern Studies* 24 (Spring 1985): esp. 32–34. On the Irish helping slaves

Probably only a tiny fraction of those poor whites who aided slave runaways engaged in conscious efforts to subvert a slave regime that they opposed on moral or ideological grounds. Those poor whites who did so gave themselves an outlet through which to express their convictions. Determining which poor whites helped runaways or stole bondspeople for the purpose of attacking slavery or the slave system in general proved difficult for contemporaries, however, much less historians. Slaveholder Josiah Crudup of Granville County, North Carolina, was not entirely sure why a mysterious peddler who had "befriended" his "negro man named GID" carried away the bondsman. According to Crudup, the peddler "may be taking him off clandestinely to sell him in some of the Western or Southern States, or be taking him to some free State."[86] Historians have made clear that abolitionists lacked a smooth-running, secret network to whisk slaves off to Canada; slaves themselves were the most active agents in obtaining their freedom. To the extent that an "underground railroad" did exist, scholarship has shown that Quakers and northern abolitionists were the whites most likely to be involved.[87] Nevertheless, very rare glimpses survive of poor whites apparently helping runaways or stealing slaves to liberate them from bondage. In August 1859, authorities in Lunenburg County, Virginia, arrested an illiterate poor white man named May George, who had in his possession "two negro boys" belonging to one of George's slaveholding neighbors in Wake County, North Carolina. According to newspaper accounts, George "was endeavoring to convey [them] to the North via the 'underground railroad.'"[88]

The only offense a poor white could commit that alarmed masters more than slave stealing was joining with bondspeople in outright rebellion.[89] Slaveholders

---

run off, see Ira Berlin, *Slaves without Masters: The Free Negro in the Antebellum South* (New York: Pantheon Books, 1974), 43–44, 263.

86. *Richmond Enquirer,* June 28, 1836. See also *North Carolina Standard* (Raleigh), June 30, 1836, in Parker, *Stealing a Little Freedom,* 859.

87. Larry Gara, *The Liberty Line: The Legend of the Underground Railroad* (1961; Lexington: University Press of Kentucky, 1996), 18.

88. *Richmond Enquirer,* August 19, 1859. The Seventh Census of the United States, 1850: Wake County, North Carolina, 224, lists May George as thirty-eight years old, illiterate, with no occupation and only $30 in real estate, married, with three children. For reasons not entirely clear, George appears twice in the 1860 census, once as a fifty-year-old illiterate day laborer and convict, with no real or personal estate, married and with two children, another time as a fifty-five-year-old farmer in jail for kidnapping. See Eighth Census of the United States, 1860: Wake County, North Carolina, 161, 354.

89. Books and articles recognizing white involvement in slave rebellions or conspiracies include James Hugo Johnston, "The Participation of White Men in Virginia Negro Insurrections," *Journal of Negro History* 16 (April 1931): 161; Harvey Wish, "American Slave Insurrections Before 1861," *Journal*

in the antebellum South looked with suspicion upon anyone without ties to the local community, who might attempt to undermine the institution of slavery. They carefully scrutinized northern travelers, itinerants, peddlers, gamblers, and steam doctors (medical quacks who practiced hydrotherapy)—all possible abolitionists in disguise. But slaveholders need not search beyond their own communities, or even neighbors, to find potential threats to the slave regime. Poor whites, although indigenous to the South, counted among those social "outsiders" whose presence demanded wariness and vigilance.

Historians have noted that throughout American history, slaves and whites (poor whites in particular) occasionally acted in concert, participating together in rebellious actions and conspiracies.[90] As early as Bacon's Rebellion of 1676, a "giddy multitude" of white indentured servants and landless freemen joined forces with black slaves in Virginia to express their grievances.[91] Many in the upper ranks of southern society feared that common interests could unite slaves and lower-class whites in rebellion. Indeed, some discontented slaves did see poor whites as potential allies in their struggle against slavery as an institution.[92] Slave autobiographer Henry Bibb, for one, felt certain that the "class of poor white people in the South . . . would be glad to see slavery abolished in self defence . . . because it is impoverishing and degrading to them and their children."[93] Pru-

of Negro History 22 (July 1937): 316–317, 320; Wish, "The Slave Insurrection Panic of 1856," *Journal of Southern History* 5 (May 1939): 210, 218, 220; Aptheker, *American Negro Slave Revolts;* Davidson Burns McKibben, "Negro Slave Insurrections in Mississippi," *Journal of Negro History* 34 (January 1949): 76–78, 79; Edwin A. Miles, "The Mississippi Slave Insurrection Scare of 1835," *Journal of Negro History* 42 (January 1957): 50–51, 60; Jeffrey J. Crow, "Slave Rebelliousness and Social Conflict in North Carolina, 1775–1802," *William & Mary Quarterly* 3d ser., 37 (January 1980), 85; Laurence Shore, "Making Mississippi Safe for Slavery: The Insurrectionary Panic of 1835," in *Class, Conflict, and Consensus: Antebellum Southern Community Studies,* ed. Orville Vernon Burton and Robert C. McMath, Jr. (Westport, Conn.: Greenwood Press, 1982), 96–98, 103, 111–112, 119; Christopher Morris, "An Event in Community Organization: The Mississippi Slave Insurrection Scare of 1835," *Journal of Social History* 22 (Fall 1988): 99; and Douglass R. Egerton, *Gabriel's Rebellion: The Virginia Slave Conspiracies of 1800 and 1802* (Chapel Hill: University of North Carolina Press, 1993), 182–185.

90. See, for example, Johnston, "Participation of White Men," 161; Aptheker, *American Negro Slave Revolts,* 79, 163, 327, 349, 373; and Robert S. Starobin, ed., *Letters of American Slaves* (New York: New Viewpoints, 1974), 124.

91. Edmund S. Morgan, *American Slavery, American Freedom: The Ordeal of Colonial Virginia* (New York: W. W. Norton & Company, 1975). See Aptheker, *American Negro Slave Revolts,* 165, for an earlier but less famous instance of white indentured servants and black slaves conspiring together to rebel against their masters.

92. Aptheker, *American Negro Slave Revolts,* 225; Starobin, *Letters of American Slaves,* 124.

93. *Narrative of the Life and Adventures of Henry Bibb, an American Slave, Written by Himself with an Introduction by Lucius C. Matlack* (New York: published by the author, 1849), 24–25.

dently, slaves remained wary, for the color line separating them from poor whites militated against absolute trust. Any participant welcomed into confidence could betray their plot to authorities at will, and bring death upon the conspirators. Though slaves and many poor whites proved virtually indistinguishable economically, the racial divide made any alliance between them tenuous at best. Nevertheless, slaves sometimes anticipated or hoped for poor white assistance, and a few, mostly anonymous poor whites, united with them in their bids to overturn the social order. Actual slave uprisings proved extremely rare in the antebellum South, however, and one should be careful not to overestimate poor white involvement in them. The evidentiary base for poor white complicity in antebellum slave plots and revolts is remarkably thin. Slaveholders' exaggerated fears of poor white support for slave rebellions were wildly disproportional to the tiny number of actual incidents of joint revolutionary action. Their acute concern over such interracial cooperation underscored the latent class tensions that underlay social relations in the antebellum South.

In each of the most famous slave conspiracies and rebellions of the nineteenth century, including those of Gabriel, Denmark Vesey, and Nat Turner, slaves either predicted that poor whites would side with them or received encouragement or assistance from them. In the summer of 1800, Gabriel, a slave artisan belonging to Thomas Prosser of Henrico County, Virginia, conspired to kill his master and neighboring whites, obtain arms, and seize the city of Richmond. According to the testimony of slave Ben, "[A]ll the whites were to be massacred, except the Quakers, the Methodists, and the Frenchmen," whom the slaves deemed "friendly to liberty." The planned bloodbath would also "spare all the poor white women who had no slaves." Two unnamed white Frenchmen had purportedly cast their lot with Gabriel, who "expected the poor white people would also join him." Originating in Gabriel's plot of 1800, the Easter slave conspiracy of 1802 marked a joint effort of slaves in Virginia and North Carolina. Implicated in the plot, slave Lewis confessed that Arthur, a bondsman belonging to William Farrer of Goochland County, Virginia, had allied himself with blacks, mulattoes, and the "common men of poor white people." Arthur reportedly said of the conspiracy that "all of the free blacks and a great number of poor white people were to join in it."[94]

94. H. W. Flournoy, ed., *Calendar of Virginia State Papers*, vol. 9 (1890; reprint, New York: Kraus Reprint Corporation, 1968), 152, 164, 299, 301. See also Starobin, *Letters of American Slaves*, 126, 130, 134; Johnston, "Participation of White Men," 161; and Aptheker, *American Negro Slave Revolts*, 233–234. On the Frenchmen, see Egerton, *Gabriel's Rebellion*, 182–185. Egerton states that the slaves spared poor white women from the planned 1800 massacre for reasons of class. The exclusion in no way rep-

During the alleged Denmark Vesey conspiracy of 1822 (the subject of a recent historical controversy), Charleston, South Carolina, authorities tried four white men for "inciting slaves to insurrection." None of these men had helped plan or engage in any rebellion, but a court did find them guilty of encouraging slaves to rise up. Three of the offenders were poor, European immigrants, victims of southern xenophobia: a Scottish sailor, a Spanish seaman, and a German peddler. The other white man was native-born shopkeeper and alleged swindler and counterfeiter Andrew S. Rhodes, the same individual whose dwelling would later be disassembled by neighbors irate over his frequent trading with local slaves. Rhodes reportedly had expressed his opinion to three free black men that "the negroes ought to fight for their liberty." All of those convicted received between three and twelve months in jail and fines ranging from $100 to $1,000, but they nevertheless heightened slaveholding South Carolinians' fears of interracial solidarity. In response, the state legislature passed a law in December 1822 that stiffened the penalties for such collaboration. The revised statute held that any individuals convicted of "counsel[ing], aid[ing], or hir[ing], any slave or slaves, free negroes, or persons of color, to raise a rebellion or insurrection within this State, whether any rebellion or insurrection do actually take place or not, . . . shall be adjudged felons, and suffer death without benefit of clergy."[95]

During Nat Turner's bloody 1831 insurrection in southside Virginia, early reports implicated "*three white men*" among the "marauders." A North Carolina

---

resented proof of white men's sexualized racial fears (200). On the 1802 conspiracy, see Douglas R. Egerton, "'Fly across the River': The Easter Slave Conspiracy of 1802," *North Carolina Historical Review* 68 (April 1991): 87–110; Egerton, *Gabriel's Rebellion;* and John Scott Strickland, "The Great Revival and Insurrectionary Fears in North Carolina: An Examination of Antebellum Southern Society and Slave Revolt Panics," in *Class, Conflict, and Consensus: Antebellum Southern Community Studies,* ed. Orville Vernon Burton and Robert C. McMath, Jr. (Westport, Conn.: Greenwood Press, 1982), 57–95.

95. Lionel H. Kennedy and Thomas Parker, *An Official Report of the Trials of Sundry Negroes, Charged with an Attempt to Raise an Insurrection in the State of South-Carolina: Preceded by an Introduction and Narrative; and in an Appendix, a Report of the Trials of Four White Persons, on Indictments for Attempting to Excite the Slaves to Insurrection* (Charleston: James R. Schenck, 1822), i, viii. See also Robert S. Starobin, ed., *Denmark Vesey: The Slave Conspiracy of 1822* (Englewood Cliffs, N.J.: Prentice-Hall, Inc., 1970), 4, 151; and Edward A. Pearson, ed., *Designs against Charleston: The Trial Record of the Denmark Vesey Slave Conspiracy of 1822* (Chapel Hill: University of North Carolina Press, 1999), 147. On the recent controversy over whether the Vesey conspiracy actually existed or was simply the product of wildly imaginative white minds, see Michael P. Johnson, "Denmark Vesey and His Co-Conspirators," *William & Mary Quarterly* 3d ser., 58 (October 2001): 915–976, and the second part of "The Making of a Slave Conspiracy" forum in *William & Mary Quarterly* 3d ser., 59 (January 2002).

newspaper reported "that one *white* man, at least, was found amongst the dead conspirators, disguised and blackened as a negro."[96] The turmoil surrounding the massacre produced wild rumors and exaggerations, however, and no solid evidence confirms these accounts. Nevertheless, in the wake of the Turner insurrection, anxious and sensitized whites detected numerous plots, both real and imagined, that did involve whites. In North Carolina's Sampson and Duplin counties, for example, "rascally whites" purportedly assisted rebellious slaves.[97] More compelling, in Chesterfield County, Virginia, a self-described poor white named Williamson Mann wrote a letter to a slave suggesting that poor whites were willing to ally themselves with bondspeople in an upcoming rebellion. According to the letter, Mann had corresponded with slaves in Norfolk, Amelia, Nottoway, and several other Virginia counties, directing "how they must act in getting their liberation they must set afire to the city [of Richmond] begin[n]ing at Shokoe Hill then going through east west north south Set fire to the birdges [*sic*]." Under the guidance of "a methodist of the name edmonds," slaves were instructed to set another town ablaze at the same time.[98] As Mann explained to his black co-conspirator, "[E]very white in this place is sceared [*sic*] to death except myself & a few others." He ended his intriguing missive urging, "[P]ush on boys push on."[99]

Very fragmentary evidence suggests that these few poor white conspirators recognized the injury the system of slavery did to themselves. Some thought, for instance, that slavery denied them opportunities for work. Regarding the slave–poor white plot in Chesterfield County, Williamson Mann explained, "I do wish they may succeed by so doing we poor whites can get work as well as slaves or collord."[100] Whereas Mann implied that slavery kept poor whites at society's economic margins, other poor whites believed the peculiar institution responsible for frustrating their innermost dreams. George Boxley of Virginia offers one example. Boxley, though "a man generally thought to be in desperate circumstances" and "with no great respectability of character," possessed a "restless and aspiring mind; wild and visionary in his theories, and ardent in pursuit of his

---

96. *Norfolk Herald*, reprinted in *Richmond Enquirer*, August 30, 1831; Robert N. Elliott, "The Nat Turner Insurrection as Reported in the North Carolina Press," *North Carolina Historical Review* 38 (January 1961), 6.

97. Quoted in Aptheker, *American Negro Slave Revolts*, 304.

98. Quoted in Johnston, "Participation of White Men," 163.

99. Quoted in ibid., 164.

100. Quoted in ibid., 163.

designs." Slaveholding society, he believed, had denied him both a seat in the state legislature and an important military appointment during the War of 1812. Boxley accused the gentry of looking down upon him as too poor and unworthy of such high-ranking positions.[101] According to one source, "These repeated disappointments seem to have imbittered his mind. On many occasions he has declared that the distinctions between the rich and poor was too great; that offices were given rather to wealth than to merit; and seemed to be an advocate for a leveling system of government." Soon, Boxley began to proclaim publicly his belief that slaves should be set free. He betrayed no conviction that black people were his social equals, but to spite the social system that had stymied his ambitions, he began to conspire with slaves. Boxley "kept a shop for selling whiskey, and some articles of merchandize" in Spotsylvania County, Virginia.[102] Slaves gathered there to hatch a plot of rebellion with Boxley and "to consult with him about the means of obtaining their freedom by force of arms" sometime in June or July 1816. The conspirators had reportedly decided to assemble, "on horse back," near Boxley's, "armed with Scythes or any other weapons they could lay their hands on," then proceed to Fredericksburg. They would seize that city, then move on to Richmond and take control of the armory there.[103] The sense that slaveholders somehow kept poor whites in their degraded condition was evident elsewhere, too. In 1860, one resident observed of an Alabama rebellion that "the instigators of the insurrection were found to be the low-down, or poor, whites of the country," who along with the slaves demanded the redistribution of "the land, mules, and money."[104]

While the realization that slavery in many ways harmed poor whites surely motivated some to assist rebellious slaves, admittedly scant evidence suggests that at least a few poor whites genuinely held a revolutionary belief in the equality of the races. In 1821, an informant overheard an "elderly white man with red whiskers"—"a gardener in or about Richmond"—whispering with "an old tall and very black negro man who walked lame." Both were known to sell vegetables and produce at the local market. The two allegedly "set up all night talking," the white man intimating to his black acquaintance his belief "that they were all of Adams race or words to that purport & that you all ought to be free."[105] In an-

101. Quoted in ibid., 166.
102. Quoted in ibid., 167.
103. Quoted in ibid., 166.
104. Quoted in Aptheker, *American Negro Slave Revolts,* 357.
105. Quoted in Johnston, "Participation of White Men," 162.

other case, one of the European immigrants accused of inciting rebellion during the purported Vesey conspiracy confessed that "though he had a white face, he was a negro in heart." [106]

Such sentiments proved drastically aberrant among poor whites, however. During the very same slave conspiracies and rebellions in which some poor whites aided slaves, others informed on them. Slaves in the Easter conspiracy of 1802 sought out possible allies in poor whites, but one liquored-up poor white man named Jarvis singled out a slave "of bad character" named Will, who he contended was among the "sons of bitches" conspiring to rebel. [107] While planning the Turner insurrection with his compatriots, slave Nat quickly changed the subject when he detected poor whites eavesdropping on their meetings. [108] Early on, as many as three whites were reported to have participated in the massacre, but afterwards, "country bullies and the poor whites" participated in searching the homes of blacks for anything suspicious. "It was a grand opportunity for the low whites," wrote famous North Carolina fugitive Harriet Jacobs, "who had no negroes of their own to scourge. They exulted in such a chance to exercise a little brief authority." [109] That poor whites straddled the line between friend and enemy mandated that slaves exercise extreme discretion when deciding which ones to trust.

Poor whites took their chances, too, when they agreed to help slaves. Though unable to testify against whites in court, slaves could inform masters about poor whites who consorted with them. To escape a whipping in December 1860, a slave named Dave, near Rock Hill, South Carolina, proposed "to disclose a matter of great interest to the community." Dave revealed that a son of the local Pugh family, "long suspected of trafficking with negroes," "was engaged in training the negroes of the country, to the art of loading and shooting guns." The Pughs had previously been expelled from Chester District for associating with slaves, and in the tense atmosphere of secession, respectable whites had little patience for such shenanigans. According to Dave, Pugh allegedly vowed to help slaves "kill the men who were at home, the old women, and the children, divide the property[,] and the negroes should have their choice of the young for wives." The night fol-

106. Kennedy and Parker, *Official Report,* iv. See also Starobin, *Denmark Vesey,* 4.

107. Egerton, "Fly across the River," 102–103.

108. Marion Wilson Starling, *The Slave Narrative: Its Place in American History* (Boston: G. K. Hall and Co., 1981), 98.

109. Harriet (Brent) Jacobs, *Incidents in the Life of a Slave Girl,* ed. L. Maria Child (1861; reprint, Detroit: Negro History Press, 1969), 97–98.

lowing this startling confession, a company of whites, two of whom had "blacked themselves," converged on Pugh's house. The whites ordered Dave in, hoping to find incriminating evidence against Pugh. Before long, they saw Pugh, brandishing a gun, exclaiming to Dave, "You damned rascal I mean to punish you for betraying me." The slave informant bolted from the house but took a shot in the thigh. The company of whites came out of hiding and arrested three members of the Pugh household, "the old man and his two sons." Rather than sentencing them to hang, the twelve citizens who sat at the examination of the Pughs "agreed to shave one half of the head, give each fifty stripes, dispose of their property, give them the proceeds and send them out of the country."[110]

A clear majority of all southern poor whites made no attempt to provide assistance to slave runaways and rebels. Those scattered, infrequent instances of collaborative slave–poor white resistance to planter authority suggest that the poor whites involved were only very rarely committed ideologically to the overthrow of slavery. And none can be shown to have forged direct ties with the northern abolitionist movement. Slave rebellions and conspiracies produced no overwhelming evidence to support the notion of an incipient, biracial, lower-class consciousness in the Old South. Poor whites cooperated with slaves far less often to subvert or overturn the social order than for pecuniary gain or some other less revolutionary end. Indeed, conducting an investigation into the events surrounding the purported Vesey conspiracy of 1822, slaveholders presumed that poor whites would merely take advantage of the anticipated chaos to pilfer money and loot from their social superiors. South Carolina authorities believed that the four "white men of the lowest characters" convicted of inciting slaves to revolt during the unrest "determined to avail themselves of the occasion, and by exciting the slaves, to hasten an event . . . they vainly imagined might be beneficial to themselves." Charleston was a city filled with "desperate men," they acknowledged, "who hold themselves in readiness at a moment's warning, to engage in any enterprise of blood and ruin, from which plunder may be gained."[111] Put another way, the vast preponderance of poor whites cultivated contacts with bondspeople to pursue material gain, not to help insurgent slaves undermine the southern social structure. Combined with the fact that many poor whites fig-

110. A. Whyte to ? December 29, 1860, Folder 115, Springs Family Papers #4121, SHC. According to this letter, the Pughs owned approximately $300 in land, three slaves, and "some Bags of Cotton." Though objectively yeomen, their behavior suggests that they qualify as poor whites.

111. Kennedy and Parker, *Official Report*, i, ii. See also Starobin, *Denmark Vesey*, 57–58.

ured prominently in suppressing episodes of slave resistance, slaveholders might have congratulated themselves on their ability to maintain hegemony in the Old South.

But masters could not be absolutely confident of poor white commitment to the southern social order. Slave–poor white conspiracies in every southern state preceding and during the Civil War fueled slaveholder doubts.[112] Across the South, there were poor whites who identified with slaves and apparently recognized that, despite skin color, their condition differed little from that of enslaved blacks. For any number of reasons, a small percentage of poor whites saw fit to write passes for slaves, harbor them, steal them away from their masters, or, in very rare cases, join them in rebellion. To slaveholders' consternation, these were members of the very same poor white class upon whom masters depended, as overseers, patrollers, and slave catchers, to keep slaves in check. To be sure, most poor whites proved dependable and submissive neighbors, but some took actions counter to the slaveholding interest, calling into question the allegiance of the entire class. Poor whites could easily erect a facade of trustworthiness and subservience that obscured their simultaneous, surreptitious intriguing with slaves. Nothing prevented poor whites, who as overseers, patrollers, or slave hunters served as the agents of slaveholders, from cooperating with particular slaves, whether out of sincere friendship, simple opportunism, or other motive. Those poor whites who assisted individual slaves, however, did not necessarily consider themselves enemies of the system, any more than they thought of their work for slaveholders as an explicit endorsement of slavery. Poor whites, in short, engaged in a range of partially contradictory and partially overlapping behaviors, none of which necessarily required any self-conscious ideological commitment to or against the southern social structure. The elusive and unpredictable nature of poor white loyalty kept slaveholders in a chronic state of confusion and anxiety.

112. Aptheker, *American Negro Slave Revolts*, 360, 363–367; Winthrop D. Jordan, *Tumult and Silence at Second Creek: An Inquiry into a Civil War Slave Conspiracy*, rev. ed. (Baton Rouge: Louisiana State University Press, 1995).

CHAPTER 4

A MASCULINE SUBCULTURE
OF VIOLENCE

More often than not, slaves and poor whites in the antebellum South coexisted peacefully, at times even amiably, but violence nevertheless frequently erupted between them. Policing a slave society, as we saw in the last chapter, naturally required the use of force. To varying degrees, poor white overseers and patrollers used violence, or at least the threat of it, to manage the bondspeople under their charge. Conversely, slaves who had reached their breaking point occasionally lashed out violently at their white oppressors in individual confrontational acts. Probably the most famous instance of a lone slave resisting white authority was Frederick Douglass's fight against the poor, brutal "nigger-breaker" Edward Covey.[1] These types of violent encounters comprised a substantial portion of the total number of cases of interracial violence between slaves and poor whites.

Slaves and poor whites did not always face one another within a framework of inequality, however. They sometimes worked side by side, gambled and drank together, or traded with one another. Such peaceable interactions, too, had the potential to turn suddenly violent. Indeed, a pervasive culture of violence infused the habitually rowdy and disorderly interracial underworld that lower-class southerners of both races shared. When slaves and poor whites took umbrage at their treatment by the other, even erstwhile companions could quickly come to blows. Although mutual hostility and resentment accounted for much of the violence between slaves and poor whites, an examination of court records, petitions, slave narratives, and other sources suggests that slaves' and poor whites' own routine fraternization in southern society engendered some of the physical conflicts between them.

Slaves and poor whites—almost exclusively men—frequently became entangled in minor scrapes, tussles, and brawls.[2] Most of these incidents consti-

1. David W. Blight, ed., *Narrative of the Life of Frederick Douglass, An American Slave, Written by Himself* (New York: Bedford Books of St. Martin's Press, 1993), 78–79.

2. Slave and poor white women in the antebellum South surely fought with one another as well, but I have found no instances in North or South Carolina court records of their committing physi-

tuted simple cases of assault and battery, brought about by any number of circumstances that have gone unrecorded. In Gates County, North Carolina, for instance, the nonslaveholding Job Blanchard went to trial in 1830 for an assault on Henry Bond's slave Jim. Bond alleged that Blanchard "did . . . beat, wound & ill treat" Jim "to his great damage." Another Gates County slaveholder, James R. Riddick, informed a justice of the peace in 1859 that Thomas Matthews, a landless, unemployed white man in his early twenties, had "made divers threat[s] against a certain slave named Miles." Riddick feared that, if left unchecked, Matthews "may do bodily harm" to his slave.[3] Barring a severe beating or maiming of a slave, perhaps by an overzealous overseer or patroller, poor white assaults went largely unprosecuted and unpunished, although in cases like these, in which a slave's life or value seemed endangered, masters often elected to take legal action. Similarly, slaves who assaulted poor whites (or any white, for that matter) rarely went before a court of law, unless the attack resulted in the white person's death. More commonly, slaves faced retribution at the hands of the white victim, the victim's friends, and perhaps the master. The machinery of the slave society—the master, the community, and the legal system—all functioned to keep slave–poor white conflicts from escalating and posing any real danger to so-

---

cal violence upon each other. Their sparring was probably more often verbal than physical, and when they did fight, masters and husbands probably more than the lawful authorities were likely to know about it. Consequently, my lack of sources prevents me from including women in this chapter. On lower-class women and violence in the Old South, see Victoria E. Bynum, *Unruly Women: The Politics of Social and Sexual Control in the Old South* (Chapel Hill: University of North Carolina Press, 1992); Laura F. Edwards, "Law, Domestic Violence, and the Limits of Patriarchal Authority in the Antebellum South," *Journal of Southern History* 65 (November 1999): 733–770; and Edward E. Baptist, "'My Mind Is To Drown You and Leave You Behind': 'Omie Wise,' Intimate Violence, and Masculinity," in *Over the Threshold: Intimate Violence in Early America*, ed. Christine Daniels and Michael V. Kennedy (New York: Routledge, 1999), 94–110. Kathleen M. Brown, *Good Wives, Nasty Wenches, and Anxious Patriarchs: Gender, Race, and Power in Colonial Virginia* (Chapel Hill: University of North Carolina Press, 1996), 305, shares the example of the white Catherine Hedman attacking Robert Carter's slave Sarah in 1705.

3. Gates County, Slave Records, n.d., 1783–1867, Criminal Actions Concerning Slaves, n.d., 1803–1861, folder 1830, NCDAH. According to the Fifth Census of the United States, 1830: Gates County, North Carolina, 102, Job Blanchard's household consisted of two people, a male age 20–29 and a female 30–39. Gates County, Slave Records, n.d., 1783–1867, Criminal Actions Concerning Slaves, n.d., 1803–1861, folder 1859, NCDAH. The Eighth Census of the United States, 1860: Gates County, North Carolina, 281, lists Thomas Matthews as twenty-two years old, with no occupation, and $120 in personal estate.

ciety. In the vast majority of cases, assaults and batteries involving slaves and poor whites seemed routine, easily handled and no cause for alarm.

Scholars have neglected the examination of slave–poor white violence in favor of that involving exclusively white male participants. They agree that, by all accounts, violence permeated the Old South. Violence routinely erupted between and among all classes of southern white men, over the most trivial of matters. What explains the southern penchant for violence? Some contemporary observers, including the distinguished slaveholder Thomas Jefferson, attributed southerners' violent proclivities to the institution of slavery. Children watched and learned as masters employed the whip to correct their charges. Based as it was on force, the argument went, the system of slavery itself bred violent passions.[4] Historians have suggested that the antebellum South's frontier character and its lack of institutional controls provided the conditions in which violence and lawlessness flourished. Others contend that southern violence resulted from a singularly pessimistic southern world view, in which a collective insecurity about human relationships convinced southerners of the necessary role that violence played in their society. Yet another interpretation holds that southern violence marked a continuation of a Celtic cultural tradition transplanted in America. According to this view, brawls and duels represented expressions of southern white males' own ancestral heritage.[5]

The most persuasive explanation for the rampant violence among southern white men hinges on the concept of honor. Restricted to adult white males, honor referred to a value system or set of cultural beliefs that emphasized one's manliness, reputation, and standing in the community. Southern white men could not claim honor for themselves; rather, the community bestowed it upon

4. Michael A. Bellesiles, ed., *Lethal Imagination: Violence and Brutality in American History* (New York: New York University Press, 1999), 4.

5. W. J. Cash, *The Mind of the South* (New York: Alfred A. Knopf, 1941; reprint, New York: Vintage Books, 1991), 42–43, 73; John Hope Franklin, *The Militant South, 1800–1861* (Cambridge, Mass.: Harvard University Press, 1956), ch. 3; Dickson D. Bruce, Jr., *Violence and Culture in the Antebellum South* (Austin: University of Texas Press, 1979), 3–7, 12, 17–18, 240; Grady McWhiney, *Cracker Culture: Celtic Ways in the Old South* (Tuscaloosa: University of Alabama Press, 1988), ch. 6. On the subject of southern violence after the first half of the nineteenth century, see Sheldon Hackney, "Southern Violence," *American Historical Review* 74 (February 1969): 906–925; and John Shelton Reed, *One South: An Ethnic Approach to Regional Culture* (Baton Rouge: Louisiana State University Press, 1982), ch. 11.

them.[6] Southern white men from all classes subscribed to this notion of honor,[7] but honor was not distributed equally throughout white society. The higher a man's rank, the more honor he received. Because slavery served as the basis for the southern social hierarchy, slaveholders occupied a position at the center of the circle of honor. As one scholar has explained, "the master's sense of honor was derived directly from the degradation of his slave" and the power he exercised over his chattel.[8] Slaveowners therefore tended to exclude poor whites from the circle of honor. They reasoned that slaveless poor whites, often struggling on a daily basis to survive, perhaps working alongside slaves, could stake no valid claim to it.[9] Southern gentlemen expected deference and obedience from such obviously inferior men. But as Orlando Patterson and others have observed, even the poorest nonslaveholding men shared in the honor of the slaveholding class simply by virtue of their white skin and their freedom, two traits enslaved men lacked.[10]

The pervasiveness of this code of honor among all classes of southern white men was inextricably linked to the South's reputation for violence.[11] In a society bound together by notions of honor, men jealously defended their reputations.

6. Bertram Wyatt-Brown, *Southern Honor: Ethics and Behavior in the Old South* (New York: Oxford University Press, 1982), 114; Edward L. Ayers, *Vengeance and Justice: Crime and Punishment in the 19th-Century American South* (New York: Oxford University Press, 1984), 13; Elliott J. Gorn, "'Gouge and Bite, Pull Hair and Scratch': The Social Significance of Fighting in the Southern Backcountry," *American Historical Review* 90 (February 1985): 39.

7. Wyatt-Brown, *Southern Honor*, 66, 88; Orlando Patterson, *Slavery and Social Death: A Comparative Study* (Cambridge, Mass.: Harvard University Press, 1982), 99; Ayers, *Vengeance and Justice*, 13; Michael Stephen Hindus, *Prison and Plantation: Crime, Justice, and Authority in Massachusetts and South Carolina, 1767–1878* (Chapel Hill: University of North Carolina Press, 1980), 32; Kenneth S. Greenberg, "The Nose, the Lie, and the Duel in the Antebellum South," *American Historical Review* 95 (February 1990): 58; Franklin, *Militant South*, 34–35; Cash, *Mind of the South*, 73.

8. Patterson, *Slavery and Social Death*, 95.

9. Horn, "Gouge and Bite," 41; Wyatt-Brown, *Southern Honor*, 46.

10. Patterson, *Slavery and Social Death*, 99; Wyatt-Brown, *Southern Honor*, 66; Ariela J. Gross, *Double Character: Slavery and Mastery in the Antebellum Southern Courtroom* (Princeton: Princeton University Press, 2000), 49.

11. This argument finds its best expression in Wyatt-Brown, *Southern Honor*; Ayers, *Vengeance and Justice*; Gorn, "Gouge and Bite"; and Kenneth S. Greenberg, *Honor & Slavery: Lies, Duels, Noses, Masks, Dressing as a Woman, Gifts, Strangers, Humanitarianism, Death, Slave Rebellions, the Proslavery Argument, Baseball, Hunting, and Gambling in the Old South* (Princeton: Princeton University Press, 1996). For a psychological study of honor and violence in the South, see Richard E. Nisbett and Dov Cohen, *Culture of Honor: The Psychology of Violence in the South* (Boulder, Col.: Westview Press, 1996).

Any insult that might call their manhood into question and jeopardize their standing in the community demanded a violent response.[12] On this point, southern white men—regardless of class standing—could agree. They differed, however, in the expressive form the violence took. Lower-class white men engaged in riotous brawls, rough-and-tumbles, and eye-gouging matches that left visible reminders of past violent confrontations.[13] Poor white violence tended to scar or maim its victims, leaving them with an empty eye socket, part of a nose, or half an ear. The poor white Warren Jones of Anson County, North Carolina, for instance, reportedly always had "fresh marks of violence on his face." As one observer recorded, "I never saw a person so scratched and scar[r]ed from previous fighting as Jones was."[14] Honor entailed an acute concern with external appearances, so a mutilated or disfigured body became an object of shame. To southern gentlemen, scarred and grotesque poor whites differed little from slaves with telltale lash marks on their backs, and therefore deserved no respect. This concern with outward appearances manifested itself in southern law through the persistence of shaming punishments such as branding, at a time when northern states gradually dispensed with them. A permanently scarred thumb or cheek guaranteed a public loss of honor for the remainder of one's days.[15] For southern gentlemen, the duel supplanted these more brutal means of fighting by the close of the eighteenth century, giving elites a more genteel way to settle disputes and to distinguish themselves socially from the unrefined, un-

12. Wyatt-Brown, *Southern Honor,* 43; Gorn, "Gouge and Bite," 28, 40.

13. Gorn, "Gouge and Bite," 22–23. For a fascinating and detailed example of an exceptional poor white man who conducted his life within a framework of violence, see Scott P. Culclasure, "'I Have Killed a Damned Dog': Murder by a Poor White in the Antebellum South," *North Carolina Historical Review* 70 (January 1993): 14–39. This article also appears as a chapter in Charles C. Bolton and Scott P. Culclasure, eds., *The Confessions of Edward Isham: A Poor White Life of the Old South* (Athens: University of Georgia Press, 1998).

14. William A. Morris to D. L. Swain, June 9, 1834, in Governor's Papers, Gov. David L. Swain, vol. 69, 644, NCDAH; Jeremiah Benton to D. L. Swain, June 7, 1834, in Governor's Papers, Gov. David L. Swain, vol. 69, 634, NCDAH. The poor white Edward Isham suffered a gouged eye and a bitten finger. See Culclasure, "I Have Killed a Damned Dog," 22.

15. Bertram Wyatt-Brown, "Community, Class, and Snopesian Crime: Local Justice in the Old South," in *Class, Conflict, and Consensus: Antebellum Southern Community Studies,* ed. Orville Vernon Burton and Robert C. McMath, Jr. (Westport, Conn.: Greenwood Press, 1982), 182; Greenberg, "The Nose, the Lie, and the Duel," 67–68; Edward E. Baptist, "Accidental Ethnography in an Antebellum Southern Newspaper: Snell's Homecoming Festival," *Journal of American History* 84 (March 1998): 1376; Hindus, *Prison and Plantation,* 102.

cultured masses.[16] No less than lower-class brawls, dueling could also result in indelible scars, but an injury sustained through such dignified custom could itself be worn as a badge of honor.

When participants came from disparate social backgrounds, violence found still other forms. A gentleman would never challenge a lower-class white man to a duel, for that would imply an equality of station; he might horsewhip or knock down a poor white man instead. A lower-class white man, in turn, could take his revenge through what Bertram Wyatt-Brown has dubbed "Snopesian crime," by secretly burning down the gentleman's barn or outbuildings; by destroying his crops; or by beating, maiming, stealing, or killing his favorite horse or slave.[17] Whatever form it took, for southern white men of all classes, violence provided a means of securing honor for themselves.

If slaveholders occupied the center of the circle of honor, and poor whites dwelled at its margins, slaves stood wholly outside of it, according to southern whites. As Orlando Patterson has noted, a slave was by definition "a person without honor." The slave's dependence, powerlessness, and absence of an identity independent from that of the master stripped him of honor altogether. Slaveholders' preferred mental image of their chattel as Sambos—docile, dependent, and childlike—itself implied unmanliness and dishonor. Masters kept their slaves in that degraded condition through threats and physical punishments.[18] As at least one slaveholder argued, slaves suffered no shame or disgrace from being whipped, precisely because they had no honor to lose.[19]

Slave men saw matters differently, however. The masculine notions of honor so exalted in white society—and the violence attending it—took root in slave culture as well. Historians have paid little attention to the topic of violence among slaves. For years, scholars glorified a harmonious slave community and shied away from exploring the hostilities, disagreements, and physical confrontations in the quarters. Because masters often intervened in and managed disputes between slaves, relatively few cases of slave-on-slave violence entered formal le-

16. Gorn, "Gouge and Bite," 22–23. Gorn contends that rough-and-tumble fighting marked not a lower-class imitation of the gentlemanly duel, but an inversion of it, in which cool decorum gave way to unrestrained passion.

17. Ibid., 41; Wyatt-Brown, "Snopesian Crime," 184–185.

18. Patterson, *Slavery and Social Death*, 10–12, 78, 96–97; quote 12. On the Sambo personality, see Stanley M. Elkins, *Slavery: A Problem in American Institutional and Intellectual Life*, 3rd ed. (Chicago: University of Chicago Press, 1976), 81–89.

19. Bruce, *Violence and Culture*, 124–125.

gal channels, so few court records documenting discord among slaves survive. When slaves owned by the same master committed violence upon each other, masters had no legal recourse. Only in those cases in which a slave of one master maimed or murdered the slave of another would the aggrieved master have the opportunity to sue in court for damages. Yet violence did mar the purportedly idyllic slave community.[20] In Wake County, North Carolina, for instance, the bondsman Gabriel uttered "a gross insult" in reference to slave Nelson's wife. Nelson promptly struck Gabriel a blow with a fence rail, killing him.[21] As this incident illustrates, slave men violently defended their honor from other male slaves to redress grievances and to establish rank among themselves. But while bondsmen prized honor as avidly as their white counterparts, observes Wyatt-Brown, "slave honor was confined to the slave quarters."[22]

If honor explains much of the violence between poor white men as well as that between slave men, did it play any role in the violence between slave and poor white men? Slaveholders charged that slaves had no honor whatsoever, poor whites barely more than that. Any white man who associated socially with slaves immediately forfeited any last shred of honor he may have possessed.[23] Thus, southern gentlemen argued, in fights between slaves and poor whites, no one's honor could possibly have been at stake. Furthermore, as historian Kenneth S. Greenberg has explained, "the code of honor demanded that all participants . . . regard each other as equals." Contests of honor, such as the duel, were by their nature designed to correct an imbalance in the relationship of the two parties in-

20. Peter Kolchin, "Reevaluating the Antebellum Slave Community: A Comparative Perspective," *Journal of American History* 70 (December 1983): 579–601, esp. 581–582, 601; Bertram Wyatt-Brown, "The Mask of Obedience: Male Slave Psychology in the Old South," *American Historical Review* 93 (December 1988): 1249, 1251. Lawrence T. McDonnell, "Money Knows No Master: Market Relations and the American Slave Community," in *Developing Dixie: Modernization in a Traditional Society,* ed. Winfred B. Moore, Jr., Joseph F. Tripp, and Lyon G. Tyler (Westport, Conn.: Greenwood Press, 1988), 31–44, suggests that slave participation in the market economy could foster tensions and violence among slaves. On domestic abuse within slave families, see Christopher Morris, "Within the Slave Cabin: Violence in Mississippi Slave Families," in *Over the Threshold: Intimate Violence in Early America,* ed. Christine Daniels and Michael V. Kennedy (New York: Routledge, 1999), 268–285; and Brenda Stevenson, "Distress and Discord in Virginia Slave Families, 1830–1860," in *In Joy and In Sorrow: Women, Family, and Marriage in the Victorian South, 1830–1900,* ed. Carol Bleser (New York: Oxford University Press, 1991), 103–124.

21. Governor's Papers, Gov. Edward B. Dudley, G.P. 90, folder October 1839, NCDAH.

22. Wyatt-Brown, "Mask of Obedience," 1249; Gross, *Double Character,* 51.

23. Wyatt-Brown, "Snopesian Crime," 188.

volved, caused when one had insulted or otherwise publicly shamed the other. Violence reestablished the social equality of the participants.[24] Clearly the vast majority of slaves and poor whites did not consider themselves equals, even though they sometimes spent their leisure time together or became friends.

Notions of honor nevertheless probably played some small part in the violence between slave and poor white men. As white males reared in a culture of honor, most poor white men demanded from slaves the same respect shown wealthy gentlemen. Many bondspeople, however, ranked poor whites much lower on the social scale than prominent slaveholders, sometimes even below slaves themselves. Slaves' behavior toward poor whites, sometimes based on their unflattering assessments of them, periodically clashed with poor whites' expectations to produce violent outcomes. When slave and poor white men encountered one another in their daily lives, working together, gambling and drinking, or transacting business, they met in contested spaces where lines between slavery and freedom blurred. In these situations, in which the inequality of the races seemed unfixed, slaves sometimes challenged their subordination to poor white men. Civility and camaraderie could abruptly lurch into violence as slave and poor white men negotiated the boundaries of power.

Slave and poor white boys often scrapped with one another during childhood, and while not altogether harmless, the violence of youth paled in comparison to that of adulthood. Once slave and poor white boys had matured into men, violence between them could produce deadly results. As adults, some poor whites seemingly took perverse pleasure in committing arbitrary acts of violence upon slaves. They targeted no specific victim, sought retribution for no particular offense. Perhaps out simply to entertain themselves, to assert their racial superiority over slaves, or to release their own pent up resentment and frustration over their impoverishment and lowly social status, these poor whites sometimes randomly beat the first unfortunate slave they stumbled across. Such violence typically took the form of harmless bullying at the slaves' expense, often at the hands of inebriated poor whites. Kenneth Mizell and a man named Brickhouse, for example, traveled to Jameston, in Martin County, North Carolina, one afternoon in August of 1848. The two men "drank spirits in the town of Jameston, until they were both intoxicated." Near nightfall, the two men retired to the home of a Mr. Cahoon, "for the purpose of staying all night." Mizell and Brickhouse "went

24. Greenberg, *Honor & Slavery*, 58, 62.

to bed together" for a short while, when Mizell awakened and "proposed that they should get up and walk out." They decided to head back into town. Armed once again with "a bottle of spirits, . . . each took a drink while crossing the old field." With the two poor whites still probably under the influence of alcohol, no slave's personal safety was guaranteed. Passing by a storehouse in Jameston around eleven o'clock, Mizell and Brickhouse "found two negro men lying on the ground," bondsmen named Dick and Caesar. Jokingly, Brickhouse informed the two slaves that he and Mizell—both strangers—were patrollers, at which point Brickhouse "took up a piece of board" and delivered each bondsman "two or three slight blows." Dick and Caesar "laughed." All four "then entered into a conversation" as if nothing had happened. As Dick would later testify, the blows "did not hurt," and he simply "thought it was done in sport by Brickhouse." Their degraded position in society demanded that slaves tolerate such random acts of violence from even the lowest and most drunken of white men.[25]

This incident only turned serious after the arrival of "a third negro named Charles" and the threat of an impending whipping. Continuing his jest, Brickhouse asked the newcomer Charles if he knew that he and Mizell were patrollers. He then "took hold of Charles and ordered Dick to go and get a whip for him to whip Charles with." Dick began to obey but changed his mind. When he stopped, Brickhouse released Charles, grabbed Dick, and began pummeling him with his free hand. Caesar looked to Charles and said that "he could not stand that." Running to a nearby fence, Caesar grabbed a rail and delivered a sudden, unexpected blow upon Brickhouse's head, knocking him unconscious. He then reeled upon Mizell "and felled him to the ground at full length." When Brickhouse revived, he saw Mizell's apparently lifeless body lying on the ground, the slaves nowhere in sight. Brickhouse staggered to Cahoon's for a gun, probably to take vengeance upon the slaves, but not procuring one, returned to Mizell, lying "some twenty yards from where he left him." Brickhouse helped Mizell to Cahoon's house, where the two retired to bed. Despite his immense pain, Mizell asked Brickhouse "if he would go with him on Thursday night after the negroes," presumably to seek retribution for the blow. Still drunk, both men fell asleep again. Around two or three in the morning, Brickhouse awoke to find "*blood and*

25. *State v. Caesar*, 31 N.C. 391 (1849), 270–271, 273. For an examination into this case in terms of slave law, see Timothy S. Huebner, "The Roots of Fairness: *State v. Caesar* and Slave Justice in Antebellum North Carolina," in *Local Matters: Race, Crime, and Justice in the Nineteenth-Century South*, ed. Christopher Waldrep and Donald G. Nieman (Athens: University of Georgia Press, 2001), 29–52.

froth" oozing from Mizell's mouth and nose. Mizell died within minutes. A Martin County jury found Caesar guilty of murder and sentenced him to death, finding that no "ordinary assault and battery, inflicted by a free white man on a slave," justified such a violent response, "however worthless and degraded the white man might be."[26]

Whiteness conferred upon even poor whites certain social privileges, including the expectation of respect and deference from slaves. That many poor whites were often little better off than slaves economically, if at all, surely fueled a desire among some "to degrade blacks to a level beneath themselves."[27] Brickhouse's play-fighting with slaves perhaps nourished a craving for power and authority that he lacked in real life. Mizell and Brickhouse had no significant ties to the community. Socially marginal, neither appeared in 1840 or 1850 census records. Caesar's legal counsel referred to the pair as "worthless vagabonds"; a judge described them unflatteringly as "two drunken ruffians."[28] Yet both demanded the respect of slaves they had never encountered before and over whom they exercised no special authority. As countless other bondspeople almost certainly had to on a daily basis, the slaves Dick and Caesar grudgingly endured poor whites' mild abuse. But once the prospect of a whipping loomed, they did not submit meekly. Whipping carried the game too far. Taking a lashing from the master or overseer was one thing, but under no circumstances, the slaves felt, should they subject themselves to that kind of mistreatment at the hands of such degraded white men. After the slaves denied Brickhouse a whip, and the poor white's beating of Dick acquired more sinister and menacing overtones, the slaves resisted violently.

The character of all parties involved in the affray became a pivotal issue in Caesar's appeal before the North Carolina state supreme court. In a somewhat similar case twenty-six years before Caesar's trial, a white man appeared before the North Carolina supreme court for inflicting "wanton injury" upon a slave. A justice at that time opined that such violent offenses upon slaves "are usually committed by men of dissolute habits, hanging loose upon society, who, being repelled from association with well disposed citizens, take refuge in the company of colored persons and slaves, whom they deprave by their example, embolden by their familiarity, and then beat, under the expectation that a slave dare not resent

26. *State v. Caesar*, 31 N.C. 391 (1849), 271–272, 274.

27. Bill Cecil-Fronsman, *Common Whites: Class and Culture in Antebellum North Carolina* (Lexington: University Press of Kentucky, 1992), 77.

28. Huebner, "Roots of Fairness," 42; *State v. Caesar*, 31 N.C. 391 (1849), 280.

a blow from a white man."[29] Caesar's counsel attempted to show that Mizell and Brickhouse belonged in that category of degraded white men. Hired by the father of Caesar's two infant masters, the attorney showcased their depravity by noting that, early in the encounter, Brickhouse solicited the slaves' help in securing "some girls" for sex.[30] Meanwhile, the court judged Caesar an "obedient" and "submissive" slave. The supreme court therefore granted the bondsman a new trial, in which he was found guilty of manslaughter rather than murder. Ultimately, Caesar escaped with only a branded left thumb. Caesar's murder of a lowly poor white man could not go entirely unpunished, but neither did the southern legal machinery judge the crime worthy of the execution of a valuable bondsman.[31]

Most examples of discord at work between slaves and poor whites have gone undocumented, but inevitably, slave and poor white laborers sometimes came into conflict. One notable case in South Carolina involved the slave Ky and a laboring white man named McCallister. On an April Sunday in 1848, Ky and McCallister were working together at an unspecified task. It is not clear whether the slave and the poor white were laboring for someone else that day, or whether Ky was working for McCallister. They apparently had known one another for some time. McCallister had hired Ky to work for him at some point prior to that Sunday, for, as one witness stated, the fray between the two began that day when "Ky asked McCallister for what he owed him for building a fence." Not amenable to that topic of conversation, McCallister replied curtly, "[D]o not Jaw me." The slave then informed McCallister that he would brook that tone neither from "you nor any other white man," and repeated, "I want you to pay me for my work." Perhaps Ky was aware of the terms of a contract between his master and McCallister, or maybe Ky had hired out himself. For whatever reason, the slave felt emboldened enough to press the poor white for his wages and defiantly defend his position. McCallister picked up a cane to punish Ky's insolence, but the slave anticipated the attack. Ky then hit McCallister, seized him by the collar, and struck him "one severe blow" with a rock upon his head, "cutting a hole through his hat." Ky exclaimed "that he would not work with any such a damned rascal" as McCallister, who quickly "drew his knife." Ky then ran off, with McCallister throwing rocks at the fleeing slave. That night, the bondsman paid a visit to

29. *State v. Hale,* 9 N.C. 582 (1823), 327. Also quoted in Ayers, *Vengeance and Justice,* 131.
30. *State v. Caesar,* 31 N.C. 391 (1849), 271; Huebner, "Roots of Fairness," 30, 45.
31. Huebner, "Roots of Fairness," 37, 40–41.

the house of William and Margaret Burnett, where McCallister stayed, hoping "to make up the scrape." That Ky sought forgiveness suggested some erstwhile friendship between the slave and white laborers, or at the very least, the slave's desire to put the episode behind them. What happened to their relationship remains a mystery, but a court did find Ky guilty of insulting and assaulting a white man and sentenced the slave to receive "fifteen lashes on the bare Back." [32]

The landless and illiterate poor white Ira Westbrook of Jones County, North Carolina, also had a "scrape" with a slave laborer, but their encounter turned lethal. Westbrook had hired Lot to work for him, but "the negro was insolent and impudent in his language" toward his poor white employer. What the slave said specifically is not clear, although it is probably safe to speculate that he verbally attacked Westbrook's poverty or his lowly position in society. When the poor white "took a cow hide to whip him," Lot defiantly proclaimed "that he would not be whipped by any such man, and began to move off." Probably surprised by the brazenness of the slave, "Westbrook then took down his gun." Lot persisted in his "impudence," repeatedly egging him "to shoot." Unable to control his rage any longer, Westbrook shot the slave in the leg, a wound that proved fatal three days later. Because, in the eyes of the law, Lot had provoked the incident, Westbrook faced charges not of murder but of manslaughter only. The jury found him not guilty, however, since it determined the slave to be in a state of rebellion at the time of the shooting. [33]

As white men, both McCallister and Westbrook expected but did not receive the customary deference from the slaves they had hired. For both Ky and Lot, the poor whites for whom they were supposed to work neither commanded nor deserved their respect. Each slave seemingly considered his poor white employer an inferior breed of white man, and they boldly made their feelings known. Ky dismissed McCallister's order not to "jaw" him, asserted his intention not to submit to the "damned rascal," and instead inverted the dynamics of power by pressing McCallister for payment for past work. Likewise, Lot refused a thrashing "by any such man" as Westbrook. Ky and Lot clearly challenged the poor whites who had hired them, and, by extension, the system of racial slavery. McCallister and Westbrook had to respond to the slaves' insubordination. Any challenge to their control threatened the slave system, and, more immediately, undermined their own authority. Not to retaliate was to concede that the bondsmen were their so-

32. Spartanburg District, Court of Magistrates and Freeholders, Trial Papers, microfilm reel C2920, SCDAH.

33. *Raleigh Register* (weekly), April 2, 1847. See also Cecil-Fronsman, *Common Whites*, 76.

cial equals, and, as historian Bill Cecil-Fronsman has explained, "Any white man who allowed blacks the right to behave as his equal might lose the status ascribed to him." McCallister and Westbrook could allow no blurring of racial lines if they expected to maintain their own position in society above that of slaves.[34] According to Cecil-Fronsman, "Deviations from established patterns" of proper slave behavior attacked poor whites' cherished "sense of superiority": "The system of racial etiquette had to be enforced even if enforcing it required violence."[35] McCallister employed a cane and a knife, Westbrook a whip and a gun, in their attempts to restore the refractory slaves to their subordinate place in society. Even then, Ky physically resisted, while the injured Lot dared his employer to empty "the other barrel of the gun" into his head. Achieving mastery over slaves confounded even the wealthiest of gentlemen; for poor whites, who rarely received the same respect bondspeople granted the "big bugs," slave management must have proven doubly vexing.[36]

If violence erupted in the work setting as poor whites tried to maintain control over their recalcitrant hires, affrays also broke out when slaves and poor whites gambled, drank, and caroused together in their leisure time. When poor whites socialized with slaves, they degraded themselves by becoming the bondsmen's equals. Aboard a stage from South Carolina en route to Charlotte, North Carolina, English geologist George W. Featherstonhaugh sat opposite "a young white man . . . about twenty-five years old, with legs *fettered* and *manacles* on his hands." Bob Chatwood, "a desperate, gambling, dissolute fellow, from his earliest years," had made a habit of gambling with slaves. According to Featherstonhaugh, he persuaded them to steal from their masters, convert their plunder into money, then play the game "all fours" with him. Recently, Chatwood had met his match. He had played all night with a skillful "black amateur . . . in a shed by the light of an old lamp." His black opponent "won every game," but Chatwood refused to pay up. Instead, he produced "two silver dollars" and proposed a challenge. If he lost those two coins, he promised to pay his debt in full.[37]

34. Cecil-Fronsman, *Common Whites*, 76.

35. Ibid., 77.

36. For an outstanding account of one frustrated planter, see Drew Gilpin Faust, *James Henry Hammond and the Old South: A Design for Mastery* (Baton Rouge: Louisiana State University Press, 1982), ch. 5.

37. G. W. Featherstonhaugh, *Excursion Through the Slave States, from Washington on the Potomac to the Frontier of Mexico; with Sketches of Popular Manners and Geological Notices*, vol. 2 (London: John Murray, 1844), 345–346. See also Wyatt-Brown, "Snopesian Crime," 199–200.

Slaves must have realized the inherent dangers of gambling with whites. Bondspeople made excellent gaming partners, as long as they lost. But sometimes luck smiled upon them, and they defeated their white opponents. In Marlboro District, South Carolina, for example, "a white person" named John Jones bet on cards with William B. Lee's slave Bob in 1858, "at or near . . . Lee's plantation." Bob "did win from him . . . the sum of one dollar and forty-eight cents."[38] Whites did not always readily accept losing to a slave, as a contemporary folk rhyme suggests:

> Nigger an' er white man playin' seven-up,
> Nigger won de money, scared to pick it up,
> Nigger drew back and de white man fell,
> Nigger grab de money, an' run like hell.[39]

Slaves understood that, when they emerged victorious, the racial harmony of the game could quickly disappear. When the gambler Chatwood's losing streak continued, his black opponent—in the spirit of the verse—"snatched up the money and ran off." Chatwood gave chase, "and in the scuffle which ensued, finding the black man too strong, he ran a knife into his throat and mortally wounded the poor fellow." As Featherstonhaugh explained, Chatwood "had committed the unpardonable sin of playing at cards with a *slave* for stolen property," then destroyed the valuable bondsman. Because "the example was too dangerous," two separate South Carolina courts ruled Chatwood guilty of murder and sentenced him to hang.[40]

Other poor whites who gambled with slaves received more lenient sentences commensurate with the seriousness of the slave victim's injuries. In Greenville District, South Carolina, for instance, Murrell Massey, Matthew Potts, Jr., and John B. Griffin gathered in a kitchen to bet "at a certain game of Cards called

---

38. Marlboro District, Court of General Sessions, Indictments, item 688, SCDAH.

39. Newman I. White, *American Negro Folk-Songs* (Hatboro, Penn.: Folklore Associates, Inc., 1965), 203. For variations on the above rhyme, for its inclusion as a verse in other songs, and for other mentions of interracial gambling in folk songs and verse, see Howard W. Odum, "Folk-Song and Folk-Poetry as Found in the Secular Songs of the Southern Negroes," *Journal of American Folk-Lore* 24 (July–September 1911): 267; Howard W. Odum and Guy B. Johnson, *The Negro and His Songs: A Study of Typical Negro Songs in the South* (Chapel Hill: University of North Carolina Press, 1925), 7, 255; Thomas W. Talley, *Negro Folk Rhymes Wise and Otherwise with a Study* (1922; reprint, Port Washington, N.Y.: Kennikat Press, 1968), 91; Dorothy Scarborough, *On the Trail of Negro Folk-Songs* (Hatboro, Penn.: Folklore Associates, Inc., 1963), 227; and White, *American Negro Folk-Songs*, 196–197.

40. Featherstonhaugh, *Excursion Through the Slave States*, 346–347.

'all fours' otherwise called 'seven up'" with Alexander McKinney's slave Jacob. Massey, perhaps like Chatwood enraged from losing money to a slave, "beat and wound[ed]" Jacob "by knocking him with a Stool and Stab[b]ing him with a dirk in the back." For the infraction, a court sentenced Massey to a $20 fine, two weeks in jail, and twenty lashes.[41]

For upper-class southern gentlemen, gaming was fraught with meaning. Gambling provided an important way to distinguish themselves from the masses unable to afford such casual risk-taking, and it served as a means to distribute honor and status among the socially equal participants. The winner earned respect and recognition that lasted as long as the memory of victory remained. Slaveholders condemned poor whites who gambled with slaves because sitting together at the gaming table implied equality among the players. As "respectable" southern whites saw it, by consorting socially with slaves, poor whites instantly dishonored themselves. Moreover, gambling between unequals rendered the pastime meaningless. In gambling with slaves, poor whites engaged in contests that inherently conferred status, when, under the circumstances, status could not have been at stake. From a gentleman's perspective, poor whites who gambled with slaves placed themselves in a psychologically ungratifying position. On the one hand, if poor whites defeated slaves in games of chance, they confirmed white superiority over obvious racial inferiors; they gained not honor and status but merely the material wealth that had been wagered. On the other hand, when slaves outplayed or outwitted poor whites at cards, they compounded the shame and disgrace brought upon the loser for gaming with slaves in the first place. To preserve the very meaning of gambling, southern lawmakers took steps to prohibit contests between whites and blacks. They deemed the dishonorable punishment of whipping, normally reserved for slaves, appropriate for white men so degraded as to participate in interracial gaming. Surely lawmakers hoped such a harsh and symbolic penalty would deter the practice, for it made poor white men even more vulnerable to losing whatever status they had.[42]

Most poor whites probably lacked southern gentlemen's understanding of gaming and failed to grasp the significance their social superiors attached to it. Most who gambled with slaves were probably in search of entertainment or a quick buck and nothing more. At the same time, poor whites themselves were not immune to southern notions of honor. Conceivably, frustrated poor whites

41. Greenville District, Court of General Sessions, Indictments, item 1102, SCDAH. Massey does not appear in the South Carolina census of 1840.

42. Greenberg, *Honor & Slavery*, 141; Wyatt-Brown, *Southern Honor*, 340, 344.

who lashed out violently upon defeat by an enslaved opponent may have been reestablishing respect they had lost in the game. Even more likely, however, poor whites who physically attacked slave victors were simply poor losers. Already impoverished, they had frittered away to a slave the little money they possessed. But as southern gentlemen agreed, the truly honorable man cared little about the material goods he won or lost. That was precisely what made gambling a sport of gentlemen.[43]

Slaves also lost their tempers while gambling, with violent and tragic results. In Person County, North Carolina, Thomas Chatham, eighteen or nineteen years old, went in company with fourteen-year-old John T. Brooks "to a fish-trap in the neighborhood, where several slaves were collected, on [a] Saturday night" in 1840. Prophetically, Chatham said en route that "he wished that he had borrowed Mr. Long's knife, for he might get into a scrape, and if so, he would need it." The only two whites present, Chatham and Brooks stayed until a few hours before dawn. At the fish-trap, a twenty-three-year-old slave named Jarrott was playing cards with Jack Hughes, a free black man, when a dispute broke out. Jarrott and Hughes called upon the white man Chatham "to keep the game for them, which he did for some time, until a second difference took place between the parties." Fed up, "Hughes refused to play longer." Jarrott snatched up the handkerchief upon which he and Hughes had been playing, sending "a 12½-cent piece of coin" of Jarrott's flying "off among the leaves." Jarrott searched unsuccessfully for his missing money, when he turned accusingly to Chatham. With extreme daring, or imprudence, Jarrott charged Chatham with taking his coin, saying "that he saw his ninepence walk into a white man's pocket, and that any white man who would steal a negro's money was not too good to unbutton a sheep's collar." He then asserted that Chatham "was raised and had lived on stolen sheep."[44]

Being accused of theft by a slave must have been an intolerable insult, yet Chatham demonstrated remarkable restraint. After simmering a while longer, Jarrott threatened to kill Chatham if he did not surrender his coin, and "brandished a stick" over Chatham's head. Still, Chatham remained passive. Jarrott then alleged that Chatham "had his ninepence in his left jacket pocket." As if to mock the enraged and hysterical slave, Chatham offered Jarrott the opportunity to search him. When the slave refused, possibly recognizing the boundaries between black and white, Chatham "turned out his pockets." No ninepence forth-

43. Greenberg, *Honor & Slavery*, 142.
44. *State v. Jarrott*, 23 N.C. 76 (1840), 66, 64.

coming, Jarrott cursed him and charged that the money must be in Chatham's shoes. Obligingly, Chatham removed "his shoes and stockings," revealing nothing. Finally, "some of the company . . . got a light, and in searching, found the piece of money in the leaves, . . . six or seven steps" from where Jarrott had jerked up the handkerchief but near the spot Chatham "stood when he turned out his pockets and pulled off his shoes." Nothing conclusively proved Chatham guilty of theft, however, and the tension subsided briefly. But a short time later, Jarrott renewed his verbal abuse of Chatham, "using very indecent and insolent language."[45]

Sitting by the fire, Chatham's patience at last wore thin. He asked Brooks for his pocketknife, noting that "he wished to cut his nails." Blade in hand, Chatham explained to Jarrott "that if he did not hush, he . . . would stick his knife in him." One free black witness recalled Chatham saying that if he did not kill Jarrott himself, "he would go to his master on Monday morning and have him whipped to his satisfaction, and he would then waylay him and shoot him with a rifle." Undeterred by such threats, and prepared for a fight, Jarrott drew his three-foot hickory stick and dared Chatham on. As Jarrott continued to harass Chatham, the white man clutched his knife in one hand, "took up a piece of a fence rail" in the other, and chased Jarrott "twice around the fire," running off the slave. Undaunted, Jarrott returned "within ten or eleven steps of the fire" and muttered something that provoked Chatham to surge forward again with the knife and fence rail, swinging but missing. In response, Jarrott struck Chatham several blows with his stick, knocking him to the ground, dead.[46]

The Old South's culture of honor demanded that Chatham respond violently to the slave's insults, or risk his own reputation.[47] Had Chatham been alone with Jarrott, he might have dismissed the slave's challenge. In this case, however, another young white witness was present, so it could not go unanswered.[48] Yet the poor white Chatham endured a slew of insults from a bold and abrasive slave

45. Ibid., 64.

46. Ibid., 64–66. Jarrott was subsequently found guilty of murder and sentenced to death in superior court. The state supreme court reversed the ruling, however, because it judged Chatham's assault upon the slave as excessive. The court permitted a white who did not own the slave to correct that slave in moderation, but it also recognized a slave's right to resist excessive punishment. See Ernest James Clark, Jr., "Aspects of the North Carolina Slave Code, 1715–1860," *North Carolina Historical Review* 39 (April 1962), 161.

47. Bellesiles, *Lethal Imagination*, 4.

48. On the importance of an affront being witnessed by other whites, see Peter Kolchin, *Unfree Labor: American Slavery and Russian Serfdom* (Cambridge: Belknap Press of Harvard University Press, 1987), 267.

before he took action. Why did he tolerate such verbal abuse for so long? Perhaps Chatham did not adhere as strictly to the code of honor as other southern white men did. Maybe he had met Jarrott socially before that night, or knew him personally. Perhaps he feared the response of the other slaves and free blacks who greatly outnumbered the two young whites. Whatever might explain the delayed response, Chatham eventually reached the limits of his restraint. Through violent retribution, he hoped to correct the slave's insolence and to remind him of his proper place in society. The confrontation led instead to his own death.

Like socializing with slaves, trading illicitly with slaves severely damaged a poor white's already low standing among "respectable" whites. Because slave testimony against whites proved inadmissible in southern courts, whites who traded with slaves generally need not fear that a slave would betray them to the law. Nevertheless, if a slave publicly admitted to trading with a poor white, the poor white's estimation declined in the eyes of his social superiors. A slave's word might have been useless in a court of law, but in the court of community opinion, it carried some weight, at least against lower-class whites. Gilbert Fanny of Gates County, North Carolina, offers an instructive example. In 1859, Fanny, a marginal farmer in his midthirties, struggling to support a household of eleven, allegedly sold "one piece of tobacco" to a slave named Mike and spiritous liquors to three other slaves. In January of the following year, he reportedly traded "with negro slave, Jet, in the night time." Sometime in the first half of 1860, Jet reported either this or another unlawful transaction with Fanny to a white or whites of some influence. In doing so, the slave imperiled his own life.[49]

With several charges of trading with slaves already filed against him, Fanny probably felt vulnerable in the eyes of the white community when Jet exposed him, and he determined to take revenge upon the slave for dishonoring his name. In June 1860, Fanny, along with his seventeen-year-old son Benjamin, invited Lemuel and Exum Everett out on patrol. Armed with guns loaded with buckshot and "a very large hickory stick," the company spotted the loose-lipped slave. As Exum Everett recalled, Fanny said, "there is Jet and I mean to beat him or kill

49. Gates County, Slave Records, n.d., 1783–1867, Criminal Actions Concerning Slaves, n.d., 1803–1861, folder 1859, NCDAH. In the Seventh Census of the United States, 1850: Gates County, North Carolina, 22, Fanny appears as a twenty-six-year-old illiterate farmer with no real estate, heading a household of six. In the Eighth Census of the United States, 1860: Gates County, North Carolina, 263, Fanny's household had increased to eleven members. Fanny was thirty-six, with $300 in real estate and $440 in personal estate. Gates County, Slave Records, n.d., 1783–1867, Criminal Actions Concerning Slaves, n.d., 1803–1861, folder 1860, NCDAH.

him." Outside the gate of Willis Boyett, Fanny overtook Jet, who was sitting in a horse-drawn buggy. Fanny asked what "he brought that meat to his house for" and why he "had gone of[f] & told white Folks that he bought it." When Jet denied telling anyone, Fanny "struck him two licks on the head" and "ordered the boy out of the buggy." Fanny informed Jet that he intended "to tie him & Jet told him he should not." Resisting Fanny's effort to restrain him, Jet "took Fanny by the shoulders to prevent him putting the line over his neck, but did not attempt to strike or harm him." Rebuffed, Fanny ordered Jet to tie up his horse. The slave requested that he be allowed "inside the field to tie so that his horse could not get away." Fanny permitted the request, but when he believed Jet was taking too long, he warned the slave that, "damn him he would shoot." Jet "jumped off to run" from the company, when Fanny screamed to his son, "Ben God damn him shoot him, shoot him." Benjamin Fanny obeyed his father's order and shot the fleeing slave, about twenty steps distant. The elder Fanny then departed, telling the rest of the company "to say nothing & know nothing about it."[50]

Despite the fact that Fanny's son Benjamin ultimately pulled the trigger, this episode smacked of premeditated murder on the part of Gilbert Fanny. Fanny's neighbor, Neverson Roundtree, testified that the elder Fanny had ventured over to his field to engage in conversation more than a week before the shooting. "Fanny said to me that Jet come to him," Roundtree explained, and "brought him pieces of meat," apparently stolen from a man named Bryant Sanders. Jet had requested that Fanny "weigh the meat," so Fanny "went in the smoke house & got the steelyard." He "weighed it & told Jet to come & see it weighed if he choosed [sic]. The boy came in & saw it weighed," but then took the meat with him when he departed. Apparently, in this particular instance, Fanny bought nothing from the slave, yet, as he explained to Roundtree, "Jet had told white Folks of it." With a history of trading with slaves, Fanny did not want neighborhood whites to consider him the type of man who would do a slave the favor of measuring his plunder. Perhaps trying to restore his reputation in "respectable" white society, Fanny responded angrily to the charge, even though a slave had uttered the incriminating words. By virtue of skin color, Jet was not Fanny's social equal, yet Fanny still took the accusation seriously. When Jet reportedly said later that "no white man should tie him," the challenge was complete. Fanny explained to Roundtree that "he intended to have him [Jet]" and that "he would give him five hundred lashes or he would kill him." Fanny followed through on his threat, indirectly, through the accurate aim of his son. As Roundtree recalled, when he heard gunfire "about bedtime" the night of the crime, he turned to his wife and said, "[T]hat [is] Jet & they have shot him."[51]

Violence could also erupt between slaves and poor whites when a planned transaction soured. This was the case involving the poor white Jesse Hassell and the slave George. Approximately twenty years old, George belonged to John W. Littlejohn of Chowan County, in northeastern North Carolina. Some time before Christmas Eve in 1823, George had made a deal with Hassell, an "old, infirm & poor" white man who "kept a grog shop in his dwelling house" a mile outside the town of Edenton and about three miles from Littlejohn's plantation. George and Hassell had agreed to swap shoes, with Hassell giving George an extra "fifty cents to boot." That they mutually assessed the value of George's shoes at fifty cents more than Hassell's suggests the degree of the white man's poverty. But when George paid a visit to Hassell's on Christmas Eve night, Hassell refused to make the trade, prompting the slave to attack the white man.[52]

Like slaves throughout the South, George had been celebrating the Christmas season before he ventured to Hassell's. In George's neighborhood, slaves' holiday reveling took an unconventional form. Dr. James Norcom, Edenton slaveholder and master of the famous runaway Harriet Jacobs, explained to North Carolina's governor that "during the season of Christmas our slaves in this part of the State have been in the habit of enjoying a state of comparative freedom; of having dances & entertainments among themselves; & of celebrating the season in a manner almost peculiar to this part of the world." Masters permitted these festivities, and "habitually overlooked and never punished" the widespread drunkenness that commonly marked such occasions, for, as Norcom observed, "[w]ithout his bottle at Christmas, a negro . . . relapses into his bonds & feels himself doubly a slave!" On the night of the affray with Hassell, "George had been with a party of negroes a playing at John Canoe, a diversion that negroes in

51. Gates County, Slave Records, n.d., 1783–1867, Criminal Actions Concerning Slaves, n.d., 1803–1861, folder 1860, NCDAH. Roundtree started in the direction of the noise when he encountered Jet, who said, "Oh Lord Mr. Roun[d]tree help me for I am shot to death." Roundtree took the slave to the home of Willis Boyett, where Jet expired.

52. Jonathan H. Jacobs to Gov. Gabriel Holmes, May 29, 1824; Leonard Martin to Gov. Gabriel Holmes, undated; Affidavit of William D. Rascoe, June 18, 1824; and Leonard Martin to Gov. Gabriel Holmes, April 23, 1824; all in General Assembly, Session Records, November 1824–January 1825, Petitions and Papers Concerning Pardon of Negro, George, Charged With Murder, NCDAH, hereinafter cited as Petitions Concerning George.

this section of the state, indulge in, upon Christmas holidays." A marriage between Christmas caroling and Halloween trick-or-treating, the John Canoe ritual was "a sport common in this part of the state with slaves on holy-days." Bands of young male slaves traveled from plantation to plantation, dressed in extravagant costume, playing boisterous music, serenading and dancing for the whites they encountered, and demanding money, whiskey, or some other token in payment for their performance. White folks, "even the most respectable and worthy," made donations to the John Canoers, "sometimes of liquor and sometimes of money to buy it." In the tenor of the season, whites typically gave generously. Slave witnesses recalled George "wishing to beat the box they carried with them" that night, and by the time George came "staggering along the road" near Hassell's, his intoxication likely was complete.[53]

Passing by Hassell's sometime after midnight, George decided to transact their prearranged bargain. He "knocked at the door," planning on trading shoes. Emboldened by both the liquor and the spirit of the John Canoe season, George, instead of taking the additional half dollar due him in coin, resolved to ask to substitute "for his fifty cents one half gallon of rum." Awakened by George's rapping, Hassell sent the slave "to the kitchen for fire." With the fire lighted, George "requested the half gallon of rum for the fifty cents." Hassell, "in bed," refused. As the keeper of a grog shop, Hassell almost certainly would have had the rum available, but perhaps he considered the late hour an inopportune time to trade shoes or he did not like the change in terms. Like poor whites generally, he probably resented the financial imposition of the John Canoe ritual itself. During the holiday season, slaves often coerced donations that poor whites could not easily afford, and if denied a treat, they broke into humiliating songs ridiculing the poverty of their white audience. Whatever Hassell's reasons for turning down the

53. James Norcom to Gov. Gabriel Holmes, June 18, 1824; and Petition to Gov. Gabriel Holmes, undated; Leonard Martin to Gov. Gabriel Holmes, undated; all in Petitions Concerning George. On the John Canoe ritual, see Elizabeth A. Fenn, "'A Perfect Equality Seemed to Reign': Slave Society and Jonkonnu," *North Carolina Historical Review* 65 (April 1988): 127–153; Michael Craton, "Decoding Pitchy-Patchy: The Roots, Branches and Essence of Junkanoo," *Slavery & Abolition* 16 (April 1995): 14–44, esp. 29–30; Wayne K. Durrill, "Routine of Seasons: Labour Regimes and Social Ritual in an Antebellum Plantation Community," *Slavery & Abolition* 16 (August 1995): 161–187, esp. 161–162, 185n3; Stephen Nissenbaum, *The Battle for Christmas: A Cultural History of America's Most Cherished Holiday* (New York: Vintage Books, 1996), 285, 289; and Sylvia R. Frey and Betty Wood, *Come Shouting to Zion: African American Protestantism in the American South and British Caribbean to 1830* (Chapel Hill: University of North Carolina Press, 1998), 54–55. Petitions to Gov. Gabriel Holmes, undated; and Leonard Martin to Gov. Gabriel Holmes, undated; both in Petitions Concerning George.

slave, George grew angry at the poor white's inflexibility. The slave's likely drunkenness only added to the volatility of the situation. Tension rising, "George took hold of the shoes he had swap[p]ed & delivered" to Hassell. The white man got out of bed, and a fight ensued. Patience, a female slave who witnessed part of the affray, heard Hassell tell George to "take all I have but spare my life," and saw the young and healthy slave overpower the old man by "choaking him." When Patience called out to George, the slave fled, taking Hassell's shoes and leaving his own, as per part of their agreement. Hassell died two days later. Authorities arrested George, without resistance, on the night of December 27 in his master's kitchen. Fearing the impossibility of a fair trial in Chowan County, John Littlejohn secured a change of venue for his slave to neighboring Perquimans County. At Perquimans County Superior Court in the spring of 1824, a jury convicted George of murdering Jesse Hassell. The judge slated his execution for May 28.[54]

The incident, and George's subsequent death sentence, divided area whites. George's many supporters argued that the slave had no malicious intent to kill Hassell. Had the victim not been such a feeble old man, with "but one step between him & the grave," they observed, no injury whatsoever would have resulted from the assault. Immediately afterward, George had rejoined his companions "*with a merry heart*" to partake further in the festivities, and he had never attempted to escape justice, suggesting that he never realized the severity of Hassell's injuries. Although his detractors contended that he was a "desperado & midnight murderer" and "a fellow of notoriously bad character, having committed several outrageous thefts before the perpetration of this last most horrible crime," several "respectable witnesses," including a former overseer of Littlejohn's, testified that George "had always been a quiet, orderly, submissive and well disposed slave." Area citizens sent at least three petitions to the governor, totaling nearly 130 signatures, asking for George's pardon on the condition that he be removed from the state. Prominent signers included the sheriff and register of Chowan County, clerks from the Chowan, Pasquotank, and Perquimans county superior courts, the cashier of the Edenton Bank, the deputy marshal of Edenton Dis-

---

54. Leonard Martin to Gov. Gabriel Holmes, April 23, 1824; Leonard Martin to Gov. Gabriel Holmes, undated; Affidavit of William D. Rascoe, June 18, 1824; all in Petitions Concerning George; *State v. George*, Chowan County, Minute Docket, Superior Court, 1809–1828, 310, NCDAH; *State v. George*, Perquimans County, Minute Docket, Superior Court, 1807–1847, Spring Term 1824, NCDAH; Fenn, "A Perfect Equality Seemed to Reign," 143, 148–149. No available records can confirm that George actually was executed.

trict, several justices of the peace, and eight of the twelve Perquimans County jurors who convicted him.[55]

No one on either side of the debate over George's fate had much good to say
about the elderly victim. Although Hassell owned two slaves, Jim and Patience,
locals described him as "poor," "feeble," and even "emaciated." Hassell lost stat-
ure among "respectable" whites because he "was in the habit of intercourse and
dealing with slaves." As one report to the governor explained, the chronically ill
Hassell "was the keeper of a dram shop, which was accessible to slaves at all times
of the day and night and had thus accustomed them to a familiarity which was
inconsistent with the respect and deference due from a slave to a Freeman." Un-
beknownst to his master, George "had long been upon terms of intimacy" with
Hassell, "and was a sort of inmate in the family of the deceased." He had apparently grown accustomed to trading with Hassell in the middle of the night. Jim
and Patience stated that Hassell was "fond" of George, "& had frequently sent
him for fire in the night to trade with him." Even those who wished to see George
hang from the gallows conceded that Hassell "kept a grog shop and traded with
negroes and had the character of being a drunken trifling fellow." Indeed, the
death of such a degraded poor white benefited neighborhood slaveholders whose
goods had been pilfered and secretly sold to him. They called for George's execution not so much for his specific crime but to provide an example to other slaves
in the area.[56]

<hr />

55. Petition to Gov. Gabriel Holmes, April 22, 1824; George Hair, Jr., to Gov. Gabriel Holmes,
May 28, 1824; James Norcom to Gov. Gabriel Holmes, June 18, 1824; Leonard Martin to Gov. Ga-
briel Holmes, undated; and J. R. Creecy to John Taylor, May 28, 1824; all in Petitions Concerning
George.

56. James Norcom to Gov. Gabriel Holmes, June 18, 1824; Petition to Gov. Gabriel Holmes,
April 22, 1824; Petition to Gov. Gabriel Holmes, undated; Leonard Martin to Gov. Gabriel Holmes,
undated; Jonathan H. Jacobs to Gov. Gabriel Holmes, May 29, 1824; all in Petitions Concerning
George. George's detractors had many reasons for wanting to see his execution, none of which concerned George's specific crime. In northeastern North Carolina, blacks outnumbered whites. Other
blacks recently convicted of burglaries had been pardoned, and a black murderer and other robbers
remained at large in Gates County. Citizens there felt "almost beseiged [sic] in their dwellings" and
dared not "venture . . . beyond their thresholds unarmed." Moreover, no black had faced capital punishment in that region for the past two decades. All of this combined to undermine whites' sense of
control over their slave population. Thus, for the sake of public safety, many whites wanted to make
an example out of George, even though they had no particular ties of communal affection with Jesse
Hassell. On May 21, 1824, Governor Gabriel Holmes postponed George's scheduled May 28 execution until June 28. The news reportedly generated a "triumph of feeling" among other slaves, who

George and Hassell had traded with one another clandestinely on a number of occasions, so the slave must have been puzzled by his poor white trading partner's stubborn refusal to supply him liquor that Christmas Eve night. Likely drunk, reveling in the unusual holiday license of John Canoe, George probably assumed Hassell would keep with the spirit of the season and agree to his proposal. When Hassell declined the trade, George may have perceived the poor white as suddenly asserting his racial authority, precisely during those precious few days when coastal North Carolina slaves enjoyed a fleeting moment of social inversion. In the context of the season, George probably felt justified in requesting a minor adjustment to their bargain, so when Hassell refused, violence ensued.[57]

As long as slave–poor white violence crossed the color line, slaveowners never felt threatened. They correctly identified poor whites as the segment of the white population with the weakest ties to the slave regime, so they were pleased to find proof of animosity between slaves and poor whites, whatever its origin. What they found more troubling was slave–poor white collusion in violent crime. Typically this meant "degraded" whites supplying news or material support to the slaves who actually committed the violent acts. In Gates County, North Carolina, the same month George was slated to be executed in a neighboring county, "three negroes . . . prosecuted for Burglary" broke jail and quickly multiplied into a "gang" of six. Petitioners attributed "sixteen burglaries one murder & three highway robberies" over the past two years to this band of convicts. Worst of all, the memorialists stated, "They are supposed to be protected and provision'd by the whites who inhabit their neighbourhood and receive information of the approach of the guards & easily escape." In nearby Southampton County, Virginia, the following year, Jeremiah Delk's slave Moses committed many "depradations [sic]" with a gun, including shooting at white people. As one correspondent informed Virginia's governor, "[H]e is no doubt protected Harboured and fur-

---

"are . . . declaring that negroes are too valuable to be hung." Nevertheless, in an eight-page letter to the governor defending George, Edenton slaveholder James Norcom complained that a "contagion" of "unexampled rage for vindictive & sanguinary justice" had swept over the community. Those who wanted George dead displayed a "nefarious & diabolical spirit." See Joseph B. Skinner to Gov. Gabriel Holmes, May 27, 1824; Petition to Gov. Gabriel Holmes, May 27, 1824; George Hair, Jr., to Gov. Gabriel Holmes, May 28, 1824; all in Petitions Concerning George; Gov. Gabriel Holmes, Letter Book, 1821–1824, G.L.B. 25, 230, NCDAH; James Norcom to Gov. Gabriel Holmes, June 18, 1824, in Petitions Concerning George.

57. Penn, "A Perfect Equality Seemed to Reign," 148–153.

nished with arms and everything he wants, by some desperately mean white persons, who I have no doubt he furnishes with plunder in return."[58]

Incidents like these in which slaves and poor whites collaborated in committing violent acts proved rare in comparison to violence between slaves and poor whites. To the perpetual annoyance and frustration of slaveholders, slaves and poor whites—usually men—sometimes associated in improper ways, drinking, gambling, and trading with one another. These unsanctioned activities supplied the conditions conducive to violence.[59] When slaves and poor whites met in society on terms of equality, frequently awash in alcohol, the bonds of social restraint loosened. Conviviality could quickly descend into fisticuffs as the slave and poor white participants more boldly revealed their perceptions of themselves in relation to the other.

While honor cannot be held directly responsible for the violence between slave and poor white men in the same way that it can between two southern gentlemen, the Old South's culture of honor provided the framework in which much of this interracial violence occurred. Despite their poverty, poor whites enjoyed the perks of belonging to the master race. Some of the more depraved examples, such as Brickhouse, clearly overextended their privileges by physically abusing slaves at will. As free white men, poor whites did stake a claim to the honor of wealthy slaveholders, and therefore expected the deference of slaves. When they believed slaves showed them a lack of respect, insulted them, or exposed their underground dealings to the "respectable" white community, poor whites felt the sting of dishonor and responded violently.

Honor becomes a much more problematic concept when applied to the violence committed by slaves. Slave men might have battled for honor in the quarters, but white society considered them wholly devoid of honor. The system of slavery itself tried to emasculate slave men, stripping them of almost all power and authority. Slave husbands and fathers did what they could to protect and provide for their families, but masters exercised the lion's share of control. They

58. Governor's Papers, Gov. Gabriel Holmes, vol. 53, May 20, 1824, NCDAH; Silas Summerall to Gov. James Pleasants, April 6, 1825, Executive Papers, Gov. James Pleasants, box 288, folder April 1–10, 1825, LVA. For other instances of poor whites paying slaves to commit destructive acts, see Herbert Aptheker, *American Negro Slave Revolts* (New York: Columbia University Press, 1943), 148. Two possible cases of poor whites committing violent acts with slaves along highways may also be found in Davidson County, Records of Slaves and Free Persons of Color, n.d., 1826–1896, folder 1852, 1854, 1859, NCDAH; and Governor's Papers, Gov. William A. Graham, G.P. 117, folder March 1847, NCDAH.

59. Ayers, *Vengeance and Justice*, 131.

denied slave men their manhood by whipping them in front of their women and children, by raping and flogging their wives, and by co-opting the supervision of the slave household. The master, rather than the slave man, supplied many of the slave family's needs. The male slave endured a lifetime of being called "boy" or "uncle," depending on his age, but never "man."[60] Masters took great comfort in thinking of their bondsmen as unmanly, childlike, and harmless Sambos, rather than as dangerous, violent criminals waiting for a convenient opportunity to strike. But slaves never internalized the Sambo personality, and instead felt what Orlando Patterson has described as an "irrepressible yearning for dignity and recognition."[61] Perhaps in their violent confrontations with poor whites, they achieved this. Historian Edward L. Ayers has observed that, statistically, "whites other than owners and overseers were the most frequent victims of slave violence."[62] Slave men who became embroiled in disputes with poor white men perhaps seized the opportunity to flex their masculinity against lower-class whites. In physically asserting themselves, they may have shared the same emotional uplift Frederick Douglass experienced after his violent resistance against the "nigger-breaker" Edward Covey. That incident, Douglass wrote, "revived within me a sense of my own manhood. . . . My long-crushed spirit rose, cowardice departed, [and] bold defiance took its place."[63] Violent confrontations against poor whites, while perhaps not as gratifying as a direct attack on the master, may have given slave men a taste of the honor and manliness that their condition denied them.[64]

These speculations would be more compelling, however, if slaves routinely struck the first blow in their violent interactions with poor whites. With the exception of George's assault on Jesse Hassell, a case in which the slave definitely believed himself wronged and took revenge for a specific grievance, bondsmen

---

60. Elkins, *Slavery*, 130; John W. Blassingame, *The Slave Community: Plantation Life in the Antebellum South*, rev. ed. (New York: Oxford University Press, 1979), 172–173; Eugene D. Genovese, *Roll, Jordan, Roll: The World the Slaves Made* (New York: Vintage Books, 1976), 482–494; Gross, *Double Character*, 51–52; Herbert G. Gutman, *The Black Family in Slavery and Freedom, 1750–1925* (New York: Vintage Books, 1977), 306–307.

61. Patterson, *Slavery and Social Death*, 97.

62. Ayers, *Vengeance and Justice*, 131–133; quote 131.

63. Blight, *Narrative of the Life of Frederick Douglass*, 79.

64. On the link between violence and manhood, see Richard Yarborough, "Race, Violence, and Manhood: The Masculine Idea in Frederick Douglass's 'The Heroic Slave,'" in *Haunted Bodies: Gender and Southern Texts*, ed. Anne Goodwyn Jones and Susan V. Donaldson (Charlottesville: University Press of Virginia, 1997): 159–184.

in none of the episodes examined here were the aggressors. Most of the violence slaves used against poor whites could be classified as defensive. Slaves usually attacked either as poor whites were on the verge of punishing them or their friends, or after poor whites had already initiated the violence. Rather than fighting with poor whites for the sake of honor, this tendency suggests that slaves were most likely to respond violently when their sense of justice, and of the "rights" they claimed for themselves, was violated. They resisted, in short, when their treatment at the hands of poor whites exceeded the bounds of what they considered fair.[65]

What is more certain than these questions of honor is that countless slave and poor white men together inhabited a shadowy subculture of conviviality and violence. The lower orders of southern society shared a rough-and-tumble culture in which camaraderie and play could suddenly turn into rivalry and animosity. When their social contacts turned violent, both slave and poor white men often resorted to the ear-biting and other lower-class fighting techniques shunned by southern gentlemen.[66] Once the inflamed passions subsided, combatants could just as quickly make amends and return to their amicable fraternization.[67] Surely the mutual companionship and economic benefits many slaves and poor whites derived through contact with the other militated against the abrupt severing of ties between them, despite the occasional violent outburst. This ability of slaves and poor whites to career erratically between friendship and violence—the volatility characteristic of their relationships—suggests the tensions underlying their social interaction. Poor whites could boast of light skin but not the wealth, respect, and other trappings of whiteness. Indeed, at times, they more closely resembled slaves than masters. Because poor whites occupied such an ambiguous place in society, unpredictability was bound to mark their relationships with slaves.

65. Kolchin, *Unfree Labor*, 265–267, 313–320.

66. Philip J. Schwarz, "Gabriel's Challenge: Slaves and Crime in Late Eighteenth-Century Virginia," *Virginia Magazine of History and Biography* 90 (July 1982): 283, explains that the slave Gabriel, the year before his well-known plot of 1800, bit off "a considerable part" of a white overseer's left ear.

67. This was the case with Edward Isham and a free black man. See Culclasure, "I Have Killed a Damned Dog," 23.

CHAPTER 5

THE DOUBLE STANDARD

Sex and Sexual Violence

Slaves and poor whites in the antebellum South engaged in a range of sexual contacts, from apparently loving unions of varying duration to violent sexual assaults and the myriad forms of coerced sex that seamlessly connected these extremes. While historians have examined in great detail such encounters between poor white women and slave men, they have overlooked the more elusive yet certainly far more numerous instances of sexual interaction between poor white men and slave women. But by juxtaposing relations between poor white women and slave men on one hand, and poor white men and slave women on the other, poor whites' gendered experience of sexual contact with slaves comes more clearly into focus. As a rule, "respectable" white society condemned as sexually depraved those lower-class white women who had consensual sex with slave men, sold them sexual favors, or became the victims of their violent sexual assaults. In contrast, poor white men successfully overcame their class status, appropriated for themselves a tenuous place atop the racialized patriarchy of the Old South, and claimed access to slave women, despite elite objections. Race, class, and gender collided in different ways for poor white men and women, confirming the double standard in southern white society that permitted sexual contact between white men and slave women, but not between white women and slave men.

The likelihood of any sort of interracial sexual encounter between slaves and poor whites varied greatly by locality. For sexual contact to take place, slaves and poor whites needed to live in close proximity to one another. In the South Carolina low country or in the western mountains of North Carolina and Virginia, opportunities would have been slim. Few poor whites inhabited the low country, while relatively few slaves lived in the mountains. The couple dozen total cases available for examination, however, make it exceptionally difficult to tease out geographical variations in the incidence of slave–poor white sexual contact. In North Carolina, for instance, confirmed episodes of slave–poor white sex or sexual violence in the antebellum decades are scattered across more than twelve counties, ranging from Perquimans along the Albemarle Sound to Mecklenburg in the southwest, with roughly equal numbers of cases found among counties in the coastal plain and in the Piedmont. Within this region, many neighborhoods and larger geographic pockets witnessed no incidents of sexual contact between slaves and poor whites, or those who engaged in illicit sex left no traces of their encounters. Because so many sexual interactions between slaves and poor whites have gone undocumented, any precise, statistical analysis of the frequency of such encounters is impossible. Nevertheless, while slave–poor white sex was not rampant and uncontrolled, neither was it unheard of over much of the Carolinas and Virginia. Petitions to governors and state legislatures, court records, slave narratives, and newspapers combine to offer brief snapshots of the sexual contacts between slaves and poor whites, whether consensual, forced, or coerced. They show that, while elite southerners considered poor white men and women alike dangerously promiscuous, they obsessed far more over the sexual behavior of poor white women. As the class of white woman most likely to reject men of their own race by taking black partners, and with the biological capacity to give birth to free mulatto children, poor white women possessed the potential to blur the racial boundaries that undergirded the southern social order.

Within the past decade, such historians as Victoria E. Bynum, Laura F. Edwards, and Martha Hodes have expertly pried into the sex lives of poor white women in the nineteenth-century South. As their work demonstrates, socially marginal poor white women often adhered to a moral code at odds with polite society and flouted its sexual prescriptions. Lacking status in the community and virtually any hope of gaining respectability, some poor white women believed they had little to lose by crossing the color line to indulge their sexual appetites. Far more frequently than "respectable" women, they broke taboos against interracial sex and boldly defied social convention by mingling freely within a historically murky subculture of interracial drinking, revelry, and sex, occasionally taking enslaved black men as lovers.[1] No exact figures can be determined, but a minute and elu-

---

1. Victoria E. Bynum, *Unruly Women: The Politics of Social and Sexual Control in the Old South* (Chapel Hill: University of North Carolina Press, 1992); Laura F. Edwards, "Sexual Violence, Gender, Reconstruction, and the Extension of Patriarchy in Granville County, North Carolina," *North Carolina Historical Review* 68 (July 1991): 237–260; Laura F. Edwards, "Law, Domestic Violence, and the Limits of Patriarchal Authority in the Antebellum South," *Journal of Southern History* 65 (November 1999): 733–770; Laura F. Edwards, "The Disappearance of Susan Daniel and Henderson Cooper: Gender and Narratives of Political Conflict in the Reconstruction-Era U.S. South," in *Sex, Love, Race: Crossing Boundaries in North American History*, ed. Martha Hodes (New York: New

sive fraction of all poor white women did engage in apparently consensual relations with slave men. Because they usually conducted their affairs clandestinely, the historical record can confirm only a precious few of these cases. In Virginia, for example, Jeremiah Delk's slave Moses "cohabited with a base white woman, in Southampton County by the Name of Catharine Britt."[2] Primary sources, however, typically reveal little more than tantalizing hints about poor white women's possible consensual sexual relationships with slave men.

Antebellum newspapers periodically printed advertisements for runaway slave men who absconded with "disreputable" white women. Masters generally looked with suspicion upon any form of slaves' contact with nonslaveholding free people, but slave men who ran off with poor white women proved especially troubling. Male slaves were supposed to augment the master's wealth by impregnating enslaved women and producing a subsequent generation of black laborers. When slave men pursued intimate and loving relationships with lowerclass white women, they snubbed the master's authority by choosing a mate whose potential offspring would not serve a lifetime of chattel slavery for the economic enrichment of the slaveholder.

Although Martha Hodes correctly observes that antebellum interracial romances sometimes met with at least tacit acceptance in the local community,[3] the choice to consort with slaves often forced white women to flee with their slave lovers, either preemptively to pursue their affairs in secret or to escape the reproach of disapproving neighbors. Surely not every white woman who ran off

York University Press, 1999), 294–312; Martha Hodes, *White Women, Black Men: Illicit Sex in the Nineteenth-Century South* (New Haven: Yale University Press, 1997). On the colonial period, see Kathleen M. Brown, *Good Wives, Nasty Wenches, and Anxious Patriarchs: Gender, Race, and Power in Colonial Virginia* (Chapel Hill: University of North Carolina Press, 1996), 97; and Kirsten Fischer, *Suspect Relations: Sex, Race, and Resistance in Colonial North Carolina* (Ithaca: Cornell University Press, 2002), 99–100, 110, 111, 114.

2. Silas Summerall to Gov. James Pleasants, April 6, 1825, Executive Papers, Gov. James Pleasants, box 288, folder April 1–10, 1825, LVA. See also James Hugo Johnston, *Race Relations in Virginia & Miscegenation in the South, 1776–1860* (Amherst: University of Massachusetts Press, 1970), 266; and Hodes, *White Women, Black Men,* 50.

3. Hodes, *White Women, Black Men,* 3. On unconventional interracial family arrangements, see Thomas E. Buckley, S.J., "Unfixing Race: Class, Power, and Identity in an Interracial Family," in *Sex, Love, Race: Crossing Boundaries in North American History,* ed. Martha Hodes (New York: New York University Press, 1999), 164–190; Josephine Boyd Bradley and Kent Anderson Leslie, "White Pain Pollen: An Elite Biracial Daughter's Quandary," in *Sex, Love, Race,* 213–234; and Joshua D. Rothman, *Notorious in the Neighborhood: Sex and Families across the Color Line in Virginia, 1787–1861* (Chapel Hill: University of North Carolina Press, 2003), ch. 2.

with a slave man was romantically linked to him, but most probably were. In taking up with a bondsman, and in finding companionship across the color line, these white women defied the organizing principles of southern society. Accompanying their slave companions in flight, they confirmed their guilt and fled the disgrace of taking up with a slave man. In Mecklenburg County, Virginia, the poor white Susan Percy ran off with a slave named John in 1857. When apprehended, Susan confessed "that an intimacy had grown up" between them, and together they resolved "to make their escape to a free State," giving John his freedom and Susan the chance to "hide her shame" for falling in love with a slave.[4]

A white woman's decision to abscond with a slave man demonstrated a strong commitment to their relationship, and evinced their hope of forging a lasting union away from the master and neighborhood scrutiny. Slaveholder Neil Brown of Robeson County, North Carolina, suspected that his bondsman Atta ran off with a white girl to find "some place where they may live in the habits of the relationship of man and wife unmolested."[5] Joel Harris of Halifax County, North Carolina, offered a $25 reward for "a bright complexioned negro man, named AUSTIN." Harris believed his slave was accompanied by Sally Doile, "a white woman with whom he was intimate, and who has left the neighborhood." Sometime during their flight, Austin and Sally got separated. Austin trekked more than a hundred miles to Fluvanna, Virginia, "before he was apprehended." Harris recovered the troublesome slave, then promptly sold him to Peter Epes of Warren County, "on account of his taking up with a white woman." Newspapers made no mention of Sally Doile's fate, but fourteen months later Austin fled from his new master, perhaps to rejoin his white lover.[6]

Loving relationships between slave men and poor white women sometimes lasted for several years. In one extraordinary case, the "large and portly" slave known as Bay Ben "eloped from the county of Pitt," in North Carolina, reportedly destined "for Indiana or some part of the western country." According to his owners, Ben "went off in company with a white woman who has several children, two or three of whom are nearly grown. . . . The woman calls her name GATSY TOOTLE, and considers herself the wife of Ben." "The children," the advertise-

4. *Richmond Enquirer,* November 20, 1857. See also Rothman, *Notorious in the Neighborhood,* 239–240.

5. Quoted in Freddie L. Parker, *Running for Freedom: Slave Runaways in North Carolina, 1775–1840* (New York: Garland Publishing, Inc., 1993), 82.

6. *Free Press* (Halifax), February 18, 1825, in Parker, *Running for Freedom,* 96; *Raleigh Register* (weekly), April 28, 1826.

ment noted, "are all supposed to be sired by Ben." If that were true, and some of the children were "nearly grown," Gatsy Tootle had been together with Ben for many years.[7]

Many of these apparently consensual affairs between antebellum poor white women and slave men originated in their close working contact. When poor whites occupied positions of servitude, they belied the notion that whiteness equaled freedom. Laboring together with slaves in the master's household blurred the lines of color and status, nurturing the conditions ripe for mutual attraction. The abovementioned Susan Percy lived, probably as a servant, with Mecklenburg County, Virginia, slaveholder Lucy Harris, the master of Susan's enslaved lover John. Likewise, in Davidson County, North Carolina, an affinity developed between the elderly Abraham Peppinger's poor white servant girl Polly Lane, and his slave Jim, during the summer of 1825. According to one neighborhood slave, "Jim was in the habit of crawling through a hole between the house logs into the loft where [Polly] slept." He had also spied Polly "late at night in the kitchen lying on the bed with Jim when all the white person[s] were asleep." Another witness "once watched and surprised Jim & Polly Lane together on Sunday in a by place and near indecent." Jim himself claimed that he "kept her as a wife for several months." Although Polly would ultimately accuse Jim of raping her, the evidence strongly suggests that they had had consensual relations for some time. Clearly the close proximity of poor white women and slave men working in slaveholding households sometimes cultivated interracial relationships of love, warmth, and affection.[8]

Less often, the working lives of poor white women made them vulnerable to assault by a small number of sexually predatory slave men. The incidence of rape or attempted rape by bondsmen upon white women (of any class) in the ante-

7. *Raleigh Register* (weekly), October 21, 1834.

8. *Richmond Enquirer,* November 20, 1857; Governor's Papers, Gov. Hutchins G. Burton, G.P. 55, 124–125, NCDAH; Governor's Papers, Gov. Hutchins G. Burton, G.P. 56, 257, NCDAH. The case of Polly Lane and Jim is analyzed with the greatest care and sophistication in Hodes, *White Women, Black Men,* ch. 3. It also earns mention in Diane Miller Sommerville, "The Rape Myth in the Old South Reconsidered," *Journal of Southern History* 61 (August 1995): 505–509; Bill Cecil-Fronsman, *Common Whites: Class and Culture in Antebellum North Carolina* (Lexington: University Press of Kentucky, 1992), 89; Bertram Wyatt-Brown, *Southern Honor: Ethics and Behavior in the Old South* (New York: Oxford University Press, 1982), 317–318; and Guion Griffis Johnson, *Ante-Bellum North Carolina: A Social History* (Chapel Hill: University of North Carolina Press, 1937), 71.

bellum decades is difficult to calculate with any precision. Countless rapes and rape attempts went unreported, and white men's willingness to dispense extralegal justice at times precluded the need to visit the courtroom. Nevertheless, the total number of slave men's sexual assaults upon white women appears quite small. In Virginia, from 1785 to 1865, only fifty-eight slaves were executed for raping white women: less than one per year for the entire state. Between 1830 and 1865, perhaps as few as thirty-six slaves were hanged for the rape or attempted rape of a white woman. The numbers were even smaller in the less populous states of North and South Carolina.[9]

Of all southern white women, those of the lower classes proved far more likely to charge a slave man with committing a sex crime. Surely some of these allegations were false. Consensual relationships between poor white women and slave men inevitably resulted in pregnancy on occasion. Ignorance of human biology combined with the rudimentary contraceptive technologies available to produce mixed-race children that betrayed interracial sexual liaisons. White women of all classes understood that giving birth to a nonwhite child invited the contempt of the community. If a poor white woman discovered she was pregnant by a slave man, she might seek an abortion. Upon realizing she carried the slave Jim's child, Polly Lane explained to an enslaved acquaintance that "she was big and would give him a dollar to get her something to destroy it."[10] Rumors circulated that Polly made "many efforts, by bleeding, Physicing, [and] jumping off high places . . . to produce an abortion."[11] Although the black father of her child cannot be positively identified, poor white Nancy Wallis of Orange County, North Carolina, also attempted to terminate her pregnancy early. She consulted Dr. Eli Watson while "at a singing meeting" in 1837 and eventually asked for "something to destroy the child." When Watson refused, Nancy grew distraught. She threatened to "kill herself by drowning or hanging if he did not. That owing to the misconduct of her sisters, her father thought much of her, and she would kill herself if he did not give her something."[12] Both Polly and Nancy ultimately saw their pregnancies to term. They then both adopted another tack available to poor white women who violated taboos against interracial sex. They cried rape

9. Philip J. Schwarz, *Twice Condemned: Slaves and the Criminal Laws of Virginia, 1705–1865* (Baton Rouge: Louisiana State University Press, 1988), 209, 293.

10. Governor's Papers, Gov. Hutchins G. Burton, G.P. 55, 124, NCDAH.

11. Ibid., 154, NCDAH.

12. Governor's Papers, Gov. Edward B. Dudley, vol. 84, 1522, NCDAH.

to disguise their illicit relationships, screen themselves from shame, and preserve their own and their family's honor and reputation.[13]

Claiming rape offered poor white women no guarantee that society would absolve them of their perceived wrongdoing. Prevailing medical wisdom in the rural South held that rape probably could not lead to pregnancy. Four doctors commenting on Polly Lane's predicament informed North Carolina's governor that, "without an excitation of lust, or the enjoyment of pleasure in the venereal act, no conception can probably take place. So that if an absolute rape were to be perpetrated, it is not likely she would become pregnant." Dr. Watson concurred. When he asked Nancy Wallis the circumstances under which she had become pregnant, the poor white woman replied that the sexual encounter had happened "partly against her consent" or "partly by force." Watson unilaterally dismissed her response, insisting that that "could not be the case or she would not be in her present condition." To become pregnant, the medical community contended, Polly and Nancy both must have enjoyed the sex with their enslaved partners.[14]

Sources from three rape trials in antebellum North Carolina nevertheless suggest that the poor white women involved may have levied charges of rape against slave men to shield themselves from the public scorn and humiliation of willfully crossing the color line for sex. Many residents of Davidson County believed that Polly Lane accused the bondsman Jim of rape only "to screen this unhappy girl from the reproach of being found alone with him in private lamenting her sad fate of Pregnancy & disgrace with Jim."[15] Similarly, when Nancy Wallis found herself "delivered of a black child" in October 1837, she accused Isaac Griffey's slave Juba with rape. Juba, however, made an unlikely rapist. Sources described him as a "feeble" man between sixty and seventy years old, "very infirm and not able to walk without a staff." Because "his hands and arms shook like a person with palzy," he worked only half time. Observing that Nancy, by contrast, was

13. Thomas D. Morris, *Southern Slavery and the Law, 1619–1860* (Chapel Hill: University of North Carolina Press, 1996), 314, 304; Catherine Clinton, "'Southern Dishonor': Flesh, Blood, Race, and Bondage," in *In Joy and In Sorrow: Women, Family, and Marriage in the Victorian South, 1830–1900*, ed. Carol Bleser (New York: Oxford University Press, 1991), 58; Bynum, *Unruly Women*, 45.

14. Governor's Papers, Gov. Hutchins G. Burton, G.P. 55, 167, NCDAH; Governor's Papers, Gov. Edward B. Dudley, vol. 84, 1522, NCDAH. Such medical wisdom, that women had to enjoy sex to become pregnant, conflicts with the widespread notion that many white women were "passionless" and did not much enjoy sexual intercourse. See Nancy F. Cott, "Passionlessness: An Interpretation of Victorian Sexual Ideology, 1790–1850," *Signs* 4 (Winter 1978): 219–236.

15. Governor's Papers, Gov. Hutchins G. Burton, G.P. 56, 258, NCDAH.

young, physically "robust and stoutly made"—far superior in strength to the decrepit Juba—and that she identified the slave as the rapist only *after* she had delivered a mulatto baby, many whites in the community considered her accusation "a false and base fabrication," a story contrived by a desperate Nancy "to cover an odious Illicit intercourse this unfortunate base woman has had with another negro who . . . she is unwilling to expose." [16] In Mecklenburg County, Elizabeth C. Rodgers, who lived with her husband Harvey on the land of Matthew Wallace, may have engaged in a consensual relationship with Wallace's slave Jeff. Though not pregnant by the slave, she ultimately accused him of rape. After Jeff's trial, one of the bondsman's attorneys remarked, "I was fully satisfied that [the rape charge] was a trumped up story of an abandoned woman to conceal her own infamy." [17]

Certainly not all accusations of rape masked consensual interracial relations. Extant court records fuel the impression that slave men sexually preyed upon poor white women more often than elite white women.[18] The patterns and routines of poor white women's daily lives made them more susceptible to sexual attack. Poor white women sometimes toiled at home, by themselves, performing household chores or other work such as sewing or laundry that they took in to help make ends meet. Whether single, or left alone on a daily basis or for days or weeks on end by husbands scouring the countryside for employment, the isolation of poor white women laboring at home made them likely targets of sexual assault. After the slave Hartwell attempted to rape the twenty-six-year-old Elizabeth J. Baxter in Prince George's County, Virginia, the victim's husband Richard, a cooper with no land or personal property, testified that the slave "was well acquainted with his habits of leaving home at an early hour before day" to go to work. One morning in 1855, after Richard had departed but still two hours before dawn, Hartwell, posing as a "waggoner," rapped at the Baxters' door, "scratching like a dog would" and asking for fire. When Elizabeth opened the door to give him fire, the slave muscled his way inside and refused to leave. Elizabeth warned him "that if her husband came he would kill him," but Hartwell knew Richard Baxter was not available to come to her rescue. Confident of no interference, he

16. Governor's Papers, Gov. Edward B. Dudley, vol. 84, 1489, 1521, 1522, NCDAH.

17. *State v. Jefferson*, 28 N.C. 305 (1846), Supreme Court Original Case #3699; Nathaniel Boyden to Gov. William A. Graham, September 15, 1846, in Governor's Papers, Gov. William A. Graham, G.P. 115, folder September 1846, NCDAH.

18. Sommerville, "Rape Myth," 514.

pushed Elizabeth to the floor "and with his knee indeavoured [*sic*] to open her legs for the purpose of having intercourse with her."[19]

Laboring poor white women who ventured outside the home to work found themselves in direct contact with slave men, working in the same households, business establishments, or fields. In 1860, some five thousand white women in North Carolina, and another twenty-two hundred in South Carolina, labored as seamstresses, with thousands more filling servant positions for wealthier neighbors. Hundreds of others worked as factory operatives or as hired agricultural hands.[20] In these occupations, poor white female laborers confronted sexual dangers in the workplace. Not only did prosperous white employers sometimes take sexual advantage of them, but so too did a few of their enslaved male co-workers. Mary Dunn likely worked as a servant for the widow Henson in Anson County, North Carolina, in 1825. The two women were the only whites in Henson's household, although a slave man named Warrick "& other negroes belonged & lived at the same place." One Monday in March, Mrs. Henson went on an extended visit, leaving Mary alone with the slaves. That night, Warrick gained entry into Mary's room, "had his will of her against her consent," and departed.[21] At Warrick's trial for rape, a neighbor testified that Mary and Warrick were altogether "too thick." Mary had engaged in fortune-telling with Warrick "sometime before" the attack, and she had once been seen "in the negro house alone" with him, "talking but not touching each other."[22] Mary conceded during the trial that she had once spent time in the slave quarters prior to the rape, "when Mrs. Henson would not let them spin in the dwelling house."[23] It was perhaps while together spinning cloth in the slave quarters that Warrick first took a fancy to Mary Dunn.

19. Executive Papers, Gov. Henry A. Wise, box 1, folder 2, LVA; Eighth Census of the United States, 1860: Prince George's County, Virginia, 411. In the colonial period, indentured servant women confronted the same brand of vulnerability. See, for example, Brown, *Good Wives*, 98; and Fischer, *Suspect Relations*, 110, 111.

20. Joseph C. G. Kennedy, *Population of the United States in 1860; Compiled from the Original Returns of the Eighth Census, Under the Direction of the Secretary of the Interior* (Washington: Government Printing Office, 1864), 363, 455.

21. Governor's Papers, Gov. Hutchins G. Burton, G.P. 55, 10, NCDAH. See also Hodes, *White Women, Black Men*, 62–63; Cecil-Fronsman, *Common Whites*, 75; and Wyatt-Brown, *Southern Honor*, 316.

22. Governor's Papers, Gov. Hutchins G. Burton, G.P. 55, 11, NCDAH.

23. Ibid., 12, NCDAH. The jury found Warrick guilty, but North Carolina's governor, apparently not convinced of the slave's wrongdoing, pardoned him, contingent upon his leaving the state. See ibid., 8, 7, NCDAH.

*   *   *

With husbands or fathers absent, and often with no male protector at all to intervene on their behalf, poor white women turned to the court system as their only recourse against the sexual assaults of slave men.[24] The courtroom, however, offered an unfavorable if not overtly hostile atmosphere for poor white women to air their charges. There, economically dependent poor white women, especially those who lacked husbands to monitor and govern their sexual conduct, faced the suspicion, scrutiny, and reproach of the surrounding community. As Victoria Bynum has argued, poverty "defeminized" poor white women.[25] Lacking wealth, property, or meaningful connections to prominent families, poor white women dwelled at the margins of southern society, laboring as seamstresses, domestic servants, or common field hands in a constant struggle for survival. Their lives fell far short of the domestic ideal for southern white women, but their impoverished circumstances left them no alternative.[26]

Poor white women's reputation for violating prescribed sexual behavior compounded their difficulties in court. Many in polite society regarded poor white women as not merely promiscuous but as sexually "deviant" or "depraved." Observing some "rather good-looking" sandhiller girls in South Carolina, one gentleman expressed the opinion of many middling and elite southern whites when he informed traveler Frederick Law Olmsted "that a very slight value is placed upon female virtue among this class."[27] Many southerners believed that poor women were unchaste and lacking in the virtue and restraint necessary to withhold consent, a necessary precondition for rape. They instead presumed that poor white women shared in the responsibility for the alleged sexual assault and regarded their charges of rape or attempted rape with skepticism.[28] In practice, the law discriminated against poor white women, failing to provide them the same protections granted elite women. Many verdicts ultimately hinged less

24. Victoria Bynum, "On the Lowest Rung: Court Control Over Poor White and Free Black Women," *Southern Exposures* 12 (November/December 1984): 41; Edwards, "Sexual Violence," 240; Sommerville, "Rape Myth," 514–515.

25. Bynum, *Unruly Women*, 7; Sommerville, "Rape Myth," 515.

26. Bynum, *Unruly Women*, 6, 7, 45–46, 110.

27. Frederick Law Olmsted, *A Journey in the Seaboard Slave States, with Remarks on Their Economy* (New York: Dix & Edwards, 1856), 507–508.

28. Bynum, *Unruly Women*, 109–110; Karen A. Getman, "Sexual Control in the Slaveholding South: The Implementation and Maintenance of a Racial Caste System," *Harvard Women's Law Journal* 7 (Spring 1984): 136; Peter W. Bardaglio, "Rape and the Law in the Old South: 'Calculated to excite indignation in every heart,'" *Journal of Southern History* 60 (November 1994): 766.

upon the race of the perpetrator and the victim than on the class standing of the accuser.[29] "Respectable" white society condemned poor white women's sexual behavior, and excluded them from the ranks of the delicate and virtuous "ladies" more worthy of protection from slave sex offenders.[30]

White society's need to punish a slave convicted for the capital offenses of rape or attempted rape of a socially marginal poor white woman often paled in comparison to the desire to preserve the life of a valuable bondsman.[31] As a rule, landed and at least moderately prosperous southern white men determined the fate of accused slaves. South Carolina's courts of magistrates and freeholders, the lawful bodies that adjudicated slave crimes in each district, consisted of two justices and three to five freeholders. For slave trials in Virginia, five justices of the peace, with no jury, served as the courts of oyer and terminer in each county. North Carolina granted accused slaves a jury trial, but state law mandated that only slaveholders could serve as jurors. This requirement, explains historian Daniel J. Flanigan, was designed specifically to protect the interests of slaveholders. The measure alleviated slaveholder fears that disaffected nonslaveholders would take revenge upon their wealthier neighbors in court by indiscriminately handing down guilty verdicts against slave defendants. Slaveholding jurors' sympathies toward fellow masters militated against any knee-jerk decisions that would culminate in the death of an accused bondsman.[32] A sample of three high-

29. Sommerville, "Rape Myth," 515, 517; Bardaglio, "Rape and the Law," 751; Edwards, "Sexual Violence," 238–239; Edwards, "Disappearance," 298, 304.

30. Bynum, "On the Lowest Rung," 40; Diane Miller Sommerville, "Rape, Race, and Castration in Slave Law in the Colonial and Early South," in *The Devil's Lane: Sex and Race in the Early South*, ed. Catherine Clinton and Michele Gillespie (New York: Oxford University Press, 1997), 75, 82; Sommerville, "Rape Myth," 518; Edwards, "Sexual Violence," 239.

31. Bynum, *Unruly Women*, 109–110. On the legal statutes surrounding sex crimes, see A. Leon Higginbotham, Jr., and Barbara K. Kopytoff, "Racial Purity and Interracial Sex in the Law of Colonial and Antebellum Virginia," *Georgetown Law Journal* 77 (August 1989): esp. 2008–2009; and Bardaglio, "Rape and the Law," 750, 753. Prior to 1823, a black man's conviction for the *attempted* rape of a white woman brought a sentence of castration in Virginia. The penalty became death in 1823. See Schwarz, *Twice Condemned*, 206, 292; and Bardaglio, "Rape and the Law," 753. For specific laws on assaults with intent to commit rape, see *Acts Passed at a General Assembly of the Commonwealth of Virginia* (Richmond: Thomas Ritchie, 1823), 37; *Acts Passed By the General Assembly of the State of North Carolina, At its Session, Commencing on the 17th of November, 1823* (Raleigh: J. Gales & Son, 1824), 42; and *The Statutes at Large of South Carolina*, vol. 11 (Columbia: Republican Printing Company, 1873), 279.

32. Daniel J. Flanigan, "Criminal Procedures in Slave Trials in the Antebellum South," *Journal of Southern History* 40 (November 1974): 540, 544, 550–551.

profile North Carolina cases in which poor white women charged slaves with rape or attempted rape shows that the average juror in these trials owned approximately nine, thirteen, and seventeen slaves.[33] The mere fact of slave ownership among jurors was no guarantee of an acquittal of an enslaved defendant, but it does raise questions of potential class bias in the court system. In many of the cases of sexual assaults committed by slaves on white women, slaveholding jurors united in defense of slave property. In reality, the master of but one or two slaves may have had more in common with a poor white female accuser than with his fellow jurymen, but the substantial planters owning twenty, fifty, or one hundred slaves, whose presence on each of the three sample juries skewed the slaveholding average high for the entire group, likely wielded considerable influence among less prosperous jurors. With a vested interest in slave property, they made certain that verdicts took into account the individual circumstances surrounding each case and not merely the race of the accused.

Preconceived notions of poor white female sexual deviance raised the burden of proof required for a slave's conviction for a sex crime. Courts required that poor white victims of sexual violence convince them of the truthfulness of their allegations and prove that they in fact deserved justice. Simply put, poor white women who charged slave men with a sex crime needed to establish their own good character.[34] Those who could successfully secure reputable third-party testimony that they were irrefutably "poor but respectable" often received the benefit of the doubt. In Perquimans County, North Carolina, a jury found slave

33. These figures are based, respectively, on the cases of *State v. Jefferson* (1846), *State v. Jim* (1856), and *State v. Juber* (1838). For the lists of jurors in each case, see, respectively, Mecklenburg County, Minute Book, Superior Court, 1829–1851, 420; Johnston County, Minute Docket, Superior Court, 1831–1868, March term 1856; and Orange County, Minute Docket, Superior Court, 1834–1848, March term 1838. All twelve of the jurors in *State v. Jefferson* may be located in the 1850 slave schedule for Mecklenburg County. Jurors on that case owned between one and twenty-five slaves. For *State v. Jim*, I also identified all twelve jurors in census records—eleven in the 1860 slave schedule for Johnston County, and juror David Avera in the 1850 slave schedule for Johnston County. Slaveholdings among these jurors ranged from three to thirty-two. I traced eleven of the twelve jurors in *State v. Juber* using the 1840 population schedule for Orange County. These eleven jurors owned a total of 185 slaves, with a minimum of four and a maximum of fifty-four. These figures of course do not represent the actual number of slaves each juror owned at the precise time of the trial, but they do provide a rough estimate. The possibility does exist, however, that I have mistakenly identified someone sharing the same name with a juror as a juror himself.

34. Sommerville, "Rape, Race, and Castration," 76; Edwards, "Disappearance," 298; Bynum, *Unruly Women,* 118; Morris, *Southern Slavery and the Law,* 315.

Henry guilty of assault with intent to ravish fourteen-year-old Mary Laura Elliott as she walked to Sunday school. Witnesses attested that the victim possessed "good" character. Likewise, slave Elick was found guilty of committing sexual violence upon Davidson County's Susannah Pickett in part because her character "was proved to be very good for truth and chastity." Predisposed to sympathize with "respectable" white women who accused black men of sexual violence, courts ruled against the enslaved defendants in these cases.[35]

Most poor white women, however, struggled to establish their "good" character in court. Any thorough assessment of a poor white woman's character required a detailed investigation into her sexual history, as her sexual past spoke directly to her credibility.[36] For white men serving in southern courts, female virtue was inextricably tied to her sexual conduct. Chastity correlated with trustworthiness.[37] If a poor white woman had a reputation for engaging in interracial sex or for giving birth out of wedlock (as far more lower-class white women than elite white women did), her entire character was cast into doubt, and the court would be less likely to accept her statements as true.[38] At the 1856 rape trial of Dixon Spivey's slave Jim, in Johnston County, North Carolina, the defense asked openly in court if the alleged poor white victim Elizabeth Sikes's word under oath could be believed, since her "general character . . . was bad for want of chastity, drinking, for illicit intercourse with negroes and for truth." Trials for accused slave rapists, in effect, metamorphosed into assessments of the poor white female plaintiffs, implicitly suggesting that the women themselves invited the sexual assault. The hours of probing questions any poor white woman who accused slaves of rape or attempted rape endured at trial, and the shame and embarrassment of the public airing of her sexual past, surely deterred countless numbers from ever filing complaints of sexual violence.[39]

35. Peter W. Bardaglio, *Reconstructing the Household: Families, Sex, and the Law in the Nineteenth-Century South* (Chapel Hill: University of North Carolina Press, 1995), 78; Edwards, "Disappearance," 299, 304; Edwards, "Sexual Violence," 244; *State v. Henry,* 50 N.C. 66 (1857), Supreme Court Original Case #7244, NCDAH; *State v. Elick,* 52 N.C. 68 (1859), 68–69. See also William D. Valentine Diary, February 17, 1838, #2148, SHC.

36. Clinton, "Southern Dishonor," 59; Bardaglio, "Rape and the Law," 766–767; Sommerville, "Rape Myth," 497; Sommerville, "Rape, Race, and Castration," 74.

37. Bardaglio, "Rape and the Law," 766–767; Fischer, *Suspect Relations,* 141.

38. Sommerville, "Rape, Race, and Castration," 81, 82.

39. Governor's Papers, Gov. Thomas Bragg, G.P. 140, folder April 1856, NCDAH; Edwards, "Sexual Violence," 244. Eighth Census of the United States, 1860: Wayne County, North Carolina, 876, lists Sikes as a landless woman of forty-five with $20 worth of personal property. On Sikes, see also Cecil-Fronsman, *Common Whites,* 77; and Hodes, *White Women, Black Men,* 62.

*   *   *

Perhaps more than any other case from the antebellum Carolinas and Virginia, that of Rachael Holman illustrates poor white women's struggle for impartial treatment in southern courts of law. In August 1856, Rachael, of Anderson District, South Carolina, swore before a magistrate that William Nevitt's slave Lewis "did make an Assault with an intent to Ravish her." As Rachael walked through the woods at dusk, "singing" and carrying a basket of "tomattoes," Lewis came from behind and reportedly "threw her down on the ground, choked her, pul[l]ed her clothes over her face and threatened to kill her, if she did not yeald [sic] to him." Rachael replied "that she was not prepared for death and would rather give up than die." She "hallowed" and begged the slave to release her, but otherwise put up little physical resistance. Lewis penetrated her and "was about ten minutes trying to accomplish his object," she estimated, before he ran away "stark naked." Presumably because the slave failed to ejaculate, court documents describe the rape attempt as unsuccessful, although Rachael assumed "that he could have succeeded if he had not been scared."[40]

Southern courts more readily believed a poor white woman's allegations of sexual abuse if she filed her complaint immediately after an attack, rather than weeks or months later; if respectable witnesses vouched that they heard cries for help or saw signs of struggle in the dirt; or if visible bruises appeared on her body. By these criteria, Rachael should have earned the benefit of the doubt. She promptly reported the assault. The bruises on her throat and arms, her ripped petticoat, her "[d]ress . . . stained by tommattoes," and "the appearance of a scuffle upon the ground" at the crime scene, where additional tomatoes were found the day after the attack "mashed lying about the place," all operated in the poor white woman's favor. Her purported sexual exploits prior to the attack did not.[41]

Rachael unquestioningly grew up in a state of dire poverty. By 1860, nearly eleven thousand individuals in Virginia, the two Carolinas, and Georgia, counted among the South Atlantic region's official "paupers." The overwhelming preponderance of these were white women of all ages, with no visible means of support. Widowed at an early age, Rachael's mother Anna Smith appears in the 1850 census as a thirty-five-year-old pauper living in the Anderson District poor house, along with a seven-year-old boy named Newton. By 1850 she already must have indentured her other, older son—never identified by name—to serve as

40. Anderson District, Court of Magistrates and Freeholders, Trial Papers, microfilm reel C2919, case #309, SCDAH.

41. Bardaglio, "Rape and the Law," 767, 769; Fischer, *Suspect Relations,* 182; Anderson District, Court of Magistrates and Freeholders, Trial Papers, microfilm reel C2919, case #309, SCDAH.

an apprentice or farm hand to a local family with the means to support him. Her daughter Rachael, listed as thirteen years old in 1850, had been sent to live with the wealthy farmer David Anderson, probably as a servant girl. Over the next few years, Rachael also lived with a man named Holman in the household of Basil Davis, but Davis "[d]id not know whether they were married." A James Holman is listed in the 1850 census as a seventeen-year-old laborer living with the elderly William Acker, a farmer from Virginia. Rachael must have married Holman prior to 1856, for she used his surname to identify herself in court records, but by the time of the attempted rape, she was around the age of twenty, living with her mother, who by then had vacated the poor house and obtained her own home. What became of Rachael's husband James remains unclear, but he did not appear in court to testify on behalf of his one-time wife.[42]

At the slave Lewis's trial, no fewer than eight witnesses, each acquainted with Rachael Holman for several years, contradicted the young poor white woman's claim that she "kept herself as free from connection with the colored population as a woman of virtue should do." "Her reputation for chastity throughout the neighborhood is bad," they stated. "[H]er character for virtue is not good." Why they testified against Rachael is not clear. Perhaps they held some personal grudge against her or hoped to shame her out of the neighborhood. Or maybe they looked with unease at her consorting with blacks, both slave and free, and saw her as a potential threat to the social order. Witnesses repeatedly claimed that Rachael "is too familiar with the colored population" and that she "is altogether too common in her embraces both with black and white." By the time of the attempted rape, Rachael had purportedly had sexual intercourse with no fewer than four or five different white men, counting her husband. Henry Howard, a boarder in Anna Smith's home for some "five to Eight months" before the trial, testified that "youngsters" who "[s]ometimes . . . set up late at night" frequented the house, but he had "not noticed any squeezing going on." Howard did acknowledge seeing "men at the house of Mrs. Smith both in the day and night," including one Benjamin Chastain, a local farmer. Another witness posited that Howard himself "had connection" with Rachael. Someone else caught

42. Rudolph M. Lapp, "The Ante Bellum Poor Whites of the South Atlantic States" (Ph.D. diss., University of California–Berkeley, 1956), 83, 84; Seventh Census of the United States, 1850: Anderson District, South Carolina, 171, 192, 252; Anderson District, Court of Magistrates and Freeholders, Trial Papers, microfilm reel C2919, case #309, SCDAH. On the subject of poor relief, see Timothy J. Lockley, "Public Poor Relief in Buncombe County, North Carolina, 1792–1860," *North Carolina Historical Review* 80 (January 2003): 28–51.

Rachael "bedded up" with Newton Majors, "a white man." John J. Brown admitted going to Anna and Rachael's house "several times," but when asked if Rachael "permit[ted] him to have connection with her," Brown "refused to answer." He confessed, however, that he "[d]id ask her once to go as far as the fence with him and she went."[43]

Compounding the developing picture of Rachael's promiscuity, witnesses also intimated that she had previously had sexual relationships with black men. Mary Chastain testified that she "[h]as frequently seen negroes slipping about the premises" when she went to Anna and Rachael's home "too [sic] see whether her . . . husband [the aforementioned Benjamin] was at the house or not." Basil Davis once spied Rachael, her one brother ("a good chunk of a boy"), "and a negro fellow running through his . . . field." "[S]ome of the Party" at Davis's "pursued the negro with the avowed object of chastising him for his intiming" with Rachael. One witness saw Rachael "whispering" with "a negro man" one Sunday, while another surprised her "covered up in bed with the two daughters" of a free black man. Upon hearing these stories, the court began to agree with witnesses' claims that Rachael "will lend herself to the embraces of a negro as quick as a white man" and that she did not properly "discriminate . . . between colors."[44]

Rachael had apparently socialized with blacks for several years without provoking community outrage, supporting Martha Hodes's contention that southerners sometimes greeted such relationships with a degree of "toleration."[45] Yet Rachael's story simultaneously reveals the limits of southern whites' willingness to condone interracial romance. Her relationship with Elias, a slave of the prosperous farmer and merchant Daniel Brown, magnified the strain her behavior placed on the community and inflicted the greatest damage to her reputation during Lewis's trial.[46] Little is known about the bondsman Elias. His master Daniel Brown had purchased him from the elderly farmer William Acker, and owned him just a year before the slave's death. What work Elias performed, and how he died, remains a mystery, but Rachael Holman likely first met the slave through her association with her husband James, who worked for Acker. In

43. Anderson District, Court of Magistrates and Freeholders, Trial Papers, microfilm reel C2919, case #309, SCDAH.

44. Anderson District, Court of Magistrates and Freeholders, Trial Papers, microfilm reel C2919, case #309, SCDAH.

45. Hodes, *White Women, Black Men*, 3.

46. Seventh Census of the United States, 1850: Anderson District, South Carolina, 189; Eighth Census of the United States, 1860: Anderson District, South Carolina, 157.

1854, one witness saw Rachael and Elias "lying on a bed together" at Acker's. "Both parties were awake and talking," according to the witness, with Rachael's two brothers, her mother Anna Smith, and Henry Howard in the same room. Rachael and Elias "remained in the same bed . . . until midnight," her mother voicing no objection. Howard, the witness went on, "staid all night" but "did not sleep at all" because he "was jealous of the negro," since Rachael "rather preferred him." (Howard had had relations with Rachael before, but "[t]he negro was not in his way at the time.") A second witness reported seeing Rachael, Elias, and others "playing hide and go seek." Rachael and Elias "went to hide together," during which time the slave held her hand, "and after a while put his arm gently around her as if in the act of kissing her." Rumors reached Elias's master Daniel Brown "that he had better remove his boy as he was too intimate with a white woman in Acker's neighborhood." Probably to preserve the social order as well as the life of his valuable slave property, Brown heeded the advice.[47]

Several of Rachael's violations of southern racial etiquette seemed to stem from her work-related activities. Coming from such a humble economic background, Rachael learned to work hard from an early age. Unfortunately for her, "respectable" southern whites often looked not with pity but with scorn upon poor white women forced to work outside the home for a living. Impoverished widows, orphans, and others who comported themselves respectably might earn public sympathy and charity, but Rachael's drive to support herself and her mother sometimes led to an inversion of the usual social order. Witness James Reeves swore "that a free negro by the name of Morris" once hired Rachael "to pick cotton for him," and that she stayed with him that night. Morris may have had the kindest of intentions, not wishing Rachael to trudge all the way home after a long day in the fields, but the surrounding community viewed the circumstances with suspicion. As one South Carolina planter informed Frederick Law Olmsted, "[A]ny white girl who could be hired to work for wages would certainly be a girl of easy virtue." A Virginia slaveholder likewise confirmed, "No girl hereabouts, whose character was good, would ever hire out to do menial service." Rachael Holman, however, routinely ventured out into public in pursuit of paid employment.[48]

47. Anderson District, Court of Magistrates and Freeholders, Trial Papers, microfilm reel C2919, case #309, SCDAH.

48. Anderson District, Court of Magistrates and Freeholders, Trial Papers, microfilm reel C2919, case #309, SCDAH; Olmsted, *Seaboard Slave States,* 508; Virginia slaveholder from Olmsted, *Seaboard Slave States,* quoted in Bynum, *Unruly Women,* 7.

She frequently took work into her mother's house as well, transforming the domicile into a very public space. The elderly shoemaker Dempsey Hill testified that one night, after passing out "drunk," he found himself near Rachael's house. He took refuge inside and slept there until midnight, when he "was waked up by a negro man who came into the house and dropped a bag [probably containing meal] near the door." The man awakened Rachael, and asked her "to get up and give him his socks." Hill saw Rachael give him something and accompany him out of the house. In this case, Rachael apparently received foodstuffs in exchange for doing either sewing, mending, or laundry. Rachael "frequently washed" for the white Samuel Smith, who described her as "an industrious poor woman." Once, Smith and his brother stopped by Rachael's house, perhaps to make arrangements for work, when they "found a free negro man in the house without a pass." The free black explained "that he expected to stay all night." Enraged at the black man's presumption, Smith "whipped the negro and sent him home."[49]

As a poor white woman, Rachael worked hard to earn a livelihood, but in so doing she blurred the boundaries between domesticity and paid work. Ideally, the home represented a tranquil sanctuary from the bustling economic activity of the marketplace. Rachael, however, like the working poor in general, found it impossible to maintain any clear distinction between home and market. Her mother's residence served as an establishment where boarders slept off their liquor, where black men stopped at a late hour to transact business, and where Rachael herself did laundry for paying customers. This economic activity had profound moral implications. It profaned the dwelling by compromising the sanctity of the space, converting what should have been a quiet home into a public, or disorderly, house. Likewise, it made Rachael Holman a public woman—a prostitute, in some sense—willing to barter or to sell her services. Indeed, as Samuel Smith testified, "Rumor says she gained her livelihood principally by having connection with the opposite sex rather than by any manual labor."[50]

No evidence can confirm that Rachael exchanged sexual favors for money, but some poor white women did choose or resort to prostitution to help make ends meet. Although presumably free to reject certain customers, poor white prosti-

49. Anderson District, Court of Magistrates and Freeholders, Trial Papers, microfilm reel C2919, case #309, SCDAH.

50. Wendy Gamber, "Tarnished Labor: The Home, the Market, and the Boardinghouse in Antebellum America," *Journal of the Early Republic* 22 (Summer 2002): 177, 180–181; Anderson District, Court of Magistrates and Freeholders, Trial Papers, microfilm reel C2919, case #309, SCDAH.

tutes sometimes had sexual contact with slave men.[51] Some of these women casually disregarded the racial characteristics of their clients. Others may have been more repulsed by the prospect of interracial sex, but dire economic need forced them to overcome their reservations.[52] Poor white prostitutes in the antebellum South were most likely to have sex with slave men in densely populated cities such as Richmond. As E. Susan Barber has found, no fewer than 180 prostitutes plied the streets of Virginia's capital city between 1853 and 1868 alone,[53] and some certainly counted black men among their johns. Urban newspapers modestly reported hints of poor white women's sexual misconduct across the color line. In March 1859, one white female in Richmond stood accused of "carrying, not war, but affection into Africa."[54] In August, "two youthful white girls, not of uncomely features or shape," were "caught pandering for lucre's sake to the passions of negroes" in that city.[55] The previous year, "two dissolute looking white women" named Peggy Cousins and Maria Powell appeared before the mayor's court, "charged with pandering to the gross appetites and moral turpitude of negroes, and allowing unlawful assemblies of negro men on their premises by day and night, for all kinds of lewd purposes." While Cousins cannot be located in the 1860 Virginia census, Powell appears as an illiterate seamstress of forty-seven, with no personal property whatsoever. Census takers sometimes employed "seamstress" as a euphemism for prostitute, so Powell may not have sewed much at all. If she did, she may have nevertheless depended upon prostitution to supplement her meager income.[56]

Prostitution was not an option limited only to women in the Old South's few major cities. For impoverished white women in small towns and rural areas, prostitution also represented a viable occupational alternative.[57] The 1860 census

51. Bynum, *Unruly Women*, 45.

52. On prostitution, see also Timothy J. Lockley, "Crossing the Race Divide: Interracial Sex in Antebellum Savannah," *Slavery & Abolition* 18 (December 1997): 167.

53. E. Susan Barber, "Depraved and Abandoned Women: Prostitution in Richmond, Virginia, across the Civil War," in *Neither Lady Nor Slave: Working Women of the Old South*, ed. Susanna Delfino and Michele Gillespie (Chapel Hill: University of North Carolina Press, 2002), 158.

54. *Richmond Enquirer*, March 18, 1859.

55. Quoted in Richard C. Wade, *Slavery in the Cities: The South, 1820–1860* (New York: Oxford University Press, 1964), 260.

56. *Richmond Enquirer*, December 24, 1858; Eighth Census of the United States, 1860: Henrico County, Virginia, 224; Suzanne Lebsock, *The Free Women of Petersburg: Status and Culture in a Southern Town, 1784–1860* (New York: W. W. Norton & Company, 1984), 297n70. Cousins and Powell received $5 fines. Newspapers neglected to publish what became of their black clients.

57. On prostitution as an avenue of employment in the urban South and North, respectively, see Barber, "Depraved and Abandoned Women," 155; and Christine Stansell, *City of Women: Sex and*

lists no fewer than twenty-two prostitutes in the South Carolina upcountry district of Spartanburg, while twenty-four lived in central North Carolina's Wake County. The census of Fredericksburg, Virginia, lists four "whores," all natives of Virginia. Likely many more poor white women sold their bodies occasionally to meet immediate needs and therefore did not appear in the census as prostitutes. And an untold number of the more than seven thousand "seamstresses" in the two Carolinas in 1860 earned little of their income by sewing.[58]

Disorderly houses catering to an interracial clientele dotted the rural landscape, providing men of all colors and complexions a convivial atmosphere for drinking, gambling, and illicit sex. The shadowy subculture of these establishments remains largely hidden from view, but the disreputable white women who ran some of them do surface periodically in court records. In rural Wayne County, North Carolina, for example, the poor whites Patsey and Biddy Warr "became a publick nuisance" for keeping "an old school House" "as a kind of brothell, and a place of resort for the basest sort of both sexes, . . . frequented by the blacks of said neighborhood." The Warrs had arrived in the area as strangers, "entirely unknown as to character." Sympathetic neighbors deemed them "objects of charity" and generously granted them possession of the building, but they soon determined that the newcomers were unwelcome and took steps to rid themselves of the "nuisance."[59]

Because teenage orphans, widows, and other female household heads were known to engage in prostitution or operate disorderly houses, at least a few slave men may have looked upon poor white women as possible sex partners whose services were available for purchase. A slave in Spartanburg District, South Carolina, "behave[d] rudely" toward one white woman in 1846 by "pulling out his private member and proposeing [sic] to have Intercourse with her," promising to "give her a dollar."[60] This episode might indicate the slave's striking lack of socialization and his inability to interact in socially acceptable ways with white

Class in New York, 1789–1860 (Urbana: University of Illinois Press, 1987), 185–192. On the social condition and poverty of poor white women in the South, see Timothy J. Lockley, "A Struggle for Survival: Non-Elite White Women in Lowcountry Georgia, 1790–1830," in *Women of the American South: A Multicultural Reader,* ed. Christie Anne Farnham (New York: New York University Press, 1997), 26–42.

58. Lapp, "Ante Bellum Poor Whites," 83, 82.

59. Governor's Papers, Gov. John Owen, vol. 60, 323, NCDAH; Wayne County, Minute Docket, Superior Court, 1826–1834, NCDAH, 67, 68, 89; Wayne County, Criminal Action Papers, 1827–1829, NCDAH. On white women and disorderly houses, see Bynum, *Unruly Women,* 93–94.

60. Spartanburg District, Court of Magistrates and Freeholders, Trial Papers, microfilm reel C2920, case #78, SCDAH. See also Morris, *Southern Slavery and the Law,* 314–315.

women. Or perhaps he was drunk. In another case from Spartanburg District, in 1859, the inebriated slave Daniel "talked scandalous" to the poor white Mary M. Demsey, asking "if he might have intercourse with her." He, too, "unbuttoned his breeches & showed his person to her." (A witness later saw the drunken Daniel wearing "two hats on his head" and loudly proclaiming his candidacy "to be overseer of the roads for the next term, as he found them to be in bad condition.")[61] As aberrant as these incidents seem, they may nevertheless suggest that these two slave men acted under the reasonable expectation that the poor white women they accosted would welcome their offers.

The legal counsel representing slaves accused of sex crimes commonly adopted the tactic of portraying the alleged poor white female victim as a prostitute. In 1829, Pleasant Burnett's slave Lewis reportedly raped the poor white Amy Baker in Mecklenburg County, Virginia. Even though Lewis was apprehended in Amy's bed, without his trousers, the defense attempted to depict the poor white woman as a harlot. One white witness called to testify on Lewis's behalf stated "that he has been to the house of Mrs. Baker for the purpose of unlawful intercourse with females and have known others to do so." A second witness stated that not only white men visited Amy Baker for sex, reporting that "he has several times passed by Drucilla Kirkland's where Mrs. Baker resides and have seen four negro men there at one time and three negro men there at another time." The night of the purported attack, Lewis had burst into the house, explaining "in the grossest language" that "he came for *cunt* and *cunt* he would have." The defense's witnesses implied that many men, like Lewis, knew "there was plenty of it there" at the residence of "old Mrs. Kirkland."[62]

Poor white women did not have to sell their bodies for money to be considered prostitutes, however.[63] Any cavorting or socializing between a poor white woman and a slave man that captured the public's attention might earn her that label, especially evidence of prior consensual sexual relations with the accused. For many southern whites, by previously consenting to sex, a white woman forfeited her right to refuse a slave man's sexual advances on subsequent occasions. At the 1803 rape trial of slave Carter in King and Queen County, Virginia, court

---

61. Spartanburg District, Court of Magistrates and Freeholders, Trial Papers, microfilm reel C2921, case #221, SCDAH; Eighth Census of the United States, 1860: Spartanburg District, South Carolina, 367.

62. Executive Papers, Gov. James Pleasants, box 311, folder June 11–20, 1829, LVA. On this case, see also Sommerville, "Rape Myth," 498–502; Hodes, *White Women, Black Men,* 58; and Schwarz, *Twice Condemned,* 207. Schwarz incorrectly identifies Amy as a free black woman.

63. Bynum, *Unruly Women,* 110.

records noted that the poor white Catherine Brinal, "a woman of the worst fame" and "of the most abandoned" character, with "no visible means of support," "permitted the said Carter to have peaceable sexual intercourse with her, before the time of his forcing her."[64] Likewise, in Mecklenburg County, North Carolina, the slave Jeff maintained that he had "had connection" with Elizabeth C. Rodgers prior to the alleged rape, "but it was by her consent, . . . a previous intimacy existed between him and her." The defense contended that Elizabeth had allowed Jeff into her home "when her Husband was absent" and that the slave "had been allowed into the Kitchen of his master to lay his hands on [Elizabeth's] body . . . in a familiar manner." Elizabeth also purportedly permitted "other . . . Slaves to take liberties with her such as Kissing her" in Jeff's absence.[65] The Johnston County, North Carolina, jury that convened to decide the fate of the slave Jim for raping Elizabeth Sikes heard testimony that the poor white woman "has had habitual intercourse with negroes and particularly with the convict; . . . he went there to her home, frequently for sexual intercourse and got it," and "he went there from time to time with her encouragement." Although available sources make no direct mention of payment for sex, one observer pronounced "Elizabeth Sikes a base prostitute of the very worst fame."[66]

The assembled evidence in the case of Rachael Holman convinced the Anderson District Court of Magistrates and Freeholders that she, too, was a prostitute. Whether this meant the court believed that she actually sold sexual favors or merely that it considered her a woman of undoubtedly depraved character is not clear. Regardless, the court judged Lewis not guilty of attempting to rape her. A short two and a half years later, Rachael faced two separate indictments for keeping a disorderly house, presumably an establishment that catered to an interracial clientele.[67] One indictment named her alone, the other her, her mother Anna Smith, and a poor, sixty-year-old carpenter Larkin Moore, who eventually married Anna.[68] In October 1859, the Anderson District Court of General Sessions ruled Rachael guilty on both counts and sentenced her the following March to four months' imprisonment and a $50 fine.[69] When the census taker visited

64. Quoted in Johnston, *Race Relations in Virginia*, 260. See also Rothman, *Notorious in the Neighborhood*, 161–162.

65. *State v. Jefferson*, 28 N.C. 305 (1846), Supreme Court Original Case #3699, NCDAH.

66. Governor's Papers, Gov. Thomas Bragg, G.P. 140, folder April 1856, NCDAH.

67. On white women and disorderly houses, see Bynum, *Unruly Women*, 93–94.

68. Anderson District, Court of General Sessions, Criminal Journal, 1840–1859, 516, SCDAH; Eighth Census of the United States, 1860: Anderson District, South Carolina, 154.

69. Anderson District, Court of General Sessions, Criminal Journal, 1859–1874, 7, 29, SCDAH.

Anderson District in 1860, he found Rachael Holman sitting in jail alongside her mother and stepfather. He listed her simply as age twenty-six, "convict."[70]

Rachael Holman's story underscores the difficult financial circumstances poor white women of the Old South confronted, as well as the circumscribed economic opportunities available to them in the southern countryside. Poor white women performed their own domestic chores at home, while also taking in extra work such as sewing or washing in exchange for money or needed goods. Moreover, they frequently ventured out into the marketplace in search of employment as domestics, factory operatives, field hands, or other menial positions. In the course of their working lives, poor white women often came into contact with slave men. At times, these interactions bred ties of mutual attraction in spite of surrounding white communities that proscribed the range of appropriate behavior between poor white women and slave men. On a smaller number of occasions, the working lives of poor white women made them vulnerable to sexual assault by a few deviant bondsmen with whom they toiled or encountered while on the job.

As Rachael Holman's courtroom struggles so vividly illustrate, white society in the antebellum South did not blindly rally behind any white woman who accused a black man of rape. Indeed, her case confirms historian Diane Miller Sommerville's scholarship on the "rape myth." Despite long-standing stereotypes of black men as extraordinarily well endowed, passionate, and sexual creatures, southern white authorities in the antebellum years typically granted accused black rapists the due process under the law that they would be systematically denied after the Civil War. Only when emancipation and the demise of racial slavery removed the institutional constraints from black men did white hysteria over black male sexuality and white obsession with the "black beast rapist" become widespread. Not until the racially charged postbellum years would elite whites bestow the privileges of white womanhood upon poor white women. In the Old South, they continued to chastise lower-class white women for violating elite prescriptions of appropriate sexual conduct. The need to execute a valuable slave for the capital offenses of rape or attempted rape was mitigated when the victim was a poor white woman such as Rachael Holman.[71]

70. Eighth Census of the United States, 1860: Anderson District, South Carolina, 154.

71. Sommerville, "Rape Myth," 483, 485, 490, 496, 514–517. For a previous generation of scholarship arguing that white men obsessively feared black male sexuality from the colonial period onward, see Winthrop D. Jordan, *White Over Black: American Attitudes toward the Negro, 1550–1812* (Chapel Hill: University of North Carolina Press, 1968), 148–152. Historians who rely more heavily

Courtroom decisions demonstrated an acute understanding of the ramifications of verdicts on southern class and race relationships. When poor white women accused slave men of a sex crime, they placed slaveholders in an awkward position, pitting masters' own economic interests in their chattel against the desire to maintain racial supremacy. The conflicting pressures produced no consistent pattern of verdicts. Individual sets of circumstances weighed heavily in determining the outcomes at trial. In about one-third of the cases, southern courts sided with the enslaved defendants and found them not guilty. In the other two-thirds of the cases, the poor white female plaintiffs marshaled sufficiently convincing evidence to earn a ruling in their favor. On some occasions when courts returned a judgment against an accused slave, the verdict seemed based less on the merits of the case in question or on any compelling need to punish the bondsman appropriately for his sexual transgression than on the widespread goal of ridding the neighborhood of a long-standing troublemaker. Reflecting on the bad character his slave Juba had sustained for decades prior to his conviction for the rape of poor white Nancy Wallis, master Isaac Griffey admitted that Juba had been destined "for the Gallows ever since he was born."[72] In fully half of the instances in which southern courts determined a slave man's guilt for raping or attempting to rape a poor white woman, however, the bondsman ultimately escaped the gallows. Sometimes the judgment was reversed on appeal; other times, petitions to the state capital earned condemned bondsmen gubernatorial clemency. In Virginia, for example, governors stayed the executions of nearly half the total number of black men, both slave and free, sentenced to death for sexual crimes committed upon a white woman.[73] To strike a balance between the competing goals of upholding both racial supremacy and the sanctity of slave property, southern justices and juries recommended mercy in sentencing for almost half of all slaves found guilty of committing sexual violence upon white women.[74] In so doing, they cleverly rendered a verdict that reinforced the southern racial order while simultaneously acknowledging masters' property rights. At sentencing, judges proved far less likely to order a convicted slave's execution if his victim was a poor white woman rather than a woman of the "respectable"

---

on legal statutes for their evidence persist in this belief. See, for example, Bardaglio, "Rape and the Law," 752. On the "Negro as beast," see George M. Fredrickson, *The Black Image in the White Mind: The Debate on Afro-American Character and Destiny, 1817–1914* (New York: Harper & Row, 1971), 275–282.

72. Governor's Papers, Gov. Edward B. Dudley, vol. 84, 1506, NCDAH.

73. Sommerville, "Rape Myth," 485.

74. Johnston, *Race Relations in Virginia*, 258.

class.[75] Because the law authorized compensation to the master of an executed slave, sparing the life of a condemned bondsman worked to the fiscal benefit of the state. Legislators were never anxious to reimburse slaveholders the cost of a bondsman, especially one slated to die for a crime committed upon what they typically regarded as a worthless, inconsequential poor white woman.[76] In many ways, the scales of justice routinely tilted against poor white women when valuable slave property was at stake.

That the court records provide a detailed account of Rachael Holman's sexual past, while mentioning nothing whatsoever of the alleged slave rapist Lewis (technically the individual on trial), suggests the importance that southern courts attached to social class when rendering their verdicts. Precisely because poor white women often worked outside the home, "respectable" white society questioned their sexual ethics and denied them the same social and legal protections granted elite "ladies." The ubiquitous assumption of poor white female promiscuity and sexual depravity, so intimately linked to poor white women's conspicuous roles in the public sphere, in many cases suggested to southern courts that the victim likely had some hand in inviting the alleged assault. Under such circumstances, the southern legal system reinforced the boundaries of class by ruling in favor of the accused slave man rather than the socially marginal poor white female victim. Because poor white women violated conventions of southern white womanhood, southern white society sought to impose controls on their sexuality. Poor white men in the Old South did not confront such rigid constraints.

Without a doubt, poor white men had sex with slave women, whether by consent, by force, or by coercion, far more often than poor white women had sex with slave men.[77] Paradoxically, however, the wealth of sources relating instances of sexual encounters between poor white men and slave women pales in comparison, conveying precisely the opposite impression. Biology accounts for much of this discrepancy. When poor white women gave birth to mixed-race children,

75. Bynum, *Unruly Women*, 109–110; Hodes, *White Women, Black Men*, 61; Bardaglio, "Rape and the Law," 768; Sommerville, "Rape Myth," 496, 515–516; Sommerville, "Rape, Race, and Castration," 81; Tim Lockley, "The Strange Case of George Flyming: Justice and Gender in Antebellum Savannah," *Georgia Historical Quarterly* 84 (Summer 2000): 250.

76. Higginbotham and Kopytoff, "Racial Purity and Interracial Sex," 2017.

77. Eugene D. Genovese, *Roll, Jordan, Roll: The World the Slaves Made* (New York: Vintage Books, 1976), 418; Brown, *Good Wives*, 355.

they produced offspring that exposed their illicit behavior and aroused the curiosity of the surrounding community. To be sure, determining the race of a poor white woman's baby sometimes posed a distinct challenge. Gatsy Tootle was fortunate in that the true "color" of her children sired by the slave Bay Ben "can be detected" only "on close inspection." As Ben's owners explained, "[T]hey may be taken for white children without strict examination."[78] After Polly Lane gave birth in 1826, a swarm of inquisitive neighbors and authorities descended on her house to inspect the child and ascertain its race to judge if the slave Jim was the father. Observers initially disputed the infant's parentage, but after diligent poking and prodding finally reached the general consensus that the baby was "of mixed blood" and therefore almost certainly Jim's.[79] If a genetic quirk erased any outward appearance of black fatherhood, a white woman's sexual transgressions against the South's racial mores might never be discovered, but most poor white women who had sex with black men could not so easily disguise the paternity of their children. Fully nineteen of the twenty-three men in Virginia who petitioned for divorce on grounds of interracial adultery had wives who had given birth to biracial children. Stunned husbands expressed a combination of shock, outrage, disgust, and dismay at being cuckolded by local black males.[80] Some women forthrightly acknowledged their unconventional sexual comportment. Catherine Brinal, for one, had "three mulatto children, which by her own confession were begotten by different negro men."[81] Others denied it. Defending her character at the rape trial of the bondsman Jim, Elizabeth Sikes disavowed ever having "had a negro child or children," yet when the census taker arrived in 1860, he indicated that her ten-year-old son James was a mulatto.[82] In con-

78. *Raleigh Register* (weekly), October 21, 1834.

79. For sources discussing the race of Polly Lane's baby, see Governor's Papers, Gov. Hutchins G. Burton, G.P. 55, 189 (quotation), 197, 186, NCDAH. For the definitive assessment, see Governor's Papers, Gov. Hutchins G. Burton, G.P. 56, 247, NCDAH.

80. Rothman, *Notorious in the Neighborhood,* 174. See, for example, the divorce petitions of Benjamin Butt, Abraham Newton, Joseph Gresham, Thomas Cain, and William Rucker, among others. Petition of Benjamin Butt, Norfolk County, December 7, 1803, Reel 138, Box 181, Folder 87; petition of Abraham Newton, Fauquier County, November 16, 1816, Reel 51, Box 72, Folder 97; petition of Joseph Gresham, James City County, December 10, 1833, Reel 93, Box 124, Folder 43; petition of Thomas Cain, Frederick County, January 9, 1841, Reel 62, Box 84, Folder 32; petition of William Rucker, Allegheny County, March 5, 1849, Reel 7, Box 8, Folder 57; all in Legislative Petitions, Virginia General Assembly, LVA.

81. Quoted in Johnston, *Race Relations in Virginia,* 260.

82. Eighth Census of the United States, 1860: Wayne County, North Carolina, 876.

trast to these instances, physical evidence substantiating poor white men's sexual contact with slave women proves almost impossible to come by.[83] When a slave woman bore a mixed-race child, the father may have been her master, the master's son or other relative, the overseer, a local yeoman or poor white man, or any number of other white males in the area. Unless the infant bore a striking resemblance to a particular white man, no one could pinpoint with absolute certainty the paternity of the child.

Legal distinctions in the Old South exacerbate the difficulty in uncovering sexual relationships between poor white men and slave women. White society viewed slave men as far more sexually threatening to the social order than slave women. If a slave man impregnated a white woman, and she gave birth to a mulatto child, she undermined the racial categories that grounded southern society. Any increase in the region's free black population called into question the notion that blackness equaled slavery and whiteness freedom. Slave men who fathered children of white mothers fomented a subtle form of rebellion, certainly not in as direct a manner as Nat Turner but nonetheless menacing to the preservation of southern white society. Legislators throughout the South therefore implemented statutes to deter sexual contact between black men and white women. Laws punished black men for the rape and attempted rape of white women, white women for the voluntary sex crimes of prostitution, fornication, and bastardy. The regulation of white female sexuality, with its intent to protect the purity of the white race, formed the cornerstone of the region's racial hierarchy.[84]

Conversely, white men faced no equivalent regulations geared toward their sexual control. Lawmakers' preoccupation with interracial sex failed to extend to that between white men and black women. Southern law did not acknowledge that any man, black or white, could rape a bondswoman. Legally, men of all colors and classes had virtually unrestricted sexual license to female slave bodies. Only men's own, individual consciences and, if they conducted their liaisons with insufficient discretion, possible community opprobrium stood between them and the sexual exploitation of slave women. Female slaves' lack of access to the

83. Thomas E. Buckley, S.J., *The Great Catastrophe of My Life: Divorce in the Old Dominion* (Chapel Hill: University of North Carolina Press, 2002), 140.

84. Higginbotham and Kopytoff, "Racial Purity and Interracial Sex," 1968, 2008. The regulation of white female sexuality as a means of maintaining a racial hierarchy began in the colonial era. See Brown, *Good Wives;* and Fischer, *Suspect Relations,* esp. 7, 9.

courtroom to prosecute for sexual offenses and their inability to testify against whites denied them access to justice. It also meant that, since southern society did not deem the rape or attempted rape of slave women a crime, scholars are deprived of court records—the richest source for information on interracial sex between poor white women and slave men—detailing the sexual contact between poor white men and slave women.

The elusive sexual liaisons between free men and female slaves reinforced the South's racial hierarchy in two important ways. First, any resulting offspring only supplemented the wealth of the master. Second, the wanton sexual abuse of slave women marked an important manifestation of white male hegemony over southern society. Historians have established that many masters regarded the sexual exploitation of female slaves as their prerogative. They frequently cornered house slaves or sneaked into the slave quarters in search of sexual gratification. The number of mulatto slave children with physical features resembling the master's testified to these interracial liaisons, but as long as slaveholders conducted their affairs in secret, white society tolerated them.[85] And slaveowners need not necessarily employ physical force to elicit sex from slave women. As masters, they possessed the coercive power to manipulate female slaves by manufacturing situations that severely limited a slave woman's ability to resist unwanted sexual advances. Slaveholders executed carefully laid plans to get themselves alone with favorite slave women to take advantage of their powerlessness. North Carolina slave Harriet Jacobs documented the nightmare of enduring her master Dr. Flint's unrelenting sexual overtures. From the time Harriet reached fifteen years of age and Flint first "began to whisper foul words in my ear," the master

85. On masters' sexual exploitation and abuse of slave women, see Catherine Clinton, *The Plantation Mistress: Woman's World in the Old South* (New York: Pantheon Books, 1982), 199–222; Clinton, "Southern Dishonor," 61–64; Thelma Jennings, "'Us Colored Women Had to Go Through A Plenty': Sexual Exploitation of African-American Slave Women," *Journal of Women's History* 1 (Winter 1990): 45–74; Nell Irvin Painter, "Of *Lily*, Linda Brent, and Freud: A Non-Exceptionalist Approach to Race, Class, and Gender in the Slave South," *Georgia Historical Quarterly* 76 (Summer 1992): 241–259; Sharon Block, "Lines of Color, Sex, and Service: Comparative Sexual Coercion in Early America," in *Sex, Love, Race: Crossing Boundaries in North American History*, ed. Martha Hodes (New York: New York University Press, 1999), 141–163; Hélène Lecaudey, "Behind the Mask: Ex-Slave Women and Interracial Sexual Relations," in *Discovering the Women in Slavery: Emancipating Perspectives on the American Past*, ed. Patricia Morton (Athens: University of Georgia Press, 1996), 260–277; Carolyn J. Powell, "In Remembrance of Mira: Reflections on the Death of a Slave Woman," in *Discovering the Women in Slavery*, 47–60; Bradley and Leslie, "White Pain Pollen"; and Fischer, *Suspect Relations*, 153.

reminded his slave that she belonged to him and was therefore obligated to submit to his wishes.[86]

But what about poor white men? Unlike wealthy slaveholders, they lacked the authority that accompanied slave ownership. Were their sexual relationships with slave women therefore, as one historian argued recently, "almost by their very nature, . . . voluntary"?[87] Deciphering the nature of the sexual interactions between poor white men and slave women proves challenging given the limited evidentiary base. Like male slaveholders, some poor white men surely committed outright rapes upon slave women, while others carried on long-term, loving affairs with female slaves. Some relationships may well have been genuinely consensual, if only for a time. On the continuum of sexual contact, however, it seems likely that the greatest percentage of sexual encounters between poor white men and slave women fell somewhere between these extremes. More often than not, some degree of coercion or exploitation was probably involved.[88]

Only in their capacity as overseers, or as occasional slave hirers, could some poor white men approximate the coercive power of the master. Although poor white men represented only a small portion of the total number of overseers,[89] contemporary accounts often echoed the belief that overseers "are taken from the lowest grade of society, and seldom have had the privilege of a religious education, and have no fear of offending God, and consequently no check on their natural propensities; they give way to passion, intemperance, and every sin, and become savages in their conduct."[90] Overseers of all economic backgrounds frequently slept with the very slaves they were assigned to control, many regarding their sexual indulgences with slave women as nothing less than a perk of the job.[91] Yet slaveholders most commonly vilified poor white men for the practice, believing that they, like poor white women, were inherently promiscuous.[92] Rice

86. Block, "Lines of Color, Sex, and Service," 143; Clinton, *Plantation Mistress*, 213; Harriet A. Jacobs, *Incidents in the Life of a Slave Girl, Written by Herself*, ed. Jean Fagan Yellin (Cambridge: Harvard University Press, 2000), 27, 28.

87. Lockley, "Crossing the Race Divide," 159.

88. Here I am in agreement with Brown, *Good Wives*, 237.

89. William Kauffman Scarborough, *The Overseer: Plantation Management in the Old South* (Baton Rouge: Louisiana State University Press, 1966), 5.

90. Quoted in Olmsted, *Seaboard Slave States*, 486.

91. Bertram Wyatt-Brown, "Community, Class, and Snopesian Crime: Local Justice in the Old South," in *Class, Conflict, and Consensus: Antebellum Southern Community Studies*, ed. Orville Vernon Burton and Robert C. McMath, Jr. (Westport, Conn.: Greenwood Press, 1982), 188.

92. Sommerville, "Race, Rape, and Castration," 89.

planter Charles Manigault, for one, suspected local poor whites he hired as overseers of fornicating with his slave women.[93] Masters resoundingly condemned overseers and other local poor white men for their sexual transgressions in the slave quarters, even as they hypocritically overlooked their own.[94] Planters discouraged sex and all other forms of social fraternization between overseers and female slaves.[95] Such familiar contacts not only undermined plantation discipline but also, in some cases, threatened a planter's sexual mastery in the quarters. To reduce the likelihood of illicit sex between overseers and slave women, some planters specifically advertised for married men "with a small family" to fill the position.[96] Despite such precautions, overseers' sexual abuse of female slaves went largely unchecked, especially on the isolated absentee estates of the low country.[97] As overseers, some poor white men surely savored their small taste of the master's authority.

Seven decades after emancipation, slave men and women alike remembered the overseers who sexually exploited their charges. Annie Coley, a former South Carolina slave, recalled that "ole Boss Jones had a mean overseer who tuk 'vantage of the womens in the fiel's."[98] Another South Carolina ex-slave reported that his "father was a Irishman," with no land or slaves, who served as "a overseer in Edgefield County. His name was Ephraim Rumple."[99] Former slave John C. Brown explained that his wife Adeline had such light skin because "[h]er daddy was a full-blooded Irishman. He come over here from Ireland and was overseer for Marse Bob Clowney." The Irishman "took a fancy for Adeline's mammy, a bright 'latto gal slave on de place. . . . Marse Bob stuck to him, and never 'jected to it."[100] One Edgefield master did not look so approvingly upon

93. William Dusinberre, *Them Dark Days: Slavery in the American Rice Swamps* (New York: Oxford University Press, 1996), 112.

94. Genovese, *Roll, Jordan, Roll*, 419, 421.

95. Scarborough, *Overseer*, 75.

96. Kenneth M. Stampp, *The Peculiar Institution: Slavery in the Ante-Bellum South* (New York: Vintage Books, 1956), 354. For sample advertisements, see *Richmond Enquirer*, August 19, 1831; October 29, 1833; and August 17, 1860; *Charleston Daily Courier*, November 15, 1853; and January 18, 1854.

97. Scarborough, *Overseer*, 6, 75.

98. George P. Rawick, ed., *The American Slave: A Composite Autobiography, Supplement, Series 1*, vol. 7, pt. 2 (Westport, Conn.: Greenwood Press, 1977), 441–442.

99. George P. Rawick, ed., *The American Slave: A Composite Autobiography*, vol. 10, pt. 6 (Westport, Conn.: Greenwood Publishing Company, 1972), 103. See also Orville Vernon Burton, *In My Father's House Are Many Mansions: Family and Community in Edgefield, South Carolina* (Chapel Hill: University of North Carolina Press, 1985), 188.

100. George P. Rawick, ed., *The American Slave: A Composite Autobiography*, vol. 2, pt. 1 (Westport, Conn.: Greenwood Publishing Company, 1972), 128.

his overseer's dalliance in the quarters. Ex-slave Rachel Sullivan recalled that three slaves "had chillun by de overseer, Mr. Whitefield, and Marster put 'em on de block. No ma'am he wouldn't tolerate dat. He say you keep de race pure."[101]

Although poor white men lacked the authority over slave women that derived from slave ownership, and a majority never commanded slaves as overseers, their impoverishment failed to emasculate them.[102] Poor white men's sex and race permitted them to maintain some degree of coercive power over female slaves. Like their male social superiors, they, too, claimed access to the bodies of slave women.[103]

Divorce petitions filed by their wives to the state legislature afford one of the few promising avenues into understanding poor white men's carnal relationships with slave women. Although the state of South Carolina prohibited legislative divorce, North Carolina permitted it between 1800 and 1835, Virginia for a longer period, from 1803 to 1850.[104] In recent studies, Thomas E. Buckley and Joshua D. Rothman have thoroughly investigated divorce in early national and antebellum Virginia. Of 583 total petitions for divorce in that state, fifty-three (9 percent), representing forty-three total petitioners, involved accusations of interracial adultery.[105] The state legislature granted divorces to sixteen of the twenty-three (70 percent) male and eleven of the twenty (55 percent) female petitioners,[106] compared to an overall rate of 33 percent for all petitioners, regardless of reason.[107] Clearly it worked to the petitioner's benefit if his or her spouse had cheated

101. Rawick, vol. 13, pt. 4, 227. See also Burton, *In My Father's House*, 188.

102. Bynum, *Unruly Women*, 7.

103. Dusinberre, *Them Dark Days*, 112.

104. Glenda Riley, *Divorce: An American Tradition* (New York: Oxford University Press, 1991), 54, 62, 69, 94. Riley explains that South Carolina wanted to preserve the institution of the family and maintain social harmony, and therefore withheld from the general assembly the power to dissolve marriages.

105. Rothman, *Notorious in the Neighborhood*, 170, 289n4. Of the 266 divorce petitions to the North Carolina state legislature between 1800 and 1835, 8 percent involved accusations of interracial adultery, making it the second most common reason for applying for divorce in that state, following desertion. See Riley, *Divorce*, 35; and Glenda Riley, "Legislative Divorce in Virginia, 1803–1850," *Journal of the Early Republic* 11 (Spring 1991): 56. For the most detailed look at interracial sex as a cause for divorce, see Rothman, *Notorious in the Neighborhood*, ch. 5, and its earlier incarnation, Joshua D. Rothman, "'To Be Freed From Thate Curs and Let at Liberty': Interracial Adultery and Divorce in Antebellum Virginia," *Virginia Magazine of History and Biography* 106 (Autumn 1998): 443–481.

106. Rothman, *Notorious in the Neighborhood*, 193–194; Buckley, *Great Catastrophe*, 123, 125. Buckley identified only nineteen women who petitioned for divorce on the grounds of interracial adultery, compared to Rothman's twenty. As a result, Buckley maintains that 58 percent of those women, rather than 55 percent, received their divorce. See Buckley, *Great Catastrophe*, 123.

107. Buckley, *Great Catastrophe*, 123.

with a black person. Of all divorces granted, twenty-seven of 153 (17.6 percent) involved interracial adultery.[108]

As a group, poor whites were not likely to appeal to the general assembly to terminate their marriages formally. Landless white men composed one-third of all of Virginia's male petitioners citing interracial adultery; poor white women made up an even smaller proportion of all female applicants.[109] Illiteracy surely prevented some poor whites from petitioning to secure a legislative divorce, but more than any other factor, the requisite legal fees probably dissuaded them.[110] For poor white men who no longer wished to remain married, desertion and abandonment presented more expedient alternatives. More constrained in the range of options available to them, poor white women in unsatisfying marriages usually suffered miserably through them. Nevertheless, the handful of women who sought legislative divorces from poor white husbands whose philandering crossed the color line offer a revealing initial look into poor white men's views of marriage, sexuality, and race.

Divorce petitions impart the heart-rending stories of poor white women trapped in a state of matrimony. Women typically emphasized their husbands' virtually chronic intoxication and the physical and mental abuse the men inflicted. Accusations of interracial adultery played only a secondary role in their pleas to the general assembly. Petitions rarely detail the marital infidelity that occurred, but it is mentioned. Sarah Robinson knew when she married her husband Samuel that he "was poor having no property." Optimistically, Sarah "hope[d] that although he was penniless," they could forge a life together and achieve a "competency." They began married life in the Lynchburg home of Sarah's widowed mother, but Robinson "was idle and dissolute making no kind of exertion whatever for the support of himself or family." He soon vacated his mother-in-law's home and rented a house to himself, where he "notoriously lived in habits of illicit intercourse with lewd women, both white and black, and . . . had children by them." In Culpeper County, Mary Lawry's husband Newsome, a "labourer," "took up with a female coloured slave in the neighborhood by the name of Cynthia." Newsome "carried on a considerable illicit intercourse with . . . Cynthia for a considerable time until he at length determined to carry her off altogether," presumably to a free state. Apprehended in Wheeling, Newsome was arrested for carrying off a slave and stealing a horse and sentenced to a total of eight years in

108. Rothman, *Notorious in the Neighborhood,* 171.
109. Buckley, *Great Catastrophe,* 123.
110. Rothman, *Notorious in the Neighborhood,* 179.

prison. Mary Lawry, the divorce petition summarized, "is poor and penniless and is the disgraced wife of a miserable convict."[111]

Several of the women who petitioned state legislatures for divorces from poor white men, however, were not themselves economically disadvantaged. Ann Eliza Eubank of King William County, Virginia, brought property to her marriage with Alfred, for example, and the poor James B. Norman married the wealthy Henry County widow Lucy Harris Price in 1842. In North Carolina, Harriet J. Smith, who wed Thomas D. Foy in 1844, stood to inherit her mother's $1,200 worth of real estate. She regarded herself and her mother as "both Ladies of high standing." All of these women, whether or not they realized it at the time, married "down" socioeconomically.[112]

In retrospect, they comprehended that their poor white husbands had tricked them into marriage.[113] Harriet Smith conceded that, at the time of her marriage, she was a "very young" and naive woman of sixteen, approximately ten years Thomas Foy's junior. She confessed to not knowing Foy well and stated that she had married him under the mistaken impression "that he was a Gentleman." Foy had erected a facade of respectability, toyed with the affluent young woman's emotions, and seduced her for fiscal gain. In this respect, Foy and other poor whites like him represented rural counterparts to the shady, duplicitous "confidence men" who stalked the nation's cities in the mid-nineteenth century, preying upon innocent young people. The confidence man mastered the ability to manipulate the superficial impression he conveyed to others. The masquerade cloaked a vast disparity between his polished outward appearance and his

111. Petition of Sarah Robinson, Campbell County, December 7, 1841, Reel 34, Box 48, Folder 3, Legislative Petitions, Virginia General Assembly, LVA; Petition of Mary Lawry, Culpeper County, January 18, 1843, Reel 43, Box 60, Folder 33, Legislative Petitions, Virginia General Assembly, LVA. On Sarah Robinson, see also Buckley, *Great Catastrophe*, 138; and Rothman, *Notorious in the Neighborhood*, 183–184, 189. On Mary Lawry, see also Rothman, *Notorious in the Neighborhood*, 188–189. The state legislature granted neither woman her divorce.

112. Petition of Ann Eliza Eubank, King William County, December 9, 1836, Reel 103, Box 134, Folder 85, Legislative Petitions, Virginia General Assembly, LVA; Petition of Lucy W. Norman, Henry County, December 20, 1848, Reel 89, Box 120, Folder 6, Legislative Petitions, Virginia General Assembly, LVA; *Foy v. Foy*, 35 N.C. 90 (1851), Supreme Court Original Case #6535, NCDAH; Seventh Census of the United States, 1850: Craven County, North Carolina, 279, lists Harriet J. Foy as a woman of twenty-one, living in the household of her mother E. Smith, a forty-four-year-old woman with $1,200 in real estate. On Ann Eliza Eubank, see also Buckley, *Great Catastrophe*, 144; and Rothman, *Notorious in the Neighborhood*, 185, 188. On Lucy Norman, see also Buckley, *Great Catastrophe*, 146–147, 169; and Rothman, *Notorious in the Neighborhood*, 184, 187, 190–191.

113. Rothman, *Notorious in the Neighborhood*, 192.

depraved inner character. A victim of such deception herself, Janet Hunter likely regarded her husband as a confidence man. After her marriage to Samuel Hunter, she stated, he "immediately . . . threw off the mask and became the most abandoned and profligate of men."[114]

Several poor white men frankly acknowledged that they married for money and property.[115] Legally, any property a woman in antebellum America owned transferred to her husband upon marriage. Thus, upon exchanging vows with Lucy Price, James Norman "found himself the undisputed owner" of his new wife's substantial holdings. Edward Womack of Halifax County, Virginia, owned "very little property except the property acquired . . . by his marriage" to his wife Sarah, which instantaneously made him the master of more than a dozen slaves. Thomas Foy admitted in a private letter to his wife Harriet that he had married her not "from affection but for the property she was entitled to." Similarly, Alfred Eubank "declared on divers occasions that he had married" Ann Eliza "for her property." Because "she did not possess as much as he expected," Alfred "therefore quit her." "[A]fter spending and carrying off nearly the whole of her property," he abandoned her three months into their marriage.[116]

Absent ties of love or affection to their well-off wives, poor white husbands pursued sex across the color line. Most petitions conveyed only the vaguest sense of poor white men's sexual transgressions. Alfred Eubank, for instance, "frequently left the marriage Bed to seek the Bed of a colored woman." On rare occasion, however, a petition details the sexual relationship between a poor white man and slave woman more explicitly. James Norman, for one, "lived in the most licentious immorality" and "formed a mischievous connection with one *not of his own color*." Norman "habitually had illicit & criminal intercourse" with a black "servant girl" named Maria: "He frequently slept with her" flagrantly, "sometimes on a pallet in his wife's chamber" or "in an adjoining room of the house."

114. *Foy v. Foy*, 35 N.C. 90 (1851), Supreme Court Original Case #6535, NCDAH; Karen Halttunen, *Confidence Men and Painted Women: A Study of Middle-class Culture in America, 1830–1870* (New Haven: Yale University Press, 1982); Petition of Janet Hunter, Petersburg (Town), December 15, 1823, Reel 217, Box 222, Folder 59, Legislative Petitions, Virginia General Assembly, LVA. On Samuel and Janet Hunter, see also Buckley, *Great Catastrophe*, 140; and Rothman, *Notorious in the Neighborhood*, 184, 187, 188, 192, 193.

115. Buckley, *Great Catastrophe*, 168–169, 175; Rothman, *Notorious in the Neighborhood*, 185.

116. Petition of Lucy W. Norman; Petition of Sarah Womack, Halifax County, March 1, 1848, Reel 73, Box 99, Folder 51, Legislative Petitions, Virginia General Assembly, LVA; *Foy v. Foy*, 35 N.C. 90 (1851), Supreme Court Original Case #6535, NCDAH; Petition of Ann Eliza Eubank. On Sarah Womack, see also Rothman, *Notorious in the Neighborhood*, 185.

According to one deponent, Norman "often embraced & kissed her in my presence" and "invited her to a seat at the dinning [*sic*] table with himself & family." Ultimately, he left his wife "in company with . . . Maria," taking her "to the southern country." [117]

Although it is impossible to determine the precise nature of the relationships between most poor white men and their enslaved partners, James Norman, Newsome Lawry, and others may have genuinely loved the female slaves with whom they consorted. A few isolated cases, however, clearly imply that poor white men sexually objectified slave women and expected them to cater to their lascivious desires. Thomas D. Foy and George W. Miller were two landless farmers living in the household of George E. and Olivia Pritchett in Jones County, North. Carolina. One day in 1847, Foy wanted sex, and asked Miller "to go out with him in search of some girls." Miller assented, and the pair "went out to where some negro Girls were washing." Foy approached Milly, a slave woman belonging to the Pritchetts. He "had some conversation with her," then "retired to a hog pen," where Miller "saw them down on the ground together." On a separate occasion, Miller watched Foy "take the Girl Milly into a shed room and they were in the room together about twenty five minutes." Miller does not mention the use of physical force in these situations, but he also fails to report the nature of Foy's "conversation" with Milly. Foy may have threatened Milly to submit to his wishes or promised her material rewards in exchange for sex. That he consorted with her at least twice implies only that he enjoyed the pleasure of her company and does not necessarily indicate that he felt any love, affection, or sense of commitment toward her.[118]

Foy, in fact, copulated with slave women other than Milly. In 1849, while at his brother's house in Jones County, Foy invited an acquaintance named Custis "to go out among the negro Girls" with him. Foy matched up his friend with a "yellow woman," then proceeded to the house of slave Hannah, on "Miss [Emily] Burgwins plantation." Foy and Hannah stayed "in the house together and the door shut and no person with them except a small negro child." Before

117. Petition of Ann Eliza Eubank; Petition of Lucy W. Norman.

118. *Foy v. Foy*, 35 N.C. 90 (1851), Supreme Court Original Case #6535, NCDAH; Seventh Census of the United States, 1850: Jones County, North Carolina, 120, lists Thomas D. Foy as a thirty-one-year-old farmer with no real estate, living in the household of Carolina Foscue, a wealthy woman of thirty; Seventh Census of the United States, 1850: Jones County, North Carolina, 113, lists George W. Miller as a twenty-five-year-old farmer with no real estate.

long, Custis's arrival at Hannah's quarters interrupted their rendezvous. Foy asked if his friend "had been accommodated." Custis "replyed he had not for he did not like the appearance of the woman." Ever the obliging host, Foy suggested a "likely maid" of Miss Emily's. On his way to retrieve her, however, Foy and Custis "met a negro boy," whom they feared "would go and tell the overseer." Rather than risk a confrontation, they decided "they had better leave." The threat of being captured cavorting in the slave quarters convinced the men to depart, suggesting their recognition of the impropriety of their behavior and their fear of retaliation at the hands of the plantation mistress.[119]

Foy's exploits in the slave quarters conformed to a broad pattern of marital infidelity on his part. Within six months of his marriage to Harriet J. Smith, Thomas left his young bride "for whole days and nights" at a time "and consorted with evil and abandoned company." Harriet eventually filed for divorce, noting that during her lengthy separation from her husband, he had surrendered "to loose and desolute [sic] habits," having "habitual and indiscriminate adulterous intercourse with slaves and other abandoned women." She contended—and all evidence bears out—that Thomas lived "in adulterous intercourse with a negro slave woman named Milly the property of George E. Pritchett and Olivia Pritchett," "with a negro slave woman named Hannah the property of Sarah E. Burguyn . . . , and also with a negro slave woman, the property of one John E. Fortiscue [Foscue]," all of Jones County. Harriet further claimed that, while in Wilmington, Foy "contracted, from some abandoned woman, a foul and loathsome disease, the consequence of his illicit conduct." Weighing the evidence, a court in Carteret County granted Harriet her divorce.[120]

If some poor white men coerced female slaves to submit to their sexual advances, others offered to pay for sex with slave women. When poor whites Kenneth Mizell and his companion, a man identified only as Brickhouse, encountered the slaves Dick and Caesar while on a drunken spree in Martin County, North Carolina, in 1848, Brickhouse asked Dick "if he could not get some girls for them," remarking, probably falsely, "that he had money a plenty." Dick successfully defended the women of his race by refusing to secure female slaves to satisfy the

119. *Foy v. Foy,* 35 N.C. 90 (1851), Supreme Court Original Case #6535, NCDAH.

120. Ibid. Like Foy, Janet Hunter's husband Samuel was afflicted "by the worst loathsome diseases contracted in his adulterous intercourse with negroes." See Petition of Janet Hunter. The North Carolina state supreme court would ultimately overturn Harriet Foy's divorce. See Bynum, *Unruly Women,* 72.

poor white men's sexual appetites.[121] Other slaves, by contrast, did act as agents in abetting the interracial sex between slave women and white men. In 1834, Virginia slaveholder John Walker complained about his neighbor Ben Pollard, a King and Queen County master who allegedly kept an "abominable Brothel" catering to the salacious desires of local white men. According to Walker, for the past ten years Pollard had dispatched his slaves to Walker's to gather clandestinely "my negro women to whore it with." Unlike Dick and Caesar, Pollard's bondsmen were under direct orders from a white authority figure to procure female slaves for lecherous purposes. Whereas Dick felt justified in refusing to comply with the request of the lowly Brickhouse, Pollard's slaves dared not disobey their master's commands. Hence, on consecutive Sundays in June 1834, some of them persuaded Walker's "Bartlet to bring to him my young woman Mary." On July 2, Walker soundly whipped Bartlet and Mary, as well as slaves Richard and Sillah, for colluding with "the abominable low life insignificant low bred skurf of the earth in the shape of human beings that Ben Pollard keeps at his house."[122] Walker lost all patience with Pollard when his thirty-four-year-old "coloured woman Eliza" succumbed to "the venereal complaint," presumably contracted through her sexual activities at Pollard's.[123] Eliza "left 4 children," all of whom she had purportedly conceived "by whoredom[,] most of them gotten by white men at Ben Pollards whos[e] house is a compleat Brothel where the Devil reigned at full power."[124]

The lack of poor white men's own voices leaves the significance of their willingness to pay for sex with slave women open to interpretation. Perhaps these poor white men, in contrast to others, did not feel sexually entitled to slave women. They may have acknowledged female slaves' right to their own bodies, and understood that it would cost them to gain access. In this sense, poor white men and slave women met in a sexual marketplace where, for a price, poor white men could obtain a desired product or service, while slave women themselves earned some material benefit.

More poor white men probably subscribed to the widespread belief among whites that female slaves were passionate and promiscuous Jezebels who craved

121. *State v. Caesar,* 31 N.C. 391 (1849), 271–272.

122. John Walker Plantation Journal, July 2, 1834, ser. 1, vol. 2, [typescript 111–112], John Walker Papers #2300, SHC. Fifth Census of the United States, 1830: King and Queen County, Virginia, 282, lists Ben Pollard as a man in his forties, with eighteen slaves.

123. John Walker Plantation Journal, July 2, 1834, [typescript 108, 109], SHC.

124. Ibid., [typescript 110], SHC.

sex with white men.[125] But to seek slave women out publicly brought shame and disgrace upon white men. Even the wealthiest of masters knew to keep affairs with female slaves discreet or risk community censure. This rule held for poor white men as well. Soon after Brickhouse solicited Dick's and Caesar's aid in procuring slave women for sex, the encounter turned violent, ending in the death of the poor white Kenneth Mizell. A Martin County jury convicted Caesar of the murder, but on appeal, the slave's attorney highlighted the alleged depravity of the poor whites. "Here are two drunken, worthless white men found at a late hour of the night," argued Caesar's counsel, "placing themselves below the rank which the law assigns them in deference to their color," by "appealing to the slaves to become their pimps, and assisting in acts of lewdness and prostitution." The poor white men's candid pursuit of slave women had blatantly overstepped the bounds of propriety. Judge Richmond Pearson, for one, believed that the poor white men's "fury and disappointed lusts" led to their bullying the slaves in the first place. Pearson condemned the behavior of Mizell and Brickhouse, providing a rare example of a southern court criticizing poor white men rather than poor white women for their sexual interactions with slaves.[126]

While scholars within the past decade have taken a great interest in the sex lives of poor white women, they have yet to conduct any parallel investigation into those of poor white men. Certainly a frustrating lack of readily accessible primary sources explains this neglect. Yet even a brief, preliminary comparison of poor white women and men in the antebellum Carolinas and Virginia reveals their disparate experiences of sexual contact—whether consensual, forced, or somewhere in between—with slaves, despite their shared race and class status. "Respectable" white society condemned the alleged sexual depravity of all poor whites, but proved far more anxious over the sexual behavior of poor white women. Although communities sometimes proved flexible, "respectable" white society typically condemned the lower-class white women who took slave men as lovers, and blamed sexual violence committed on them by slaves on poor white

125. On the Jezebel, see Deborah Gray White, *Ar'n't I a Woman?: Female Slaves in the Plantation South* (New York: Norton, 1985), 29–46.

126. Timothy S. Huebner, "The Roots of Fairness: *State v. Caesar* and Slave Justice in Antebellum North Carolina," in *Local Matters: Race, Crime, and Justice in the Nineteenth-Century South*, ed. Christopher Waldrep and Donald G. Nieman (Athens: University of Georgia Press, 2001), 36. The supreme court granted Caesar a new trial, in which he was found guilty of manslaughter rather than murder. Ultimately, the slave escaped with only a branded left thumb.

women's own perceived depravity and licentiousness. Elite economic interests in slaveholding combined with preconceived notions of poor white women as collectively lewd and abandoned to challenge the credibility of poor white women's charges of sexual assault. In contrast, poor white men successfully capitalized upon the privileges of their race and sex to transcend their class status and, like slaveholders themselves, appropriate the bodies of slave women for their own libidinous purposes, momentarily joining male slaveholders as equals in the sexual domination of enslaved women.

Masters of course disapproved of poor white men sneaking into the slave quarters to elicit sex from female slaves. When poor white men satisfied their prurient urges with slave women, they usurped the master's rights to his enslaved property. But, should children result, the offspring only added to the slaveholders' wealth. Poor white women, on the other hand, possessed the reproductive power to blur the racial categories of "black" and "white," by giving birth to free mixed-race children. Because they had the ability to erode the racial distinctions that ordered southern society, lower-class white women were the especial targets of elite scrutiny. Whereas poor white men defied elite prescriptions against interracial sex and conferred upon themselves the license to take sexual liberties with slave women, poor white women's opportunities for sex with slaves were far more constricted. Throughout the antebellum era, white society denied them the sexual leeway grudgingly permitted poor white men, closely monitored their sexual activities, and condemned any seemingly errant behavior. The gendered experiences of poor white men and women in their sexual encounters with slaves both reflected and affirmed the sexual double standard of the Old South.

EPILOGUE

The preceding chapters have attempted to illustrate the unappreciated complexity of slave–poor white relations in the antebellum Carolinas and Virginia. While conflict and contention characterized some of their interracial contacts, others were notable for the cooperation and camaraderie shown by the enslaved and poor white participants. How strong were the cords that bound those slaves and poor whites who worked, drank, and gambled together, traded with one another, plotted, or made love? The Civil War provided the barometer to measure the strength of their ties, flushing out precisely where poor white allegiance truly lay.

Roughly 75 percent of all southern white men of military age served in the Confederate army. Over the four-year course of the Civil War, a majority of non-slaveholding southern white men fought for the Confederacy at some point, willingly or not. Most adamantly opposed secession from the Union, so it comes as no surprise that few poor white men volunteered for service during the first year of the conflict. A handful enlisted out of patriotism and loyalty to the Confederate cause, but most felt no compelling desire to preserve southern society as it existed. Their poverty offered them ample and undeniable proof that the present system benefited them little. Moreover, many transient poor whites were unattached to any particular locality. The war therefore aroused no emotional need to defend the homeland from northern attacks. The Confederacy, however, could not permit its human resources to go untapped. When the Confederate draft began in April 1862, poor white men, who composed a significant minority of potential recruits, became the disproportional targets of conscription. The onerous "twenty nigger" rule excluded slaveholders with the requisite number of bondspeople from such impressment. Other wealthy southern white men willingly forked over an exemption fee or paid their impoverished neighbors to serve as substitutes. Such practices gave rise to the oft-repeated "rich man's war, poor man's fight" slogan.[1]

1. Charles C. Bolton, *Poor Whites of the Antebellum South: Tenants and Laborers in Central North Carolina and Northeast Mississippi* (Durham: Duke University Press, 1994), 157; J. William Harris, *Plain Folk and Gentry in a Slave Society: White Liberty and Black Slavery in Augusta's Hinterlands* (Middletown, Conn.: Wesleyan University Press, 1985; reprint, Baton Rouge: Louisiana State Uni-

Many Northerners maintained that, beneath the veneer of Confederate allegiance, most poor whites were latent Unionists and possible allies against "the despotism of the Slave Power."[2] Antislavery northern newspaper correspondent James Redpath, who toured the South incognito in the 1850s, interviewing slaves, small farmers, and others, went one step further, insisting that substantial numbers of poor whites and a majority of nonslaveholders in general were in fact "secret abolitionists."[3] To be sure, many poor whites welcomed the arrival of northern armies in the South and offered them aid when possible. According to one Union officer, "[T]he negroes and poor whites . . . are very willing to communicate all the information they are in possession of."[4] Nonslaveholding southern whites resisted the rebel draft and deserted the Confederate army at unusually high rates, and they made up virtually all of the approximately 100,000 whites from Confederate states who defected to serve in Union blue.[5] But perhaps most poor whites sided with neither the Confederacy nor the Union, treating the war with indifference, as a conflict that had little if anything to do with them.[6] In North Carolina, letters to the governor complained that "the comon people is drove of[f] in the ware to fight for the big mans negro" and that "our pore clas of men are all gonn to the Ware to fight to save our country & the Rich mans negroes & land."[7]

---

versity Press, 1998), 149–153. There remains a heated debate over the role that internal dissent within the South played in the downfall of the Confederacy. For a clear and forceful but not entirely convincing argument downplaying divisions on the southern home front, see Gary W. Gallagher, *The Confederate War* (Cambridge: Harvard University Press, 1997), esp. 3–4, 12, ch. 1. For recent works emphasizing wartime divisions among southern whites, see David Williams, Teresa Crisp Williams, and R. David Carlson, *Plain Folk in a Rich Man's War: Class and Dissent in Confederate Georgia* (Gainesville: University Press of Florida, 2002); William W. Freehling, *The South vs. the South: How Anti-Confederate Southerners Shaped the Course of the Civil War* (New York: Oxford University Press, 2001), esp. xi–xiii, 20–22, 145, 201–202; David Williams, *Rich Man's War: Class, Caste, and Confederate Defeat in the Lower Chattahoochee Valley* (Athens: University of Georgia Press, 1998); Wayne K. Durrill, *War of Another Kind: A Southern Community in the Great Rebellion* (New York: Oxford University Press, 1990); and Fred Arthur Bailey, *Class and Tennessee's Confederate Generation* (Chapel Hill: University of North Carolina Press, 1987).

2. Stephen V. Ash, "Poor Whites in the Occupied South, 1861–1865," *Journal of Southern History* 57 (February 1991): 46.

3. John R. McKivigan, ed., *The Roving Editor, or Talks with Slaves in the Southern States, by James Redpath* (University Park, Penn.: Pennsylvania State University Press, 1996), 55, 90.

4. Quoted in Ash, "Poor Whites," 48.

5. Freehling, *The South vs. the South*, 145, xiii.

6. Ash, "Poor Whites," 56.

7. Quoted in Bill Cecil-Fronsman, *Common Whites: Class and Culture in Antebellum North Carolina* (Lexington: University Press of Kentucky, 1992), 203, 212.

The incongruity of poor white men marching off to war to preserve and protect the slaveholding interest did not escape the notice of contemporaries. Some
ex-slaves pointed out the anomaly of poor white men heading into battle, dispatched for the purpose of defending the property of the wealthy.[8] The former
slave Willie Blackwell of Granville County, North Carolina, declared that "dem
poor whites dat fought on de Southern side didn't have no business fightin'." According to Blackwell, "de big man" enticed "de poor man" into battle with promises of slave ownership upon his return.[9] An ex-slave from Alabama claimed that
poor white "counterscript soldiers" who "refused to go to war . . . got shot down
like a dog," so most took their chances in battle instead of "get[ting] shot widout a doubt" back home. She reflected sympathetically that "dey had to go and
fight a rich man's war but dey couldn't help demselves no better'n us slaves
could."[10] Slave autobiographer H. C. Bruce correctly observed that poor white
men "contributed their full share to the death roll of the Southern Army."[11]
Whether they joined as volunteers, conscripts, substitutes, or as the result of de-
ceit, threats, or intimidation, many poor white men of military age marched off
to war for a cause that was not their own.

This begs the long-standing question: why did slaves and poor whites (and
free blacks) not form a coalition of the downtrodden and dispossessed and
bring slaveholder fears of a southern, lower-class alliance to fruition? Historian
Charles C. Bolton cites several valid reasons in his excellent study of antebellum
poor whites. Ties of kinship and neighborhood, shared social and religious experiences, cultural values, and educational opportunities all helped unite disparate classes of southern whites. The geographic mobility of poor whites prevented
them from forging sustained biracial alliances, and the Old South's criminal justice system maintained social boundaries by punishing wayward poor whites
(and equally subversive free blacks) whose activities with slaves threatened the
social structure. The constraints of enslavement also made it difficult for blacks
to organize. Masters kept their slaves busy at work, and they swiftly corrected
disobedient chattel. Finally, as the *Herrenvolk* thesis states, racial animosities of-

8. Eugene D. Genovese, "'Rather Be a Nigger Than a Poor White Man': Slave Perceptions of
Southern Yeomen and Poor Whites," in *Toward a New View of America: Essays in Honor of Arthur C.
Cole*, ed. Hans L. Trefousse (New York: Burt Franklin & Company, Inc., 1977), 90.

9. George P. Rawick, ed., *The American Slave: A Composite Autobiography, Supplement, Series 2*,
vol. 2, pt. 1 (Westport, Conn.: Greenwood Press, 1979), 315–316.

10. George P. Rawick, ed., *The American Slave: A Composite Autobiography*, vol. 11, Missouri
(Westport, Conn.: Greenwood Publishing Company, 1972), 302.

11. H. C. Bruce, *The New Man: Twenty-Nine Years a Slave, Twenty-Nine Years a Free Man* (York,
Penn.: P. Anstadt & Sons, 1895; reprint, New York: Negro Universities Press, 1969), 31.

ten drove a wedge between the slaves and poor whites who otherwise shared similar lives of dependence and poverty. All of these factors combined to militate against the creation of a biracial alliance against the planters.[12]

To this list we must add the nature of the relationship between slaves and poor whites itself. Bolton rightly observes that race alone did not pit slaves and poor whites against one another; indeed, he offers perhaps the single most comprehensive look at the array of reasons why they would not forge ties in wartime. But slaves and poor whites themselves engaged in such competing and contradictory types of relationships that it would have been incredibly difficult for them to unite unequivocally. While some poor whites drank and gambled with slaves, exchanged goods with them illicitly, helped them run away, or had consensual sex with them, others competed with bondspeople for work, made their livelihood doing the masters' bidding as overseers, inflicted violence upon slaves, and engaged in forced or coerced sex with them. And when slaves and poor whites did cooperate, they often did so for practical and mutually beneficial reasons rather than necessarily out of friendship, camaraderie, or compassion. Relations between slaves and poor whites proved complex, and while shared impoverishment and degradation sometimes brought them together as individuals, they typically showed no clear ideological commitment to the other's plight as a class.

The ambivalent relationship between slaves and poor whites continued during the war. Despite the war, and in many instances because of it, mutually supportive exchanges between slaves and poor whites persisted and flourished. Many slaves and poor whites evinced an acute understanding of the position in which the war placed the other. As ex-slave George Briggs of South Carolina recalled, "When dese poor white men went to de war, dey left deir little chillun and deir wives in de hands of de darkies dat was kind and de rich wives of our marsters to care fer. Us took de best care of dem poor white dat us could under de circumstances dat prevailed."[13] Slaves often stole provisions to feed and supply suffering poor whites and deserters from the Confederate army.[14] Former North Caro-

---

12. Bolton, *Poor Whites*, 9, 51–58, 65, 136–137, 184. Moreover, poor white tenants and laborers held disparate interests from the numerically superior and more politically astute yeoman class. As Bolton observes, "Poor whites might have viewed the split between the landed and the landless as equally or more significant than the dividing line that separated nonslaveowner and slaveowner" (113, 120, 136–137). See also Bruce Collins, *White Society in the Antebellum South* (London: Longman, 1985), 7, 158.

13. Rawick, vol. 2, pt. 1, 87.

14. Rawick, vol. 14, pt. 1, 266.

lina slave Anthony Dawson remembered that poor whites would sometimes render slaves aid in running away during wartime "if you could bring 'em sumpin you stole, lak a silver dish or spoons or a couple big hams." Poor whites in desperate circumstances provided assistance only conditionally, as Dawson recalled, but, he continued, "I couldn't blame them poor white folks, wid the men in the War and the women and children hongry. The niggers didn't belong to them nohow, and they had to live somehow." [15] Much to slaveholders' alarm, other slaves and poor whites took advantage of wartime opportunities to cooperate in pillaging neighborhoods and plundering unguarded homes and smokehouses.[16]

Fellow North Carolina slave William Henry Singleton insisted, probably too optimistically, that "poor white people naturally sympathized with us." During the war, he stated, "the plantation owners were afraid that because of this they might teach us to read or might give us some information about what the North was trying to do." [17] From the slaveholders' perspective, the everyday contacts between slaves and poor whites assumed increasingly ominous undertones after secession. Poor whites undermined slaveholders by apparently helping dispel the rumors that masters promulgated among their slaves about the nature of the war. In the Sea Islands, for example, slaveholders informed their chattel that the Union army planned to gather them up and sell them to Cuba. Through eavesdropping on white conversations or reading local newspapers, slaves acquired some sense of the war's meaning, but communications with poor whites sometimes served to clarify northern intentions.[18]

But if the Civil War drew some slaves and poor whites closer together, its onset also profoundly disrupted the racial climate in which contact occurred, imposing strains on slaves' and poor whites' ability to forge bonds across the color line. Historian Stephen V. Ash has shown that wartime intensified poor whites' racism as they competed with the freedpeople for increasingly scarce jobs and housing. The shared racial hostility of many slaves and poor whites prevented them from recognizing their mutual desires to acquire land and an education. Rather than creating a biracial alliance of the poor and dispossessed to pursue their common goals, many poor whites identified with their white social superiors and united with the master class. They assisted slaveholders by tracking down

15. Rawick, vol. 7, Oklahoma, 66. See also B. A. Botkin, ed., *Lay My Burden Down: A Folk History of Slavery* (1945; reprint, Athens: University of Georgia Press, 1989), 253.

16. Ash, "Poor Whites," 44; Bolton, *Poor Whites,* 156.

17. William Henry Singleton, *Recollections of My Slavery Days* (Peekskill, N.Y.: Highland Democrat, 1922), 6.

18. Genovese, "Rather Be a Nigger Than a Poor White Man," 89.

fugitives attempting to exploit wartime chaos to gain their freedom, or by supplying runaways misinformation that would lead to their apprehension. "Yes,
dat's de way it was," reminisced Anthony Dawson about the confused relationships with poor whites during war. "Devils and good people walking in de road
at de same time, and nobody could tell one from t'other."[19]

Historians have noted the "dual nature of emancipation" resulting from the
Civil War.[20] Former slaves observed that emancipation freed "not only the slaves,
but the poor whites of the South as well, for they occupied a condition nearly approaching that of slavery."[21] To the detriment of the ex-slaves, poor white gains
often came at the freedpeople's expense. Slaves' release from bondage did nothing to change the color of their skin, and without slavery to keep blacks in check,
southern whites found other means to maintain racial supremacy. Southern
whites instituted a widespread system of segregation in the South, requiring the
physical separation of the races in churches, schools, hospitals, and other public
accommodations.[22] Meanwhile, formerly marginalized poor whites were welcomed into a fuller participation in the benefits of whiteness. Whereas before the
war, white society distinguished the respectable poor from the undeserving and
degraded "poor whites," the postbellum years saw blacks relegated to the "undeserving" category while poor whites increasingly counted among the "deserving,"
becoming the objects of missionary work.[23] Employers banished black workers entirely from the textile mills of the New South in favor of working-class
white operatives,[24] and society at last ushered poor white women into the fold of
"southern womanhood." In the last third of the nineteenth century, black men

19. Ash, "Poor Whites," 58–59; Rawick, vol. 7, Oklahoma, 67. See also Botkin, *Lay My Burden
Down*, 253.

20. Ash, "Poor Whites," 40. See also C. Vann Woodward, *Origins of the New South, 1877–1913*
(Baton Rouge: Louisiana State University Press, 1951), 175; and Robert Gilmour, "The Other Emancipation: Studies in the Society and Economy of Alabama Whites during Reconstruction" (Ph.D.
diss., Johns Hopkins University, 1972).

21. Bruce, *New Man*, 30.

22. On the debate over when segregation took hold in the South, see C. Vann Woodward, *The
Strange Career of Jim Crow*, 3rd ed. (New York: Oxford University Press, 1974); Howard N. Rabinowitz, "From Exclusion to Segregation: Southern Race Relations, 1865–1890," *Journal of American
History* 63 (September 1976): 325–350; and Rabinowitz, "More Than the Woodward Thesis: Assessing the Strange Career of Jim Crow," *Journal of American History* 75 (December 1988): 842–856.

23. Nina Silber, "'What Does America Need So Much as Americans?': Race and Northern Reconciliation with South Appalachia, 1870–1900," in *Appalachians and Race: The Mountain South from
Slavery to Segregation*, ed. John C. Inscoe (Lexington: University Press of Kentucky, 2001), 247.

24. Norris W. Preyer, "The Historian, the Slave, and the Ante-Bellum Textile Industry," *Journal of Negro History* 46 (April 1961): 81.

who raped or attempted to rape even the poorest of white women risked swift justice at the hands of a lynch mob.[25] In short, racial lines hardened in postwar southern society, generally to the benefit of poor whites and to the detriment of the freedpeople. As former South Carolina slave Waters McIntosh insisted, "It was the poor white man who was freed by the War, not the Negroes."[26]

In the postbellum years, the political arena offered the last possible avenue of biracial cooperation between freedpeople and poor whites. Initially after the war, possibly as a natural outgrowth of their mutually beneficial antebellum contacts, large numbers of poor whites and debt-ridden yeomen joined black men in the ranks of the Republican Party. Typically wartime Unionists who had opposed secession altogether, these southern-born white Republicans, contemptuously dubbed "scalawags" both by their political enemies and by subsequent generations of uncharitable scholars, saw, in W. E. B. DuBois's words, "a vision of democracy across racial lines."[27] In the North Carolina Piedmont, a biracial coalition of freedmen and disaffected lower-class whites, resentful of planter domination, channeled their frustrations into politics, ushering into state and local offices Republican administrations of a reformist bent, pursuing measures calculated to end aristocratic privilege and forge a more democratic society.[28]

25. Martha Hodes, *White Women, Black Men: Illicit Sex in the Nineteenth-Century South* (New Haven: Yale University Press, 1997), ch. 8.

26. Rawick, vol. 10, pt. 5, 20.

27. The scalawags were actually an eclectic combination of former Whig planters and elite businessmen, nonslaveholding whites, and wartime Unionists. For the basic contours of the debate over the composition of the scalawags, see David H. Donald, "The Scalawag in Mississippi Reconstruction," *Journal of Southern History* 10 (November 1944): 447–460; and Allen W. Trelease, "Who Were the Scalawags?" *Journal of Southern History* 29 (November 1963): 445–468. Donald contends that the scalawags were antebellum Whig planters, while Trelease finds that they were predominantly poorer-than-average "hill-country farmers." Donald and Trelease both conceded an element of truth in the other's interpretation. For more on the debate, see also Vernon Lane Wharton, *The Negro in Mississippi, 1865–1890* (Chapel Hill: University of North Carolina Press, 1947), 157; Thomas B. Alexander, "Persistent Whiggery in the Confederate South, 1860–1877," *Journal of Southern History* 27 (August 1961): 305–329; William C. Harris, "A Reconsideration of the Mississippi Scalawag," *Journal of Mississippi History* 32 (February 1970): 3–42; Warren A. Ellem, "Who Were the Mississippi Scalawags?" *Journal of Southern History* 38 (May 1972): 217–240; Sarah Woolfolk Wiggins, *The Scalawag in Alabama Politics, 1865–1881* (University, Ala.: University of Alabama Press, 1977); Peter Kolchin, "Scalawags, Carpetbaggers, and Reconstruction: A Quantitative Look at Southern Congressional Politics, 1868–1872," *Journal of Southern History* 45 (February 1979): 63–76. DuBois quoted in Trelease, "Who Were the Scalawags?" 446.

28. Paul D. Escott, "White Republicanism and Ku Klux Klan Terror: The North Carolina Piedmont During Reconstruction," in *Race, Class, and Politics in Southern History: Essays in Honor of Robert F. Durden,* ed. Jeffrey J. Crow, Paul D. Escott, and Charles L. Flynn, Jr. (Baton Rouge: Louisiana

Throughout the Reconstruction South, Republican lawmakers helped draft and pass legislation concerning education and economic development, designed to uplift both the freedpeople and poor whites.[29] After Reconstruction as well, blacks and whites continued to form potent independent and fusion political parties that southern Democrats could not take lightly. The Readjuster Party, with its biracial constituency, governed the state of Virginia from 1879 to 1883. Indeed, every southern state witnessed experiments in interracial political coalitions in the decades after the Civil War.[30] The Populist Party of the late 1880s and 1890s marked the last concerted effort in the nineteenth century to unify impoverished blacks and whites under a single political banner. In Georgia and North Carolina especially, Populists courted the suffering and discontented farmers of both races and urged their cooperation to effect reform.[31]

Southern white Democrats did not stand idly by and cede political power to these biracial coalitions. They feared any political alliances that transcended racial lines, arguing that when white men split their votes, black men held the balance of power in determining the outcome of closely contested elections. The overwhelming majority of white voters who cast ballots for non-Democratic candidates did so for pragmatic political reasons of their own rather than out of any particular commitment to the advancement of black rights, so time and again, whether in the case of the Republicans, the Readjusters, or the Populists, southern Democrats lured whites back into the fold by co-opting the opposition platform that had successfully unified black and white voters. They then directed the electorate's attention away from substantive issues toward the polarizing issue

State University Press, 1989), 4–5, 21–23, 25, 28; Eric Foner, *Reconstruction: America's Unfinished Revolution, 1863–1877* (New York: Harper & Row, 1988), 301.

29. Genovese, "Rather Be a Nigger Than a Poor White Man," 91.

30. Jane Dailey, *Before Jim Crow: The Politics of Race in Postemancipation Virginia* (Chapel Hill: University of North Carolina Press, 2000), 1, 2, 155. For other instances of biracial political alliances in the 1870s and 1880s, see Kenneth C. Barnes, *Who Killed John Clayton?: Political Violence and the Emergence of the New South, 1861–1893* (Durham: Duke University Press, 1998), 3; Michael R. Hyman, *The Anti-Redeemers: Hill-Country Political Dissenters in the Lower South from Redemption to Populism* (Baton Rouge: Louisiana State University Press, 1990), ch. 8; Steven Hahn, *The Roots of Southern Populism: Yeoman Farmers and the Transformation of the Georgia Upcountry, 1850–1890* (New York: Oxford University Press, 1983), 236; Carl N. Degler, *The Other South: Southern Dissenters in the Nineteenth Century* (New York: Harper & Row, 1974), ch. 9; Woodward, *Origins of the New South*, 75–106.

31. Hahn, *Roots of Southern Populism*, 283; J. Morgan Kousser, *The Shaping of Southern Politics: Suffrage Restrictions and the Establishment of the One-Party South, 1880–1910* (New Haven: Yale University Press, 1974), 216; C. Vann Woodward, *Tom Watson: Agrarian Rebel* (1938; New York: Oxford University Press, 1963), 220–222.

of race. Flagrant race-baiting, playing to whites' racial fears and anxieties, ce-
mented loyalty to the party of white supremacy. Intimidation, violence, and elec-
toral fraud rounded out the Democratic arsenal of tactics.[32] When poor white
voters aided in the restoration of Democratic governments, they removed from
power the very politicians most sympathetic to their plight.[33] In time, Democratic lawmakers accomplished the nearly complete disfranchisement of black
men through a creative array of voting restrictions. That many of these, including literacy tests, poll taxes, and property qualifications, also eliminated some
poor white men from the rosters of eligible voters seemed a salutary fringe benefit for southern Democrats concerned over poor white loyalties to the party and
their race.[34] Certainly by the end of the nineteenth century, antebellum cooperation between slaves and poor whites was forgotten, replaced by the reality of
racial hatred and Jim Crow segregation.

32. Bolton, *Poor Whites*, 184; Foner, *Reconstruction*, 299, 303; Degler, *The Other South*, ch. 9.
33. Genovese, "Rather Be a Nigger Than a Poor White Man," 91.
34. Kousser, *Shaping of Southern Politics*, 6–7, 58–59; Bolton, *Poor Whites*, 184.

BIBLIOGRAPHY

Primary Sources

NORTH CAROLINA DEPARTMENT OF ARCHIVES AND HISTORY, RALEIGH

Caldwell County, Slave Records
Chatham County, Records of Slaves and Free Persons of Color
Chowan County
    Minute Docket, Superior Court
    Slave Records, Criminal Actions Concerning Slaves
Cleveland County, Records of Slaves and Free Persons of Color
Craven County
    Criminal Actions Concerning Slaves and Free Persons of Color
    Superior Court, Minutes
    Superior Court, State Docket
Davidson County, Records of Slaves and Free Persons of Color
Gates County, Slave Records, Criminal Actions Concerning Slaves
General Assembly, Session Records
Governor's Letter Books
    Hutchins G. Burton, William A. Graham, Gabriel Holmes
Governor's Papers
    Thomas Bragg, Hutchins G. Burton, Edward B. Dudley, John W. Ellis, William A. Graham, Gabriel Holmes, Charles Manly, John M. Morehead, John Owen, Montfort Stokes, David L. Swain
Granville County, Criminal Actions Concerning Slaves and Free Persons of Color
Johnston County, Minute Docket, Superior Court
Mecklenburg County, Minute Book, Superior Court
Nash County, Slave Records, Civil Action Records and Criminal Action Records
New Hanover County, Records of Slaves and Free Persons of Color
Northampton County, Slave Records
Orange County, Minute Docket, Superior Court

Perquimans County
    Minute Docket, Superior Court
    Slave Records
Randolph County, Records of Slaves and Free Persons of Color
Richmond County, Slave Records, Criminal Action Papers Concerning Slaves
Robeson County, Records Concerning Slaves and Free Persons of Color
Stanly County, Records of Slaves and Free Persons of Color
Stokes County, Slave Records
State Supreme Court Records
    State v. Hale, 9 N.C. 582 (1823)
    State v. Jim, 12 N.C. 508 (1828)
    Skinner v. White, 18 N.C. 471 (1836)
    State v. Jarrott, 23 N.C. 76 (1840)
    State v. Jefferson, 28 N.C. 305 (1846), Supreme Court Original Case #3699
    State v. George, 29 N.C. 321 (1847), Supreme Court Original Case #4188
    State v. Caesar, 31 N.C. 391 (1849)
    State v. Boyce, 32 N.C. 536 (1849)
    State v. Moses Dean, 35 N.C. 63 (1851), Supreme Court Original Case #6985
    Foy v. Foy, 35 N.C. 90 (1851), Supreme Court Original Case #6535
    State v. Nat, 35 N.C. 154 (1851)
    State v. Alvin G. Thornton, 44 N.C. 252 (1853)
    State v. Jim, 48 N.C. 348 (1856), Supreme Court Original Case #3631
    State v. Henry, 50 N.C. 66 (1857), Supreme Court Original Case #7244
    State v. Eli Carroll, 51 N.C. 458 (1859)
    Lucas v. Nichols, 52 N.C. 32 (1859)
    State v. Elick, 52 N.C. 68 (1859)
Wayne County
    Criminal Action Papers
    Minute Docket, Superior Court
    Records of Slaves and Free Persons of Color
Wilson County, Slave Records

SOUTHERN HISTORICAL COLLECTION, WILSON LIBRARY,
UNIVERSITY OF NORTH CAROLINA AT CHAPEL HILL

Burwell Family Papers
David Gavin Diary
Springs Family Papers
William D. Valentine Diary
John Walker Papers

SOUTH CAROLINA DEPARTMENT OF ARCHIVES AND HISTORY, COLUMBIA

Anderson District
    Court of General Sessions, Criminal Journals
    Court of Magistrates and Freeholders, Trial Papers
Charleston District, Grand Jury Presentments, Legislative Papers
Chesterfield District, Grand Jury Presentments, Legislative Papers
Church Minutes
    Antioch Baptist Church
    Barnwell Baptist Church
    Ebenezer Baptist Church
    First Baptist Church
    New Providence Baptist Church
Committee Reports, Legislative Papers
Darlington District, Grand Jury Presentments, Legislative Papers
Fairfield District, Court of General Sessions, Indictments
Grand Jury Presentments, Legislative Papers
Greenville District, Court of General Sessions, Indictments
Kershaw District
    Court of Magistrates and Freeholders, Trial Papers
    Grand Jury Presentments, Legislative Papers
Laurens District
    Court of General Sessions, Indictments
    Court of Magistrates and Freeholders, Trial Papers
Marlboro District
    Court of General Sessions, Indictments
    Grand Jury Presentments, Legislative Papers
Petitions, Legislative Papers
Spartanburg District
    Court of General Sessions, Indictments
    Court of Magistrates and Freeholders, Trial Papers
    Grand Jury Presentments, Legislative Papers
Union District
    Court of General Sessions, Indictments
    Grand Jury Presentments, Legislative Papers
York District, Clerk of Court of General Sessions, General Sessions Papers

SOUTH CAROLINIANA LIBRARY, UNIVERSITY OF SOUTH CAROLINA, COLUMBIA

Henry Calvin Conner Papers
James S. M. Davis Papers
Historical Sketch of DeTreville House (Walterboro, S.C.)
Preamble and Regulations of the Savannah River Anti–Slave Traffick Association
William G. Roberds Papers

COLEMAN KARESH LAW LIBRARY, UNIVERSITY OF SOUTH CAROLINA, COLUMBIA

State v. Sonnerkalb, 2 Nott & McCord 280 (1820), *South Carolina Law Reports*, vol. 11
Rhodes v. Bunch, 3 McCord 66 (1825), *South Carolina Law Reports*, vol. 14
State v. Fife, 1 Bailey 1 (1828), *South Carolina Law Reports*, vol. 17
State v. Berhman and Peters, Riley 92 (1836), *South Carolina Law Reports*, vol. 22
State v. Lefronty, Riley 155 (1836), *South Carolina Law Reports*, vol. 22
State v. Schroder, 3 Hill 61 (1836), *South Carolina Law Reports*, vol. 21
State v. Nates, 3 Hill 200 (S.C. 1836)
State v. Hardy, Dudley 236 (1838), *South Carolina Law Reports*, vol. 23
State v Turner, 2 McMullan 399 (1842), *South Carolina Law Reports*, vol. 27
State v. Anderson, 1 Strobhart 455 (1847), *South Carolina Law Reports*, vol. 32
State v. Chandler, 2 Strobhart 266 (1848), *South Carolina Law Reports*, vol. 33
State v. Scates, 3 Strobhart 106 (1848), *South Carolina Law Reports*, vol. 34
State v. Thomas Motley; State v. William Blackledge, 7 Richardson 327 (1854), *South Carolina Law Reports*, vol. 41
State v. Rollins, 12 Richardson 297 (1859), *South Carolina Law Reports*, vol. 46

LIBRARY OF VIRGINIA, RICHMOND

Dinwiddie County, Minute Book 1
Martin Duralde Letter Book
Executive Papers
    James Pleasants, Henry A. Wise
Legislative Petitions, Virginia General Assembly
        Campbell County
        Culpeper County
        Halifax County
        Henry County
        King William County
        Petersburg (Town)

Lunenburg County, Justice of the Peace Records
Moseley v. Moss, 6 Grattan 534 (1850), 47 Va. 534

CENSUS RECORDS

DeBow, J. D. B. *The Seventh Census of the United States: 1850.* Washington: Robert Armstrong, 1853.

Kennedy, Joseph C. G. *Population of the United States in 1860; Compiled from the Original Returns of the Eighth Census, Under the Direction of the Secretary of the Interior.* Washington: Government Printing Office, 1864.

U.S. Bureau of the Census. Population Schedules. Fifth through Eighth Censuses. 1830–1860.

———. Slave Schedules. Seventh and Eighth Censuses. 1850–1860.

SLAVE NARRATIVES

Andrews, William L., and Henry Louis Gates, Jr., eds. *The Civitas Anthology of African American Slave Narratives.* Washington, D.C.: Civitas/Counterpoint, 1999.

An Autobiography of the Reverend Josiah Henson. Reading, Mass.: Addison-Wesley Publishing Company, 1969.

Ball, Charles. *Fifty Years in Chains.* 1837. Reprint. New York: Dover Publications, Inc., 1970.

Blassingame, John W. *Slave Testimony: Two Centuries of Letters, Speeches, Interviews, and Autobiographies.* Baton Rouge: Louisiana State University Press, 1977.

Blight, David W., ed. *Narrative of the Life of Frederick Douglass, An American Slave, Written by Himself.* New York: Bedford Books of St. Martin's Press, 1993.

Botkin, B. A., ed. *Lay My Burden Down: A Folk History of Slavery.* 1945. Reprint. Athens: University of Georgia Press, 1989.

Brown, Wm. Wells. *My Southern Home: or, The South and Its People.* Boston: A. G. Brown & Co., 1880.

Bruce, H. C. *The New Man: Twenty-Nine Years a Slave, Twenty-Nine Years a Free Man.* York, Penn.: P. Anstadt & Sons, 1895. Reprint. New York: Negro Universities Press, 1969.

Bruner, Peter. *A Slave's Adventures Toward Freedom: Not Fiction, but the True Story of a Struggle.* Oxford, Ohio: n.p., 1918.

Chamerovzow, L. A., ed. *Slave Life in Georgia: A Narrative of the Life, Sufferings, and Escape of John Brown, a Fugitive Slave, Now in England.* London: n.p., 1855.

Colyer, Vincent. *Brief Report of the Services Rendered by the Freed People to the United States Army in North Carolina, in the Spring of 1862, after the Battle of Newbern.* New York: Vincent Colyer, 1864.

Douglass, Frederick. *My Bondage and My Freedom.* New York: Miller, Orten & Mulligan, 1855.

Eakin, Sue, and Joseph Logsdon, eds. *Twelve Years a Slave, by Solomon Northup.* Baton Rouge: Louisiana State University Press, 1968.

Hughes, Louis. *Thirty Years a Slave: From Bondage to Freedom.* Milwaukee: South Side Printing Company, 1897.

Jacobs, Harriet (Brent). *Incidents in the Life of a Slave Girl.* Edited by L. Maria Child. 1861. Reprint. Detroit: Negro History Press, 1969.

Jacobs, Harriet A. *Incidents in the Life of a Slave Girl, Written by Herself.* Edited by Jean Fagan Yellin. Cambridge: Harvard University Press, 2000.

Katz, William Loren, comp. *Flight from the Devil: Six Slave Narratives.* Trenton: Africa World Press, Inc., 1996.

Long, Rev. John Dixon. *Pictures of Slavery in Church and State.* 2nd ed. Philadelphia: published by the author, 1857.

Mellon, James, ed. *Bullwhip Days: The Slaves Remember.* New York: Weidenfeld & Nicolson, 1988.

Narrative of the Life and Adventures of Henry Bibb, an American Slave, Written by Himself with an Introduction by Lucius C. Matlack. New York: published by the author, 1849.

A Narrative of the Life and Labors of the Rev. G. W. Offley. Hartford, Conn.: n.p., 1859.

Narrative of the Sufferings of Lewis Clarke, During a Captivity of More Than Twenty-Five Years, Among the Algerines of Kentucky, One of the So Called Christian States of North America. Boston: David H. Ela, 1845.

Osofsky, Gilbert, ed. *Puttin' on Ole Massa: The Slave Narratives of Henry Bibb, William Wells Brown, and Solomon Northup.* New York: Harper & Row, 1969.

Parker, Allen. *Recollections of Slavery Times.* Worcester, Mass.: Chas. W. Burbank & Co., 1895.

Parker, William. "The Freedman's Story. In Two Parts. Part I." *Atlantic Monthly* 17 (February 1866): 152–166.

Pennington, J. W. C. *A Narrative of Events of the Life of J. H. Banks, an Escaped Slave, from the Cotton State, Alabama, in America.* Liverpool: M. Rourke, 1861.

Perdue, Charles L., Jr., Thomas E. Barden, and Robert K. Phillips, eds. *Weevils in the Wheat: Interviews with Virginia Ex-Slaves.* Charlottesville: University Press of Virginia, 1976.

Rawick, George P., ed. *The American Slave: A Composite Autobiography.* 19 vols. Westport, Conn.: Greenwood Publishing Company, 1972.

———. *The American Slave: A Composite Autobiography, Supplement, Series 1.* 12 vols. Westport, Conn.: Greenwood Press, 1977.

————. *The American Slave: A Composite Autobiography, Supplement, Series 2.* 10 vols. Westport, Conn.: Greenwood Press, 1979.

The Rev. J. W. Loguen, as a Slave and as a Freeman: A Narrative of Real Life. 1859. Reprint. New York: Negro Universities Press, 1968.

Roberts, Ralph. "A Slave's Story." *Putnam's Monthly Magazine of American Literature, Science, and Art* 9 (June 1857): 614–620.

Robinson, W. H. *From Log Cabin to the Pulpit, or, Fifteen Years in Slavery.* 3rd ed. Eau Claire, Wis.: James H. Tifft, 1913.

Roper, Moses. *A Narrative of the Adventures and Escape of Moses Roper, from American Slavery; with a Preface, by the Rev. T. Price, D.D.* London: Darton, Harvey and Darton, 1838. Reprint. New York: Negro Universities Press, 1970.

Singleton, William Henry. *Recollections of My Slavery Days.* Peekskill, N.Y.: Highland Democrat, 1922.

Steward, Austin. *Twenty-Two Years a Slave, and Forty Years a Freeman.* Rochester, N.Y.: William Alling, 1857.

Thompson, Charles. *Biography of a Slave; Being the Experiences of Rev. Charles Thompson, a Preacher of the United Brethren Church, While a Slave in the South.* Dayton, Ohio: United Brethren Publishing House, 1875.

Webb, William. *The History of William Webb, Composed By Himself.* Detroit: Egbert Hoekstra, 1873.

SLAVE RUNAWAY ADVERTISEMENTS

Meaders, Daniel, ed. *Advertisements for Runaway Slaves in Virginia, 1801–1820.* New York: Garland Publishing, Inc., 1997.

Parker, Freddie L. *Stealing a Little Freedom: Advertisements for Slave Runaways in North Carolina, 1791–1840.* New York: Garland Publishing, Inc., 1994.

Smith, Billy G., and Richard Wojtowicz. *Blacks Who Stole Themselves: Advertisements for Runaways in the* Pennsylvania Gazette, *1728–1790.* Philadelphia: University of Pennsylvania Press, 1989.

Windley, Lathan A., comp. *Runaway Slave Advertisements: A Documentary History from the 1730s to 1790.* 4 vols. Westport, Conn.: Greenwood Press, 1983.

TRAVELERS' ACCOUNTS

Barnard, Henry. Edited by Bernard C. Steiner. "The South Atlantic States in 1833, as Seen By a New Englander." *Maryland Historical Magazine* 13 (December 1918): 295–386.

Bremer, Frederika. *The Homes of the New World; Impressions of America.* Vol. 1. Translated by Mary Howitt. London: Arthur Hall, Virtue, & Co., 1853.

Buckingham, J. S. *The Slave States of America.* 2 vols. London: Fisher, Son, & Co., 1842.

Crayon, Porte [David Hunter Strother]. "North Carolina Illustrated. II. —The Piny Woods." *Harper's New Monthly Magazine* 14 (May 1857): 741–755.

Featherstonhaugh, G. W. *A Canoe Voyage Up the Minnay Sotor.* Vol. 2. London: Richard Bentley, 1847.

————. *Excursion Through the Slave States, from Washington on the Potomac to the Frontier of Mexico; with Sketches of Popular Manners and Geological Notices.* Vol. 2. London: John Murray, 1844.

Hall, Basil. *Travels in North America, in the Years 1827 and 1828.* Vol. 2. Philadelphia: Carey, Lea & Carey, 1829.

McKivigan, John R., ed. *The Roving Editor, or Talks with Slaves in the Southern States, by James Redpath.* University Park, Penn.: Pennsylvania State University Press, 1996.

Olmstead, Denison. "On the Gold Mines of North Carolina." *American Journal of Science* 9 (1825).

Olmsted, Frederick Law. *The Cotton Kingdom: A Traveller's Observations on Cotton and Slavery in the American Slave States.* Edited by Arthur M. Schlesinger. New York: Alfred A. Knopf, 1953.

————. *The Cotton Kingdom: A Traveller's Observations on Cotton and Slavery in the American Slave States, 1853–1861.* Edited by Arthur M. Schlesinger. New York: Da Capo Press, 1996.

————. *A Journey in the Back Country.* 1860. Reprint. New York: Burt Franklin, 1970.

————. *A Journey in the Seaboard Slave States, with Remarks on Their Economy.* New York: Dix & Edwards, 1856.

Parsons, C. G. *Inside View of Slavery: or A Tour Among the Planters.* Boston: John P. Jewett and Company; Cleveland: Jewett, Proctor and Worthington, 1855.

Singleton, Arthur [Henry Cogswell Knight]. *Letters from the South and West.* Boston: Richardson and Lord, 1824.

Stirling, James. *Letters from the Slave States.* London: John W. Parker and Son, 1857.

NEWSPAPERS

Charleston Daily Courier
Miners' & Farmers' Journal (Charlotte)
New York Daily Times
North Carolina Whig (Charlotte)
Raleigh Register (weekly)

Richmond Enquirer
Western Democrat (Charlotte)

LAWS

Acts of the General Assembly of the State of South Carolina, Passed in December, 1850. Columbia: I. C. Morgan, 1850.

Acts of the General Assembly of Virginia. Richmond: Samuel Shepherd, 1848.

Acts of the General Assembly of Virginia. Richmond: William F. Ritchie, 1858.

Acts Passed at a General Assembly of the Commonwealth of Virginia. Richmond: Thomas Ritchie, 1823.

Acts Passed at a General Assembly of the Commonwealth of Virginia. Richmond: Thomas Ritchie, 1829.

Acts Passed at a General Assembly of the Commonwealth of Virginia. Richmond: Thomas Ritchie, 1831.

Acts Passed at a General Assembly of the Commonwealth of Virginia. Richmond: Thomas Ritchie, 1832.

Acts Passed at a General Assembly of the Commonwealth of Virginia. Richmond: Thomas Ritchie, 1834.

Acts Passed By the General Assembly of the State of North Carolina, At Its Session, Commencing on the 17th of November, 1823. Raleigh: J. Gales & Son, 1824.

Acts Passed By the General Assembly of the State of North Carolina, At Its Session, Commencing on the 21st of Nov. 1825. Raleigh: Bell & Lawrence, 1826.

Acts Passed By the General Assembly of the State of North Carolina, At Its Session, Commencing on the 25th of December, 1826. Raleigh: Lawrence & Lemay, 1827.

Acts Passed By the General Assembly of the State of North Carolina, at the Session of 1830 – 31. Raleigh: Lawrence & Lemay, 1831.

The Laws of North-Carolina, Enacted in the Year 1821. Raleigh: Thomas Henderson, 1822.

Laws of the State of North-Carolina, Enacted in the Year 1819, Transmitted According to Law, to One of the Justices of the Peace for the County of . . . Raleigh: Thomas Henderson, Jr., 1820.

Laws of the State of North Carolina, Passed By the General Assembly, at the Session of 1838–'39. Raleigh: J. Gales and Son, 1839.

Laws of the State of North-Carolina, Passed By the General Assembly, At the Session of 1850 –'51. Raleigh: T. J. Lemay, 1851.

Laws of the State of North Carolina, Passed By the General Assembly, at the Session of 1852. Raleigh: Wesley Whitaker, Jr., 1853.

McCord, David J. *The Statutes at Large of South Carolina; Edited, Under Authority of the Legislature.* Vol. 6. Columbia: A. S. Johnston, 1839.

———. *The Statutes at Large of South Carolina; Edited, Under Authority of the Legislature.* Vol. 7. Columbia: A. S. Johnston, 1840.

The Statutes at Large of South Carolina. Vol. 11. Columbia: Republican Printing Company, 1873.

BOOKS & ARTICLES

Avirett, James Battle. *The Old Plantation: How We Lived in Great House and Cabin Before the War.* New York: F. Tennyson Neely Co., 1901.

Cairnes, J. E. *The Slave Power: Its Character, Career, and Probable Designs.* 2nd ed. New York: Carleton, 1862.

Catterall, Helen Tunnicliff. *Judicial Cases Concerning American Slavery and the Negro.* Vols. 1, 2, and 4. Washington, D.C.: Carnegie Institute of Washington, 1926, 1929, 1936.

Clinkscales, J. G. *On the Old Plantation: Reminiscences of His Childhood.* Spartanburg, S.C.: Band & White, 1916.

Elliott, Colleen Morse, and Louise Armstrong Moxley. *The Tennessee Civil War Veterans Questionnaires.* Compiled by Gustavus W. Dyer and John Trotwood Moore. 5 vols. Easley, S.C.: Southern Historical Press, Inc., 1985.

Flournoy, H. W., ed. *Calendar of Virginia State Papers.* Vol. 9. 1890. Reprint. New York: Kraus Reprint Corporation, 1968.

Gilmore, James R. "Poor Whites of the South." *Harper's Magazine* 29 (June 1864): 115–124.

———. [Edmund Kirke, pseud.]. *Down in Tennessee, and Back By Way of Richmond.* New York: Carleton, 1864.

Hundley, D. R. *Social Relations in Our Southern States.* New York: Henry B. Price, 1860. Reprint. New York: Arno Press, 1973.

Jones, Henry B. "Farming in Virginia." *DeBow's Review* 18 (January 1855): 59–60.

Kennedy, Lionel H., and Thomas Parker. *An Official Report of the Trials of Sundry Negroes, Charged with an Attempt to Raise an Insurrection in the State of South-Carolina: Preceded by an Introduction and Narrative; and in an Appendix, a Report of the Trials of Four White Persons, on Indictments for Attempting to Excite the Slaves to Insurrection.* Charleston: James R. Schenck, 1822.

Martin, Isabella D., and Myrta Lockett Avary, eds. *A Diary from Dixie, as Written By Mary Boykin Chesnut.* New York: D. Appleton and Company, 1914.

Morris, John [John O'Connor]. *Wanderings of a Vagabond: An Autobiography.* New York: published by the author, 1873.

Partz, August. "Examinations and Explorations on the Gold-Bearing Belts of the Atlantic States." *Mining Magazine* 3 (1854): 161–168.

Pollard, Edward A. *Black Diamonds Gathered in the Darkey Homes of the South.* New York: Pudney & Russell, 1859.

Weston, George M. "The Poor Whites of the South: The Injury Done Them By Slavery." Washington, D.C.: Republican Executive Congressional Committee, 1860.

Secondary Sources

Alexander, Thomas B. "Persistent Whiggery in the Confederate South, 1860–1877." *Journal of Southern History* 27 (August 1961): 305–329.

Aptheker, Herbert. *American Negro Slave Revolts.* New York: Columbia University Press, 1943.

Arroyo, Elizabeth Fortson. "Poor Whites, Slaves, and Free Blacks in Tennessee, 1796–1861." *Tennessee Historical Quarterly* 55 (Spring 1996): 56–65.

Ash, Stephen V. "Poor Whites in the Occupied South, 1861–1865." *Journal of Southern History* 57 (February 1991): 39–62.

Ayers, Edward L. *Vengeance and Justice: Crime and Punishment in the 19th-Century American South.* New York: Oxford University Press, 1984.

Bailey, Fred. "Tennessee's Antebellum Society from the Bottom Up." *Southern Studies* 22 (Fall 1983): 260–273.

Bailey, Fred Arthur. *Class and Tennessee's Confederate Generation.* Chapel Hill: University of North Carolina Press, 1987.

Baptist, Edward E. "Accidental Ethnography in an Antebellum Southern Newspaper: Snell's Homecoming Festival." *Journal of American History* 84 (March 1998): 1355–1383.

———. "'My Mind Is To Drown You and Leave You Behind': 'Omie Wise,' Intimate Violence, and Masculinity." In *Over the Threshold: Intimate Violence in Early America,* edited by Christine Daniels and Michael V. Kennedy, 94–110. New York: Routledge, 1999.

Barber, E. Susan, "Depraved and Abandoned Women: Prostitution in Richmond, Virginia, across the Civil War." In *Neither Lady Nor Slave: Working Women of the Old South,* edited by Susanna Delfino and Michele Gillespie, 155–173. Chapel Hill: University of North Carolina Press, 2002.

Bardaglio, Peter W. "Rape and the Law in the Old South: 'Calculated to excite indignation in every heart.'" *Journal of Southern History* 60 (November 1994): 749–772.

———. *Reconstructing the Household: Families, Sex, and the Law in the Nineteenth-Century South.* Chapel Hill: University of North Carolina Press, 1995.

Barnes, Kenneth C. *Who Killed John Clayton?: Political Violence and the Emergence of the New South, 1861–1893*. Durham: Duke University Press, 1998.

Barney, William. *The Road to Secession: A New Perspective on the Old South*. Washington: Praeger Publishers, 1972.

Barney, William L. *The Secessionist Impulse: Alabama and Mississippi in 1860*. Princeton: Princeton University Press, 1974.

Beatty, Bess. "I Can't Get My Bored on Them Old Lomes: Female Textile Workers in the Antebellum South." In *Neither Lady Nor Slave: Working Women of the Old South*, edited by Susanna Delfino and Michele Gillespie, 249–260. Chapel Hill: University of North Carolina Press, 2002.

———. "Textile Labor in the North Carolina Piedmont: Mill Owner Images and Mill Worker Response, 1830–1900." *Labor History* 25 (Fall 1984): 485–503.

Bellesiles, Michael A., ed. *Lethal Imagination: Violence and Brutality in American History*. New York: New York University Press, 1999.

Bellows, Barbara L. "'My Children, Gentlemen, Are My Own': Poor Women, the Urban Elite, and the Bonds of Obligation in Antebellum Charleston." In *The Web of Southern Social Relations: Women, Family, & Education*, edited by Walter J. Fraser, Jr., R. Frank Saunders, Jr., and Jon L. Wakelyn, 52–71. Athens: University of Georgia Press, 1985.

Berlin, Ira. *Many Thousands Gone: The First Two Centuries of Slavery in North America*. Cambridge: Belknap Press of Harvard University Press, 1998.

———. *Slaves without Masters: The Free Negro in the Antebellum South*. New York: Pantheon Books, 1974.

———. "Time, Space, and the Evolution of Afro-American Society on British Mainland North America." *American Historical Review* 85 (February 1980): 44–78.

Berlin, Ira, and Herbert G. Gutman. "Natives and Immigrants, Free Men and Slaves: Urban Workingmen in the Antebellum South." *American Historical Review* 88 (December 1983): 1175–1200.

Blassingame, John W. *The Slave Community: Plantation Life in the Antebellum South*. Rev. ed. New York: Oxford University Press, 1979.

Block, Sharon. "Lines of Color, Sex, and Service: Comparative Sexual Coercion in Early America." In *Sex, Love, Race: Crossing Boundaries in North American History*, edited by Martha Hodes, 141–163. New York: New York University Press, 1999.

Bode, Frederick A., and Donald E. Ginter. *Farm Tenancy and the Census in Antebellum Georgia*. Athens: University of Georgia Press, 1986.

Boles, John B. "Introduction." In *Masters & Slaves in the House of the Lord: Race and Religion in the American South, 1740–1870*, edited by John B. Boles, 1–18. Lexington: University Press of Kentucky, 1988.

Bolton, Charles C. "Edward Isham and Poor White Labor in the Old South." In *The Confessions of Edward Isham: A Poor White Life of the Old South,* edited by Charles C. Bolton and Scott P. Culclasure, 19–31. Athens: University of Georgia Press, 1998.

————. *Poor Whites of the Antebellum South: Tenants and Laborers in Central North Carolina and Northeast Mississippi.* Durham: Duke University Press, 1994.

Bolton, Charles C., and Scott P. Culclasure, eds. *The Confessions of Edward Isham: A Poor White Life of the Old South.* Athens: University of Georgia Press, 1998.

Boney, F. N. *Southerners All.* Macon: Mercer University Press, 1984.

Bonner, James C. "Profile of a Late Ante-Bellum Community." *American Historical Review* 49 (July 1944): 663–680.

Bradley, Josephine Boyd, and Kent Anderson Leslie, "White Pain Pollen: An Elite Biracial Daughter's Quandary." In *Sex, Love, Race: Crossing Boundaries in North American History,* edited by Martha Hodes, 213–234. New York: New York University Press, 1999.

Breen, T. H. "A Changing Labor Force and Race Relations in Virginia, 1660–1710." *Journal of Social History* 7 (Fall 1993): 3–25.

————. "Horses and Gentlemen: The Cultural Significance of Gambling among the Gentry of Virginia." *William & Mary Quarterly* 3d ser., 34 (April 1977): 239–257.

Breen, T. H., and Stephen Innes. *"Myne Owne Ground": Race and Freedom on Virginia's Eastern Shore, 1640–1676.* New York: Oxford University Press, 1980.

Bridner, Elwood L., Jr. "The Fugitive Slaves of Maryland." *Maryland Historical Magazine* 66 (Spring 1971): 33–50.

Brown, Kathleen M. *Good Wives, Nasty Wenches, and Anxious Patriarchs: Gender, Race, and Power in Colonial Virginia.* Chapel Hill: University of North Carolina Press, 1996.

Brown, W. O. "Role of the Poor Whites in Race Contacts of the South." *Social Forces* 19 (December 1940): 258–268.

Bruce, Dickson D., Jr. *And They All Sang Hallelujah: Plain-Folk Camp-Meeting Religion, 1800–1845.* Knoxville: University of Tennessee Press, 1974.

————. *Violence and Culture in the Antebellum South.* Austin: University of Texas Press, 1979.

Buck, Paul H. "The Poor Whites of the Ante-Bellum South." *American Historical Review* 31 (October 1925): 41–54.

Buckley, Thomas E., S.J. *The Great Catastrophe of My Life: Divorce in the Old Dominion.* Chapel Hill: University of North Carolina Press, 2002.

————. "Unfixing Race: Class, Power, and Identity in an Interracial Family." In *Sex,*

Love, Race: Crossing Boundaries in North American History, edited by Martha Hodes, 164–190. New York: New York University Press, 1999.

Burton, Orville Vernon. *In My Father's House Are Many Mansions: Family and Community in Edgefield, South Carolina.* Chapel Hill: University of North Carolina Press, 1985.

Bynum, Victoria. "On the Lowest Rung: Court Control Over Poor White and Free Black Women." *Southern Exposures* 12 (November/December 1984): 40–44.

Bynum, Victoria E. *Unruly Women: The Politics of Social and Sexual Control in the Old South.* Chapel Hill: University of North Carolina Press, 1992.

Camp, Stephanie H. M. "The Pleasures of Resistance: Enslaved Women and Body Politics in the Plantation South, 1830–1861." *Journal of Southern History* 68 (August 2002): 533–572.

Campbell, John. "As 'A Kind of Freeman'?: Slaves' Market-Related Activities in the South Carolina Up Country, 1800–1860." *Slavery & Abolition* 12 (May 1991): 131–169.

———. "As 'A Kind of Freeman'?: Slaves' Market-Related Activities in the South Carolina Up Country, 1800–1860." In *The Slaves' Economy: Independent Production by Slaves in the Americas,* edited by Ira Berlin and Philip D. Morgan, 131–169. London: Frank Cass, 1991.

———. "As 'A Kind of Freeman'?: Slaves' Market-Related Activities in the South Carolina Up Country, 1800–1860." In *Cultivation and Culture: Labor and the Shaping of Slave Life in the Americas,* edited by Ira Berlin and Philip D. Morgan, 243–274. Charlottesville: University Press of Virginia, 1993.

Campbell, Randolph B. "Planters and Plain Folk: Harrison County, Texas, as a Test Case, 1850–1860." *Journal of Southern History* 40 (August 1974): 369–398.

Cash, W. J. *The Mind of the South.* New York: Alfred A. Knopf, 1941. Reprint. New York: Vintage Books, 1991.

Cecelski, David S. "The Shores of Freedom: The Maritime Underground Railroad in North Carolina, 1800–1861." *North Carolina Historical Review* 71 (April 1994): 174–206.

Cecil-Fronsman, Bill. *Common Whites: Class and Culture in Antebellum North Carolina.* Lexington: University Press of Kentucky, 1992.

Clark, Ernest James, Jr. "Aspects of the North Carolina Slave Code, 1715–1860." *North Carolina Historical Review* 39 (April 1962): 148–164.

Clinton, Catherine. *The Plantation Mistress: Woman's World in the Old South.* New York: Pantheon Books, 1982.

———. "'Southern Dishonor': Flesh, Blood, Race, and Bondage." In *In Joy and In Sorrow: Women, Family, and Marriage in the Victorian South, 1830–1900,* edited by Carol Bleser, 52–68. New York: Oxford University Press, 1991.

Collins, Bruce. *White Society in the Antebellum South.* London: Longman, 1985.

Cott, Nancy F. "Passionlessness: An Interpretation of Victorian Sexual Ideology, 1790–1850." *Signs* 4 (Winter 1978): 219–236.

Crane, J. Michael. "Controlling the Night: Perceptions of the Slave Patrol System in Mississippi." *Journal of Mississippi History* 61 (Summer 1999): 119–136.

Craton, Michael. "Decoding Pitchy-Patchy: The Roots, Branches and Essence of Junkanoo." *Slavery & Abolition* 16 (April 1995): 14–44.

Craven, Avery O. "Poor Whites and Negroes in the Ante-Bellum South." *Journal of Negro History* 15 (January 1930): 14–25.

Crow, Jeffrey J. "Slave Rebelliousness and Social Conflict in North Carolina, 1775–1802." *William & Mary Quarterly* 3d ser., 37 (January 1980): 79–102.

Culclasure, Scott P. "'I Have Killed a Damned Dog': Murder by a Poor White in the Antebellum South." *North Carolina Historical Review* 70 (January 1993): 14–39.

———. "'I Have Killed a Damned Dog': Murder by a Poor White in the Antebellum South." In *The Confessions of Edward Isham: A Poor White Life of the Old South,* edited by Charles C. Bolton and Scott P. Culclasure, 45–70. Athens: University of Georgia Press, 1998.

Dailey, Jane. *Before Jim Crow: The Politics of Race in Postemancipation Virginia.* Chapel Hill: University of North Carolina Press, 2000.

Degler, Carl N. *The Other South: Southern Dissenters in the Nineteenth Century.* New York: Harper & Row, 1974.

Delfino, Susanna. "Invisible Woman: Female Labor in the Upper South's Iron and Mining Industries." In *Neither Lady Nor Slave: Working Women of the Old South,* edited by Susanna Delfino and Michele Gillespie, 285–307. Chapel Hill: University of North Carolina Press, 2002.

Den Hollander, A. N. J. "The Tradition of 'Poor Whites.'" In *Culture in the South,* edited by W. T. Couch, 403–431. Chapel Hill: University of North Carolina Press, 1935.

Donald, David H. "The Scalawag in Mississippi Reconstruction." *Journal of Southern History* 10 (November 1944): 447–460.

Dunaway, Wilma A. *Slavery in the American Mountain South.* New York: Cambridge University Press, 2003.

Durrill, Wayne K. "Routine of Seasons: Labour Regimes and Social Ritual in an Antebellum Plantation Community." *Slavery & Abolition* 16 (August 1995): 161–187.

———. *War of Another Kind: A Southern Community in the Great Rebellion.* New York: Oxford University Press, 1990.

Dusinberre, William. *Them Dark Days: Slavery in the American Rice Swamps.* New York: Oxford University Press, 1996.

Eaton, Clement. "Class Differences in the Old South." *Virginia Quarterly Review* 33 (Summer 1957): 357–370.

———. "Slave-Hiring in the Upper South: A Step toward Freedom." *Mississippi Valley Historical Review* 46 (March 1960): 663–678.

Edwards, Laura F. "The Disappearance of Susan Daniel and Henderson Cooper: Gender and Narratives of Political Conflict in the Reconstruction-Era U.S. South." In *Sex, Love, Race: Crossing Boundaries in North American History*, edited by Martha Hodes, 294–312. New York: New York University Press, 1999.

———. "Law, Domestic Violence, and the Limits of Patriarchal Authority in the Antebellum South." *Journal of Southern History* 65 (November 1999): 733–770.

———. "Sexual Violence, Gender, Reconstruction, and the Extension of Patriarchy in Granville County, North Carolina." *North Carolina Historical Review* 68 (July 1991): 237–260.

Egerton, Douglas R. "'Fly across the River': The Easter Slave Conspiracy of 1802." *North Carolina Historical Review* 68 (April 1991): 87–110.

———. *Gabriel's Rebellion: The Virginia Slave Conspiracies of 1800 and 1802.* Chapel Hill: University of North Carolina Press, 1993.

Elkins, Stanley M. *Slavery: A Problem in American Institutional and Intellectual Life.* 3rd ed. Chicago: University of Chicago Press, 1976.

Ellem, Warren A. "Who Were the Mississippi Scalawags?" *Journal of Southern History* 38 (May 1972): 217–240.

Elliott, Robert N. "The Nat Turner Insurrection as Reported in the North Carolina Press." *North Carolina Historical Review* 38 (January 1961): 1–18.

Escott, Paul D. "White Republicanism and Ku Klux Klan Terror: The North Carolina Piedmont During Reconstruction." In *Race, Class, and Politics in Southern History: Essays in Honor of Robert F. Durden*, edited by Jeffrey J. Crow, Paul D. Escott, and Charles L. Flynn, Jr., 3–34. Baton Rouge: Louisiana State University Press, 1989.

Fabian, Ann. *Card Sharps, Dream Books, and Bucket Shops: Gambling in 19th-Century America.* Ithaca: Cornell University Press, 1990.

Faust, Drew Gilpin. *James Henry Hammond and the Old South: A Design for Mastery.* Baton Rouge: Louisiana State University Press, 1982.

———, ed. *The Ideology of American Slavery: Proslavery Thought in the Antebellum South, 1830–1860.* Baton Rouge: Louisiana State University Press, 1981.

Fellman, Michael. "Getting Right With the Poor White." *Canadian Review of American Studies* 18 (Winter 1987): 527–539.

Fenn, Elizabeth A. "'A Perfect Equality Seemed to Reign': Slave Society and Jonkonnu." *North Carolina Historical Review* 65 (April 1988): 127–153.

Fields, Barbara J. "Ideology and Race in American History." In *Region, Race, and*

Reconstruction: Essays in Honor of C. Vann Woodward, edited by J. Morgan Kousser and James M. McPherson, 143–177. New York: Oxford University Press, 1982.

Fischer, Kirsten. *Suspect Relations: Sex, Race, and Resistance in Colonial North Carolina.* Ithaca: Cornell University Press, 2002.

Flanigan, Daniel J. "Criminal Procedures in Slave Trials in the Antebellum South." *Journal of Southern History* 40 (November 1974): 537–564.

Flynt, J. Wayne. *Dixie's Forgotten People: The South's Poor Whites.* Bloomington: Indiana University Press, 1979.

———. *Poor but Proud: Alabama's Poor Whites.* Tuscaloosa: University of Alabama Press, 1989.

Fogel, Robert William, and Stanley L. Engerman, *Time on the Cross: The Economics of American Negro Slavery.* Boston: Little, Brown, 1974.

Foner, Eric. *Reconstruction: America's Unfinished Revolution, 1863–1877.* New York: Harper & Row, 1988.

Ford, Lacy K., Jr. *Origins of Southern Radicalism: The South Carolina Upcountry, 1800–1860.* New York: Oxford University Press, 1988.

Forret, Jeff. "Slave Labor in North Carolina's Antebellum Gold Mines." *North Carolina Historical Review* 76 (April 1999): 135–162.

Forret, Jeffrey P. "African Americans and Gold Mining in North Carolina." In *Gold in History, Geology, and Culture: Collected Essays,* edited by Richard F. Knapp and Robert M. Topkins, 207–222. Raleigh: Division of Archives and History, North Carolina Department of Cultural Resources, 2001.

Franklin, John Hope. *The Militant South, 1800–1861.* Cambridge, Mass.: Harvard University Press, 1956.

———. "Slaves Virtually Free in Ante-Bellum North Carolina." *Journal of Negro History* 28 (July 1943): 284–310.

Franklin, John Hope, and Loren Schweninger. *Runaway Slaves: Rebels on the Plantation.* New York: Oxford University Press, 1999.

Fredrickson, George M. *The Black Image in the White Mind: The Debate on Afro-American Character and Destiny, 1817–1914.* New York: Harper & Row, 1971.

Freehling, William W. *The South vs. the South: How Anti-Confederate Southerners Shaped the Course of the Civil War.* New York: Oxford University Press, 2001.

Frey, Sylvia R. "Shaking the Dry Bones: The Dialectic of Conversion." In *Black and White Cultural Interaction in the Antebellum South,* edited by Ted Ownby, 23–44. Jackson: University Press of Mississippi, 1993.

Frey, Sylvia R., and Betty Wood. *Come Shouting to Zion: African American Protestantism in the American South and British Caribbean to 1830.* Chapel Hill: University of North Carolina Press, 1998.

Gallagher, Gary W. *The Confederate War.* Cambridge: Harvard University Press, 1997.

Gamber, Wendy. "Tarnished Labor: The Home, the Market, and the Boardinghouse in Antebellum America." *Journal of the Early Republic* 22 (Summer 2002): 177–204.

Gara, Larry. *The Liberty Line: The Legend of the Underground Railroad.* 1961. Reprint. Lexington: University Press of Kentucky, 1996.

Genovese, Eugene D. *The Political Economy of Slavery: Studies in the Economy and Society of the Slave South.* New York: Vintage Books, 1974.

———. "'Rather Be a Nigger Than a Poor White Man': Slave Perceptions of Southern Yeomen and Poor Whites." In *Toward a New View of America: Essays in Honor of Arthur C. Cole,* edited by Hans L. Trefousse, 79–96. New York: Burt Franklin & Company, Inc., 1977.

———. *Roll, Jordan, Roll: The World the Slaves Made.* 1974. Reprint. New York: Vintage Books, 1976.

———. "Yeoman Farmers in a Slaveholders' Democracy." *Agricultural History* 49 (April 1975): 331–342.

Getman, Karen A. "Sexual Control in the Slaveholding South: The Implementation and Maintenance of a Racial Caste System." *Harvard Women's Law Journal* 7 (Spring 1984): 115–152.

Gilmour, Robert. "The Other Emancipation: Studies in the Society and Economy of Alabama Whites during Reconstruction." Ph.D. diss., Johns Hopkins University, 1972.

Glass, Brent D. "The Miner's World: Life and Labor at Gold Hill." *North Carolina Historical Review* 62 (October 1985): 420–447.

———. "'Poor Men with Rude Machinery': The Formative Years of the Gold Hill Mining District, 1842–1853." *North Carolina Historical Review* 61 (January 1984): 1–35.

Gorn, Elliott J. "'Gouge and Bite, Pull Hair and Scratch': The Social Significance of Fighting in the Southern Backcountry." *American Historical Review* 90 (February 1985): 18–43.

Green, Fletcher Melvin. "Gold Mining: A Forgotten Industry of Ante-Bellum North Carolina." *North Carolina Historical Review* 14 (January 1937): 1–19.

Greenberg, Kenneth S. *Honor & Slavery: Lies, Duels, Noses, Masks, Dressing as a Woman, Gifts, Strangers, Humanitarianism, Death, Slave Rebellions, the Proslavery Argument, Baseball, Hunting, and Gambling in the Old South.* Princeton: Princeton University Press, 1996.

———. "The Nose, the Lie, and the Duel in the Antebellum South." *American Historical Review* 95 (February 1990): 57–74.

Griffin, Richard W. "Poor White Laborers in Southern Cotton Factories, 1789–1865." *South Carolina Historical Magazine* 61 (January 1960): 26–40.

Gross, Ariela J. *Double Character: Slavery and Mastery in the Antebellum Southern Courtroom.* Princeton: Princeton University Press, 2000.

Gutman, Herbert G. *The Black Family in Slavery and Freedom, 1750–1925.* New York: Pantheon Books, 1976.

———. *The Black Family in Slavery and Freedom, 1750–1925.* New York: Vintage Books, 1977.

Hackney, Sheldon. "Southern Violence." *American Historical Review* 74 (February 1969): 906–925.

Hadden, Sally E. *Slave Patrols: Law and Violence in Virginia and the Carolinas.* Cambridge, Mass.: Harvard University Press, 2001.

Hahn, Steven. *The Roots of Southern Populism: Yeoman Farmers and the Transformation of the Georgia Upcountry, 1850–1890.* New York: Oxford University Press, 1983.

Hall, Robert L. "Black and White Christians in Florida, 1822–1861." In *Masters & Slaves in the House of the Lord: Race and Religion in the American South, 1740–1870,* edited by John B. Boles, 81–98. Lexington: University Press of Kentucky, 1988.

Halttunen, Karen. *Confidence Men and Painted Women: A Study of Middle-class Culture in America, 1830–1870.* New Haven: Yale University Press, 1982.

Harris, J. William. *Plain Folk and Gentry in a Slave Society: White Liberty and Black Slavery in Augusta's Hinterlands.* Middletown, Conn.: Wesleyan University Press, 1985. Reprint. Baton Rouge: Louisiana State University Press, 1998.

Harris, William C. "A Reconsideration of the Mississippi Scalawag." *Journal of Mississippi History* 32 (February 1970): 3–42.

Henry, H. M. *The Police Control of the Slave in South Carolina.* 1914. Reprint. New York: Negro Universities Press, 1968.

Heyrman, Christine Leigh. *Southern Cross: The Beginnings of the Bible Belt.* Chapel Hill: University of North Carolina Press, 1997.

Higginbotham, A. Leon, Jr., and Barbara K. Kopytoff. "Racial Purity and Interracial Sex in the Law of Colonial and Antebellum Virginia." *Georgetown Law Journal* 77 (August 1989): 1967–2029.

Hindus, Michael Stephen. *Prison and Plantation: Crime, Justice, and Authority in Massachusetts and South Carolina, 1767–1878.* Chapel Hill: University of North Carolina Press, 1980.

Hodes, Martha. *White Women, Black Men: Illicit Sex in the Nineteenth-Century South.* New Haven: Yale University Press, 1997.

Hoetink, H. *Slavery and Race Relations in the Americas: Comparative Notes on Their Nature and Nexus.* New York: Harper & Row, 1973.

Howe, Barbara J. "Patient Laborers: Women at Work in the Formal Economy of West(ern) Virginia." In *Neither Lady Nor Slave: Working Women of the Old South,* edited by Susanna Delfino and Michele Gillespie, 121–151. Chapel Hill: University of North Carolina Press, 2002.

Hudson, Larry E., Jr. "'All That Cash': Work and Status in the Slave Quarters." In *Working Toward Freedom: Slave Society and Domestic Economy in the American South*, edited by Larry E. Hudson, Jr., 77–94. Rochester: University of Rochester Press, 1994.

———. *To Have and to Hold: Slave Work and Family Life in Antebellum South Carolina*. Athens: University of Georgia Press, 1997.

Huebner, Timothy S. "The Roots of Fairness: *State v. Caesar* and Slave Justice in Antebellum North Carolina." In *Local Matters: Race, Crime, and Justice in the Nineteenth-Century South*, edited by Christopher Waldrep and Donald G. Nieman, 29–52. Athens: University of Georgia Press, 2001.

Hyman, Michael R. *The Anti-Redeemers: Hill-Country Political Dissenters in the Lower South from Redemption to Populism*. Baton Rouge: Louisiana State University Press, 1990.

Ignatiev, Noel. *How the Irish Became White*. New York: Routledge, 1995.

Ingle, Edward. *Southern Sidelights: A Picture of Social and Economic Life in the South a Generation Before the War*. Boston: Thomas Y. Crowell & Company, 1896.

Inscoe, John C. "Mountain Masters: Slaveholding in Western North Carolina." *North Carolina Historical Review* 61 (April 1984): 143–173.

———. *Mountain Masters: Slavery and the Sectional Crisis in Western North Carolina*. Knoxville: University of Tennessee Press, 1989.

Isaac, Rhys. *The Transformation of Virginia, 1740–1790*. New York: W. W. Norton & Company, 1982.

James, Larry M. "Biracial Fellowship in Antebellum Baptist Churches." In *Masters & Slaves in the House of the Lord: Race and Religion in the American South, 1740–1870*, edited by John B. Boles, 37–57. Lexington: University Press of Kentucky, 1988.

Jennings, Thelma. "'Us Colored Women Had to Go Through A Plenty': Sexual Exploitation of African-American Slave Women." *Journal of Women's History* 1 (Winter 1990): 45–74.

Johnson, Charles A. *The Frontier Camp Meeting: Religion's Harvest Time*. 1955. Reprint. Dallas: Southern Methodist University Press, 1985.

Johnson, Guion Griffis. *Ante-Bellum North Carolina: A Social History*. Chapel Hill: University of North Carolina Press, 1937.

———. "Recreational and Cultural Activities in the Ante-Bellum Town of North Carolina." *North Carolina Historical Review* 6 (January 1929): 17–37.

Johnson, Michael P. "Denmark Vesey and His Co-Conspirators." *William & Mary Quarterly* 3d ser., 58 (October 2001): 915–976.

———. "Runaway Slaves and the Slave Communities in South Carolina, 1799–1830." *William & Mary Quarterly* 3d ser., 38 (July 1981): 418–441.

Johnston, James Hugo. "The Participation of White Men in Virginia Negro Insurrections." *Journal of Negro History* 16 (April 1931): 158–167.

———. *Race Relations in Virginia & Miscegenation in the South, 1776–1860.* Amherst: University of Massachusetts Press, 1970.

Jones, Jacqueline. "Encounters, Likely and Unlikely, between Black and Poor White Women in the Rural South, 1865–1940." *Georgia Historical Quarterly* 76 (Summer 1992): 333–353.

Jordan, Winthrop D. *Tumult and Silence at Second Creek: An Inquiry into a Civil War Slave Conspiracy.* Rev. ed. Baton Rouge: Louisiana State University Press, 1995.

———. *White Over Black: American Attitudes Toward the Negro, 1550–1812.* Chapel Hill: University of North Carolina Press, 1968.

Kay, Marvin L. Michael, and Lorin Lee Cary. "Slave Runaways in Colonial North Carolina, 1748–1775." *North Carolina Historical Review* 63 (January 1986): 1–39.

———. "'They are Indeed the Constant Plague of Their Tyrants': Slave Defence of a Moral Economy in Colonial North Carolina, 1748–1772." *Slavery & Abolition* 6 (December 1985): 37–56.

Kolchin, Peter. *American Slavery, 1619–1877.* New York: Hill and Wang, 1993.

———. "Reevaluating the Antebellum Slave Community: A Comparative Perspective." *Journal of American History* 70 (December 1983): 579–601.

———. "Scalawags, Carpetbaggers, and Reconstruction: A Quantitative Look at Southern Congressional Politics, 1868–1872." *Journal of Southern History* 45 (February 1979): 63–76.

———. *Unfree Labor: American Slavery and Russian Serfdom.* Cambridge: Belknap Press of Harvard University Press, 1987.

Kousser, J. Morgan. *The Shaping of Southern Politics: Suffrage Restrictions and the Establishment of the One-Party South, 1880–1910.* New Haven: Yale University Press, 1974.

Lander, E. M., Jr. "Slave Labor in South Carolina Cotton Mills." *Journal of Negro History* 38 (April 1953): 161–173.

Lander, Ernest McPherson, Jr. *The Textile Industry in Antebellum South Carolina.* Baton Rouge: Louisiana State University Press, 1969.

Lapp, Rudolph M. "The Ante Bellum Poor Whites of the South Atlantic States." Ph.D. diss., University of California–Berkeley, 1956.

Lebsock, Suzanne. *The Free Women of Petersburg: Status and Culture in a Southern Town, 1784–1860.* New York: W. W. Norton & Company, 1984.

Lecaudey, Hélène. "Behind the Mask: Ex-Slave Women and Interracial Sexual Relations." In *Discovering the Women in Slavery: Emancipating Perspectives on the*

American Past, edited by Patricia Morton, 260–277. Athens: University of Georgia Press, 1996.

Levine, Lawrence W. *Black Culture and Black Consciousness: Afro-American Folk Thought from Slavery to Freedom.* New York: Oxford University Press, 1977.

Lichtenstein, Alex. "'That Disposition To Theft, With Which They Have Been Branded': Moral Economy, Slave Management, and the Law." *Journal of Social History* 21 (Spring 1988): 413–440.

Lockley, Tim. "The Strange Case of George Flyming: Justice and Gender in Antebellum Savannah." *Georgia Historical Quarterly* 84 (Summer 2000): 230–253.

Lockley, Timothy J. "Crossing the Race Divide: Interracial Sex in Antebellum Savannah." *Slavery & Abolition* 18 (December 1997): 159–173.

———. "Partners in Crime: African Americans and Non-Slaveholding Whites in Antebellum Georgia." In *White Trash: Race and Class in America,* edited by Matt Wray and Annalee Newitz, 57–72. New York: Routledge, 1997.

———. "Public Poor Relief in Buncombe County, North Carolina, 1792–1860." *North Carolina Historical Review* 80 (January 2003): 28–51.

———. "Spheres of Influence: Working White and Black Women in Antebellum Savannah." In *Neither Lady Nor Slave: Working Women of the Old South,* edited by Susanna Delfino and Michele Gillespie, 102–120. Chapel Hill: University of North Carolina Press, 2002.

———. "A Struggle for Survival: Non-Elite White Women in Lowcountry Georgia, 1790–1830." In *Women of the American South: A Multicultural Reader,* edited by Christie Anne Farnham, 26–42. New York: New York University Press, 1997.

———. "Trading Encounters between Non-Elite Whites and African Americans in Savannah, 1790–1860." *Journal of Southern History* 66 (February 2000): 25–48.

Lockley, Timothy James. *Lines in the Sand: Race and Class in Lowcountry Georgia, 1750–1860.* Athens: University of Georgia Press, 2001.

Lomax, John A. "Self-Pity in Negro Folk-Songs." *The Nation* 105 (August 9, 1917): 141–145.

Malone, Bill C. "Blacks and Whites and the Music of the Old South." In *Black and White Cultural Interaction in the Antebellum South,* edited by Ted Ownby, 149–170. Jackson: University Press of Mississippi, 1993.

Mann, Ralph. "Mountains, Land, and Kin Networks: Burkes Garden, Virginia, in the 1840s and 1850s." *Journal of Southern History* 58 (August 1992): 411–434.

Mathews, Donald G. *Religion in the Old South.* Chicago: University of Chicago Press, 1977.

McCurry, Stephanie. *Masters of Small Worlds: Yeoman Households, Gender Relations, and the Political Culture of the Antebellum South Carolina Low Country.* New York: Oxford University Press, 1995.

———. "Producing Dependence: Women, Work, and Yeoman Households in Low-Country South Carolina." In *Neither Lady Nor Slave: Working Women of the Old South*, edited by Susanna Delfino and Michele Gillespie, 55–71. Chapel Hill: University of North Carolina Press, 2002.

McDonnell, Lawrence T. "Money Knows No Master: Market Relations and the American Slave Community." In *Developing Dixie: Modernization in a Traditional Society*, edited by Winfred B. Moore, Jr., Joseph F. Tripp, and Lyon G. Tyler, 31–44. Westport, Conn.: Greenwood Press, 1988.

———. "Work, Culture, and Society in the Slave South, 1790–1861." In *Black and White Cultural Interaction in the Antebellum South*, edited by Ted Ownby, 125–147. Jackson: University Press of Mississippi, 1993.

McIlwaine, Shields. *The Southern Poor-White from Lubberland to Tobacco Road*. Norman: University of Oklahoma Press, 1939.

McKibben, Davidson Burns. "Negro Slave Insurrections in Mississippi." *Journal of Negro History* 34 (January 1949): 73–90.

McNeill, John Charles. *Lyrics from Cotton Land*. Charlotte: Stone Publishing Co., 1907.

McWhiney, Grady. *Cracker Culture: Celtic Ways in the Old South*. Tuscaloosa: University of Alabama Press, 1988.

Meaders, Daniel E. "South Carolina Fugitives as Viewed Through Local Newspapers with Emphasis on Runaway Notices, 1732–1801." *Journal of Negro History* 60 (April 1975): 288–319.

Mell, Mildred Rutherford. "Poor Whites of the South." *Social Forces* 17 (December 1938): 153–167.

Miles, Edwin A. "The Mississippi Slave Insurrection Scare of 1835." *Journal of Negro History* 42 (January 1957): 48–60.

Miller, Randall M. "The Enemy Within: Some Effects of Foreign Immigrants on Antebellum Southern Cities." *Southern Studies* 24 (Spring 1985): 30–53.

Moore, John Hebron. "Simon Gray, Riverman: A Slave Who Was Almost Free." *Mississippi Valley Historical Review* 49 (December 1962): 472–484.

Morgan, Edmund S. *American Slavery, American Freedom: The Ordeal of Colonial Virginia*. New York: W. W. Norton & Company, 1975.

Morgan, Philip D. "Colonial South Carolina Runaways: Their Significance for Slave Culture." *Slavery & Abolition* 6 (December 1985): 57–78.

———. "The Ownership of Property by Slaves in the Mid-Nineteenth-Century Low Country." *Journal of Southern History* 49 (August 1983): 399–420.

———. *Slave Counterpoint: Black Culture in the Eighteenth-Century Chesapeake & Lowcountry*. Chapel Hill: University of North Carolina Press, 1998.

———. "Work and Culture: The Task System and the World of Low Country Blacks, 1700–1880." *William & Mary Quarterly* 3d ser., 39 (October 1982): 563–599.

Morgan, Philip D., and George D. Terry. "Slavery in Microcosm: A Conspiracy Scare in Colonial South Carolina." *Southern Studies* 21 (Summer 1982): 121–145.

Morris, Christopher. "An Event in Community Organization: The Mississippi Slave Insurrection Scare of 1835." *Journal of Social History* 22 (Fall 1988): 93–111.

———. "Within the Slave Cabin: Violence in Mississippi Slave Families." In *Over the Threshold: Intimate Violence in Early America,* edited by Christine Daniels and Michael V. Kennedy, 268–285. New York: Routledge, 1999.

Morris, Thomas D. *Southern Slavery and the Law, 1619–1860.* Chapel Hill: University of North Carolina Press, 1996.

Moton, Robert Russa. *What the Negro Thinks.* Garden City, N.Y.: Doubleday, Doran and Company, Inc., 1932.

Mullin, Gerald W. *Flight and Rebellion: Slave Resistance in Eighteenth-Century Virginia.* New York: Oxford University Press, 1972.

Newby, I. A. *Plain Folk in the New South: Social Change and Cultural Persistence, 1880–1915.* Baton Rouge: Louisiana State University Press, 1989.

Nisbett, Richard E., and Dov Cohen. *Culture of Honor: The Psychology of Violence in the South.* Boulder, Col.: Westview Press, 1996.

Nissenbaum, Stephen. *The Battle for Christmas: A Cultural History of America's Most Cherished Holiday.* New York: Vintage Books, 1996.

Oakes, James. *The Ruling Race: A History of American Slaveholders.* New York: W. W. Norton & Company, 1982.

Odum, Howard W. "Folk-Song and Folk-Poetry as Found in the Secular Songs of the Southern Negroes." *Journal of American Folk-Lore* 24 (July–September 1911): 255–294.

Odum, Howard W., and Guy B. Johnson. *The Negro and His Songs: A Study of Typical Negro Songs in the South.* Chapel Hill: University of North Carolina Press, 1925.

Olwell, Robert. "'Loose, Idle and Disorderly': Slave Women in the Eighteenth-Century Charleston Marketplace." In *More Than Chattel: Black Women and Slavery in the Americas,* edited by David Barry Gaspar and Darlene Clark Hine, 97–110. Bloomington: Indiana University Press, 1996.

———. *Masters, Slaves, & Subjects: The Culture of Power in the South Carolina Low Country, 1740–1790.* Ithaca: Cornell University Press, 1998.

Otto, John Solomon, and Augustus Marion Burns III. "Black Folks and Poor Buckras: Archeological Evidence of Slave and Overseer Living Conditions on an Antebellum Plantation." *Journal of Black Studies* 14 (December 1983): 185–200.

Outland, Robert B., III. "Slavery, Work, and the Geography of the North Carolina

Naval Stores Industry, 1835–1860." *Journal of Southern History* 62 (February 1996): 27–56.

Owsley, Frank L. *Plain Folk of the Old South.* 1949. Reprint. Baton Rouge: Louisiana State University Press, 1982.

Page, Thomas Nelson. "Uncle Gabe's White Folks." In *Library of Southern Literature.* Vol. 9. Edited by Edwin Anderson Alderman and Joel Chandler Harris. Atlanta: Martin & Hoyt Company, 1909.

Painter, Nell Irvin. "Of *Lily,* Linda Brent, and Freud: A Non-Exceptionalist Approach to Race, Class, and Gender in the Slave South." *Georgia Historical Quarterly* 76 (Summer 1992): 241–259.

Parker, Freddie L. *Running for Freedom: Slave Runaways in North Carolina, 1775–1840.* New York: Garland Publishing, Inc., 1993.

Patterson, Orlando. *Slavery and Social Death: A Comparative Study.* Cambridge, Mass.: Harvard University Press, 1982.

Pearson, Edward A., ed. *Designs against Charleston: The Trial Record of the Denmark Vesey Slave Conspiracy of 1822.* Chapel Hill: University of North Carolina Press, 1999.

Penningroth, Dylan C. *The Claims of Kinfolk: African American Property and Community in the Nineteenth-Century South.* Chapel Hill: University of North Carolina Press, 2003.

Perrow, E. C. "Songs and Rhymes from the South." *Journal of American Folk-Lore* 28 (April–June 1915): 129–190.

Phillips, Ulrich Bonnell. *American Negro Slavery: A Survey of the Supply, Employment and Control of Negro Labor as Determined by the Plantation Régime.* 1918. Reprint. New York: Peter Smith, 1952.

Powell, Carolyn J. "In Remembrance of Mira: Reflections on the Death of a Slave Woman." In *Discovering the Women in Slavery: Emancipating Perspectives on the American Past,* edited by Patricia Morton, 47–60. Athens: University of Georgia Press, 1996.

Powell, Richard E., Jr. "Sport, Social Relations and Animal Husbandry: Early Cockfighting in North America." *International Journal of the History of Sport* 10 (December 1993): 361–381.

Powell, William S., ed. *Dictionary of North Carolina Biography.* Vol. 4. Chapel Hill: University of North Carolina Press, 1991.

Presley, Delma E. "The Crackers of Georgia." *Georgia Historical Quarterly* 60 (Summer 1976): 102–116.

Preyer, Norris W. "The Historian, the Slave, and the Ante-Bellum Textile Industry." *Journal of Negro History* 46 (April 1961): 67–82.

Prude, Jonathan. "To Look Upon the 'Lower Sort': Runaway Ads and the Appearance of Unfree Laborers in America, 1750–1800." *Journal of American History* 78 (June 1991): 124–159.

Rabinowitz, Howard N. "From Exclusion to Segregation: Southern Race Relations, 1865–1890." *Journal of American History* 63 (September 1976): 325–350.

———. "More Than the Woodward Thesis: Assessing the Strange Career of Jim Crow." *Journal of American History* 75 (December 1988): 842–856.

Reed, John Shelton. *One South: An Ethnic Approach to Regional Culture.* Baton Rouge: Louisiana State University Press, 1982.

Reidy, Joseph P. "Obligation and Right: Patterns of Labor, Subsistence, and Exchange in the Cotton Belt of Georgia, 1790–1860." In *Cultivation and Culture: Labor and the Shaping of Slave Life in the Americas,* edited by Ira Berlin and Philip D. Morgan, 138–154. Charlottesville: University Press of Virginia, 1993.

Riley, Glenda. *Divorce: An American Tradition.* New York: Oxford University Press, 1991.

———. "Legislative Divorce in Virginia, 1803–1850." *Journal of the Early Republic* 11 (Spring 1991): 51–67.

Roberts, B. W. C. "Cockfighting: An Early Entertainment in North Carolina." *North Carolina Historical Review* 42 (July 1965): 306–314.

Rorabaugh, W. J. *The Alcoholic Republic: An American Tradition.* New York: Oxford University Press, 1979.

Rothman, Joshua D. *Notorious in the Neighborhood: Sex and Families across the Color Line in Virginia, 1787–1861.* Chapel Hill: University of North Carolina Press, 2003.

———. "'To Be Freed From Thate Curs and Let at Liberty': Interracial Adultery and Divorce in Antebellum Virginia." *Virginia Magazine of History and Biography* 106 (Autumn 1998): 443–481.

Scarborough, Dorothy. *On the Trail of Negro Folk-Songs.* Hatboro, Penn.: Folklore Associates, Inc., 1963.

Scarborough, William Kauffman. *The Overseer: Plantation Management in the Old South.* Baton Rouge: Louisiana State University Press, 1966.

Schechter, Patricia A. "Free and Slave Labor in the Old South: The Tredegar Ironworkers' Strike of 1847." *Labor History* 35 (Spring 1994): 165–186.

Schlotterbeck, John T. "The Internal Economy of Slavery in Rural Piedmont Virginia." *Slavery & Abolition* 12 (May 1991): 170–181.

Schwarz, Philip J. "Gabriel's Challenge: Slaves and Crime in Late Eighteenth-Century Virginia." *Virginia Magazine of History and Biography* 90 (July 1982): 283–309.

———. *Twice Condemned: Slaves and the Criminal Laws of Virginia, 1705–1865.* Baton Rouge: Louisiana State University Press, 1988.

Schweninger, Loren. "Slave Independence and Enterprise in South Carolina, 1780 – 1865." *South Carolina Historical Magazine* 93 (April 1992): 101–125.

———. "The Underside of Slavery: The Internal Economy, Self-Hire, and Quasi-Freedom in Virginia." *Slavery & Abolition* 12 (September 1991): 1–22.

Shirley, Michael. "Yeoman Culture and Millworker Protest in Antebellum Salem, North Carolina." *Journal of Southern History* 57 (August 1991): 427–452.

Shore, Laurence. "Making Mississippi Safe for Slavery: The Insurrectionary Panic of 1835." In *Class, Conflict, and Consensus: Antebellum Southern Community Studies*, edited by Orville Vernon Burton and Robert C. McMath, Jr., 96–127. Westport, Conn.: Greenwood Press, 1982.

Silber, Nina. "'What Does America Need So Much as Americans?': Race and Northern Reconciliation with South Appalachia, 1870–1900." In *Appalachians and Race: The Mountain South from Slavery to Segregation*, edited by John C. Inscoe, 245–258. Lexington: University Press of Kentucky, 2001.

Sobel, Mechal. "Whatever You Do, Treat People Right: Personal Ethics in a Slave Society." In *Black and White Cultural Interaction in the Antebellum South*, edited by Ted Ownby, 55–82. Jackson: University Press of Mississippi, 1993.

Sommerville, Diane Miller. "The Rape Myth in the Old South Reconsidered." *Journal of Southern History* 61 (August 1995): 481–518.

———. "Rape, Race, and Castration in Slave Law in the Colonial and Early South." In *The Devil's Lane: Sex and Race in the Early South*, edited by Catherine Clinton and Michele Gillespie, 74–89. New York: Oxford University Press, 1997.

Sparks, Randy J. "Gentlemen's Sport: Horse Racing in Antebellum Charleston." *South Carolina Historical Magazine* 93 (January 1992): 15–30.

———. "Religion in Amite County, Mississippi, 1800–1861." In *Masters & Slaves in the House of the Lord: Race and Religion in the American South, 1740–1870*, edited by John B. Boles, 58–80. Lexington: University Press of Kentucky, 1988.

Stampp, Kenneth M. *The Peculiar Institution: Slavery in the Ante-Bellum South*. New York: Vintage Books, 1956.

Stansell, Christine. *City of Women: Sex and Class in New York, 1789–1860*. Urbana: University of Illinois Press, 1987.

Starobin, Robert S. *Industrial Slavery in the Old South*. New York: Oxford University Press, 1970.

———, ed. *Denmark Vesey: The Slave Conspiracy of 1822*. Englewood Cliffs, N.J.: Prentice-Hall, Inc., 1970.

———, ed. *Letters of American Slaves*. New York: New Viewpoints, 1974.

Strickland, John Scott. "The Great Revival and Insurrectionary Fears in North Carolina: An Examination of Antebellum Southern Society and Slave Revolt Panics." In *Class, Conflict, and Consensus: Antebellum Southern Community Studies*, edited by

Orville Vernon Burton and Robert C. McMath, Jr., 57–95. Westport, Conn.: Greenwood Press, 1982.

Talley, Thomas W. *Negro Folk Rhymes Wise and Otherwise with a Study.* 1922. Reprint. Port Washington, N.Y.: Kennikat Press, 1968.

Taylor, Alan. *Liberty Men and Great Proprietors: The Revolutionary Settlement on the Maine Frontier, 1760–1820.* Chapel Hill: University of North Carolina Press, 1990.

Taylor, Rosser H. *Ante Bellum South Carolina: A Social and Cultural History.* Chapel Hill: University of North Carolina Press, 1942.

Terrill, Tom E. "Eager Hands: Labor for Southern Textiles, 1850–1860." *Journal of Economic History* 36 (March 1976): 84–99.

Tindall, George Brown, with David E. Shi. *America: A Narrative History.* Vol. 1. 3rd ed. New York: W. W. Norton & Company, 1992.

Trelease, Allen W. "Who Were the Scalawags?" *Journal of Southern History* 29 (November 1963): 445–468.

Twyman, Robert W. "The Clay Eater: A New Look at an Old Southern Enigma." *Journal of Southern History* 37 (August 1971): 439–448.

Tyrrell, Ian R. *Sobering Up: From Temperance to Prohibition in Antebellum America, 1800–1860.* Westport, Conn.: Greenwood Press, 1979.

Wade, Richard C. *Slavery in the Cities: The South, 1820–1860.* New York: Oxford University Press, 1964.

Waldstreicher, David. "Reading the Runaways: Self-Fashioning, Print Culture, and Confidence in Slavery in the Eighteenth-Century Mid-Atlantic." *William & Mary Quarterly* 3d ser., 56 (April 1999): 243–272.

Walvin, James. "Slaves, Free Time and the Question of Leisure." *Slavery & Abolition* 16 (April 1995): 1–13.

Wharton, Vernon Lane. *The Negro in Mississippi, 1865–1890.* Chapel Hill: University of North Carolina Press, 1947.

White, Deborah Gray. *Ar'n't I a Woman?: Female Slaves in the Plantation South.* New York: Norton, 1985.

———. *Ar'n't I a Woman?: Female Slaves in the Plantation South.* Rev. ed. New York: W. W. Norton & Company, 1999.

White, Newman I. *American Negro Folk-Songs.* Hatboro, Penn.: Folklore Associates, Inc., 1965.

White, Shane, and Graham White. *Stylin': African American Expressive Culture from Its Beginnings to the Zoot Suit.* Ithaca: Cornell University Press, 1998.

Wiggins, D. "Good Times On the Old Plantation: Popular Recreations of the Black Slave in Ante Bellum South, 1810–1860." *Journal of Sport History* 4 (Fall 1977): 260–284.

Wiggins, David K. "The Play of Slave Children in the Plantation Communities of the Old South, 1820–1860." *Journal of Sport History* 7 (Summer 1980): 21–39.

Wiggins, Sarah Woolfolk. *The Scalawag in Alabama Politics, 1865–1881.* University, Ala.: University of Alabama Press, 1977.

Williams, David. *Rich Man's War: Class, Caste, and Confederate Defeat in the Lower Chattahoochee Valley.* Athens: University of Georgia Press, 1998.

Williams, David, Teresa Crisp Williams, and R. David Carlson. *Plain Folk in a Rich Man's War: Class and Dissent in Confederate Georgia.* Gainesville: University Press of Florida, 2002.

Williams, Jack Kenny. *Vogues in Villainy: Crime and Retribution in Ante-Bellum South Carolina.* Columbia: University of South Carolina Press, 1959.

Windley, Lathan Algerna. *A Profile of Runaway Slaves in Virginia and South Carolina from 1730 through 1787.* New York: Garland Publishing, Inc., 1995.

Wish, Harvey. "American Slave Insurrections Before 1861." *Journal of Negro History* 22 (July 1937): 299–320.

———. "The Slave Insurrection Panic of 1856." *Journal of Southern History* 5 (May 1939): 206–222.

Wood, Betty. "'For Their Satisfaction or Redress': African Americans and Church Discipline in the Early South." In *The Devil's Lane: Sex and Race in the Early South,* edited by Catherine Clinton and Michele Gillespie, 109–123. New York: Oxford University Press, 1997.

———. "'White Society' and the 'Informal' Slave Economies of Lowcountry Georgia, c. 1763–1830." *Slavery & Abolition* 11 (December 1990): 313–331.

———. *Women's Work, Men's Work: The Informal Slave Economies of Lowcountry Georgia.* Athens: University of Georgia Press, 1995.

Wood, Peter H. *Black Majority: Negroes in Colonial South Carolina from 1670 through the Stono Rebellion.* New York: W. W. Norton & Company, Inc., 1975.

Woodward, C. Vann. *Origins of the New South, 1877–1913.* Baton Rouge: Louisiana State University Press, 1951.

———. *The Strange Career of Jim Crow.* 3rd ed. New York: Oxford University Press, 1974.

———. *Tom Watson: Agrarian Rebel.* 1938; New York: Oxford University Press, 1963.

Wright, Gavin. "'Economic Democracy' and the Concentration of Agricultural Wealth in the Cotton South, 1850–1860." *Agricultural History* 44 (January 1970): 63–93.

Wyatt-Brown, Bertram. "Community, Class, and Snopesian Crime: Local Justice in the Old South." In *Class, Conflict, and Consensus: Antebellum Southern Community*

Studies, edited by Orville Vernon Burton and Robert C. McMath, Jr., 173–206. Westport, Conn.: Greenwood Press, 1982.

———. "The Mask of Obedience: Male Slave Psychology in the Old South." *American Historical Review* 93 (December 1988): 1228–1252.

———. "Religion and the Formation of Folk Culture: Poor Whites of the Old South." In *The Americanization of the Gulf Coast, 1803–1850,* edited by Lucius F. Ellsworth, 20–33. Pensacola: State of Florida; Department of State; Historic Pensacola Preservation Board, 1972.

———. *Southern Honor: Ethics and Behavior in the Old South.* New York: Oxford University Press, 1982.

Yarborough, Richard. "Race, Violence, and Manhood: The Masculine Idea in Frederick Douglass's 'The Heroic Slave.'" In *Haunted Bodies: Gender and Southern Texts,* edited by Anne Goodwyn Jones and Susan V. Donaldson, 159–184. Charlottesville: University Press of Virginia, 1997.

INDEX